Edward Lewes Cutts

**Turning points of general church history**

Edward Lewes Cutts

**Turning points of general church history**

ISBN/EAN: 9783337261290

Printed in Europe, USA, Canada, Australia, Japan

Cover: Foto ©Lupo / pixelio.de

More available books at **www.hansebooks.com**

# TURNING POINTS

OF

# GENERAL CHURCH HISTORY.

BY THE

REV. EDWARD L. CUTTS, B.A.,

HON. D.D. UNIVERSITY OF THE SOUTH, U.S.A.,

*Author of* "*Turning Points of English Church History*"; "*Constantine*"; "*Charlemagne*"; "*St. Jerome and St. Augustine,*" *in the Fathers for English Readers;* "*Some Chief Truths of Religion*"; "*Pastoral Counsels*"; *&c.*

SIXTH THOUSAND.

PUBLISHED UNDER THE DIRECTION OF THE TRACT COMMITTEE.

LONDON:
SOCIETY FOR PROMOTING CHRISTIAN KNOWLEDGE,
NORTHUMBERLAND AVENUE, CHARING CROSS, W.C.;
43, QUEEN VICTORIA STREET, E.C.;
26, ST. GEORGE'S PLACE, HYDE PARK CORNER, S.W.
BRIGHTON: 135, NORTH STREET.
NEW YORK: E. & J. B. YOUNG & CO.

1886.

## PREFACE.

THIS is an attempt to give, within the limits of a small book, some adequate idea of the history of the Church of Christ to the thousands of intelligent Church-people who have little previous acquaintance with the subject. The special features of the plan are these :—Pains have been taken to show what the Church is—viz., the Body of Christ informed by the Holy Spirit; the salient points of the history have been selected with a special view to our present ecclesiastical condition; instead of referring the reader to other books, to which he may not have ready access, for that sketch of secular history which is indispensable to an intelligent grasp of Church history, such a sketch is included.

# CONTENTS.

### CHAPTER I.

#### THE WORLD PREPARED FOR THE CHURCH.

PAGE

The three great races—Greek, Jewish, Roman; Greek philosophy—Epicureanism, Stoicism, Platonism, Eclecticism; Greek philosophy widely spread by the conquests of Alexander; The diffusion of the Jews—they bear witness to the unity of God and the promise of a Saviour; The Roman empire throws down the barriers which divided the nations, and prepares the world for the planting of the Church .................................................................... 1

### CHAPTER II.

#### THE CHURCH IN THE GOSPELS.

The Church called in the Gospels the kingdom of heaven or of God; This kingdom foretold in prophecy and type; The Magi came to worship the king; The charge on which He was put to death was that He claimed to be a king; John Baptist proclaimed the kingdom at hand; The parables of the kingdom; Christ anointed King—begins to call His subjects—lays the foundation of His ministry; On the confession of His divinity by the apostles, He foretells the foundation of His Church; The last parable illustrates the profoundest truth concerning the Church—its incorporation with Christ; During the forty days He is speaking to the apostles of the things pertaining to the kingdom; The ideal of this kingdom...... 7

### CHAPTER III.

#### THE APOSTOLIC CHURCH.

The beginning of the Church on the day of Pentecost; Its spread among Jews, Samaritans, Proselytes, Gentiles; Antioch the centre of missions to the Gentiles; The Church founded in Asia Minor

—Greece; St. Paul visits Rome; Internal history of individual churches in St. Paul's epistles; The Seven Churches of Asia; The principles of Church organisation found in the New Testament; A visible organisation; The Sacraments—Baptism, the Eucharist; The unity of the Church hinged on the ministry; A general council the centre of unity; A spiritual kingdom; The threefold ministry —apostles, deacons, elders; The three orders permanent; The apostles succeeded in their office by bishops; A bird's-eye view of the Apostolic Church ...................................................... 13

## CHAPTER IV.

#### SKETCH OF THE ROMAN EMPIRE TO THE CONVERSION OF CONSTANTINE.

The Roman conquests; Transfer of power from the senate to the emperor; Julius Cæsar (B.C. 46); Augustus (B.C. 27)—Christ born; Tiberius (A.D. 14)—Christ crucified; Caligula (37); Claudius (41); Nero (54)—St. Paul visits Rome—persecution of Christians at Rome; Galba (68); Otho (69); Vitellius (69); Vespasian (69)—the Judean war—destruction of the Temple; Titus (79); Domitian (81)—Christians persecuted; Nerva (96); Trajan (98)— St. John still living—Pliny's letter—martyrdom of Polycarp; Hadrian (117)—rebuilt Jerusalem; Antoninus (138); Marcus Aurelius (161)—the first persecution by order of the emperor; Commodus (180); Pertinax (193); Julius Didianus (193); Septimius Severus (193); Caracalla and Geta (211)—Roman citizenship extended to the whole empire; Macrinus (217); Eliogabalus (218), Priest of the Sun; Alexander Severus (222)—favoured Christianity; Maximin (235); The Gordians (238); Philip the Arabian (244); Decius (249)—general persecution ordered by the emperor; Gallus (251); Æmilianus (253); Valerian (253)—a reign of calamities; Gallienus (260); Claudius Gothicus (268); Aurelian (270); Probus (276); Carus (282); Carinus and Numerian (283); Diocletian reorganises the government—associates with himself Maximian as emperor, and then Galerius and Constantius as Cæsars; Galerius and Constantius (305)—discord and civil wars for eighteen years; Constantine the Great becomes emperor (306), with Licinius and Maximin as associates in the empire; Constantine sole emperor (323). ............................................................................ 34

## CHAPTER V.

#### NERO'S PERSECUTION OF THE CHRISTIANS AT ROME.

Great fire at Rome; Nero suspected—diverts public suspicion upon the Christians; Causes which led to the popular odium .................. 53

## CHAPTER VI.

### PLINY'S LETTER TO TRAJAN.

The prevalence of the Church in Pontus and Bithynia; Its persecution by Pliny the Pro-Consul; Trajan's rescript; The martyrdom of Ignatius; Trajan's journey through Antioch; The people clamour for the death of the bishop—his examination before the emperor—condemned to the wild beasts at Rome—his journey to Rome—his letters .................................................................... 58

## CHAPTER VII.

### THE RESCRIPT OF HADRIAN AND MARTYRDOM OF POLYCARP.

Persecution during the first centuries partial and occasional; Examples; Letter of the Pro-Consul of Asia to the emperor as to the treatment of Christians; Hadrian's reply; Apologies of Quadratus and Aristides; Hadrian's account of religion in Egypt; Marcus Aurelius; Spread of philosophy; Decay of ancient Roman religion; Public calamities—attributed to anger of the gods; The emperor orders revival of ancient worship, and issues persecuting edicts against the Christians; Polycarp, Bishop of Smyrna, accused and tried by the Prefect—condemned to be burnt—his prayer at his death............ 65

## CHAPTER VIII.

### THE MERCHANTMAN SEEKING GOODLY PEARLS.

Contemporary sketch of the growth of Christianity in the Recognitions of Clement; Actual example in the case of Justin Martyr........... 74

## CHAPTER IX.

### THE MARTYRS OF VIENNE.

The Church in Gaul—Lyons and Vienne; Outburst of popular rage against Christians; The story of their sufferings and death........... 85

## CHAPTER X.

### THE CHURCHES OF EGYPT AND AFRICA.

Severus favoured Christianity till towards the close of his reign, when persecution happened in Egypt and Africa; Account of the Church of Alexandria—that city a famous school of philosophy; Neo-Platonism; The Catechetical school; Clement; The persecution; Origen; Church of Pro-Consular Africa derived from Rome—flourishing in the second century; Tertullian; His Apology......... 91

## CHAPTER XI.

#### THE MARTYRDOM OF PERPETUA AND FELICITAS.

Continuation of Severus' persecution in Africa; The story of the sufferings and death of Perpetua and Felicitas ........................ 96

## CHAPTER XII.

#### PROGRESS OF THE CHURCH—MARTYRDOM OF CYPRIAN.

Close of Severus' persecution; Alexander Severus favours Christianity; Churches built; Bishops at the imperial court; Decius aims at a restoration of the ancient Roman religion and manners—endeavours to extirpate Christianity; A general and severe persecution; The *Libellatici* and *Lapsi*; Valerian issues an edict for the destruction of the churches and persecution of the bishops; Cyprian—Bishop of Carthage; The plague of Carthage; The bishop arrested under the Valerian edict—his trial by the Pro-Consul—execution ............ 102

## CHAPTER XIII.

#### THE DIOCLETIAN PERSECUTION—THE CONVERSION OF CONSTANTINE.

The Church has peace, and prospers in the early part of Diocletian's reign; In 202 and 203 a series of persecuting edicts issued, and put into force throughout the empire; Constantius discountenances cruelty in his provinces; After two years persecution relaxes in the West—continues in the East; In 311 Galerius, on his death-bed, issues edict of toleration; Christians rebuild their churches, and freely exercise their religion; Maximin continues to harass Christians in his dominions, and revives the pagan worship; The rivalry between the emperors assumes a religious character; Constantine is the hope of Christianity—his rivals seek to conciliate the old heathen party; A.D. 323 Constantine sole emperor, and Christianity triumphs with him; Issues edict of general toleration, inviting his subjects to embrace Christianity; Embraces Christianity; Builds churches; Founds a new capital on the Bosphorus; The empress-mother, Helena, not a British princess—a zealous Christian—took special interest in the holy places of Judea and in relics of saints............ 108

## CHAPTER XIV.

### THE CONSTITUTION OF THE PRIMITIVE CHURCH.

PAGE

Three theories of Church constitution—the Congregational, Presbyterian, Episcopalian ; The Congregational argument examined ; The Presbyterian argument examined ; Evidence that Episcopacy was the permanent constitution of the Church contemplated and initiated by the apostles ; Evidence that Episcopacy was universal in the primitive Church, from Ignatius, Irenæus, Clement of Alexandria, Origen, Cyprian, Firmilian, Eusebius; All bishops equal; Organised into provinces with metropolitans; Patriarchs; Rights of bishops, metropolitans, patriarchs ; This constitution recognised by the whole Church represented in the Council of Nicæa .......................... 115

## CHAPTER XV.

### RELATIONS OF CHURCH AND STATE.

The emperor sole legislator and governor, as a Christian bound to legislate and govern on Christian principles, and to promote the spread of the Gospel among his subjects ; The Church welcomed his support without any formal concordat ; Provinces of secular and spiritual power very early distinguished.................................................... 127

## CHAPTER XVI.

### THE CHURCH BUILDINGS—THE CATACOMBS.

The first places of public worship were in the houses of converts ; The upper room of Jerusalem ; Other examples ; The first Church in the house of Pudens ; Churches built earlier than is popularly supposed ; Existing churches of early date in Africa and Syria; The basilicas at Rome which Constantine gave for churches; The churches built in the time of Constantine and subsequently ; Exterior of churches plain, interior adorned with marbles, sculpture, mosaics, &c., and costly furniture ; Eusebius' description of the new church at Tyre ................................................................................ 130

## CHAPTER XVII.

### THE WORSHIP OF THE PRIMITIVE CHURCH.

Justin Martyr's sketch of Church worship. A.D. 140. The ancient Liturgies traced up to the age immediately succeeding the apostles ;

Probably represent an unwritten apostolic Liturgy; Primitive vestments of the clergy; Tunic and pallium; Sketch of a primitive church, its congregation and service .................................. 140

## CHAPTER XVIII.

#### EARLY HERESIES AND SCHISMS.

The early heresies the result of an eclectic combination of Christianity with the Oriental and Greek philosophies—Gnosticism, Manicheism, Neo-Platonism; Early schisms—Montanism, Novatianism, Donatism 147

## CHAPTER XIX.

#### SKETCH OF THE EMPIRE FROM THE DEATH OF CONSTANTINE TO THAT OF THEODOSIUS.

Division of the empire among the sons of Constantine (A.D. 337); Constantine II. makes war against Constans—is defeated and slain; Constans slain by the usurper Maxentius; Maxentius defeated, dies, and Constantius is sole emperor; His character feeble; An Arian; Makes Gallus Cæsar—executes him; Appoints Julian to be Cæsar; Constantius dies (A.D. 361), and Julian succeeds—his character and reign—tries to restore the ancient heathenism—tries to rebuild the Temple of Jerusalem; Jovian (A.D. 363); Valentinian and Valens (A.D. 364); Persecution of the Pagans in Rome; Election of Damasus Bishop of Rome; Gratian (A.D. 375); Defeat of Valens by the Goths at Hadrianople; Theodosius raised to the purple (A.D. 379); Triumph of the Church ...................................................... 156

## CHAPTER XX.

#### THE ARIAN CONTROVERSY.

Arius—his heresy—condemned by his bishop—excommunicated—his heresy spreads; Constantine summons the first general council at Nicæa, A.D. 325; The Nicene Fathers declare the ancient faith; Arianism condemned; Arianism continues to spread—favoured by the court; On the death of Constantine I. Constantius sustains Arianism with all the power of the State; The Catholics persecuted; Arianism predominant; Constantius succeeds to the empire of the West and tries to force Arianism upon it also; Council of Milan adopts an Arian Creed; Hosius and Liberius refuse it—are exiled—succumb; Council of Rimini adopts an Arian Creed; Constantius dies; The Catholic bishops return from exile.......................... 162

## CHAPTER XXI.

### THE TRIUMPH OF THE CHURCH.

PAGE

Theodosius (A.D. 380) issues edict declaring it the will of the emperors that their subjects should embrace the Catholic faith; Visits Constantinople—ejects the Arian bishops and clergy and replaces the Catholics; Arianism gradually withers (A.D. 391); Edict forbidding pagan sacrifices; Destruction of temples—of Serapis at Alexandria; Ancient religion still predominant in Rome; The heathen party petition the emperor for toleration—refused; Pagan worship occasionally performed in secret, but slowly dies out, leaving superstitious notions as its legacy.................................................. 170

## CHAPTER XXII.

### THE EXTENSION OF THE CHURCH OUTSIDE THE EMPIRE.

Armenia the first Christian kingdom; Gregory the Illuminator its apostle; Christianity adopted as the national religion; Armed resistance put down by force; Subsequent history of the Armenian Church; Conversion of the Goths; Ulphilas introduces the Arian heresy from the Eastern Church among the Goths; Foundation of the Abyssinian Church; Frumentius consecrated bishop by Athanasius; Conversion of the Georgians—receive hierarchy from Constantinople—subsequent history ............................................. 175

## CHAPTER XXIII.

### THE FATHERS OF THE CHURCH.

The majority of the Great Fathers, both Greek and Latin, flourished within a brief period (A.D. 330—461); Their various origin and character—their work; Athanasius—his character—before the Council of Tyre—excommunicated and deposed by the council—he appeals to the emperor—is banished to Trèves—on the death of Constantine returns to his see—Council of Antioch condemns him; Gregory of Cappadocia intruded into his see; Treatment of the Catholics; Athanasius retires to Rome; Constantius replaces him in his see; The Council of Milan condemns him; the prefect surrounds his church with troops, but Athanasius escapes; George of Cappadocia intruded into his see; Treatment of the Catholics; Death of Constantius; George murdered; Athanasius resumes his see; Julian excepts Athanasius from the amnesty—he takes refuge among the monks of the desert; Jovian invites his return—edict of Valens—takes refuge in the tomb of his family—returns and dies in his see; Chrysostom—birth and education—asceticism—ordained—appointed preacher at Antioch—the sermons on the statues—appointed Bishop of Constantinople—unpopular—the court hostile to him—the Synod of the Oak—he is banished—brought back—banished again to Cucussus—to Petyus–dies; Ambrose—Prefect of Liguria—elected Bishop of Milan—his influence with Gratian—opposed by Eudoxia—goes as ambassador to Maximinus; The massacre at Thessalonica; Ambrose prohibits the emperor's entry into church till he has given evidence of repentance.......... ... 179

## CHAPTER XXIV.

#### MONASTICISM.

Antony (born A.D. 251) the Father of the Hermits—sells all and follows Christ—takes up his abode in a tomb; In a ruined castle near the Red Sea—disciples people the desert—visits Alexandria during the persecution of Maximin—returns to desert—revisits Alexandria during the Arian disturbances—dies 105 years old; Pachomius draws up a monastic rule of life; Community life; Solitaries and cænobites in hills of the Nile valley; Ammon founds communities in Nitria, Macarius in Scetis; Monk-town of Tebenne; Hilarion introduces monasticism into Syria—a disciple of Antony—builds a cell near Gaza—disciples multiply; St. Sabas visits the Egyptian desert—sails to Sicily—dies there; St. Basil (born A.D. 329) introduces monkish life into Asia Minor—birth and education—ascetic life—draws up a monastic rule—returns to Cæsarea—ordained—appointed bishop; Jerome—birth and education—visits Rome—the East—adopts hermit life—his praise of solitude—returns to Antioch—goes to the synod at Rome, A.D. 381—appointed secretary to the synod—secretary to the Pope, Damasus; Roman ladies adopt the ascetic life; On the Pope's death Jerome retires to Bethlehem—Paula and Eustochium also — they found monasteries there—description of their life there; Jerome's literary labours—the Vulgate, &c.; St. Martin of Tours, a soldier, turns hermit—evangelises Gaul—introduces monastic life into Gaul .......................... 195

## CHAPTER XXV.

#### THE DISRUPTION OF THE ROMAN EMPIRE AND CONVERSION OF THE BARBARIANS

Permanent division of the empire into East and West—its causes; Slavery; The revolt of Alaric, A.D. 395—he ravages Greece and Italy—is defeated by Stilicho; Rhagasius invades the empire; Defence of Florence; Stilicho starves the barbarians into surrender; Alaric takes and sacks Rome, A.D. 410—spares the people and the churches; The Suevi and Vandals invade Spain ; The Burgundians and Franks invade Gaul; Attila and the Huns ravage Europe ; Leo the Great induces him to spare Rome ; The Vandals invade Africa ; The phantom emperors from Honorius to Augustulus; Odoacer rules Italy—conquered by Theodoric, King of the Goths ; The Saxon conquest of Britain ; The division of the empire ; The barbarians are Arian Christians, except the Franks and the Saxons; Conversion of Clovis and the Franks; The relations of the conquering barbarians to the Catholic Church ; In Italy, Gaul, and Spain they tolerate the Catholics, and in time adopt the Catholic faith; In Africa an Arian persecution for seventy-seven years ; The conversion of the Saxons 208

## CHAPTER XXVI.

#### THE EASTERN EMPIRE FROM THE DEATH OF THEODOSIUS TO THAT OF JUSTINIAN

Arcadius (395)—feebleness of his reign; Pulcheria and Theodosius II. (408) ; Marcian (450) ; Leo of Thrace (457) ; Leo II. and Zeno (474) ; Anastasius (491) ; Justin (518) ; Justinian (527) ; Belisarius reconquers Africa, Sicily, and Italy, and annexes them to the Eastern empire ; The Pandects of Justinian—his fortifications and buildings ; Churches ; Santa Sophia ; Byzantine art ; War with Persia .................................................................. 219

## CHAPTER XXVII.

#### THE SECOND, THIRD, FOURTH, AND FIFTH GENERAL COUNCILS.

Theodosius puts Gregory Nazianzen in possession of the churches of Constantinople ; Maximus irregularly consecrated as a rival bishop ; The Apollinarian heresy ; The Macedonian heresy ; The *Second General Council* of Constantinople (A.D. 381) summoned by Theodosius ; Meletius of Antioch presides ; Gregory's claim to the see confirmed ; Meletius dies, and Gregory presides over the Council ; Peter of Alexandria arrives and questions Gregory's right ; Gregory resigns ; Nectarius consecrated, and presides ; The Apollinarian heresy condemned ; The Macedonian heresy condemned, and the Niceno-Constantinopolitan Creed put forth ; The council raises Constantinople to be a Patriarchate, and gives it precedence next after Rome; Nestorius, Patriarch of Constantinople, preaches against the Word "Theotokos "; Cyril of Alexandria—his training, character, and administration—he writes against Nestorius ; Celestine of Rome and Cyril both hold synods which condemn Nestorius; Cyril's "Anathemas"; John of Antioch sides with Nestorius; The *Third General Council* of Ephesus (A.D. 434) summoned by Theodosius II.; The Fathers wait a fortnight for John of Antioch and his bishops; The representatives of the Western Church also absent; The council sits without them; Nestorius refuses to appear; The council proceeds to business and condemns Nestorius; The Oriental bishops arrive and open a rival council; The Roman delegates arrive and subscribe to acts of Cyrillan Council; The rivals appeal to the emperor; Nestorius resigns; The Greek and Latin Churches accept the council; The Oriental Churches refuse; The spread of Nestorianism in the East; Dioscorus and Eutyches—their heresy; Eutyches condemned by the Synod of Constantinople; The *Concilio Latrocinium*; The *Fourth General Council* summoned at Chalcedon (A.D. 451) by Marcian; Condemns Dioscorus and Eutyches; Arranges jurisdiction of Patriarchate of Constantinople; Raises Jerusalem to the dignity of the Patriarchate; Leo's reception of the Acts of the Council; The Monophysite heresy spreads in Africa and the East; The *Fifth General Council*; The Monophysites encouraged by Anastasius and Theodora; Pope Agapetus visits Constantinople with Vigilius; Vigilius Pope; The controversy "of the Three Chapters"; Vigilius summoned to Constantinople; His vacillation; The Fifth General Council summoned at Constantinople (A.D. 553); Vigilius excommunicated; His submission and death; The *Sixth General Council*; Sergius of Constantinople starts the Monothelite heresy; Heraclius desires to reconcile the Monophysites on this basis; Cyrus of Alexandria partially succeeds; Opposed by Sophronius of Jerusalem; Pope Honorius writes in defence of the Monothelite heresy; The *Ecthesis* of Heraclius; The *Type* of Constans II.; The Pope carried prisoner to Constantinople and banished; The Sixth General Council summoned at Constantinople (A.D. 680); The Monothelite heresy condemned; Pope Honorius and others condemned by name; The *Quinisext Council* ............................................................. 223

## CHAPTER XXVIII.

**THE EASTERN EMPIRE FROM THE DEATH OF JUSTINIAN TO THAT OF HERACLIUS.**

Justin (565); The Lombard kingdom established in Italy; The imperial dominions in Italy reduced to Ravenna, Rome, and Venice; The Persian war renewed; Tiberius (574); Maurice (582); The Avars overrun Europe; Phocas (602); Heraclius (610); Chosroes conquers the Asian and African provinces of the empire; Receives a letter from Mohammed; The Avars invade the empire on the side of Europe; Heraclius carries the war into the heart of Persia; Peace concluded; Heraclius receives an embassy from Mohammed; The Arabs finally conquer the Asiatic provinces of the empire; Leo the Isaurian (726); The Iconoclastic controversy; Constantine Copronymus (741); The Council of Constantinople abolishes images; A persecution; Irene (780) repeals the edict against images; the Council of Nicæa restores their veneration; The Council of Frankfort takes an independent course; The revolt of the Italian dominions of the empire ...................................... 245

## CHAPTER XXIX.

### THE MOHAMMEDAN CONQUESTS.

Mohammed—his early history—flight to Medina (622)—sovereign of Arabia (632)—dies (632); Succeeded by Abubekr (632)—Omar (634)—Othman (644)—Ali (660)—Moawiyeh (665); Conquest of Syria, of Palestine, of Persia, of Egypt, North Africa, of Spain ; Dynasty of the Ommiades succeeded by that of Abbassides ; Abdalrahman makes Spain an independent caliphate ; The descendants of Ali make Africa an independent caliphate ; The Spanish Moors invade France—routed by Charles Martel at Roncesvalles ; The Mohammedan religion .................................................. 251

## CHAPTER XXX.

### THE GROWTH OF THE PAPACY.

No evidence of the foundation of the Roman Church ; Tradition attributes it to St. Peter and St. Paul ; The Church territorial arrangements followed those of the empire; Honorary precedence given to the bishop of the capital city at an early period ; Claim of Rome to the primacy as representing the see of Peter examined—no evidence that St. Peter exercised any primacy over the other apostles—no evidence that he established his permanent see at Rome—no evidence that any primacy descended from St. Peter to the bishops of Rome ; Views of Gregory the Great; The great patriarchates independent ; The Council of Nicæa on the point ; The primacy of Rome based on the political status of the capital ; John of Constantinople takes title of Œcumenical Bishop ; Gregory the Great's protest ; Early Papal attempts to exercise authority ; The question of the time of Easter ; The question of heretical baptism ; Exercised no authority in the general councils ; Lapse of Liberius ; Heresy of Honorius ; Adrian's approval of the Second Council of Nicæa opposed by the Council of Frankfort ; Growth of papal power favoured by absence of emperors from Rome—by orthodoxy of the West—by undisputed precedence of Rome in the West ; Decretals of Dionysius ; Gothic kings of Italy controlled the papacy : Gothic kingdom destroyed by Belisarius ; Justinian summons Vigilius to Constantinople ; Schism of Aquileia, &c. ; Justinian greatly controls the action of the popes ; Under the Exarchate of Ravenna the popes exercise some undefined authority in Rome ; The Italian provinces throw off their allegiance to the empire ; The Lombards seize Ravenna—threaten Rome ; The Pope appeals to Pepin for aid ; The claim of the papacy on the gratitude of Pepin ; Pepin wrests the Exarchate of Ravenna out of the hands of the Lombards, and bestows it on the Pope ; The pseudo-Isidorean Decretals; Pope Nicholas I. advances large claims, which lie for 300 years in abeyance .................................................. 258

## CHAPTER XXXI.

### THE EMPIRE OF CHARLEMAGNE.

PAGE

He inherits half Pepin's kingdom—seizes the other half (772) —conquers the kingdom of the Lombards—part of Spain, Saxony, Bohemia—exercise a real sovereignty over the Papal States—crowned emperor of the West—his encouragement of learning and religion—his religious foundations—the Council of Frankfort on the iconoclastic controversy—on the "filioque"—his death—the description of his empire; Establishment of the German empire in Otho I. (962); Increase of the wealth and power of the clergy —of the papacy .................................................................. 274

## CHAPTER XXXII.

### THE DARK AGES OF THE WESTERN CHURCH.

Aggrandisement of Church benefices; Prevalence of simony—examples of it; The see of Rome; Formosus (891); Boniface VI. (896); Stephen VI. (896)—disinters Formosus—tries and condemns him; John IX. (897) reverses the sentence on Formosus; Theodora and Marozia; Sergius III. (904), the lover of Marozia; Anastasius III. (911); John X. (913), the lover of Theodora; John XI. (931), the illegitimate son of Sergius III. and Marozia; John XII. (955), grandson of Marozia; Interference of the Emperor Otho; Three rival popes—John XII., Leo VIII., and Benedict; The emperor again intervenes; Benedict IX. (1033), a boy of ten or twelve; Again three popes—Benedict IX., Sylvester III., and Gregory VI.; The Emperor Henry III. intervenes and nominates Clement II........................................................................ 281

## CHAPTER XXXIII.

### THE CONVERSION OF THE NORTHERN NATIONS.

England absorbed into heathendom; Conversion of Ireland; Palladius' mission fails; Patrick, a Scot, educated and ordained in Gaul—his mission to Ireland—its success; Ireland a famous school of learning; The island of the saints; Conversion of Scotland; Columba founds Iona; Story of Pope Gregory and the Yorkshire slave-children in the Forum—he sends Augustine to England; Conversion of Kent; Conversion of Northumbria—its relapse; Foundation of Lindisfarne; The work of the two missions; Archbishop Theodore; in the Council of Hertford unites the two schools and all the churches into a united Church of England; The schools of Deira famous for learning; The Irish and Saxon missionary adventurers; Columbanus evangelises the Vosges—founds monasteries—labours in

Switzerland and in Lombardy ; Gall labours in Switzerland—founds monastery ; Amandus in Frisia ; Eligius—his labours—his sermons ; Wilfrid of York in Frisia ; Willebrord in Frisia ; King Radbod ; Wulfram in Frisia ; Human sacrifices ; Winfrid, or Boniface, preaches in Frisia—in Hessia—is consecrated bishop at Rome, and takes oath of obedience to the Roman see—reforms Frankish Church—evangelises Western Germany—revisits Frisia—slain by the heathen ; Charlemagne's Saxon wars and evangelisation ; Conversion of Denmark—Sweden ; Conversion of Norway ; Harald Haarfager unites it into one sovereignty ; Eric ; Haco converted at the court of Athelstan—introduces Christianity—the bonders compel him to join in heathen rites ; Harold Ericsson tries to introduce Christianity—conquered by Denmark ; Yarl Hacon ; Olaf, a viking in youth, is baptized—dispossesses Yarl Hacon—introduces Christianity—the adventure at Mære—defeated in battle with Sweyn ; Olaf Haraldson sends to England for a bishop and priests ; Canute  288

## CHAPTER XXXIV.

### THE CONVERSION OF THE SLAVONIC NATIONS.

The *Bulgarians* ; The sister of the Prince Bogoris a captive in Constantinople—converted—returns home—the prince and people converted ; Greek and Roman Churches contend for the obedience of the Bulgarians ; The Bulgarians choose the Greek connection ; *Moravia* receives a bishop from Charlemagne ; King Ratislav applies to Constantinople for Christian teachers ; Methodius and Cyril translate Scriptures and Liturgy ; Methodius consecrated at Rome ; *Bohemia* receives Christianity through Moravia ; Diethmar establishes his see at Prague ; *Poland* ; Mieceslav marries the daughter of the King of Bohemia, and embraces Christianity ; See established at Griesen, &c. ; Casimir elected king—brings the Church into union with Rome ; *Russia* ; The Princess Olga converted ; Russian ambassadors at Constantinople conveited ; Vladimir converted and marries the Princess Anne ; The people baptized ; Kieff the metropolitan see ; *Pomerania* receives the Gospel through Poland ; *Livonia* converted by crusading armies ; The Brethren of the Sword ; *Prussia* converted by the Teutonic knights—revolt—twenty-two years religious war ; Conversion of *Lithuania*, the *Samoeids*, the *Laps* .........  318

## CHAPTER XXXV.

### THE HILDEBRANDINE PERIOD.

Reaction against the abuses of the Church ; A reforming party—Clement II., Damasus II., Hildebrand, Leo IX. ; Hildebrand the soul of the reforming party ; Leo IX. (1048) holds reforming visitations and synods in Italy, France, Germany ; Victor II. (1054), the emperor, dies—his son entrusted to the Pope's guardianship; Stephen IX. (1057), rival Pope; Benedict X. (1058), legitimate Pope; Nicholas II.; Affairs of Milan; Election of Pope vested in the cardinals; Rival popes—Honorius II. and Alexander II. (1061)—the latter acknowledged; Gregory VII. (Hildebrand), 1073—his scheme of universal monarchy—causes of his success; Contest between Pope and Emperor; Gregory summons Henry IV. to Rome; Council of Worms deposes the Pope; Pope excommunicates the emperor; Henry forsaken by his subjects—declared deposed unless he obtains absolution—crosses the Alps to Italy; The scene at Canossa; Rival Emperor Randolph; Henry triumphs—marches into Italy—crowned by the anti-Pope; The Normans under Guiscard take Rome, plunder, and set fire to it; Death of Gregory; Victor III. (1085) —Urban II.; The popes continue to carry out the Hildebrandine policy; The quarrel of investitures; Henry V. imprisons the Pope and cardinals; The Diet of Worms (1123); Innocent III.—papal supremacy at its highest point—his transactions with Philip of France and John of England; Boniface VIII. (1294)—his assumptions higher than those of any of his predecessors—transactions with Edward of England and Philip the Fair of France; The reaction against the papal supremacy .................................... 326

## CHAPTER XXXVI

#### THE CRUSADES.

Under the earlier caliphs Christians and pilgrims to the holy places well treated; The Turks conquer Syria—oppress the Christians, and ill-treat pilgrims, and defile the sacred places; Peter the Hermit submits the project of a crusade to Urban II.; The Councils at Piacenza and at Clermont (1075) adopt the crusade—its popularity; The expeditions under Peter and others destroyed; The main body besieges Antioch—conquers Jerusalem; Extent and constitution of the Latin kingdom of Jeruszlem—its kings—the military orders; Loss of Edessa; St. Bernard preaches the Second Crusade—its failure; Saladin unites the caliphates—defeats the Christians at Hittin; Clement III. proclaims the Third Crusade; The forces assemble at the siege of Acre—its partial success; A German Crusade; The Fourth Crusade turns aside to the conquest of Constantinople; The Latin Empire of the East; French Crusade against Egypt; German Crusade obtains possession by treaty of several towns; The Chorasinians conquer Syria; Crusade of St. Louis—defeat—his death ........................................................ 343

## CHAPTER XXXVII

#### THE WALDENSES AND ALBIGENSES.

Heresies and schisms in the mediæval Church—Patarines, Cathari, Petro-

PAGE

Brussians; Arnold of Brescia; The Waldenses founded by Peter Waldo; He asks the Pope for his sanction—their progress; The Albigenses—a crusade organised against them; Capture of Beziers of Carcassonne; Submission of Raymond of Toulouse .............. 358

## CHAPTER XXXVIII.

#### THE POPES AT AVIGNON AND THE GREAT SCHISM.

Benedict XI. (1303) rescinds the obnoxious acts of Boniface VIII.; Clement V. (1305), a French Pope, entirely in the interest of the French king—removes his see to Avignon; Rome without the popes; Avignon with the popes; Seventy years of French popes—their rapacity; The death of Gregory IX. (1378) occasions the great schism; The rival papacies of Rome and Avignon; The Council of Pisa (1409); The Council of Constance (1414)......... 363

## CHAPTER XXXIX.

#### THE REFORMING COUNCILS OF THE FIFTEENTH CENTURY.

Cause of the failure of the Council of Pisa; Policy of Council of Constance—emperor presides—held out of Italy—voting by Nations—deposes both popes — declares a general council superior to the Pope; Committee of Reformation; The council elects an Italian Pope, Martin V. (A.D. 1417)—he makes separate concordats with the sovereigns, and hurries the council to a conclusion; The council condemns Wyclif, Huss, and Jerome of Prague; The religious wars in Bohemia; Martin V. summons a council at Basle; Eugenius IV. (1431) pronounces its dissolution, but the council continues its sittings; Eugenius recognises it; Fresh dissensions; The Pope removes the council to Ferrara to meet the Greek deputies; The Council of Basle continues its sittings—deposes Eugenius and elects Amadeus of Savoy (Felix V.), 1439; The conference between the Latins and Greeks at Ferrara; History of the schism; An ambiguous reconciliation; Its terms rejected by the Greek churches; History of the Church subsequent to the Council of Basle; France adopts the Pragmatic Sanction of Bourges; The German Emperor arranges a concordat; The Church relapses into a state of corruption ................................................. 369

## CHAPTER XL.

#### THE GREEK EMPIRE AND CHURCH FROM IRENE TO THE FALL OF THE EASTERN EMPIRE

Nicephorus (A.D. 802); Basil the Macedonian (867); The dynasty lasts through eight emperors, 150 years; Ann, daughter of Romanu,

|   | PAGE |
|---|---|

married to Vladimir of Russia; Basil conquers the Bulgarians; Theodora; Final rupture of the Eastern and Western Churches; The Comnenian dynasty; Isaac Angelus dethroned by his brother—his son escapes to Venice and diverts the Crusaders of the Third Crusade to Constantinople; The Crusaders take the city and establish the Latin Empire; Theodore Lascaris founds a kingdom at Nicæa—he and his successor, John Ducas Vataces, in fifty years win back the European provinces; Michael Paleologus recovers the city and restores the Greek Empire—attends the Council of Lyons, attempts the reconciliation of the Eastern and Western Churches; Persecutes the Eastern Church; John Paleologus; The Turks conquer nearly all the empire except the city; He visits the Council of Ferrara, and attempts the reconciliation of the churches; Manuel visits Europe to ask aid; Turkish power broken by Tamerlane—reunited under Mahomet I.; Mahomet II. conquers the Empire ... 386

## CHAPTER XLI.

### MEDIÆVAL DEVELOPMENTS.

A general sketch of the mediæval Western Church; The Pope accepted as spiritual ruler of the Church; Church discipline; The clergy, monks, friars, seculars; Public worship; The devotion to the Blessed Virgin Mary; Saint worship and pilgrimages; Purgatory, its practical influence; *The doctrine of the Eucharist*—scriptural—primitive; Paschasius Radbert introduces transubstantiation — Ratramnus' confutation; Berengarius; Transubstantiation spreads—defined by the Lateran Council (1216); The Council of Trent (1551); The Creed of Pope Pius (1563); A spiritual interpretation of the doctrine held by some; *The temporal power;* Early endowments of the Roman see; Pepin makes the Pope feudatory of Rome and the exarchate of Ravenna; The pseudo-donation of Constantine; The acquisition of the estates of the Countess Matilda of Tuscany; The Papal Infallibility; The promise of Christ to the Church believed to be in a general council; The forged decretals of Isidore lay foundation for claim of Nicholas I. to be the voice of the whole Church; The claim urged by the Hildebrandine writers—Gratian and Aquinas formulate it—the University of Paris opposes it—the great schism discredits it; The Councils of Constance and Basle enunciate, and the contemporary popes admit, the superiority of a Council to a Pope; The Papal Infallibility rehabilitated—taken up by the Jesuits—the doctrine decreed in the Vatican Council (1870); *The cultus of the Blessed Virgin Mary*—the Gospel view; The Council of Ephesus calls attention to her status—exaggerated reverence; Proposal of a Feast of the Conception of Blessed Virgin Mary opposed by St. Bernard; The great Church writers opposed to the theory of the Immaculate Conception; Duns Scotus brought it into vogue—the Dominicans oppose, the Franciscans support it—

warmly disputed for centuries—popes silence the disputants—still her worship grows; The Immaculate Conception decreed by the Pope to be a doctrine of the Church in 1844 .......................... 391

## CHAPTER XLII.

### THE REFORMATION.

*The German Reformation;* Accession of Leo X.; The peaceful state of the Church; The sale of indulgences; Luther's opposition—summoned to Rome—protected by the Elector Frederick—appears before the Diet of Augsburg; The Pope issues a bull in defence of indulgences; Luther appeals to a Council; Disputations at Leipsic with Eckius; The Pope issues a bull of excommunication—Luther burns the bull at Wittemberg; The spirit of reform spreads; Luther summoned to the Diet of Worms—condemned—carried off to Wartzburg—returns to Wittemburg—abandons his monastic profession (1524), and marries; The Elector John establishes a reformation in Saxony (1527); Other princes and states of Germany follow his example; The Diet of Spires (1529) condemns the Reformation; The princes protest; The Confession of Augsburg; The diet condemns the Reformation; The League of Smalcald; War; The defeat of Muhlberg; The *Formula ad interim;* Duke Maurice seizes the emperor; The settlement of Augsburg; *The Swiss Reformation;* Zuingle at Zurich; Œcolampadius at Basle; Calvin at Geneva—his system of doctrine—of Church organisation and discipline; *The French Reformation* introduced by Swiss preachers; First Reformed Church at Paris (1555); Their opinions spread; A Reformed Synod (1559) issues a Confession of Faith; The Prince of Condé the head of the reformed; Religious war; The Massacre of St. Bartholomew (A.D. 1572); Henry IV. succeeds to the throne; The Edict of Nantes (1598); The Dragonnades; Revocation of the Edict of Nantes (1648); Louis XIV. upholds the Gallican liberties; *The Reformation in Sweden* effected by the king, Gustavus Vasa; The Swedish apostolical succession; Council of Upsal (1593); *The Danish Reformation;* Character of Scandinavian Lutheranism; *Norway; Finland; The Reformation in Italy and Spain* suppressed by the Inquisition; *The English Reformation;* Wolsey's reforms; Reforming inclinations of the English Church; The king's divorce (1534); The Church and nation repudiate the papal supremacy; Suppression of the regular clergy; The doctrinal reformation; The introduction of Calvinistic influence in reign of Edward VI.; Return to papacy under Mary; Establishment of the Reformation under Elizabeth; Pius V. (1570) excommunicates Elizabeth and originates the Roman schism; *The Scottish Reformation;* The Covenant; Knox inflames the passions of the mob; Monasteries and churches attacked and plundered; The Genevan doctrine and discipline established by Parliament, and many imprisoned by the Reform party; King James subscribes the Covenant, 1581; Bishops restored (1610) by

James; Charles attempts to introduce the Prayer-book; General resistance; The Assembly of Divines and the Parliament again sign the Covenant; Assist in the civil war against Charles; On the Restoration the Church again established; Persecution of the Covenanters—Presbyterian doctrine and discipline established under William III. .................................................................. 415

# TURNING POINTS
## OF
# GENERAL CHURCH HISTORY.

### CHAPTER I.

#### THE WORLD PREPARED FOR THE CHURCH.

GLANCE at the state of the world at the time when our Lord Jesus Christ came into it, and lived, suffered, died, rose again, ascended, and on the foundation of the apostles and prophets erected the Church, whose history is our present theme.

We are specially concerned with three great races of mankind—the Greek, the Jewish, and the Roman. First, the Greek.

The human intellect reached, perhaps, its highest development in this glorious race. In history and philosophy, in arts and literature, its productions are still the models for mankind. The Greek, first of the ancient races, learnt the falsehood and folly of the popular religion, and directed his researches to the universe around him, and to his own being, and sought from these, by use of human reason, an explanation of the phenomena of Being and of Life—an answer to the questions, What am I, and whence? what is the true method of life? what becomes of me after death?

These researches led to the establishment of the various

systems of Greek philosophy. The chief were, the Epicurean, the Stoic, and the Platonic.

Epicureanism, as taught by Lucretius, had materialism for its theory of the universe. Its theory of human life was that happiness is the highest good, and that a wise man should pursue happiness in a well-regulated enjoyment of all the pleasures which the world affords. It was a religion suited to the acute, worldly-minded, pleasure-loving man; involving no moral responsibilities, calling for no self-denials; leaving him without fear or scruple to enjoy life, with no other rule than to seek the highest pleasures, and not to indulge in them to such excess as to blunt the keen edge of enjoyment.

The Stoic philosophy had Pantheism for its basis. It believed that the universe was an organic whole, informed by a universal spirit. All individual existence has emanated from this universal spirit, and is absorbed into it again. Evil and good are only different necessary forms of the universal life. The wise man lives within himself, holding himself superior to the accidents of life, and retaining his serenity under all circumstances. He has the same divine life as the gods; it is manifested in his individuality for a little while, and then reabsorbed into the whole, and given forth again in new individuals. The whole is everything, the individual nothing. The individuals are like waves of the sea, which are but the transient forms which the mass of waters for the moment bears.

But the profoundest and noblest philosophy was the Platonic. It taught the existence of one Supreme Spirit, the Maker and Ruler of the universe, who united in His Being all perfections. It held that man was not a mere transient phenomenon, but a real permanent individual; that there was a spark of the divinity in man which was purifying him and drawing him up to a higher mode of existence. It taught a belief in virtue and vice—virtue pleasing to God and preparing man for a happy future life; vice, displeasing to God and earning for man a miserable future.

The Eclectic philosophers took one doctrine from one system, and another from another, and recast them into a system of their own.

These philosophies took the place of a religion to the educated Greek; they were an explanation of the universe, and a guide to human life. But the philosophers held that the ancient superstitions were still useful for women, children, and the unlearned vulgar, who were incapable of rising to such a knowledge of philosophy as would influence their lives; and they themselves continued to attend the temples, and to pay a certain outward respect to the ancient religious observances, in order to countenance them, and encourage the vulgar belief in them.

The Greek colonies and conquests had spread the Greek culture and philosophy widely over the world. An adventurous, maritime, commercial race, they had emigrated and established flourishing communities along the shores of almost the whole Mediterranean Sea. Southern Italy itself was largely peopled by Greeks.

The rapid conquests of Alexander the Great were, after his death, divided among his generals into four kingdoms. Ptolemy took Egypt, Arabia, and Palestine; Cassander had Macedonia and Greece; Lysimachus had Thrace, Bithynia, and other provinces beyond the Hellespont; Seleucus took all the rest of Upper Asia, including Syria and Persia, and stretching as far as to the Indus. These Greek sovereigns were enlightened and energetic rulers; they diligently introduced Greek civilisation into the countries subject to their rule, built cities, encouraged commerce, patronised learning, philosophy, and the arts. Greek culture became widely diffused among the better classes of these countries. Greek became the language of literature and commerce throughout the civilised world, and the conclusions of Greek philosophy were widely known among educated people. Plutarch recognises that the mission of Alexander was to propagate Greek culture among the barbarians.

The Jews, since their return from the Babylonian captivity, had greatly multiplied. Outgrowing the narrow limits of their own land, they had adopted commerce as their pursuit, and spread themselves over the civilised world. Every great city had its colony of Jews, who did not intermarry with, or merge into, the people around them, but retained their nationality and religion and social isolation. In some of the great cities, tempted by special privileges, they had settled in large numbers. At Alexandria its great Macedonian founder assigned to them a third part of the city, and gave them the same privileges as the Greeks. At Antioch they were allowed, by Seleucus its founder, the same political privileges as the Greeks, and were governed by their own ethnarch. Everywhere their peculiarities attracted notice, and everywhere they were witnesses to the two great truths—the Unity of God, and the Promise of a Saviour.

Greek philosophy had everywhere shaken the faith of thinking men in their ancestral heathenism, and set them speculating on the mystery of human life. Where the Jewish theology was presented to minds in such a state, it was likely to win the adhesion of some; and so it came to pass that in every city the synagogue was surrounded by a fringe of proselytes of the gate, who believed in the Jewish God, and more or less shared the Jewish hope of a Messiah. Women especially were attracted by the Jewish teaching, and many of them of all ranks [*] were its disciples and supporters.

[*] Acts xiii. 50.

The establishment of the Roman empire was the last great step in the preparation of the world for the Church. It completed the work which the Greek conquests and commerce and philosophy had begun, in breaking down the barriers of race and religion which had divided mankind. Greek commerce had found out the paths through the seas from one maritime city to another. Roman conquest made the great high-roads, which ran straight over hill and valley, over mountain and river, through forest and marsh, connecting the imperial city with the furthest frontiers of the empire. Rome had succeeded to all the Asian and African conquests of Greece, and added her own European conquests to them. The Roman government and Roman law bound the various nations together as citizens of one empire.

The fusion of these various elements was assisted by the fact that Rome adopted the Greek civilisation. Greek became the language of educated people, as Latin did in the Middle Ages. Greek models were imitated in every branch of literature and the arts and philosophy, and Greek artists and *literati* encouraged. Teachers of Greek philosophy abounded in the chief cities of the empire. The well-born youth were sent to Athens, as to a university, to complete their education. Every Roman, with even a tincture of education, considered himself something of a philosopher.

On the whole the different races of the world were brought into more intimate relations and more familiar intercourse with one another than at any previous period in history. It is astonishing to what an extent the Roman world was thrown open, and how freely and largely men moved about in it, regarding it as a common country. The same interminable straight roads led them with perfect ease and safety from one side of the world to the other; they were everywhere under the protection of the same strong government, and the same wise and just laws. In every city they came to, the houses and streets and temples and theatres wore the same aspect; the better classes of the people everywhere wore the same dress, spoke the same language, had the same manners. Greece and Rome had filled the valleys and levelled the hills, and made the crooked ways straight, and the rough places smooth, and prepared the way for the coming of the Lord, that all flesh might see the salvation of God; and Judaism, like a herald, had raised a general expectation of His coming.

## CHAPTER II.

### THE CHURCH IN THE GOSPELS.

THE extent to which the Church occupied the mind of our Lord Jesus Christ, as shown in the prominent and large space which it takes up in His discourses, is often overlooked by the cursory reader of the New Testament.

There is no question that by the phrase "kingdom of heaven," or "kingdom of God," our Lord means His Church.* A glance at the places where the phrase occurs will show that in the great majority of cases it is applied to the state of the Church militant here upon earth; in a few places it may apply more especially to its state triumphant in heaven, but these are only two phases of the same Church.

The Church had already been foretold in Daniel's great prophecy as the "kingdom of the God of heaven, which shall never be destroyed."† The kingdom of David and Solomon was a type of it, and God had promised to David that the Messiah should be of his seed and should sit upon his throne. Accordingly Christ was born at Bethlehem, David's city, " because He was of the house and lineage of David"; and the genealogy of St. Matthew traces His descent through the kings. The magi came and worshipped

---

\* See Matt. xvi. 18, 19, where our Lord says, "Thou art Peter, and upon this rock I will build My *Church* . . . and I will give unto thee the keys of the *kingdom of heaven*"—the *Church* and the *kingdom of heaven* mean the same thing. Col. i. 13, "Who hath translated us into the *kingdom of His dear Son*," means into the *Church*; and 1 Thess. ii. 12, "Who hath called you unto *His kingdom* and glory," also means into *the Church*, &c

† Daniel ii. 44, vii. 27.

Him as King of the Jews (*i.e.*, of the true Israel). For assuming this title He was arraigned before Pilate, and He claimed before him to be a king, though not in the sense in which His accusers meant. On this charge He was actually put to death, for "the title of His accusation," put, according to custom, on His cross, in Hebrew, Greek, and Latin, was, "Jesus of Nazareth, the King of the Jews." John Baptist's preaching was, "Repent, for the kingdom of heaven is at hand."* Our Lord Himself began His ministry with the same announcement, "Repent, for the kingdom of heaven is at hand" †; and He sent forth His apostles to make the same proclamation.‡ Out of thirty-two parables, nineteen are parables of the kingdom. They begin with the first of the series—the parable of the sower—and end with the last—the parable of the vine. In the thirteenth chapter of St. Matthew several of them seem to be arranged in a prophetic order. The *sower* speaks of the first proclamation of the Gospel, and foretells the different reception it would meet with from different kinds of hearts. The *tares* shows that the Church would not consist of good people only, but that hypocrites would be found in it. The *mustard-seed* prophesies the vast extension of the kingdom from its small beginning, so that the Gentile nations would seek shelter under it. The *leaven* illustrates the way in which, hidden from observation, the power of the Spirit would work in the world and leaven the mass of mankind. The *treasure* and the *pearl* show how some would come upon the Gospel as by accident, like the Ethiopian eunuch, and others, like Justin Martyr, as the end of a careful search after truth. As the first of the series spoke of the first preaching of the Gospel, the last of the series takes us to the end of the world. The *net* tells us how the Church, having swept through the ages from one end

* Matt. iii. 2.   † Matt. iv. 17.   ‡ Matt. x. 7.

of the world to the other, will finally land those whom it has caught on the shore of eternity, and there the separation (already spoken of in the *tares*) shall take place: " The angels shall gather out of His kingdom all things that offend, and them which do iniquity, and shall cast them into a furnace of fire, there shall be wailing and gnashing of teeth. Then shall the righteous shine forth as the sun in the kingdom of their Father. Who hath ears to hear let him hear." (Matth. xiii. 41, 42, 43.)

But although our Lord generally speaks of His Church under the title of kingdom, it is to Him we owe the word by which in all times, from the apostles downwards, it has been most usually called. "Upon this rock" of Peter's confession of His deity "I will build My Church, and the gates of hell shall not prevail against it "* (Matt. xvi. 18); and again, in laying down a rule of discipline for the members of it, He says that an offending brother who refuses to listen to private admonition is to be reported " to the Church; but if he neglect to hear the Church" he is to be cast out of its communion (Matt. xviii. 17). The word translated church (ἐκκλησία) means a body called out of the general mass of people; as Abraham and his seed were called out of the rest of mankind and formed a separate nation and Church, so individuals are called out of all nations and formed into a distinct kingdom and Church of Christ.

In His baptism our Lord received the Divine anointing to the kingly office. On the very day after, He began to gather His Church out of those whom John the Baptist had prepared for Him. First He called Andrew (and perhaps John), and Andrew brought his brother Simon; and the next day Christ called Philip, and Philip brought

---

* This is a prophecy of the foundation of the Church, of its endless duration, and of the name by which it should be called.

Nathanael; and so brother brought brother, and friend friend, and His disciples multiplied. A little later He laid the foundations of the sacred ministry of His Church in the twelve apostles. Having passed the previous night in prayer (Luke vi. 12), next morning He assembled His disciples, and out of the general body He chose twelve, whom He named apostles, and sent them forth to preach to the lost sheep of the house of Israel " *The kingdom of heaven is at hand,*" and gave them power to work miracles in attestation of their authority to make this proclamation of the kingdom. These men, when they returned from their mission, He kept with Him thenceforward, to be witnesses of all He did and hearers of all He said, that they might be taught and trained for their future work.

Again, the thoughtful reader of the Gospels will have observed how the life and teaching of our Lord lead up to the moment when He at length drew from the hearts of His apostles, through the mouth of Peter, the confession of His divinity:—" But whom say *ye* that I am? And Peter answered, Thou art the Christ, the Son of the living God"; and how from this moment His life and teaching assumed another tone; "the signs and wonders" became less frequent; He begins to look forward to and to speak of His death. Let it be noticed how at this great crisis our Lord's mind was occupied with the idea of His Church. In response to the apostles' confession of His divinity He prophesies to them the foundation of His Church, and gives the promise of its indefectibility: " On this rock"—the rock of this confession—" I will build My Church, and the gates of hell shall not prevail against it." At this crisis in the development of the Gospel the two things are joined together by our Lord—the confession of His divinity and His Church, the one founded on the other. Note again, as an illustration of the way in which His Church comes out continually in our Lord's teaching, that His last parable, that of the vine, was a type of the deepest mystery of the Church, viz., its incorporation with Christ; and His last act before His passion was the institution of the great means of maintaining that incorporation.

During the mysterious forty days, between His resurrection and His ascension, His Church was the chief subject of His communications with His disciples, " being seen of them forty days, and speaking of the things pertaining to *the kingdom of God*" (Acts i. 3). The evangelists record some of His sayings of these forty days pertaining to the kingdom of God. On the evening of the great Easter Day, when He appeared to the apostles assembled in the upper room, " He breathed on them and said, Receive ye the Holy Ghost: whosesoever sins ye remit, they are remitted unto them; and whosesoever sins ye retain, they are retained." When He appeared to them on the shore of the lake of Galilee He wrought the miracle of the draught of fishes, which was typical of the work of the commissioned fishers of men, and gave to Peter the command, and through Peter to the rest of the apostles, " Feed My sheep," " Feed My lambs." He appeared to His disciples and said, " All power is given unto Me in heaven and in earth"—as God He possessed all power from all eternity; it was as Son of man that, after His resurrection, He received His kingdom— " Go ye, therefore, and make disciples (*i.e.*, make Christians) of all nations, baptizing them in the name of the Father, and of the Son, and of the Holy Ghost; teaching them to observe all things whatsoever I have commanded you; and; lo, I am with you alway, even unto the end of the world. Amen" (Matt. xxviii. 19, 20). And, lastly, " Behold, I send the promise of My Father upon you; but tarry ye in the city of Jerusalem until ye be endued with power from on high" (Luke xxiv. 49).

What, then, is the idea of the Church which we gather from the Gospels? It is of a spiritual kingdom, of which Christ is the ever-present King, the Bible its code of laws, the clergy its ministers, and Christian people its citizens; a kingdom extending into every temporal kingdom, not withdrawing subjects from their temporal allegiance, for the civil magistrates are "His ministers attending to this very thing," but setting up a superior claim to a more entire obedience and more devoted allegiance, as extending over a higher province. The apostles are to go into all the world and proclaim this kingdom, and demand belief and obedience to the proclamation under the most awful sanctions. They are to admit men into it by an external act of incorporation, to appoint subordinate officers over every section, to rule the whole with Divine authority. These several sections are to spread until they have leavened the whole society in which they are placed, until the Church shall have become co-extensive with the world; and the gates of Hades shall not prevail against it. The apostles are promised supernatural guidance and assistance in the initiation of this great work, equally applying to what they taught in doctrine, and to what they ordained as to organisation.

We shall proceed in the next chapter to see how the apostles actually established and organised this kingdom of Christ.

## CHAPTER III.

### THE APOSTOLIC CHURCH.*

THE Acts of the Apostles is especially the history of the establishment and gradual development of the Church of Christ. Incidental notices in the Epistles and the Revelation complete the history of its apostolic organisation. All the principles of Church organisation will be found in the sacred volume.

The Christian Church was supernaturally begun in the upper chamber at Jerusalem on the day of Pentecost. The Lord had prepared it a body, in the 120 who were gathered together there awaiting the fulfilment of Christ's promise of the Comforter. And as the Holy Spirit breathed into Adam's body the breath of life and he became a living soul, so the same Holy Spirit came with a sound as of a rushing mighty wind and filled all the house where they were sitting, and tongues of flame lighted upon each of them who sat there, and they were all filled with the Holy Ghost; and the Church—the company of believers, called by Christ, and indwelt by the Holy Spirit, the "one Body and one Spirit"—began its life, against which the gates of hell should not prevail.

The multitude of Jews and proselytes gathered together to the feast from all parts of the world, from the Tiber to the Euphrates, from the Euxine to the cataracts of the

---

* Portions of this chapter are taken from a chapter on the same subject in "Some Chief Truths of Religion," by the same author.

Nile, flocked together at the rumour of the miracle; and the apostles, filled with the Holy Ghost, at once began their work of making disciples by the preaching of the Word. Peter preached to them the facts of the Gospel; and they were pricked in their hearts, and asked, "Men and brethren, what shall we do?" And Peter told them, "Repent, and be baptized every one of you in the name of Jesus Christ, for the remission of sins; and ye shall receive the gift of the Holy Ghost. For the promise is to you, and to your children, and to all that are afar off, even as many as the Lord our God shall call." "And they that gladly received his word were baptized," by the one Spirit into the one Body, to the number of 3,000.

Then we have a statement of the criteria of Church membership. They continued steadfastly—

1. In the apostles' doctrine.
2. In their fellowship.
3. In the breaking of the bread.
4. In the prayers.

A few verses afterwards we have a further statement about the worship and devotions of the primitive Church. They continued daily, with one accord, in the Temple (the prayers; see an instance of it a few verses farther on, Acts iii. 1), and breaking the bread (the Eucharist) at the house, *i.e.*, the upper chamber, where they had been, and continued to be, accustomed to assemble.

And the events of the next few days or weeks, or months it may be, are summed up in the words, "And the Lord added to the Church daily (οἱ σωζόμενοι) those who were being saved" (Acts ii. 47).

In the third chapter we have an instance of the way in which the working of miracles helped the preaching of the Word; for many who heard the Word preached again by St. Peter, and saw the miracle of the healing of the lame man at the Beautiful Gate, "believed; and the number of the men was about 5,000."

The foreign Jews converted on the day of Pentecost, and they who were scattered abroad by Saul's persecution, went everywhere telling what they had learned, and so preparing the ground for the future mission work of the apostles.  But the Church, as an organised body, was limited at first to Jerusalem, and all its members were Jews.

In the eighth chapter we have the history of its extension to the first circle beyond the Jewish pale. Philip the deacon went down to a city of Samaria and preached Christ unto them; and they, seeing his miracles and hearing his teaching, believed, and were baptized, both men and women, and there was great joy in that city. And when the apostles heard of it they sent down two of their own number, Peter and John, "who, when they were come down, prayed for them, that they might receive the Holy Ghost." When we call to mind the ancient enmity between the Jews and Samaritans we shall understand the full significance of this event. It was the abandonment of prejudices on both sides, and the reconciliation of these ancient religious enemies in the unity of the Church of Christ.

The next step was the admission of a Gentile proselyte, in the conversion and baptism, also by the agency of Philip, of the treasurer of Queen Candace. Philip found him as he journeyed in his chariot, reading Isaiah liii. ver. 7 and 8, and took occasion from this passage to preach unto him Jesus, teaching him that he must be baptized in His name. How could he fail to do it? Were not our Lord's words to His apostles "Go, and make disciples of all nations, baptizing them"?. And as they went on their way they came to a certain water, and the eunuch said, "See, here is water, what doth hinder *me* to be baptized?" And

Philip said, "If thou believest with all thine heart thou mayest." And in the eunuch's reply we have a catechumen's baptismal confession of faith: "I believe that Jesus is the Son of God"—the germ of all the creeds; and he baptized him, and the eunuch went on his way rejoicing.

In the tenth chapter we have the history of the extension of the Church to the Gentile world. This was a greater step than that of the admission of Samaritans, or proselytes of the gate, who were already half Jews: it was the abandonment of the strongest religious prepossessions of the Jews; it was the conclusive step out of the bondage of the law into the liberty of Christ; it was not merely the admission of Samaritans and proselytes into a new school of Judaism, it was the merging of Judaism into Christianity. This accounts for the elaborate circumstances of the transaction, and the fulness with which they are recorded. A vision of an angel bids Cornelius, the Roman centurion, send for Peter the apostle. A simultaneous vision bids Peter lay aside his Jewish scruples, and go to this Gentile who sends for him. Again, while Peter is yet speaking, the Holy Ghost falls on the Gentile company. And Peter is able to appeal to this manifest indication of the will of Jesus as his warrant for admitting these uncircumcised Gentiles by baptism into the Church of Christ.

We have seen so far how, on the day of Pentecost, the Church of Christ, as a visible company of believing people indwelt by the Holy Ghost, began to be; we have seen the Church spread in widening circles from the upper room to embrace Jews, Samaritans, proselytes, and Gentiles. So far Jerusalem has been the centre of interest, and Peter the most prominent figure of the history. Then the scene shifts, and in chap. xi. 19 we enter upon another series of events—the gradual spread of the Church among the Gentiles.

Some men of Cyprus and Cyrene (after the admission of Cornelius and his friends had opened the gates of the Church to the Gentiles) coming to Antioch, the great and luxurious capital of Syria, preached the Gospel to the heathen inhabitants of that city, and a great number of them believed and turned to the Lord. When tidings of these things came to the ears of the Church at Jerusalem, the apostles assumed the direction of this new work, and sent Barnabas to organise and conduct it. The work so prospered under his hands, that he needed help in it, and he went himself to Tarsus to induce Paul to come and help him. It was now seven years since Paul's miraculous conversion. The first three years he seems to have spent in Arabia, and then to have returned to his native city, and to have taken no active, at least no conspicuous part in the work of the Church. Barnabas knew him personally; it was he who answered for Paul when the brethren at Jerusalem had distrusted the sudden conversion of the recent persecutor. The time was now come for the fulfilment of the purpose which Jesus had revealed to Paul at his conversion: "He is a chosen vessel to bear My name among the Gentiles" (Acts x. 15, and xxvi. 17). He accepted the duty to which Barnabas invited him, and for a whole year they laboured together in the flourishing Gentile Church of Antioch.

At the end of that time the Holy Ghost bade the prophets and teachers at Antioch separate Barnabas and Saul for a special mission; and Antioch became the centre whence the Church began to spread itself over the nations of the world. Barnabas and Saul, the apostles of the Gentiles, went first to Cyprus (where Barnabas was known as a landowner) and preached in its chief cities; then crossed the sea again to the southern part of Asia Minor, and preached in some of its towns—the Pisidian Antioch, Iconium

Lystra, Derbe; on a second visit they ordained elders to take charge of the new churches; and returned in the third year to give an account of their labours to the Church at Antioch.

After about a year's interval St. Paul undertook a second missionary journey, taking Silas as his deacon. First he revisited the Churches of Derbe, Lystra, and Iconium, which he and Barnabas had founded. Then he pushed forward westward through Galatia, and a vision led him to cross over the narrow strait which separates the continents, and to carry the Gospel into Europe; and the sacred historian records his progress through the cities of Macedonia and Greece, Philippi, Thessalonica, Berea, Athens, and Corinth.

A third journey began with a two years' stay at Ephesus, whence he travelled again through Macedonia and Greece, and finally up to Jerusalem. Here he was arrested by the Roman captain of the Temple as the cause of a riot in the Temple precincts. He was detained in custody two years at Cæsarea, when at length his appeal to the emperor led to his visit as a prisoner to Rome, where he stayed two years in his own hired house, preaching the Gospel without hindrance. And when the history has thus recorded how the Church was established among the three great civilisations—Jewish, Greek, and Roman—its task is accomplished, and it ends.

The Epistles of St. Paul reveal to us incidentally something of the interior history of several of the churches of his foundation—the Churches of Corinth, Galatia, Ephesus, Philippi, Colosse, and Thessalonica.

The Revelation gives us a view, at the close of the first century, of one corner of the field of the Church, viz., of the great Ephesian Church, and the daughter Churches which had sprung from her, and were still, and continued to their end, under her jurisdiction—the Churches of Smyrna,

Pergamos, Thyatira, Sardis, Philadelphia, and Laodicea. The inspired history of the Church is thus brought down very nearly to the end of the first century, coinciding with the history of the Roman empire from Tiberius to Trajan.

All the principles of Church organisation and discipline are found to have been established by the apostles acting under Divine inspiration.

The Church is seen as a visible body of men gathered out of all nations, admitted by the external ceremony of baptism, assembling together for common worship, obeying the same laws. Though consisting of men of different races, scattered in groups in all the cities of the world, yet the Church of the New Testament is one body, an *imperium in imperio;* just as the Church's prototypes the dispersed Jews were subjects of the laws of the country in which they lived, but continued of one nationality and religion, and looked to Jerusalem as their national and religious centre. Its internal unity consists in the one Spirit which inhabits it. Its external bond of unity is the ministry, whose members all derive their authority, through the apostles, from Christ.

The Church is a visible society, into which all are bidden to enter who desire salvation through Christ. When our Lord bade His ministers go and make disciples of all nations, baptizing them, he virtually bade all men who should believe to enter by baptism into this visible society; and having entered, to conform to its laws. So at the beginning we read, when Peter preached the first sermon and his hearers asked, What are we to do? he said, Repent (as the necessary pre-requisite for baptism), and be baptized every one of you. And those who were daily, by the apostles' teaching, brought into the way of salvation, the Lord added to the Church. So the early Christian writers understood it. Irenæus says : " They who do not come into the Church do not partake of the Spirit, but deprive themselves of life; for where the Church is, there is the Spirit of God."\* And St. Cyprian says: "He cannot have God for his father who has not the Church for his mother." † The Church has not, as the synagogue had, any proselytes of the gate. Jew and Gentile are invited and required to enter into the fulness of the new covenant of God in Christ Jesus.

The two sacraments hold the same prominent place in the Church of the New Testament that they have ever since held in the Church.

Baptism is the sacrament of entrance. Our Lord had declared to Nicodemus that without baptism no man could enter into the kingdom of God, *i.e.*, the Church (John iii.). Our Lord commanded, "Make disciples of all nations, baptizing them" (Matt. xxviii. 19); and in obedience to this command the converts of the New Testament are always baptized at once as a matter of course. The three thousand converted on the day of Pentecost (Acts ii. 41); the Samaritans (Acts viii. 12); the Ethiopian proselyte (Acts viii. 38); Paul after his miraculous conversion (Acts xxii. 16); Cornelius and his friends, though they had already received the Holy Ghost (Acts x. 47, 48); Lydia and her household (Acts xvi. 15); the jailer of Philippi and all his (Acts xvi. 33); the twelve disciples of John Baptist at Ephesus, though they had received John's baptism (Acts xix. 6); Crispus and his house, and many of the Corinthians (Acts xviii. 8); the household of Stephanas (1 Cor. xvi. 15).

Holy Communion is one of the four criteria of primitive Churchmanship :—They continued steadfastly in the breaking of the bread. The first converts at Jerusalem celebrated the Holy Communion daily :—They continued daily with one accord in the Temple, and breaking the bread at the house. It was so much the centre and chief act of their

\* Irenæus, lib iii., cap. xi.　　† De Unitate Ecclesiæ

worship that the history of St. Paul's doings at Troas describes the purpose for which the disciples were accustomed to come together every Lord's day as being to break the bread : "When the disciples came together on the first day of the week to break the bread" (Acts xx. 7).

St. Paul (1 Cor. x.) alludes to the veneration in which the two sacraments were held by the primitive Christians, and warns them not to trust in these great privileges for salvation unless they continued faithful to their profession and their grace.

The unity of the Church is plainly set forth: "There is one Body and one Spirit, one Lord, one Faith, one Baptism, one God and Father of all" (Eph. iv. 4, 5). The internal bond of this unity is spiritual unity in the mystical body of Christ. Christ himself teaches it: "As the branch cannot bear fruit of itself, except it abide in the vine; no more can ye, except ye abide in Me. I am the vine (stem), ye are the branches" (John xv. 4, 5). St. Paul compares it to the oneness of a human being: "He is the head of the body, the Church" (Col. i. 18). "As the human body is one, and hath many members, and all the members of that body, being many, are one, so also is Christ (the mystical Christ); for by one Spirit are we all baptized into one body." (1 Cor. xii. 13.)

The importance of it appears from the admonition, "Be ye all of one mind"; from the anxiety of the apostle to check the rising spirit of partizanship in the Corinthian Church, "I beseech you, brethren, by the name of our Lord Jesus Christ, that there be no divisions among you" (1 Cor. i. 10, &c.); from the direction to the Romans to avoid the leaders of schism, "Mark them which cause divisions . . . and avoid them" (Rom. xvi. 17; compare 1 Tim. vi. 3, 4, 5).

The mode of maintaining this external unity of a society

scattered in groups through every city of the world is illustrated in the sacred writings. Christ is the head of the body, the centre of the Church's unity. He sent forth the apostles as His representatives: "As My Father hath sent Me, even so send I you; whoso receiveth you receiveth Me." He gave the keys of His kingdom—*i.e.*, the government of the Church—to the college of co-equal apostles. It was one of the marks of primitive Churchmanship to "continue steadfastly in the apostles' fellowship." When the Samaritans were baptized the apostles sent two of their own number to receive the converts into the unity of their fellowship; when the Gentiles were converted at Antioch they sent Barnabas to take charge of the new work.

But how was unity to be maintained when serious differences of opinion arose? The sacred history tells us. The first serious difference of opinion was whether the Mosaic institution established under such solemn sanctions was a permanent one. Some said that though the gates of God's ancient Church were to be thrown open to the Gentiles, yet the Gentiles on entering it must conform to its divinely sanctioned customs; others maintained that the Mosaic institution was a temporary addition to the covenant made with Abraham, which had served its purpose and was now to pass away, and Jews and Gentiles were to unite in the Christian Church, on the basis of the original covenant with Abraham, with new institutions ordained by Christ. The question troubled the believers everywhere, and was evidently of the utmost consequence. The way it was settled, and the unity of the Church preserved, was by the calling of a synod: "The apostles and elders came together to consider of this matter." And it appeared, from Peter's account of the miraculous sanctions under which he admitted Cornelius and his friends into the Church, and by Paul and Barnabas's account of the miracles which had attended their wholesale admission of Gentiles everywhere, that Christ had sanctioned their admission into the Church without their observance of the ceremonial law. And they drew up a canon in which they boldly affirm, "It hath seemed good to the Holy Ghost and to us" so to decree. And when the believers read the decree they did not proceed to question its authority; but, admitting it as an authoritative solution of a difficult and dangerous difference, "they rejoiced for the consolation" (Acts xv.).

This kingdom of Christ—the Church—though it is a visible kingdom, receiving its subjects by an open profession of allegiance and by an outward rite of admission, though it has written laws which its citizens are bound to obey, and officials by whom its laws are administered, and raises revenues out of the purses of its citizens, is yet a spiritual kingdom:—" My kingdom," said our Lord, "is not of this world." None are compelled to become its subjects; men enter it or not as they will, only if they will not they incur the responsibility of rejecting the invitation of God. Its citizens are not compelled by any temporal penalties to obey its laws, only they incur such punishments as God shall inflict. Its revenues are raised by a voluntary self-taxation, only Christians are God's stewards of all their property, and will have to reckon with Him at last. The utmost power the Church assumes is to refuse to allow an offender to continue a member of the kingdom whose laws he refuses to obey.

The Church is visible, spiritual, and one. There are not two Churches here on earth—a visible and a spiritual, a Church within the Church, a Church of good people within the Church of worldly, wicked people. The one visible spiritual Church contains both good and bad, as our Lord told us it would (Matt. xiii.), and the separation has not yet been made. There is not a single passage in the whole of the

New Testament where the Church is spoken of as any but an outward and visible congregation.

It is true that a man may live in the Church's outward communion, and use all the means of grace, and receive none of the inward blessings of membership of Christ's Church, because he is destitute of faith and obedience. It is also true that it is possible for a man to be excluded from the Church's outward communion, and at the same time to maintain an uninterrupted invisible communion with Christ, and to receive direct from Him grace and blessing, which is the case of the unjustly excommunicated. But it remains true that the Church is an outward and visible society, descended visibly from Christ its head, and that every man who hears the call of the Gospel, and has it in his power, is required by our Lord Jesus Christ to become a member of it: "He that believeth and is baptized shall be saved," and baptism is the outward admission into the visible Church.

The threefold ministry is seen fully constituted and established in the Church of the New Testament. Christ Himself ordained the apostles, and gave them full powers as His representatives, and guided them by the Holy Spirit in the exercise of those powers.

The history of the appointment of deacons is recorded in the sixth chapter of the Acts.* The selection of them † seems to have been left for obvious reasons to the discontented Hellenic party, but they were ordained to their office by the laying on of the apostles' hands. Their office was especially to administer the charities of the Church, but we find that some of them at least (Stephen and Philip) also preached and baptized.

---

\* It is possible that this may be only the record of an addition of some Hellenists to the body of deacons already existing; but it has usually been accepted as the record of the first institution of this order of the ministry.

† All their names are Greek.

The first appointment of presbyters is not recorded. We find them first mentioned as already existing in the Church of Judea in the eleventh chapter of the Acts, ver. 30. When the foreign churches sent their help to the brethren who dwelt in Judea during the famine, they sent them to the elders by the hands of Barnabas and Saul. We infer that wherever in the course of their labours the apostles gathered together a number of disciples, there they ordained an elder to take charge of the flock, over which they themselves, however, retained the chief oversight and supreme government. Thus Barnabas and Paul "ordained elders in every church" (Acts xiv. 23). The office of the elders was to take charge of these separate flocks; and that their appointment was made under the inspiration of the Holy Ghost we learn from St. Paul's address to the elders of Ephesus: "Take heed therefore unto yourselves, and to all the flock, over the which the Holy Ghost hath made you overseers, to feed the Church of God" (Acts xx. 28). St. Peter assumes the same principles of Church government, and similarly compares the office of an elder to that of a shepherd: "The elders among you I exhort, who am also an elder. Feed the flock of God which is among you, taking the oversight thereof, not by constraint, but willingly; not for filthy lucre (a temptation to which the payment of the ministry out of the offerings of the people made them liable), but of a ready mind; neither as being lords over God's heritage (a temptation to which the spiritual authority they wielded and the great deference commonly paid to it by the believers opened the way), but being ensamples to the flock" (1 Pet. v. 1—3). The duties of the second order of the ministry were, therefore, to rule a particular congregation of believers, subject to the superior rule of the apostles, and to minister the word and sacraments in that congregation.

We find, then, abundant evidence of the existence of three

gradations or orders of the ministry in the Apostolic Church. Was this ministry, and this gradation of orders in it, intended to be, and was it in fact, permanent?

There is little question that our Lord intended that there should always be a ministry for the preaching of the Gospel, the teaching of believers, the conduct of Divine worship, and the government of this visible society; in fact there has always been such a ministry. When our Lord commissioned some to go and make disciples of all nations, teaching them to observe "whatsoever I have taught you," and promised to be with them to the end of the world, He contemplated the permanent existence of such a body of ministers. St. Paul's direction to Timothy (2 Tim. ii. 2), "The things that thou hast heard of me, the same commit thou also to faithful men, who shall be able to teach others also," clearly contemplates a succession of authorised teachers.

The real question is as to the permanence of the highest order of the ministry. When the apostles died, were the individual congregations left to the rule of the second order, or were any successors appointed to the apostles in a higher order, in whom the office of the supreme government of the churches was continued? In other words, was the permanent government of the Church intended by our Lord to be Episcopal or Presbyterian? There are three facts in the history of the New Testament which make it at least highly probable that it was intended that the apostles should be, and in fact were, succeeded by others in their higher office and supreme authority over the other ministers, and over the general body of the Church.

The first is the appointment by the apostles of a Bishop of Jerusalem.

Before they dispersed to their missionary work throughout the world they appointed James to be the Bishop of the Church of Jerusalem. Whether this was James the son of

Alphæus the apostle, or the son of Joseph by a former wife, all agree that he was a kinsman of our Lord. The ancient fathers constantly affirm that James was Bishop of Jerusalem. The catalogues of the Bishops of Jerusalem, given by the first Christian writers, all place James at the head of the list. An episcopal throne, or chair, in which it was believed that he used to sit, was still preserved and had in veneration when Eusebius wrote his history in the former part of the fourth century. The notices of him in the New Testament confirm this statement. In the early part of the Acts, St. Peter is always spoken of as the leading person in the Church at Jerusalem; but after the twelfth chapter James always appears to be the chief person in that Church. When Peter was delivered from prison, he bids some of the disciples " go show these things to James and to the brethren "—James was the chief among the brethren. When Paul came up to Jerusalem to give a report of his missionary labours and successes he went to James, and all the elders were present (Acts xxi. 18)—the bishop and his presbyters. At the Synod of Jerusalem James authoritatively sums up the discussion and pronounces the decree of the synod. Paul speaks (Gal. ii. 9) of having conferred with "James, Cephas, and John, who seemed to be pillars," where James is put before Peter and John. The Judaising teachers who went down from Jerusalem to Antioch are said to be "certain who came from James," which implies that he was the head of the Church of Jerusalem. On the death of James the surviving apostles and disciples assembled together at Jerusalem and ordained Simeon, the son of Cleophas, another kinsman of our Lord, to be his successor. Simeon presided over this Church till the time of Trajan, and was one of the victims of the persecution under that emperor. After Simeon, succeeded thirteen bishops, all of Jewish name, before Hadrian drove out the inhabitants and razed the city to the ground. Their names are given by Eusebius, the historian of the early Church.

The second fact to which we call attention is that St. Paul, towards the close of his life, appointed Timothy to exercise in the Church of Ephesus the same authority which he himself had hitherto exercised there, and in all the other churches of his own planting. His Epistles to Timothy remain as evidences of this; they and the Epistle to Titus are the permanent written instructions which he gave them to guide them in the execution of their important office, and they were included in the sacred canon because they were intended to be the inspired directions to all the bishops of the Church of Christ. The ancient fathers constantly call Timothy Bishop of Ephesus, and the subsequent bishops of that see are always spoken of as being his successors; at the Council of Chalcedon a list of twenty-seven in uninterrupted succession from him was extant. Titus was similarly appointed, with similar authority over the churches of the island of Crete. It is the method of the New Testament history of the Church, as we have seen, to mention examples of Church principles as occasion arises, and to leave to us the inference that the principles thus incidentally mentioned were of general application. We conclude that these are instances of the transition from the rule of apostles keeping an oversight over all the churches of their own foundation, to that of bishops, each succeeding to the apostolic authority in the particular portion of the Church committed to his care.

If the apostles had been directed by their Lord, or inspired by the Holy Ghost, to prepare the churches, after their removal, for self-government on a democratic or a Presbyterian constitution, surely we should have found some intimations of it, some preparation for it. Would the churches not have been warned that this autocratic rule which the apostles had exercised was not to be permanent? Would there have been no exhortations to the people or to the presbyters as to the mode of exercising this Church power, when it should suddenly fall into their hands on the apostles' decease? But, on the contrary, the steps which St. Paul takes to prepare the churches of Ephesus and of Crete for his own departure, which he knew to be at hand, is to send Timothy and Titus to them armed with his own autocratic authority, and with directions for its firm and vigorous exercise. The transition from the apostolic constitution to the permanent constitution is seen, not in the appointment of general synods of Church members, or colleges of presbyters, but in the delegation of apostolic authority to an individual. The whole teaching and action of St. Paul, from beginning to end, tends to the permanent establishment of episcopacy; and if it was his intention to establish Presbyterianism or Congregationalism, his conduct is utterly inexplicable.

The third fact alluded to confirms this view of the question. The seven epistles in the Book of the Revelation are addressed to the "angels" of the seven principal churches of Proconsular Asia—viz., Ephesus, Smyrna, Pergamos, Thyatira, Sardis, Philadelphia, and Laodicea. The date of the book is about 95 A.D., or two or three years later; and it is clear from the letters themselves that these "angels" are individual men invested with the chief authority in those several churches.

The title angels is very nearly the same in meaning as apostles. Our Lord is called the Angel of the Covenant, and the apostles are called angels * (Rev. xxi. 12—14).

---

* These angels are typified by the seven stars : "The seven *stars* are the angels of the seven churches, and the candlesticks are the churches." Our Lord is also called a *star*—" The Morning Star" (Rev. ii. 28, xxii. 16); and the apostles are called *stars* (Rev. xxii. 1).

St. Augustine and other ancient fathers call these seven angels the bishops of the seven churches. We know from history that these churches had bishops at a very early period. Timothy had been appointed Bishop of Ephesus long before; and, as we have said, the acts of the Council of Chalcedon show that there had been an uninterrupted succession of bishops there. Polycarp, a disciple of St. John, is stated by his disciple Irenæus to have been consecrated by the apostles to be Bishop of Smyrna. Not long after St. John's time, Sagaris, who is said to have been a disciple of St. Paul, was Bishop of Laodicea. Melito was Bishop of Sardis in the time of the Emperor M. Aurelius. When Ignatius wrote his Epistle to the Philadelphians, which, at the most, was not above twelve years after St. John returned from Patmos, they had a bishop, whose gravity, modesty, and other virtues Ignatius commends, and exhorts the Philadelphians to be dutiful to him. The old Roman martyrology speaks of Carpus, Bishop of Thyatira, who suffered martyrdom under Antoninus. Antipas is said to have been Bishop of Pergamos. So that we have evidence of the presidency of bishops in the seven forementioned churches in or soon after the time in which the Revelation was written, and more than this could not be expected from the short and imperfect accounts which are left us of the Church of that age.

When we come to consider the constitution of the Church in the sub-apostolic age, we shall find abundant clear statements by the early fathers that these cases of Jerusalem, Ephesus, Crete, and the Apocalyptic Churches, are only examples of that which took place universally—viz., that the apostles everywhere appointed men to continue in the several churches the authoritative government which they themselves had first exercised in them.

Clement, Bishop of Rome towards the end of the first

century, who is said to be the Clement mentioned by St. Paul (Phil. iv. 3), says in his First Epistle to the Corinthians, the earliest uncanonical book which has come down to us, "the apostles knew through our Lord Jesus Christ that contentions would arise about the name of episcopacy, and for this reason, being endued with perfect foreknowledge, they appointed certain persons, and handed down an order of succession, so that when they should depart, other approved men should take their office and ministry." [Epis. ad Corinth, lib. I. chap. 44; I. § 44.]

Clement of Alexandria (A.D. 180—210) says, "The Apostle John, when he settled at Ephesus, went about the neighbouring regions ordaining bishops and setting apart such persons for the clergy as were signified to him by the Holy Ghost" (Strom., lib. *Quis dives Salvetur*).

Let us take our stand at the close of the period to which the sacred history of the Church of Christ brings us—viz., to the close of the first, or early part of the second, century—and look round upon the condition of the Church.

It is the reign of the Emperor Trajan. Turn first to the chief city of Pro-Consular Asia, Ephesus, for there, walking in its stately streets, passing under the shadow of its beautiful Temple of Diana, frequenting its public baths, may still be seen a venerable old man; who forms a living link between the Christians of the day and the Lord Jesus; for this is the disciple whom Jesus loved, who lay in His bosom at the Last Supper, who outran Peter to the empty sepulchre, who saw Him after His resurrection, and witnessed His ascent into heaven—the last survivor of the twelve who went up and down with Jesus. He has lately written, at the pressing request of many, a fourth Gospel, to confirm the three Gospels which have long been in the hands of Christian people, and especially to put on record some of the discourses of the Lord. During his recent exile in Patmos he was favoured with a vision of the Lord, and with revelations of the future history of the Church, and was charged by the Lord Himself with messages to the seven churches over which he specially presided.

Our eyes turn naturally to Jerusalem. Alas! the burnt and blackened walls of the Temple, standing amidst the ruins of the half-depopulated city, tell us of the Jewish war under Vespasian, ending with the assault of the city and the burning of the Temple under Titus. But there is still a feeble Church in Jerusalem, and Simeon, the brother of the Lord, is its bishop.

Few are left in the world whose bodily eyes saw the Lord. Ignatius, the Bishop of the Church in Antioch, they say, saw Him when a boy. Some say he was the child whom Jesus once took and set in the midst of the apostles to teach them a lesson of humility. But the churches still contain many who had been personally acquainted with one or other of the apostles; had heard their preaching, witnessed their miracles, been their disciples, had themselves received with the laying on of their hands miraculous gifts of the Spirit. Some of those who were appointed by the apostles themselves to preside over the churches still survive, and still occupy the bishop's seat. Ignatius is bishop of the venerated mother Church of splendid Antioch; and Polycarp, the disciple of John, is the angel of the Church of Smyrna; and Clement, the companion of Paul, rules the churches of the mistress of the world; and others.

In most of the chief cities of the empire there is a Church. Its history is nearly the same in all. It began at the synagogue, among the Jews and the proselytes, and their sympathisers. After a while it separated from the synagogue, and formed a distinct body, which was the object of hatred, and, where possible, of hindrance and persecution at the hands of the Jews and their adherents. Vulgar prejudices were excited against them by horrible stories of monstrous secret rites and licentious practices. But the Christians have steadily increased. They meet together for their simple rites in the large upper room of the house of some devoted disciple; they lead outwardly peaceful and harmless lives; they are noted for their mutual attachment; their societies are organised and affiliated to one another, and are in frequent intercommunication, so that they form a network all over the empire, and far beyond the bounds of the empire. Whatever city a Christian visits, he has only to go to the church in that city, and whether he is Jew, Greek, Roman, or barbarian, rich or poor, bond or free, there he is received as a brother among brethren.

Especially the churches are numerous in Asia Minor and in Eastern Europe, where there are organised churches not only in the towns but even in the country places. They are numerous in the cities of Egypt; from Rome and Italy they have spread to Carthage and the rest of Proconsular Africa. There are churches scattered thinly over the Parthian empire and Arabia, and other countries of the East. There are a few churches in one or two cities of Gaul and Spain. And besides and beyond these organised churches the Gospel has been preached and its doctrines embraced by scattered disciples all over the world. The Christian soldier has spoken of it to his comrades of the watch, and the Christian merchant to the dwellers of the countries to which he has travelled; and the leaven of the Spirit is spreading secretly and mysteriously among the masses of mankind.

## CHAPTER IV.

#### THE ROMAN EMPIRE FROM AUGUSTUS TO CONSTANTINE.

In the history of the apostolic age we have seen the Church founded by Christ; informed by the Holy Spirit at Pentecost; gradually organised under the direction of the apostles; spreading from Jerusalem as a centre till its widening circles have embraced the different varieties of religious condition—Jew, Samaritan, Proselyte, and Gentile—and reached the three great races—Jew, Greek, and Roman; we have seen it pass from point to point, from Jerusalem to Antioch, from Asia Minor to Greece, from Greece to Rome—Rome, the centre of the civilised world.

When we resume the history we enter upon a new phase of it. The miraculous element has almost entirely disappeared; not that Christ has ceased to be with His Church, or that the Holy Spirit has departed out of it, but that the Church, with a completed organisation, and fairly launched, is left to make its way, with its permanent spiritual forces, and by the ordinary agencies, under the special providence of God.

This portion of the history upon which we enter treats of the spread of Christianity from the time of Nero to that of Constantine, during which period it grew from the apparent condition of a mere handful of sectaries, the offspring of a schism in the synagogues, to be the dominant and established religion throughout the Roman empire.

The period is one of special importance; for while, on one hand, the Church is fully organised, and left to its normal working, on the other hand the Church is still so united, and so near to the apostolic age, as to give us some security for the purity of its doctrine and discipline. The disadvantages of the Christian profession have kept out the mere worldly professor, and no alliance with the State has yet modified its constitution. So that from these our later times we look back over all the intermediate ages and appeal to this period as affording the purest standard of the doctrine and discipline of the Church of Christ.

To obtain any clear notion of the history of the Church of this period it is necessary to have previously some knowledge of the outlines at least of the history of the Roman empire. Instead of assuming that all the readers of an elementary book have this knowledge, instead of referring them to some other book which may be inaccessible to them, we propose to supply here as briefly as may be this necessary knowledge.

Seven centuries of conquest, beginning with the difficult subjugation of rival villages, and ending with the rapid absorption of whole kingdoms, had at length made Rome the mistress of a vast congeries of kingdoms, republics, and states, of at least a hundred different races, speaking as many different languages, including along with the most ancient and the most polished civilisations barbarous tribes whose conquest by Rome was their first contact with civilisation—Egypt and Greece, Gaul and Britain. To all these nations the conquerors allowed their municipal governments and their ancestral religions.

But while Rome was rapidly completing the circle of her empire, the political power over it was passing out of the hands of the august body (the senate), which had presided over its earlier fortunes, into the hands of a single master. The wars of conquest had created vast and veteran armies, which knew no country but their camp and no master but their imperator. He who could win the affections of the legions could, if he had the ambition and daring, make himself master of Rome and of the subject world. Perhaps the political condition made the absolute rule of one man the only refuge from civil war and the disruption of the vast and ill-cemented fabric. JULIUS CÆSAR (B.C. 46) had the ambition to attempt and the genius to accomplish this design. Made perpetual imperator he retained the sole command of the armies he had so often led to victory. Made perpetual Dictator he controlled with absolute authority all the civil organisation of the State.

His assassination did not restore Rome to its ancient liberty; for after a short struggle, first with the Republican party—Brutus and Cassius and their conspirators—and then with rival aspirants for power; Antony and Lepidus, AUGUSTUS (B.C. 27) succeeded in grasping his uncle's power. Carefully eschewing all ensigns of power, affecting an antique simplicity in his mode of life, living on terms of familiar intercourse with his fellow-patricians, retaining all the forms of the Republican constitution, he was yet the absolute master of Rome and of the Roman world. The policy of his reign, which he solemnly recommended also to his successors, was to abstain from further territorial acquisitions and to consolidate the provinces together with Rome into a firm and enduring empire. A decree of this emperor, ordering a census to be taken of all the countries under the Roman authority, was the human cause of the journey of the Virgin Mary and Joseph from Galilee to their ancestral city, Bethlehem; where she brought forth her first-born son, and they called his name Jesus.

Five princes of the Julian family thus wielded absolute power under the modest guise of first citizen of Rome. On the death of Augustus the empire devolved upon his step-son, the gloomy, suspicious, and tyrannical TIBERIUS

(A.D. 14), in whose reign, under the authority of his delegate Pontius Pilate, Procurator of Judea, that same Jesus was crucified on a charge of treason.

His great-nephew, the furious CALIGULA, succeeded (A.D. 37), and reigned four years. It was his resolve to have a statue of himself erected in the Temple at Jerusalem, which so engaged the thoughts of the Jewish magistracy as to divert them from the persecution of the Christians, and to give that peace to the Church which is mentioned in the Acts of the Apostles (ix. 31).

On the assassination of Caligula in A.D. 41 the feeble CLAUDIUS (A.D. 41), uncle of the late emperor, was raised to the purple by the acclamation of the troops. He is not specially connected with our present subject, but may be remembered as the emperor in whose reign the actual conquest of Britain took place, the emperor himself paying a brief visit to the island to reap the laurels of the first decisive success of his lieutenants, and to return to Rome with the honour of a triumph and the title Britannicus.

NERO, his step-son and son-in-law, succeeded him A.D. 54, and was the Cæsar to whose personal judgment Paul of Tarsus, in the exercise of his right as a Roman citizen, appealed from the subordinate tribunal of the Procurator Festus. It was in his seventh year (A.D. 61) that Paul arrived in Rome. He spent two years in an irksome but not severe custody, when his case was at length brought before the emperor, and he was acquitted and set at liberty. In the following year (A.D. 64) occurred the great fire at Rome, and the horrible persecution of the Christians of the capital, which we shall have to speak of at greater length in a subsequent chapter. Four years after this (viz., in A.D. 68), St. Paul was again sent prisoner to Rome, and a very ancient and probable tradition says that he suffered martyrdom there, together with St. Peter, in the last year of Nero's reign, and probably only a few months before the Emperor's death.

The atrocities of Nero at length drove the nobles into conspiracy. GALBA (A.D. 68), a statesman and general full of years and honours, then governing the Spanish province, was induced, in his seventy-second year, to head the revolt against the tyrant. He was hailed as imperator by the Spanish legions, Rome welcomed the tidings, and the senate acknowledged a new master. Nero, deserted by every one, fled in disguise to the neighbouring villa of one of his freedmen, and there, in the prospect of a death of shame and torture, found courage to die a Roman's death only when his pursuers were already at the door.

Galba had only reigned seven months when OTHO (A.D. 69), the gay and gallant favourite of Nero, conspired against him, slew him, and seized the empire. But the legions in Germany, on hearing of the death of Nero, had already elected their general, the aged, good-natured, gluttonous VITELLIUS (A.D. 69), as their emperor; and Otho, being defeated by his rival in battle, put an end to his life after a reign of ninety-five days. Vitellius in turn was defeated by VESPASIAN (A.D. 69), who had been proclaimed emperor by the troops engaged under his command in the Judean war.

With the reign of Vespasian commenced a new and better era, which lasted during the reigns of the Flavian and Antonine families, embracing eight reigns and about 110 years, from the accession of Vespasian to the death of Aurelius. Though the era was founded on a military revolution, yet these princes all showed the utmost outward deference to the senate; the long struggle between the imperator and the nobility, the army and the senate, the sword and the gown, which had drained the life-blood of Rome from Marius to Nero, ceased, and the contending parties seemed to be reconciled. The real authority, no doubt, rested with the military chief, but with the complacent acquiescence of the other party. All these princes, with one exception (Domitian), were men of ability, virtue, and public spirit; it was a period of legal government, of wise, just, and beneficent administration, of tranquil obedience and general prosperity.

The Flavian family continued on the throne during three reigns—those of Vespasian and his two sons, Titus and Domitian. The reign of VESPASIAN is connected with ecclesiastical history chiefly by the events which accompanied the suppression of the Jewish rebellion. Vespasian himself, as general of the armies in Judea, had conquered the whole country, with the exception of Jerusalem. When he marched to Rome to seize the purple, he left his son Titus to conduct the siege of the Holy City. The horrors which our Lord had foretold were fulfilled in that dreadful siege.\* At length the city was taken, the Temple, in spite of the anxiety of Titus to save it, was burnt; the sacred vessels graced the conqueror's triumph on his return to Rome, and their likeness may still be seen sculptured on a panel of the triumphal arch of Titus in the Forum. Previous to the formation of the siege the Christian community, recognising the signs foretold by their Lord, had escaped and taken refuge in the little town of Pella, beyond the Jordan. Of the Jews multitudes had fled to Egypt, where there was already a numerous Jewish population at Alexandria and Cyrene; others fled to Mesopotamia, where they fell under the rule of the Parthian monarchy. Of those captured in the war, vast numbers were sold as slaves, so that the slave markets of the world were glutted with Jews. At the close of the war, Jerusalem and the great cities were left desolate; the Christians re-

\* See Josephus.

turned and a few Jews, and built huts amidst the ruins of the Holy City. But the Jewish polity was transferred to the city of Tiberias, situated amidst the most prosperous part of the country, and there took root again for a while. The Temple and the priests and the Sanhedrim were gone for ever. A new school of religious teaching sprang up under the doctors of the law and the rabbis—the new leaders of the people. Out of their teaching grew the Mishna, a commentary on the Scriptures of the Old Testament, and at a still later period grew the Gemara, a commentary on the Mishna.

TITUS succeeded his father as sole sovereign in A.D. 79, and after a brief reign of two years was succeeded by his brother DOMITIAN (A.D. 81). In him the temper of Tiberius reappeared. Cruel and dissolute, he feared the fate which he was conscious he deserved; and those who, from their virtue, ability, and conspicuous station, were likely to be put forward as his successors were the victims of his apprehensions. Cursed also with the vice of avarice, they who were wealthy were included in his executions, that he might seize their confiscated estates. One of the ten persecutions which the ancient historians count is ascribed to his reign, but it is probable that the Christians felt his cruelty because they were confounded with the Jews, who were persecuted then, as often in later times, on account of their wealth rather than upon any ground of religion. He was at length (A.D. 96) assassinated by his friends and officials, whose own lives were in danger from his increasing suspicions of all around him.

The virtuous NERVA (A.D. 96) was invited by the senate to assume the empire upon the death of Domitian. He associated the warlike Trajan with himself, who, after two years, succeeded him.

With Trajan (A.D. 98) begins the reign of the Antonine family—Trajan, Hadrian, Antoninus, Aurelius—the eighty years of whose possession of supreme power was the golden age of the Roman world.

The first Cæsars were masters of Rome, and ruled the dependent world as the representatives of the conqueror city. The Antonines embraced the whole empire in their care; not ruling the provinces specially in the interests of Rome, but seeking to wield their sovereignty in the interests of all mankind.

TRAJAN (A.D. 98), the first great military emperor since Julius Cæsar, engaged for the first time since his reign in wars of conquest, not, however, for the sake of territory, but of security. He added Dacia to the empire, extended his arms and conquests beyond the Euphrates, and secured the frontiers of the empire by the terror of the Roman discipline and valour. In his reign Pliny the Younger, who was Governor of Bithynia, wrote to inform the emperor of the growth of Christianity in his province, and to ask instructions for the treatment of its professors, and received an imperial rescript in reply. We shall presently make use of these valuable documents in illustration of the history of the Church. The life of the Apostle St. John extended into the early part of the reign of Trajan. In this reign, too, occurs the martyrdom of Polycarp, which we shall have occasion to speak of more fully.

HADRIAN (A.D. 117) abandoned the eastern conquests of his predecessor and devoted himself to the consolidation of the empire and the defence of its northern frontiers against the rising power of the northern barbarians. Trajan's genius had been especially warlike; Hadrian was especially an administrator. He devoted his attention to the internal affairs of the whole empire. He visited every part of it in person, inquiring into its condition, encouraging everywhere, by his presence and example, the development of the resources of the countries, the construction of works of public utility and civic magnificence. He took a philosophic interest in the different religions of the empire, and was especially curious about the religious mysteries; in Greece he was initiated into the Eleusinian mysteries; the Jews say that he became a Jewish proselyte; in Egypt he was very much impressed with the solemn grandeur of its ancient monuments and rites. In the fourteenth year of his reign (A.D. 132) occurred the last revolt of the Jews under Barcochebas. It was put down with great severity, and Hadrian banished all the Jews from their country. On the ruined site of Jerusalem he founded a new city, which he called, after the name of his own family, Ælia Capitolina, and a temple of Jupiter rose on the sacred site of Moriah. The emperor distinguished between the Jews and Christians, allowing the latter to remain in the country, and to live in Jerusalem, while he forbade a Jew to set foot in the city on pain of death. The Church of Jerusalem, we shall see hereafter, in time regained some degree of prosperity, and was at length, in the fifth century, raised to the dignity of a patriarchate *causâ honoris;* but its long depression had destroyed its prestige, and it is remarkable that with all the claims it had upon the veneration of Christendom there was never any tendency to claim for it the place, which Rome afterwards tried to usurp, of the Mother Church and centre of organisation of the Christian world.

ANTONINUS, worthily surnamed PIUS (A.D. 138), an upright, amiable, religious man—unlike Trajan fighting on the frontiers, or Hadrian journeying from province to province—passed his well-regulated life in tranquillity between his palace in Rome and his villa in the suburbs. He devoted himself especially, with the help of great jurisconsults, to the establishment of a wise system of imperial law throughout the empire.

His successor, MARCUS AURELIUS, surnamed the Philosopher (A.D. 161), was in his personal character one of the noblest examples of the degree of wisdom and moral excellence to which it is possible for men to attain under the influence of mere philosophy.

By the several abilities of these four great princes the provinces of the empire were gradually bound together into one majestic and harmonious whole. It is remarkable, and will hereafter be accounted for, that Christianity suffered persecution under the authority of all these virtuous sovereigns, while it was allowed to increase unmolested in the reigns of the vilest and wickedest of mankind. The reign of Aurelius especially is marked by the first general persecution expressly ordered by the emperor.

COMMODUS, his son and successor (A.D. 180), was a youth of violent passions and degraded tastes, who spent his days with the gladiators and his nights in orgies, recklessly dooming to death those who excited his suspicions or his anger. His favourite mistress, Marcia, whom he treated as empress, seems to have been a believer in Christianity or to have had Christian connections, and used her influence to protect its professors. His murder by the officers of his own household left the empire again without a natural successor.

The relations which had existed between the senate and the reigning family throughout the reigns of the Flavian family and the Antonines were now broken up; the decent forms which had respected the ancient honour of the senate, and veiled the absolute power of the prince, were rudely torn away; and in future the prize of empire was confessedly the gift of the soldiery, and their nominee did not always pay the senate the courtesy of even asking from them the customary acknowledgment of his title.

A brief note on the next two reigns will indicate the precarious condition of the empire. PERTINAX (A.D. 193), one of the few counsellors of Marcus Aurelius who had not fallen a victim to the jealousy of Commodus, was visited late at night by the chamberlain of the palace and the prefect of the Prætorians, and calmly offered himself to the death of which he concluded they were the messengers; when, instead, they announced the assassination of Commodus and offered him the purple. The strictness of his life and government, however, soon offended the mutinous and insolent Prætorians, and, after eighty-six days, they assassinated him. Having made it known that they would confer the purple on him who should promise them the largest donative, an old senator, JULIUS DIDIANUS (A.D. 193), was urged by his ambitious family to outbid the late emperor's father-in-law, who was a rival candidate, and he was actually elected by the Prætorians, and acknowledged by the complacent senate. Three of the great provincial governors, on hearing what had taken place, refused to accept the new emperor, and each took steps to win the empire for himself.

SEPTIMIUS SEVERUS (A.D. 193), a native of Africa, in command of the legions which occupied Pannonia and Dalmatia, reached Rome by forced marches, compelled the Prætorians to surrender, executed the leaders of the late disgraceful proceedings and dismissed the rest, and the senate pronounced sentence of deposition and death against Didius. Severus successively met and defeated his rivals—Pescennius Niger, the governor of Syria, on his march from Eastern Europe; and Clodius Albinus, the governor of Britain, in a great battle at Lyons. Severus held the sovereignty during a vigorous and successful reign of eighteen years, and left his two sons, CARACALLA and GETA (A.D. 211), joint heirs of the empire. The idea was thus for the first time presented, to the consternation of the ancient Roman spirit, of a partition of the empire. The murder of Geta left Caracalla sole master of the world. We may note that the honour and privileges of Roman citizenship, which in former times had been gradually extended to individuals, to cities, to whole communities, was by this emperor extended finally to all the free inhabitants of the empire. After a reign of remorse and cruelty of six years, Caracalla was in turn murdered by his minister MACRINUS, who procured his own election to the vacant throne (A.D. 217). A successful conspiracy among the relations of the late emperor replaced Macrinus by the young ELAGABALUS (A.D. 218), the nephew of Severus.

The new emperor had been priest of the Temple of the Sun at Emesa, and he introduced his worship into Rome, where he placed the new deity above all the ancient gods, and required the senate to join in the splendid rites with which the emperor-priest honoured his god. The priesthood among the heathens did not demand any special sanctity of life, and the religious zeal of Elagabalus did not prevent him from plunging into infinite luxury and infamous lusts. He was at length murdered by the Prætorians, and succeeded by his young and virtuous cousin ALEXANDER SEVERUS (A.D. 222).

For forty years the Roman world had experienced the successive and various vices of tyrants, from Commodus to Elagabalus. Under the virtuous Alexander it enjoyed thirteen years of calm and good government. Of a devotional turn of mind, he was acquainted with Christianity, esteemed Christ as one of the great religious teachers of the world, and tolerated His religion; Christian bishops, in their avowed capacity, were among the habitual attendants at his court.

At length the army revolted and elected to the throne MAXIMIN (A.D. 235), a Thracian peasant, who had won the affections of the soldiery by his gigantic stature and strength, and had gradually risen to high command in the army. A mere brutal soldier, jealous of all who were distinguished by birth, or services, or accomplishments, he never during his three years' reign even visited Italy, but from his camp on the Rhine or Danube, surrounded only by soldiers and minions, he tyrannised over the Roman world. If some Christians suffered in his reign it was, perhaps, only in common with the other friends of Alexander.

A revolt against the extortion of his African procurator compelled GORDIAN, the Proconsul of Africa, to place himself at its head and assume the purple (A.D. 238). The family of Gordian was one of the most illustrious of the Roman senate, he himself being a relic of the happy age of the Antonines. The senate determined to embrace his cause, and to make head against the domination of the soldiery and the tyranny of their nominees. The African revolt was terminated by the death of the Gordians, father and son, after six-and-thirty days; but the senate elected MAXIMUS and BALBINUS in their stead, and in compliance with the clamours of the people, associated a grandson of Gordian's with them in the imperial power, and then prepared to defend Italy against Maximin. His troops, discouraged by their ill-success before Aquileia, the first town they besieged on their march to Rome, killed their emperor, and accepted the nominee of the senate. The Prætorians, however, in a few months invaded the palace, and slew the two elder emperors, while they adopted the young GORDIAN as their choice. The promise of his virtuous reign was disappointed by another military revolution, by which PHILIP THE ARABIAN, the Prætorian prefect (A.D. 244), acquired the throne by the murder of his master.

From the accession of Philip to the death of the Emperor Gallienus, there elapsed twenty years of shame and misfortune. During that calamitous period every instant of time was marked, every province of the Roman empire was afflicted, by barbarous invaders and military tyrants, and the ruined empire seemed to approach its dissolution. The successive murders of so many emperors had loosened all the ties of allegiance. Any one of the armies might any day nominate a new emperor, and all the generals of armies were disposed to be aspirants for the dangerous honour. We may hasten over the succeeding names which serve to mark the lapse of years in this portion of our history. Philip in five years was succeeded by DECIUS (A.D. 249). In his reign took place the first invasion of that people, the Goths, who ultimately broke the Roman power, sacked the capital, and reigned in Gaul, Spain, and Italy. In his reign a deliberate and general persecution of the Christians was commanded by the emperor's edict. Decius perished, after two years of able rule, in an unsuccessful engagement with the Goths, and was succeeded by GALLUS (A.D. 251), who was dethroned by ÆMILIANUS, who in four months was murdered by his soldiers, and was succeeded by VALERIAN (A.D. 253), who associated with himself his son GALLIENUS. The whole period of the Valerian reign (fifteen years) was one uninterrupted series of confusion and calamity; the empire was, at the same time and on every side, attacked by the blind fury of foreign invaders and the wild ambition of domestic usurpers. The Franks crossed the Rhine and ravaged Gaul as far as the Pyrenees. The Alemanni crossed the Danube, and marched across the plains of Lombardy as far as Ravenna. The Goths came down the Euxine, plundering as they came, ravaged Greece and threatened Italy. The Persians, under the vigorous Sapor, conquered the allied kingdom of Armenia, and spread devastation on either side of the Euphrates. Valerian was taken prisoner by Sapor.

Gallienus spent his time in indolent neglect of public affairs, while on all sides the lieutenants of Valerian aspired to the throne, or the mutinous legions forced the pretension upon them. During the eight years of Gallienus' sole reign there were no less than nineteen pretenders to the throne in all parts of the empire, not one of whom enjoyed a life of peace, or died a natural death. Italy, Rome, and the senate constantly adhered to the cause of Gallienus.

To the worthless Gallienus succeeded a series of great princes—CLAUDIUS, AURELIAN, TACITUS, PROBUS, DIOCLETIAN and his colleagues, who during a period of thirty years triumphed over the foreign and domestic foes of the State, re-established military discipline, and restored the prosperity, and to some extent the virtue and dignity, of the Roman world. Our purpose needs no more than that we should name the brave and virtuous CLAUDIUS GOTHICUS (A.D. 268) and the warlike AURELIAN (A.D. 270). On his death it is remarkable that the army invited the senate to elect an emperor. The senate declined, fearing, probably, that its nominee might not be accepted, and that the whole senate might suffer from the jealousy of the emperor whom the army should set up against the senate's choice, and there ensued an interregnum of eight months, until at length the senate elected TACITUS (A.D. 275), who ruled, as far as possible, in accordance with the ancient Republican constitution. He was succeeded by PROBUS (A.D. 276), who imitated the policy and the virtues of his predecessor. Next came the able but cruel CARUS (A.D. 282), and his sons, CARINUS and NUMERIAN (A.D. 283), the first of whom imitated the vices of Elagabalus and the cruelty of Domitian, while the other possessed all the virtues and amiability of Alexander Severus. The natural death of the latter in 284, and the assassination of the former in A.D. 285, made way for the elevation of Diocletian, on whose reign we must bestow a more detailed attention.

DIOCLETIAN (A.D. 284), a statesman of profound and subtle

genius, was the founder of a new phase of empire. At the beginning of his reign he recognised that the task of defending and governing the empire was too great for one man, and associated with himself a colleague in MAXIMIAN, giving him equal titles and power. Diocletian was the brain and Maximian the arm of the monarchy—the Jove and Hercules of the lower sphere. Six years afterwards Diocletian carried still further this subdivision of power by giving to each of the Augusti a lieutenant with the title of Cæsar, GALERIUS and CONSTANTIUS. To knit the bonds among them more closely by domestic ties, Diocletian adopted Galerius as his son, and gave him his daughter in marriage; Maximian similarly took Constantius for his son-in-law and adopted son. The empire was thus distributed among them:—the defence of Gaul, Spain, and Britain was entrusted to Constantius; Galerius was stationed on the banks of the Danube as the safeguard of the Illyrian provinces; Italy and Africa were considered the department of Maximian; while Diocletian reserved as his peculiar portion Thrace, Egypt, and Asia. The united authority of the Augusti extended over the whole monarchy; each Emperor administered his own district; and was prepared to assist his colleagues with his counsels or presence. The Cæsars revered the majesty of the Augusti, and the three younger princes, by their gratitude and obedience, acknowledged the common parent of their fortunes. The singular arrangement worked harmoniously, and answered the purpose of the statesman who devised it, so long as he himself presided over it. Rome had virtually ceased to be the capital of the empire. Diocletian had fixed his ordinary residence at Nicomedia, Maximian at Milan; those two cities rapidly became populous and magnificent, and inferior only to Rome, Alexandria, and Antioch in extent and population. Till his triumph in the twentieth year of his reign, it is doubtful whether Diocletian had ever visited Rome, and on that occasion he only remained there two months. It was the policy of the emperor to lessen the authority of the senate and the power of the ancient Roman families. The new constitution of the empire was entirely independent of the senate. The sovereigns consulted only with their own ministers, appointed their own lieutenants, and organised their courts in imitation of the Eastern monarchies. Diocletian assumed the Eastern titles of Dominus and Basileus, maintained a magnificent appearance, and finally adopted the diadem of royalty, and affected the reserve and state and etiquette of the Eastern kings.

In the twenty-first year of his reign Diocletian laid down his power by a voluntary and public abdication. Maximian on the same day at Milan accomplished a like abdication. The two Cæsars succeeded to the higher title and authority of Augusti, and Galerius filled up the Diocletian scheme of empire by the nomination of two new Cæsars—MAXIMIN, his nephew, for the eastern division of the empire, and SEVERUS, a faithful adherent of his own, for the western.

But the balance of power established by Diocletian could only be maintained by his own political skill and personal authority, and his abdication was succeeded by eighteen years of discord and confusion. The empire was afflicted by five civil wars, into whose details we need not enter. It is enough for our purpose to glance at the main outline of events. Constantine, the son of Constantius, had been left in the service of Diocletian, and the public voice had designated him as the probable successor to his father's Cæsarship. On the appointment of the new Cæsars, Constantius obtained the tardy and reluctant leave of Galerius that his son should rejoin him. He reached Constantius at the very moment the emperor was embarking at Boulogne for Britain to repel an incursion of the wild tribes of Caledonia. Fifteen months afterwards Constantius died in the imperial palace at Eboracum (York), and the troops saluted Constantine, not as Cæsar, but by the higher title of Augustus. Galerius agreed to accord to him the title of Cæsar and the government of the provinces beyond the Alps, but asserted the authority of the second Augustus for Severus, and Constantine acquiesced in the decision.

In the same year MAXENTIUS, the son of the retired Emperor Maximian, and son-in-law of Galerius, was set up as emperor by the Romans, and was at once joined by the ex-emperor, his father. Severus, marching against them, was deserted by his troops, surrendered to Maximian, and was put to death. Maximian sought an interview with Constantine, conferred on him the title of Augustus, and gave him his daughter in marriage.

Galerius, marching into Italy against the new emperors, found the obstacles so great, and the fidelity of his troops so doubtful, that he again retreated. To balance the power of his rivals he raised LICINIUS to the dignity of Augustus in place of the dead Severus, passing over Maximin, who, however, claimed, and forced Galerius to accord to him, the higher title. There were, therefore, now six emperors dividing the empire among them. The number soon began to diminish.

Maxentius presently refused to submit to the control of his father Maximian. The ex-emperor took refuge with Galerius, but he also obliged him to leave his dominions. He fled to his son-in-law Constantine, but by an act of treachery against that emperor he brought upon himself a violent death, A.D. 310. Galerius died in the following year of a horrible disease, and Maximin and Licinius divided the whole East between them.

Maxentius having alienated the Italians by his vices and crimes, made preparations for war against Constantine, but the northern emperor anticipated him and marched into Italy; in a rapid campaign overcame his troops, and made himself master of Rome and Italy. It was while on his march to attack Maxentius, in 311, when undecided as to the truth of Christianity, that a luminous cross is said to have appeared in the sky in broad daylight, in sight of himself and his army, with this inscription in the Greek language, "In this conquer." He had the famous standard made, consisting of a cross and the letters X P* surrounded by a garland. He also, it is said, had the armour of his soldiers marked with a X, the initial of the name of Christ. His victory and his conversion followed. The triumphal arch which he erected in Rome three years after in honour of his victory still remains.

Secretly Licinius had been the ally of Constantine, Maximin the ally of Maxentius. A war broke out between the two Eastern emperors. Maximin was defeated, fled, and shortly after died. The world was now divided between the two surviving emperors, and in little more than a year (A.D. 314) their arms were turned against one another. Constantine was victorious, and claimed all Eastern Europe as the prize of victory, leaving Thrace, Asia Minor, and Egypt to Licinius. Again (A.D. 323) another war broke out between them. Licinius was defeated, and the Roman world was once more united under Constantine, thirty-seven years after it had been first divided by Diocletian. This brings us to the end of an important period both of civil and ecclesiastical history, and we turn to the consideration of the history of the Church, of which this sketch of the empire is intended to form the basis.

* The first two letters—*ch* and *r*—of the name Christ.

## CHAPTER V.

#### NERO'S PERSECUTION OF THE CHRISTIANS AT ROME.

IN tracing the history of the Church through these early ages whose secular history we have sketched in the preceding chapter, we have no contemporary consecutive history to aid us. We only at intervals catch glimpses from one source or another of what was taking place. Some incident is recorded which, like a flash of lightning, reveals the scene and the actors for a few moments, then all is dark, till the next flash again lights up the scene, and we have to infer as well as we can the intervening history.

The first of these incidents occurs A.D. 64, the seventh year of the reign of Nero, the year after St. Paul's first imprisonment at Rome, and we find it in the pages of the great Roman historian Tacitus. In that year a great fire broke out, which burnt three parts of the city. The character of the emperor led to the suspicion that he himself had wantonly set fire to his capital; and the murmurs of the multitude who had been burnt out of their houses began to assume a threatening tone. The emperor endeavoured to evade the danger which threatened him by diverting the popular suspicions upon some other object. " With this view," says the historian, "he accused those men who, under the appellation of Christians, were already branded with deserved infamy. They derived their name and origin from Christ, who in the reign of Tiberius had suffered death by the sentence of the procurator, Pontius Pilate. For a while this dire superstition was checked, but it again burst forth, and not only spread itself over Judea, the first seat of this mischievous sect, but was even introduced into Rome, the common asylum which receives and protects whatever is impure, whatever is atrocious. The confessions of those who were seized discovered a great multitude of their accomplices, and they were all convicted, not so much for the crime of setting fire to the city as for their hatred of humankind. They died in torments, and their torments were embittered by insult and derision. Some were nailed on crosses; others sewn up in the skins of wild beasts and exposed to the fury of dogs; others, again, smeared over with combustible materials, were used as torches to illuminate the darkness of the night. The gardens of Nero * were destined for the melancholy spectacle, which was accompanied with a horse-race, and honoured with the presence of the emperor, who mingled with the populace in the dress and attitude of a charioteer. The guilt of the Christians deserved indeed the most exemplary punishment, but the public abhorrence was changed into commiseration, from the opinion that those unhappy wretches were sacrificed not so much to the public welfare as to the cruelty of a jealous tyrant."

In this brief narrative we observe the statements that the Christians had become numerous, and had attracted general attention, and that the popular prejudice against them was such as to make people believe them capable of a monstrous crime. If we examine the causes which led to this popular prejudice against the Christians—a prejudice which continued through the whole of the period under our consideration— we shall have the clue to the reasons of the long series of

---

* The gardens of Nero covered the present site of the Vatican. The obelisk which now stands in the esplanade in front of St. Peter's ornamented the spina of the circus of Nero's gardens, at the period of the horrors described in the text.

acts of violence against them, of which this is the first recorded instance.

Christianity sprang out of Judaism. At first the Christians appeared to outsiders to be nothing more than a Jewish sect. The early opposition to the Gospel down to the time of Nero came entirely from the Jews. From the heathen it had nothing to fear, except what its professors might suffer from any legal action or popular violence directed against the Jews, with whom they would be confounded. For example, when Claudius banished all the Jews from Rome, in all probability the Christians would be expelled among them.

But as the number of Gentile converts increased, and the Jewish converts, abandoning their national exclusiveness, were absorbed into the body of believers, the Christian Church began to assume a new appearance in the eyes of the world. And when men began to examine this new religious body there were several features in it which were liable to animadversion.

First, it was not a national religion. The ancient heathens believed that different nations had different gods. Egypt, every one knew, worshipped Isis, and the Persians the sun; and Rome freely allowed the conquered nations the use of their national religions, and even tolerated in Rome itself the erection of the temples of foreign deities beside the temples of the gods of Rome. But Christianity had not the prestige of an ancient national religion. It was not the acknowledged religion of any country. It was a "new superstition," which seemed to have suddenly sprung up sporadically all over the empire, chiefly among the lower classes of the people.

Again, such a religion was unintelligible to the mere pagan looker-on; it was contrary to all his ideas of a religion. All the ancient religions had their temples and statues, and altars and sacrifices, and grand ceremonials; and religion had come to mean the mechanical observance of external rites. The Christians meeting (at first) in private houses, with rites which needed little apparatus, presented the spectacle of a sect destitute of all the usual appliances of religion. People who had no temples and statues seemed to the popular apprehension to have no god; and the commonest accusation which the mob flung at the Christians was, that they were Atheists—godless. Those who professed to be better informed on the tenets of the new sect reported that they worshipped as a god a certain Jew who had been crucified in Judea for sedition, under the procurator Pilate, in the time of Tiberius, which to the Greeks was foolishness.

The exclusion of strangers from their principal act of worship gave an air of secrecy to their meetings, and not unnaturally excited suspicions; and some incorrect reports of their worship afforded a foundation for the most horrible misconceptions. Some vague report of the Eucharistic sacrifice led to the story that Christians offered human sacrifice; and the doctrine that the faithful communicants partook of the body and blood of Christ led to the horrible belief that they ate of their human victims; while a similar misrepresentation of the love feast and the kiss of peace gave rise to the belief among the mob, always credulous of horrors, that they indulged in luxurious orgies and horrible lusts.

Moreover, these Christians were people who seemed to shun the ordinary intercourse of men. The fact that heathen religious ceremonies were mixed up with all the business, the public amusements, the social customs of the pagan world, made the Christian hold aloof from them. An altar was placed before the magistrate's chair; the games of the amphitheatre were celebrated in honour of the gods; the standards of the legions were idols; at the public festivities of the imperial birthday sacrifice had to be made to the divinity of the emperor; even at a neighbour's supper-table the first cup was a libation to the gods. This reserve must have given to the Christians, in the eyes of the world, the appearance of men of secret habits, and unknown objects and designs; morose neighbours, bad citizens, hostile to the gods, and " enemies of mankind."

Another circumstance calculated to excite the jealousy of the Roman authorities was that these Christians formed all over the empire associations unrecognised by the law, bound by their own rules, obedient to their own officers, all united together in a great confederation. The Church might not unreasonably appear to a Roman statesman in the light of a network of secret societies, capable at least of being employed as a political engine. Here was matter enough, on the whole, to account for popular prejudice against the Christians, and for the jealousy of the authorities of their unlawful religion and their dangerous association.

## CHAPTER VI.

#### PLINY'S LETTER TO TRAJAN. MARTYRDOM OF IGNATIUS

AFTER an interval of thirty years, in the time of the Emperor Trajan, a passage of profane history again gives us a view of the condition of the Church, and the impression it was making upon the world, in a distant province of the empire.

Pliny the Younger, who is well known to the student of Roman history as a highly educated, refined, amiable man, and an experienced statesman, was proconsul of Bithynia and Pontus. We have an official letter of his, written about A.D. 112, in which he makes a report to the emperor, and asks for instructions in the novel circumstances in which he finds himself.

It will be more satisfactory to the reader to have before him the very words of this important document. "C. Pliny to Trajan, emperor, health. It is my usual custom, sir, to refer all things of which I harbour any doubts to you. For who can better direct my judgment in its hesitation, or instruct my understanding in its ignorance? It has never been my lot to be present at any examination of Christians before. I am therefore at a loss to determine what is the usual object either of inquiry or of punishment, and to what length either of them is to be carried. It has also been with me a question very problematical whether any distinction should be made between the young and the old, the tender and the robust; whether pardon should be given on repentance, or whether retraction is not to be allowed to profit the man who has been a Christian; whether the name itself abstracted from flagitiousness of conduct, or the crimes connected with the name, be the object of punishment. In the meantime this has been my method with respect to those who were brought before me as Christians. I asked them whether they were Christians; if they pleaded guilty I interrogated them a second and a third time with a menace of capital punishment. In case of obstinate perseverance I ordered them to be executed. For of this I had no doubt, whatever was the nature of their religion, that stubbornness and inflexible obstinacy ought to be punished. Some infected with the same madness, on account of their privilege of citizenship, I reserved to be sent to Rome, to be referred to your tribunal. But this crime spreading (as is usually the case) while it was actually under persecution, more cases soon occurred. An anonymous libel was exhibited with a catalogue of names of persons, who yet declared that they were not Christians then, and never had been, and they repeated after me an invocation of the gods, and offered worship with wine and frankincense to your image, which, for this purpose, I had ordered to be brought with the images of the deities; and they likewise reviled Christ; none of which things, I am told, a real Christian can ever be compelled to do. On this account I dismissed them. Others named by an informer, first affirmed and then denied the charge of Christianity, declaring that they had been Christians, but had ceased to be so some three years ago, others still longer, some even twenty years ago. All of them worshipped your image and the statues of the gods, and also reviled Christ. And this was the account they gave of the nature of the religion they once had professed, whether it deserves the name of crime or error, namely, that they were accustomed on a stated day to meet before daylight, and to say in turns a hymn to Christ (*dicere secum invicem carmen Christo*) as to a god, and to bind themselves by an oath (*sacramentum*) not to commit any wickedness, but, on the contrary, to abstain from thefts, robberies, and adulteries; also not to violate their promise or deny a pledge; after which it was their custom to separate, and to meet again at a promiscuous harmless meal, from which last practice they, however, desisted after the publication of my edict, in which, agreeably to your orders, I forbade any associations of that sort. On which account I judged it the more necessary to inquire by torture from two females, who were said to be deaconesses (*ministræ*), what was the real truth. But nothing could I collect except a depraved and excessive superstition. Deferring, therefore, any further investigation I determined to consult you; for the number of culprits is so great as to call for serious consultation. Many persons are informed against of every age and rank and of both sexes; more still will be in the same situation. The contagion of the superstition has spread not only through cities, but even villages and the country. Not that I think it impossible to check and to correct it. The success of my endeavours hitherto forbids such desponding thoughts; for the temples, once almost desolate, begin to be frequented; and the sacred solemnities, which had long been intermitted, are now attended afresh; and the sacrificial victims are now bought up everywhere, which once could scarcely find a purchaser; whence I conclude that many might be reclaimed were the hope of impunity on repentance absolutely confirmed."

This is a very striking testimony to the all but universal prevalence of Christianity in the province of Bithynia at this early period, and there is other reason to believe that the whole of Asia Minor was more thoroughly evangelised in this earliest period than any other part of the Church (Milner, i. 120). The Christian customs spoken of seem to have been the Eucharistic service early in the morning, and the love feast in the evening, the latter of which was given up in obedience to Trajan's edict against unlawful meetings. The whole tone of the letter seems to imply that these people seemed to Pliny rather to be mere harmless enthusiasts than criminals or political intriguers, and he shrank from the wholesale cruelties which a general enforcement of the law against them would have occasioned. We give the emperor's rescript also in its very words. " Trajan to Pliny. You have done perfectly right, my dear Pliny, in the inquiry which you have made concerning Christians. For truly no one general rule can be laid down which will apply to all such cases. These people must not be sought after. If they are brought before you and convicted, let them be capitally punished, yet with this restriction, that if any one renounce Christianity and prove his sincerity by supplicating our gods, however suspected he may be for the past, let him on his repentance obtain pardon. But anonymous libels ought in no case to be attended to; for it is a very dangerous precedent, and perfectly incongruous with the maxims of our age."

Trajan himself, a little later in his reign, was brought into communication with the Christians of the East, and he treated them in the spirit of his rescript to Pliny.

The emperor had arrived at Antioch, the capital of the East, on his way to take command of the war against the Parthians. It was at a time when the public mind had been greatly excited by a series of public disasters, and the people were clamorous against the Christians as the cause of these visitations of the anger of the gods. The venerable Ignatius, the Bishop of the Christians of Antioch, was denounced to the emperor as one of the leaders of the sect in the East. Ignatius must indeed have been one of the most conspicuous persons in the Church at that time. An early tradi-

crown of martyrdom.* They reached Rome when the games were in progress and almost over; he was hurried to the amphitheatre and the wild beasts let loose upon him. A few of the larger bones only were left, which the Christians gathered together as relics, and they were afterwards buried at his own city of Antioch.

* These letters still remain to us, and are among the most valuable evidences of the sub-Apostolic Church. Three editions have descended to us. Until the middle of the seventeenth century there were twelve epistles in Greek, which laboured under great suspicion of forgery or interpolation, besides some others which existed in Latin only, and were undoubtedly spurious. About 1644 a MS. was discovered at Florence which contained seven of the epistles in a shorter form. The learned generally accepted these seven in their shorter form as genuine; but a few years ago, among some Syrian MSS. procured for the British Museum, one was found to be a translation into Syriac of three of these epistles in a still more abbreviated form. These are decided, by the majority of those competent to form an opinion, to be abridgments of the Greek; and the seven epistles of the Florentine MS. are still generally accepted as the genuine work of Ignatius.

## CHAPTER VII.

### THE RESCRIPT OF HADRIAN. THE MARTYRDOM OF POLYCARP.

WHEN the name of "the Age of Persecution" is given to the first three centuries of the Christian era, it must not be supposed that a continuous persecution was kept up against the Church of Christ throughout the Roman empire. Christians were liable to persecution at any time, in any province, but the hostile action against them was very fitful. Sometimes a private enemy would seek to get rid of a rival, or to wreak his revenge, by putting the law in motion against a Christian.

There is an example of this in the story told by Eusebius of Marinus (A.D. 259), a martyr of the time of Gallienus: "Marinus being a candidate for a Roman office at Cæsarea was informed against as a Christian by an antagonist, who pleaded that, upon that account, he ought not to have the office. The judge, upon examination finding it to be so, gave him three hours' time to consider whether he would quit his religion or his life. During this space Theotecnus, Bishop of Cæsarea, met him, and taking him by the hand, led him to the church, and set him by the Holy Table, then offered him a Bible and a sword, and bade him take his choice. He readily without any demur laid his hand upon the Bible. Whereupon the Bishop thus addressed him: 'Adhere,' said he, 'to God, and in His strength enjoy what thou hast chosen, and go in peace.' He immediately returned from the church to the judge, made his profession of faith, received sentence, and died a martyr."

Sometimes a popular clamour was raised against the Christians. If anything went wrong—a bad harvest or a military reverse—the superstitious were always ready to attribute it to the anger of the gods against the Christians, the impious contemners of their worship, and to clamour for their death. "If the Tiber rose," says Tertullian, "the cry was, 'The Christians to the lions!' if famine or pestilence threatened Rome, 'The Christians to the lions!' And this popular cry was more dangerous than, without some explanation, would be supposed. When the people, assembled in the amphitheatre at the celebration of any festival, demanded anything with tolerable unanimity, this was accepted as a declaration of the will of the people, it was the Roman mode of expressing public opinion, and the magistrate was bound by the prescription of ancient usage to defer to it. Any man might raise in the assembly the cry, '*Christiani ad leones!*' (The Christians to the lions!), and if the cry was taken up and swelled into a general acclamation, it was enough to cause a sudden outbreak of violence. The magistrate might send his officers at once to arrest the prominent members of the Christian body, and if they were found at once they might be brought before his seat in the amphitheatre in a pause of the games, and on their refusal to sacrifice to the emperor and the gods might be cast into the arena, and the wild beasts be turned in upon them, as an exciting *finale* to the exhibition. The magistrates, no doubt, acted very differently. One would turn a deaf ear to the mob clamour, even when it swelled loudly from the benches;* another would make a slight demonstration a pretext for action against the Christians. A humane prefect discouraged informers, and sometimes made a way

---

* *See* page 193 for an example.

for the accused to evade the customary tests ; while wicked magistrates are said to have used the power which the law gave them over Christians to gratify their own greed or lust."

The reign of Hadrian is marked by an edict which restrained the outbursts of popular prejudice against the Christians. Serenus Graiianus, the Proconsul of Asia, applied to the emperor for instructions. He represented that occasionally an outburst of popular fury would raise the cry for persecution, and the names of some of the most prominent Christians would be denounced. He says "that it seems to him unreasonable that the Christians should be put to death merely to gratify the clamours of the people, without trial and without any crime proved against them," and he asks what course should be taken. Hadrian's reply is addressed to Minucius Fundanus, who had meantime succeeded Graiianus in the government of the province. He desires "that men may not be disturbed without cause, and that base informers may not be encouraged in their odious practices. If the people of the province will appear publicly and make open charges against the Christians, so as to give them an opportunity of answering for themselves, let them proceed in that manner only, and not by rude demands and mere clamours. But it is very proper, if any person will accuse them, that you should take cognisance of these matters. If any then accuse them, and show that they actually break the laws, do you determine according to the nature of the crime. But, by Hercules, if the charge be a mere calumny, do you estimate the enormity of such calumny, and punish it as it deserves." The meaning is a little obscure, but the rescript seems intended to declare that Christians are not to be punished merely for being Christians; and that those who harassed Christians with false accusations of crimes are to be punished as calumniators.

Hadrian was not ignorant of Christianity. He was specially curious about all the religions of the empire, and no doubt had inquired about this which was attracting attention. He had authentic information upon it too, for two of the early Defences of Christianity—one by Quadratus, the other by Aristides—were dedicated, and no doubt presented, to him. There is extant, moreover, one of this emperor's letters, in which he gives a curious account of the impression made on his own mind by the state of religion in Egypt, and incidentally discovers to us the progress which Christianity had made in that country: " I have found the people vain, fickle, and shifting with every breath of popular rumour. Those who worship Serapis are Christians, and those who call themselves Christian bishops are worshippers of Serapis. There is no ruler of a Jewish synagogue, no Samaritan, no Christian bishop who is not an astrologer. The Patriarch himself, when he comes to Egypt, is compelled by one party to worship Serapis, by the other Christ. . . . They have but one god, him Christians, Jews, and Gentiles worship alike (viz., gold)." " The key," says Dean Milman, " to this curious statement is probably that the tone of the higher, the fashionable, society in Alexandria was to affect, either on some gnostic or philosopic theory, that all these religions differed only in form, but were essentially the same; that all adored one Deity, all one Logos or Demiurge, under different names; all employed the same arts to impose upon the vulgar, and all were equally despicable to the real philosopher." It is clear at least that Christianity and its chief officials were conspicuous in the world of Alexandria. On the whole the long and peaceful reigns of Hadrian and Antoninus Pius were favourable to Christianity, which was rapidly growing in numbers and assuming a more important position in the world. The philosophers were joining its ranks, its professors affected no disguise, its clergy were well known, its apologies were no longer mere defences of Christianity against prejudice and misrepresentation; they boldly attacked the folly and wickedness of the established polytheism.

Marcus Aurelius, whose character commands our admiration for its philosophic spirit and its many virtues, was nevertheless the first of the emperors who encouraged a general persecution of the Christians. There were probably three causes for this: 1. The growth of Christianity above mentioned, and the aggressive tone which it assumed more and more against the religion of the State, with which the institutions of the State appeared to be bound up. 2. The temper of the emperor, with whom philosophy had already taken that more earnest tone of a religion which was the characteristic of the final phase of cultured paganism. He believed that his philosophy would elevate the soul of man to higher dignity, and human life to its greatest possible happiness; and he himself, as a writer and teacher of this philosophy, was a competitor with Christianity for the ear of mankind. It was not incompatible with his philosophy to support the established polytheism, whether, with the earlier philosophers, he regarded the ancient religion as so interwoven with the constitution of the State and with the customs of the people that it could not be destroyed without danger to the whole social fabric, or as a set of superstitions adapted to the gross minds of the ignorant, and useful in controlling them.

At this period the superstitious fears of the people were deeply stirred. A series of misfortunes happened in various parts of the empire—inundations, famines, a new and virulent plague (so described by the great physician Galen) swept from east to west of the empire, earthquakes, irruptions of the barbarians all along the northern frontier, defeats of the armies. Such visitations naturally turn men's thoughts to the unseen powers which rule the world. But when their attention was now attracted to the subject, what met their gaze? The temples everywhere half deserted; the majority of the people no longer worshipped the great ancient gods to whose favour they were wont to attribute fruitful seasons; and the lesser tutelar deities, to whose special favour they had consigned the protection of this or that nation, city, guild, or family, were alike neglected. Everywhere was to be found this sect of Christians, to whom the decay of the ancient faith was owing, and, who, growing daily bolder, openly blasphemed the gods, and were drawing all men into the same impiety. A general revival of the worship of these gods was accompanied by a general demand for the suppression of Christianity, and the emperor, for whatever reason, falling in with the popular feeling, ordered the most solemn and costly religious ceremonies, offered great numbers of sacrifices, and at the same time repealed the edicts which had hitherto protected the Christians from persecution, and issued new edicts, encouraging informers by the offer of half the forfeited goods of the convicted Christians, and authorising for the first time the use of torture to force them into recantation. It was only natural that the leaders of Christianity should be sought out. Among them Justin the Philosopher, of whom we shall speak presently, suffered at Rome, and acquired the honourable title, which has ever since distinguished him, of Justin Martyr. A still more distinguished victim was Polycarp, whose death is minutely recorded in a letter from the Church of Smyrna to that of Philadelphia, which bears every mark of authenticity. Polycarp was the most remarkable person in the Eastern Church. He had been a disciple of St. John; he had been appointed by that apostle Bishop of Smyrna; he was "the angel of the Church of Smyrna" to whom was addressed one of our Lord's messages by the mouth of St. John, in the Revelation (Rev. ii. 8). He was now at least one hundred years old; he was one of the last links which united the present with the apostolic age. Many Christians had already suffered at Smyrna. Polycarp, at the solicitation of his friends, had removed from the city to a neighbouring village, and from thence to another; but his retreat having been betrayed by two slaves under torture, he was at length seized by the soldiers sent in search of him. "The will of God be done," said he, and bade food be prepared for his captors while he spent in prayer the two hours during which they rested and refreshed themselves. He was carried straight to the arena, where a great concourse was assembled at the celebration of the games. As he entered the place a voice was heard —from heaven the Christians among the spectators thought —saying, "Be strong, Polycarp, and play the man." The spectators were greatly excited at his appearance, and broke out into loud clamours. He was brought before the proconsul, Statius Quadratus, who, whether moved to compassion by his venerable age, or anxious to obtain his recantation for the effect it would have on his followers, urged him to save his life, "to have respect to his old age"; the multitude joined in the scene with their clamour. "Swear by the genius of Cæsar; Retract; say 'Away with the Atheists.'" He repeated the words, with a glance round the ranks of clamorous spectators, and a gesture which gave a different application to the words, "Away with the Atheists." "Swear," said the proconsul, "and I release thee; blaspheme Christ." "Eighty and six years," he replied, "have I served Christ, and He has never done me wrong; how can I now blaspheme my King and my Saviour?" The proconsul continued in vain to urge him with threats to retract and to address the people against

Christianity. At length he condemned him; and the herald, advancing into the midst of the amphitheatre, proclaimed thrice, " Polycarp has professed himself a Christian." The Jews and heathens replied with loud shouts, " This is the teacher of all Asia, the overthrower of our gods, who has perverted so many from sacrifice and the adoration of the gods." They demanded of the Asiarch who presided over the games that a lion should be let loose upon him. The Asiarch excused himself on the ground that the games were over. A general cry arose that he should be burned. A quantity of wood was soon collected from the neighbouring baths; the Jews, we are told, " as was their custom," being specially zealous in the work. Polycarp was unrobed, bound to the stake in the midst of the arena, and the fuel piled up about him. His prayer at the stake may be considered as embodying the sentiments of the Christians of that period: " O Lord God Almighty, the Father of Thy well-beloved and ever-blessed Son Jesus Christ, by whom we have received the knowledge of Thee; the God of angels, powers, and of every creature, and of the whole race of the righteous who live before Thee, I thank Thee that Thou hast graciously thought me worthy of this day and this hour, that I may receive a portion in the number of Thy martyrs, and drink of Christ's cup, for the resurrection to eternal life, both of body and soul, in the incorruptibleness of the Holy Spirit; among whom may I be admitted this day, as a rich and acceptable sacrifice, as Thou, O true and faithful God, hast prepared and foreshown and accomplished. Wherefore I praise Thee for all Thy mercies; I bless Thee, I glorify Thee, with the eternal and heavenly Jesus Christ, Thy beloved Son, to whom with Thee and the Holy Spirit be glory now and for ever."

The pile was kindled, but the flame swept round him " like the sail of a ship filled with wind," while his body appeared in the midst, not like flesh that is burnt, but like bread that is baked, or like gold and silver glowing in the furnace, "and a perfume as of spices and frankincense filled the air."

The confector (the man whose duty at the games it was to dispatch any beast that was dangerous) was ordered to approach and plunge his sword into his body, whereupon the blood gushed forth so that the fire was extinguished. The body was then placed in the midst of the fire and burnt. "Then we gathered up his bones, more precious than gold and jewels, and deposited them in a proper place, where if it be possible we shall meet, and the Lord will grant us, in gladness and joy, to celebrate the birthday of his martyrdom, both in commemoration of those who have wrestled before us, and for the instruction and confirmation of those who may hereafter be called upon to suffer."

## CHAPTER VIII.

### THE MERCHANTMAN SEEKING GOODLY PEARLS.

IN the Acts of the Apostles we see how Christianity was first presented to the minds of men, and how it was received by them—*e.g.*, by the Jews on the day of Pentecost,* by the Athenian philosophers on the Acropolis,† and by the rude heathen of Lystra.‡ The early Christian writings continue this branch of Church history. The arguments *pro* and *con* —between the Christian teacher on one side, and the learned Jew, the Greek philosopher, the Eastern religionist, and the Christian heretic on the other—are recorded with great fulness, and afford a subject of study of the profoundest interest. Our narrow limits forbid us to enter into it; but we have thought that a couple of brief extracts would lay before the reader in an interesting and graphic way some general notion of the mental process by which thousands of thoughtful men found their way out of the philosophical scepticism of educated Roman society into the faith of Christ.

"The Recognitions of Clement" is a kind of philosophical and theological romance. Like similar works of the present day, it constructs a plot whose gradual development is just enough to interest the reader, and into the mouths of the characters the author puts the arguments *pro* and *con* on a multitude of religious and philosophical questions. The characters of the story are apostles and the companions of apostles; Peter is the most prominent person. Clement of Rome is supposed to be the relater of the story; and the plot

\* Acts ii. † Acts xvii. ‡ Acts xvi.

turns on the adventures of Clement's family; and is just such a story of love and intrigue, adventures and escapes, with a final re-union of the characters, and clearing up of their perplexities, as a modern novelist might weave. We quote the introductory account which Clement gives of his early training, and of the motives which led him to Christianity, which represents no doubt the spiritual history of thousands of educated thoughtful heathens.

CHAPTER I.—CLEMENT'S EARLY HISTORY AND DOUBTS.

"I, Clement, who was born in the city of Rome, was from my earliest age a lover of chastity, while the bent of my mind held me bound as with chains of anxiety and sorrow. For a thought that was in me, whence originating I cannot tell, constantly led me to think of my condition of mortality, and to discuss such questions as these: whether there be for me any life after death, or whether I am to be wholly annihilated; whether I did not exist before I was born; and whether there shall be no remembrance of this life after death, and so the boundlessness of time shall consign all things to oblivion and silence, so that not only we shall cease to be, but there shall be no remembrance that we have ever been. This also I revolved in my mind: when the world was made, or what was before it was made, or whether it has existed from eternity. For it seemed certain that if it had been made it must be doomed to dissolution; and if it be dissolved, what is to be afterwards?—unless, perhaps, all things shall be buried in oblivion and silence, or something shall be which the mind of man cannot now conceive."

CHAPTER II.—HIS DISTRESS.

"While I was continually revolving in my mind these and such like questions, suggested I know not how, I was pining away wonderfully through excess of grief; and, what was worse, if at any time I thought to cast aside such cares as being of little use, the waves of anxiety rose all the higher upon me.  For I had in me that most excellent companion who would not suffer me to rest—the desire of immortality; for, as the subsequent issue showed, and the grace of Almighty God directed, this bent of mind led me to the quest of truth and the acknowledgment of the true light; and hence it came to pass that ere long I pitied those whom formerly in my ignorance I believed to be happy."

CHAPTER III.—HIS DISSATISFACTION WITH THE SCHOOLS OF THE PHILOSOPHERS.

"Having therefore such a bent of mind from my earliest years, the desire of learning something led me to frequent the schools of the philosophers.  There I saw that nought else was done, save that doctrines were asserted and controverted without end, contests were waged, and the arts of syllogisms and the subtleties of conclusions were discussed.  If at any time the doctrine of the immortality of the soul prevailed, I was thankful; if at any time it was impugned, I went away sorrowful.  Still, neither doctrine had the power of truth over my heart.  This only I understood, that opinions and definitions of things were accounted true or false, not in accordance with their nature and the truths of the arguments, but in proportion to the talents of those who supported them.  And I was all the more tortured to the bottom of my heart, because I was neither able to lay hold on any of those things which were spoken of as firmly established, nor was I able to lay aside the desire of inquiry; but the more I endeavoured to neglect and despise them, so much the more eagerly, as I have said, did a desire of this sort, creeping in upon me secretly, as with a kind of pleasure, take possession of my heart and mind."

## Chapter IV.—His Increasing Disquiet.

"Being therefore straitened in the discovery of things, I said to myself, Why do we labour in vain since the end of things is manifest? For if after death I shall be no more, my present torture is useless; but if there is to be for me a life after death, let us keep for that life the excitements that belong to it, lest, perhaps, some sadder things befall me than those which I now suffer, unless I shall have lived piously and soberly, and, according to the opinions of some of the philosophers, I be consigned to the stream of dark-rolling Phlegethon or to Tartarus, like Sisyphus and Tityus, and to eternal punishment in the infernal regions, like Ixion and Tantalus. And again I would answer to myself, But these things are fables; or if it be so, since the matter is in doubt, it is better to live piously. But again I would ponder with myself, How shall I restrain myself from the lust of sin, while uncertain as to the reward of the righteous?—and all the more when I have no certainty what righteousness is, or what is pleasing to God; and when I cannot ascertain whether the soul be immortal, and as such that it has anything to hope for; nor do I know what the future is certainly to be. Yet still I cannot rest from thoughts of this sort."

## Chapter V.—His Design to Test the Immortality of the Soul.

"What, then, shall I do? This I shall do. I shall proceed to Egypt, and there I shall cultivate the friendship of the necrophants or prophets who preside at the shrines. Then I shall win over a magician by money, and entreat him by what they call their necromantic art to bring me a soul from the infernal regions, as if I were desirous of consulting it about some business. But this shall be my consultation, whether the soul be immortal. Now the proof that the soul is immortal will be put past doubt, not from what it says, or from what I hear, but from what I see; for seeing it with my eyes I shall ever after hold the surest conviction of its immortality, and no fallacy of words or uncertainty of hearing shall ever be able to disturb the persuasion produced by sight. However, I related this project to a certain philosopher with whom I was intimate, who counselled me not to venture upon it: 'For,' said he, 'if the soul should not obey the call of the magician, you henceforth will live more hopelessly, as thinking that there is nothing after death, and also as having tried things unlawful. If, however, you seem to see anything, what religion or what piety can arise to you from things unlawful or impious? For they say that transactions of this sort are hateful to the Divinity, and that God sets Himself in opposition to those who trouble souls after their release from the body.' When I heard this I was indeed staggered in my purpose, yet I could not in any way either lay aside my longing or cast off the distressing thought."

### Chapter VI.—Hears of Christ.

"Not to make a long story of it, whilst I was tossed upon these billows of my thought, a certain report, which took its rise in the regions of the East in the reign of Tiberius Cæsar, gradually reached us; and gaining strength as it passed through every place, like some good message sent from God, it was filling the whole world, and suffered not the Divine will to be concealed in silence. For it was spread over all places, announcing that there was a certain person in Judea, who, beginning in the spring-time, was preaching the kingdom of God to the Jews, and saying that those should receive it who should observe the ordinances of His commandments and His doctrine. And that His speech might be believed to be worthy of credit and full of the Divinity, He was used to perform many mighty works, and wonderful signs and prodigies by His mere word, so that, as one having power from God, He made the deaf to hear, and the blind to see, and the lame to stand erect, and expelled every infirmity and all demons from men; yea, that he even raised dead persons who were brought to Him; that he cured lepers also, looking at them from a distance, and that there was absolutely nothing which seemed impossible to Him. These and such like things were confirmed in process of time, not now by frequent rumours, but by the plain statements of persons coming from those quarters; and day by day the truth of the matter was further disclosed."

CHAPTER VII.—ARRIVAL OF BARNABAS AT ROME.

"At length meetings began to be held in various places in the city, and this subject to be discussed in conversation, and to be a matter of wonder who this might be who had appeared, and what message He had brought from God to men; until about the same year a certain man, standing in a most crowded place in the city, made proclamation to the people, saying, 'Hear me, O ye citizens of Rome! The Son of God is now in the regions of Judea, promising eternal life to every one who will hear Him, but upon condition that he should regulate his actions according to the will of Him by whom He hath been sent, even of God the Father. Wherefore turn ye from evil things to good, from things temporal to things eternal. Acknowledge that there is one God, ruler of heaven and earth, in whose righteous sight ye unrighteous inhabit His world. But if ye be converted, and act according to His will, then coming to the world to come, and being made immortal, ye shall enjoy His unspeakable blessings and rewards.' Now, the man who spake these things to the people was from the regions of the East, by nation a Hebrew, by name Barnabas, who said that he himself was one of His disciples, and that he was sent for this end, that he should declare these things to those who would hear them."

The story goes on to tell how some of the hearers put puzzling questions, and when he ceased how the crowd raised a shout of derision. But Clement took his part; and at last brought Barnabas to lodge at his house. Next day Barnabas departs for Cæsarea; after a little while Clement follows him, and is introduced to Peter, and by Peter's instruction is converted.

Our next extract is from Justin Martyr's "Dialogue with Trypho the Jew." Justin was a native of Flavia Neapolis, a town of Greek population and language, on the site of the ancient Sychem, in Samaria. He was a philosopher by profession, a man of thought and learning. After his conversion he wrote a defence of Christianity, addressed to the Emperor Antoninus and the senate and people of Rome, which is still extant, and is one of our authorities for the condition of the Church at that early period.*

His Dialogue with Trypho is really an elaborate work on the Judeo-Christian controversy, thrown into the form of a dialogue for the sake of bringing out the argument in a more pointed and lively manner. It opens with a little adventure which at once interests the mind of the reader, and affords an opportunity to the author to give an account of his own early studies and of his conversion. We quote it as a remarkable real example of the general notions we have gained from the fictitious experience of the pseudo-Clement.

CHAPTER I.—INTRODUCTION.

"While I was going about one morning on the walks of

* Its date is usually fixed at about 138 or 140.

the Xystus,* a certain man, with others in his company, having met me, said, 'Hail, O philosopher!'† and immediately after saying this he turned round and walked along with me; his friends likewise followed him. And I in turn, having addressed him, said, 'What is there important?'

"And he replied that he had been taught to respect philosophers; 'therefore whenever I see any one in such costume I gladly approach him, and now for the same reason have I willingly accosted you; and these accompany me in the expectation of hearing for themselves something profitable from you.' In this picturesque way the subject is introduced.

——" 'Tell us,' says Trypho, smiling gently, 'your opinion of these matters, and what ideas you entertain respecting God, and what your philosophy is.' "

## Chapter II.—Justin Describes his Studies in Philosophy.

" ' I will tell you,' said I, 'what seems to me; for philosophy is in fact the greatest possession and most honourable before God, to whom it leads us and alone commends us; and there are truly holy men who have bestowed attention on philosophy. What philosophy is, however, and the reason why it has been sent down to men, have escaped the observation of most . . . Being desirous of personally conversing with one of these men, I surrendered myself to a certain Stoic; and having spent a considerable time with him, and when I had not acquired any further knowledge of God (for he did not know himself, and said such knowledge was unnecessary), I left him, and betook myself to another,

---

\* Eusebius says this was at Ephesus.

† Justin was a professed philosopher before his conversion, and still retained the garb afterwards. Eusebius says, " Justin, in philosopher's garb, preached the Word of God."

who was called a Peripatetic, and, as he fancied, shrewd. And this man, after having entertained me for the first few days, requested me to settle the fee, in order that our intercourse might not be unprofitable. Him, too, for this reason I abandoned, believing him to be no philosopher at all. But when my soul was eagerly desirous to hear the peculiar and choice philosophy, I came to a Pythagorean, very celebrated, a man who thought much of his own wisdom. And then, when I had an interview with him, willing to become his hearer and disciple, he said, "What then? Are you acquainted with music, astronomy, and geometry? Do you expect to perceive any of those things which conduce to a happy life if you have not first, &c."—he dismissed me when I confessed to him my ignorance .... In my helpless condition it occurred to me to have a meeting with the Platonists, for their fame was great. I therefore spent as much of my time as possible with one who had lately settled in our city—a sagacious man, holding a high position among the Platonists—and I progressed and made the greatest improvements daily. And the perception of immaterial things quite overpowered me, and the contemplation of ideas furnished my mind with wings, so that in a little while I supposed that I had become wise; and such was my stupidity, I expected forthwith to look upon God, for this is the end of Plato's philosophy.'"

CHAPTER III.—JUSTIN NARRATES THE MANNER OF HIS CONVERSION.

"And while I was thus disposed, when I wished at one period to be filled with great quietness, and to shun the path of men, I used to go into a certain field not far from the sea. And when I was near that spot one day, which having reached I purposed to be by myself, a certain old man, by no means contemptible in appearance, exhibiting meek and venerable manners, followed me at a little distance. And when I turned round to him, having halted, I fixed my eyes rather keenly on him." A long conversation ensues about God and the human soul, in which the stranger shows Justin that his philosophy gives no satisfactory conclusions. He concludes with this sentence :—

"'There existed long before this time certain men more ancient than all those who are esteemed philosophers, both righteous and beloved by God, who spoke by the Divine Spirit, and foretold events which would take place, and which are now taking place. They are called prophets. These alone both saw and announced the truth to men, neither reverencing nor fearing any man, not influenced by a desire for glory, but speaking those things alone which they saw and which they heard, being filled with the Holy Spirit. Their writings are still extant, and he who has read them is much helped in his knowledge of the beginning and end of things, and of those things which the philosopher ought to know, provided he has believed them. For they did not use demonstration in their treatises, seeing that they were witnesses to the truth above all demonstration and worthy of belief; and those events which have happened, and those which are happening, compel you to assent to the utterances made by them, although indeed they were entitled to credit on account of the miracles which they performed, since they both glorified the Creator, the God and Father of all things, and proclaimed His Son the Christ [sent] by Him, which, indeed, the false prophets, who are filled with the lying, unclean spirit, neither have done nor do, but venture to work certain wonderful deeds for the purpose of astonishing men, and glorify the spirits and demons of error. But pray that, above all things, the gates of light may be opened to you; for these things cannot be perceived or understood by all, but only by the man to whom God and His Christ have imparted wisdom.'

"When he had spoken these and many other things, which there is no time for mentioning at present, he went away, bidding me attend to them; and I have not seen him since. But straightway a flame was kindled in my soul, and a love of the prophets, and of those men who are friends of Christ, possessed me; and whilst revolving his words in my mind I found this philosophy alone to be safe and profitable. Thus for this reason I am a philosopher. Moreover, I wish that all making a resolution similar to my own do not keep themselves away from the words of the Saviour, for they possess a terrible power in themselves, and are sufficient to inspire them who turn aside from the path of rectitude with awe, while the sweetest rest is afforded those who make a diligent practice of them. If, then, you have any concern for yourself, and if you are eagerly looking for salvation, and if you believe in God, you may—since you are not indifferent to the matter—become acquainted with the Christ of God, and, after being initiated,* live a happy life."

This account of Justin's conversion is the more interesting because of our knowledge of his subsequent history. Having thus found the true philosophy he devoted himself to its defence and propagation. Still retaining his philosopher's garb and character, he established a school of Christian philosophy in Rome. He also wrote two Apologies (or Defences) of Christianity, the first dedicated to the Emperor Antoninus, the second to the Emperor Marcus Aurelius. During the reign of the latter emperor, probably on the accusation of Crescens, a Cynic philosopher who had been his bitter opponent, he was condemned as a Christian, behaved with great firmness and dignity, and earned the honourable title of "the Martyr," which is usually appended to his name.

* *i.e.*, Baptized.

## CHAPTER IX.

#### THE MARTYRS OF VIENNE.

THE story of the martyrs of Vienne and Lyons, in the latter part of the reign of Marcus Aurelius, may be given as an example of the more general persecutions in which the whole body of Christians in a city was occasionally involved. The history is further interesting as giving the first distinct glimpse of the state of the Church in Gaul. Vienne was an ancient Roman colony; Lyons was a town of more recent foundation, planted by merchants from Asia Minor, as an emporium of commerce, at the junction of two great rivers, which were then the commercial highways of Southern Gaul; and the churches of these two places seem to have been not very long before planted by Christians coming from Asia Minor. We notice all the features of a settled Church. Pothinus was the Bishop of Lyons; Irenæus, the pupil of Polycarp, was a presbyter of Lyons, but, being absent on a deputation to Rome, he escaped the persecution, and on his return was elected bishop in place of Pothinus, and became one of the great lights of the Church; Sanctus was a deacon of the Church of Vienne. The history is told in a letter from the churches of Vienne and Lyons to the churches of Asia and Phrygia, and is told with such circumstantiality and absence of exaggeration as to carry with it a conviction of its truth. We abbreviate it, but give it for the most part in the language of the original.

In some way, which is not told, a popular clamour had been raised against the Christians. The mob assailed them with shouts and blows, dragging them about and plundering their goods. The magistrates, to prevent the tumults, prohibited the Christians from appearing in any houses except their own, in the baths, the market, or any public place. Then they were apprehended and led to the Forum by the tribune and the magistrates, and examined before all the people whether they were Christians. On pleading guilty they were committed to prison till the arrival of the governor, who was then absent from his post. The prefect, when they were brought before him, treated them with great savageness of manner. The spirit of Vettius Epagathus, one of the brethren, a young man of rank, was roused; he could not bear to see so manifest a perversion of justice, and demanded to be heard in behalf of the brethren, and pledged himself to prove that there was nothing atheistic or impious among them. Those about the tribunal shouted against him; the governor, vexed and irritated at his interference, only asked him if he were a Christian, and on his admitting it, he also was put among the accused. Ten of them, when questioned, lapsed,\* in fear of what was to come. Persons were now apprehended daily, so that the most excellent were selected from the two churches (Vienne and Lyons), even those by whose labour they had been founded and established (which seems to imply that these churches had existed only a very short time). Some of the heathen servants of the accused were also seized, and, under threat of torture, at the suggestion of the soldiers, accused the Christians of eating human flesh, and of various abominable crimes (the old vulgar stories, as old as Nero, which were revived again from time to time as late as Gallienus). These things being commonly reported, all were incensed even to madness against them; so that if some were formerly more moderate on account of relationship or friendship, they

\* *i.e.*, denied that they were Christians.

were now transported beyond all bounds with indignation, and our Lord's word was fulfilled, "The time will come when whoso killeth you will think that he doeth God service." (John xvi. 2.) The holy martyrs now sustained tortures which exceed the power of description, Satan labouring by means of these tortures to extort something slanderous against Christianity. The whole fury of the multitude, the governor, and the soldiers, was particularly spent on Sanctus of Vienne, a deacon; and on Maturus, a late convert indeed, but a magnanimous wrestler in spiritual things, son of Attalus of Pergamus, a man who had ever been the pillar and support of our Church; and, lastly, on Blandina, through whom Christ showed that those things that appear unsightly and contemptible among men are most honourable in the presence of God on account of love to His name, exhibited in real energy, and not in boasting and pompous pretences.

While we all feared, and, among the rest, while her mistress according to the flesh, who herself was one of the noble army of martyrs, dreaded that she would not be able to witness a good confession because of the weakness of her body, Blandina was endued with so much fortitude that those who successively tortured her from morning to night were quite worn out with fatigue, and owned themselves conquered and exhausted of their whole apparatus of tortures, and were amazed to see her still breathing while her body was torn and laid open; they confessed that any single species of the torture would have been sufficient to dispatch her, much more so great a variety as had been applied. But the blessed woman, as a generous wrestler, received fresh vigour in the act of confessing Christ, and it was an evident refreshment, support, and annihilation of all her pains to say, "I am a Christian, and no evil is committed among us." Sanctus also, through long and intense tortures, "resisted so firmly that he would neither tell his own name nor that of his nation or state, nor whether he was a freeman or slave; but to every interrogation he answered, '*I am a Christian.*' This, he used to say, was to him both name and state and race and everything; and nothing else did the heathen draw from him. They were so exasperated that, having exhausted the usual tortures, they applied hot brazen plates to the most tender parts of his body, so that at length his body "was one continued wound and bruise, and contracted together, and no longer retaining the form of a human creature." Some young persons died in prison. "The blessed Pothinus, Bishop of Lyons, upwards of ninety years of age, and very infirm and asthmatic, yet strong in spirit and panting after martyrdom, was dragged before the tribunal; his body was worn out indeed with age and disease, yet he retained a soul through which Christ might triumph. Borne by the soldiers to the tribunal, and attended by the magistrates and all the multitude shouting against him as if he were Christ himself, he made a good confession. Being asked by the governor who was the God of the Christians? he answered, "If ye be worthy ye shall know." He was then unmercifully dragged about and suffered a variety of ill-treatment. Those who were near insulted him with their hands and feet without the least respect to his age, and those at a distance threw at him whatever came to hand; every one looked upon himself as deficient in zeal if he did not insult him in some way or other. For thus they imagined they revenged the cause of their gods. He was thrown into prison almost breathless, and after two days expired.

Many who had denied their Saviour had nevertheless been thrown into prison; these were dejected and spiritless, forlorn, and in every way disgraced, even insulted by the heathen as cowards; while they who had been faithful, the joy of martyrdom, and the hope of the promises, and the love of Christ, and the Spirit of the Father, supported them, so that their countenances shone with grace and glory.

An extra day having been added to the shows of the amphitheatre on account of these Christians, Maturus and Sanctus again underwent various tortures in the amphitheatre; they were beaten with stripes, dragged and torn by the wild beasts, then made to sit in a hot iron chair, in which their bodies were roasted and emitted a disgusting smell, and at length died under the tortures, not a word having been extracted from Sanctus beyond what he had at first uttered—"I am a Christian." Blandina was all the while suspended fróm a stake in the amphitheatre, but none of the wild beasts at that time touched her, and at the end of the day she was again thrown into prison and reserved for another contest. Attalus was vehemently demanded by the multitude, and was led round the amphitheatre, cheerful and serene, with a tablet carried before him with an inscription, "This is Attalus, a Christian"; but, being a Roman citizen, he was remanded to prison till instructions should arrive from the emperor.

Cæsar sent orders that the confessors of Christ should be put to death, and those who denied Him should be liberated. And they were again brought before the tribunal of the governor, in the presence of the people. Some of those who had apostatised now withdrew their denial of Christ, and were added to the list of martyrs. During this re-examination a man who had lived many years in Gaul, and was generally known for his love of God and zealous regard for Divine truth—a person of apostolical endowments, a physician by profession, a Phrygian by nation—stood near the tribunal, and by his gestures encouraged them to confess the truth. The multitude clamoured against him as the cause of the recovered firmness of the lapsed. The governor ordered him to be placed before him, and questioned him who he was, when he declared that he was a Christian, and was at once condemned to the wild beasts; and the next day he and Attalus underwent all the usual methods of torture in the amphitheatre.

On the last day of the spectacles Blandina was again introduced, with Ponticus, a youth of fifteen. They had been daily brought in to see the punishment of the rest, in hope of intimidating them; but on their refusing to swear by the idols, and treating the menaces with contempt, the people were incensed, and no pity was shown to the youth of the one or the sex of the other. The tortures were aggravated by all sorts of methods, and the whole round of barbarities was inflicted. Ponticus, animated by his sister, who was observed by the heathen to strengthen and confirm him, after a magnanimous exertion of patience, yielded up the ghost. And now the blessed Blandina, last of all, as a generous mother, having exhorted her children and sent them before her victorious to the King, reviewing the whole series of their sufferings, hastened to undergo the same herself, rejoicing and triumphing in her exit, as if invited to a marriage supper, not going to be exposed to wild beasts. After she had endured stripes, the tearing of the beasts, and the iron chair, she was enclosed in a net and thrown to a bull, and having been tossed some time by the animal, and proving quite superior to her pains, through the influence of hope, and the realising view of the objects of her faith and her fellowship with Christ, she at length breathed out her soul. Even her enemies confessed that no woman among them had ever suffered such and so great things. The bodies of those who had died in prison were cast to the dogs. All the relics of the dead were exposed for some days *in terrorem*, and at length were burnt and the ashes cast into the Rhone, that the Christians might not honour them, according to their custom.

## CHAPTER X.

### THE CHURCHES OF EGYPT AND AFRICA.

From the death of Marcus Aurelius to the death of Severus there is little of importance in the external history of the Church to demand our notice. Severus himself in the earlier part of his reign was not unfavourable to Christianity. On the occasion of an illness he had been anointed with oil by a Christian named Proculus Torpacion, and attributed his subsequent recovery to the efficacy of this unction. In his gratitude he took Proculus into his household, and perhaps it was through his influence that a Christian nurse and a Christian preceptor were provided for his son Caracalla.

Towards the end of his reign, however (A.D. 202), this emperor issued an edict forbidding any of his subjects to embrace Judaism or Christianity. The edict did not command, and did not lead to, any general persecution of those who were already Christians, but a special persecution broke out against the Christians in Egypt and Proconsular Africa, which calls for our notice.

The history of the Church in these countries is of special interest and importance.

The city of Alexandria was the Greek and subsequently the Roman capital of Egypt. Founded by Alexander the Great, it became the capital of the Ptolemies, who succeeded to that part of his conquests; the inhabitants, claiming descent from the first colonists, proudly called themselves Macedonians; their language and civilisation were

Greek; and under the patronage of an enlightened dynasty the city had become one of the great centres of learning and philosophy.

The philosophy of Alexandria had a special character; it was not merely Greek, it was a combination of all the learning of all the great schools of human thought. A great colony of Jews, attracted by the offer of special privileges, had settled there under the early Ptolemies, and the rabbis of Alexandria were famous not only for their Jewish learning, but had also diligently cultivated the philosophy of the Greeks. The mysterious monuments of Egypt pressed upon every intelligent mind which lived within their influence the study of that most ancient civilisation and religion; while in this emporium of the commerce of the East the curious inquirer came in contact with the religions of Persia and Chaldea, themselves affected by the systems of India and the further East.

The Christian Church was early planted here. St. Peter is said to have himself founded the Alexandrian Church, and to have appointed St. Mark as its first bishop. The new religion, regarded from the philosophic point of view, attracted the attention of the learned of Alexandria. It exercised a considerable influence on the existing philosophies, and was itself influenced in return. It gave rise on one side to a new philosophy, the neo-Platonic. Platonism was its basis; some of its profound but vague shadowings forth of great truths were interpreted by the light of Christianity, and other truths of the Christian revelation were incorporated into it.

On the other hand, the philosophic side of Christianity was rapidly developed in the hands of its Alexandrian professors. They found in the language of Plato a vehicle which enabled them to present Christian truth acceptably to minds trained in the schools of philosophy; they did not hesitate to recognise, and to adopt from philosophy, all which was in harmony with revelation. A famous school of Christian learning thus arose which exercised considerable influence on the mind of the Church.

The Catechetical school of Alexandria is said indeed to have existed from the time of St. Mark, but it was about the middle of the second century that it assumed the shape of a great school of thought, in which not only the clergy and the educated converts were trained, but even heathen disciples came, as they did to the great Platonic or the great Stoic school of the day, to learn the Christian philosophy. The first famous master of the school whose name has descended to us was Pantænus, a convert from the Stoic philosophy, who is described by his successor, Clement, as having been superior in learning and ability to all his contemporaries. Clement, a native of Athens, had (like so many of the inquiring minds of the time) travelled through various countries in search of wisdom till he found satisfaction in the teaching of Pantænus and settled at Alexandria, and succeeded his master as head of the Alexandrian school.

Clement of Alexandria, as he is called, was master of the Catechetical school when the persecution broke out in the end of the reign of Severus. One of its most distinguished pupils was the young Origen, a young man of seventeen or eighteen. Origen was born at Alexandria about A.D. 185, and from his childhood had been carefully trained both in literature and in the Christian religion by his father Leonidas, who was a teacher of rhetoric by profession, and a Christian.

When the persecution broke out it was thought right that one so sure to be sought as Clement should take refuge elsewhere. Some of the priests were burned. Leonidas was one of the victims; his property was seized and his widow and her seven children were in deep distress. Origen, the eldest, was compassionately received into the house of a wealthy Christian lady. Some educated heathen who wished to be instructed in Christian philosophy applied to Origen, whose extraordinary learning and abilities were known; and thus at the age of eighteen he found himself drawn into the office of a public lecturer, and soon after was appointed by Demetrius, the Bishop, to be the master of the Catechetical school. And when the persecution broke out afresh on the arrival of a new governor, and priests were burnt and virgins tortured, Origen stood by his disciples and encouraged them in their sufferings, not without himself enduring some violence at the hands of the mob. It is not our business here to follow the subsequent life and labours of Origen, but to content ourselves with this glance at the state of the Christian Church in Alexandria at the end of the reign of Severus.

The persecution extended to the neighbouring province of Africa. The north of Africa was then crowded with rich and populous cities, and formed with Egypt the granary of the Western world. Carthage, its capital, and probably most of its towns, had inherited from the conquests of Scipio and the victories of Cæsar the Roman language and civilisation. In no part of the empire had Christianity taken more deep and permanent root. Its Christianity had a special tone—severe, simple, and practical in its creed, earnest and fervent in its spirit. Africa rather than Rome was the parent of Latin Christianity. Tertullian was at this period the chief representative of African Christianity, and Tertullian is the first of the great writers of the Church who wrote in Latin. Still later Cyprian, and later still Augustine, are the representatives of the ecclesiastical organisation and the grand theology of this Latin Church. No churches in the world have been so influential as the Greek Church of Alexandria and the Latin Church of Africa—one the mother of Eastern, the other of Western theology — and no churches have so utterly passed away. To us, preoccupied with the modern insignificance of the Egyptian town, it requires an effort of the mind to realise that Alexandria was once the second largest city in the world and the second greatest patriarchate of the Church — the Church of Clement, Origen, Athanasius, and Cyril. It gives us a kind of mental shock when we recall that the land of Tertullian, Cyprian, and Augustine is the modern Tunis and Algiers.

Tertullian's first Apology was written at the time of the persecution of Severus. In it he urges with characteristic force most of the points which had been advanced by the earlier apologists, and adds many new arguments both in favour of Christianity and in refutation of heathenism. He also incidentally gives much interesting information as to the history and circumstances of the Church, and its extension at that time. He says: "We are a people of yesterday, and yet we have filled every place belonging to you — cities, islands, castles, towns, assemblies, your very camp, your tribes, companies, palace, senate, forum. We leave you your temples only. We can count your armies; our numbers, in a single province, are greater." In a second Defence, a few years later, he says to Scapula the prefect: "Thousands of both sexes, of every rank, will eagerly crowd to martyrdom, exhaust your fires, and weary your swords. Carthage must be decimated; the principal persons in the city, even perhaps your own most intimate friends and kindred, must be sacrificed." Even if we make some allowance for rhetorical exaggeration, there remains a general assertion that Christianity was widely spread in Africa at this period — the early part of the third century — an assertion which is corroborated by other independent evidence.

## CHAPTER XI.

### THE MARTYRDOM OF PERPETUA AND FELICITAS.

IT was the year after the death of Severus, and apparently as an isolated outbreak of the persecuting spirit, that somewhere in this African province there occurred the martyrdom of Perpetua and Felicitas. "Of all the histories of martyrdom none is so unexaggerated in its tone and language, none abounds in such exquisite touches of nature, or on the whole breathes such an air of truth and reality as that of Perpetua and Felicitas."* We give it for its value in helping us to realise the actual Christian life of the time. The youthful catechumens, Revocatus and Felicitas, Saturninus and Secundulus, were apprehended, and with them Vivia Perpetua, a woman of good family and liberal education. Perpetua was about twenty-two years old, married, with an infant at the breast. Her father and mother were living; she had two brothers, one of them, like herself, a catechumen. The history is related by Perpetua herself, and is said to have been written by her own hand. "When we were in the hands of the persecutors, my father, in his tender affection, persevered in his endeavours to pervert me from the faith. 'My father, this vessel—be it a pitcher, or whatever it is—can we call it anything else than what it is?' 'Certainly not,' he replied. 'Nor can I call myself by any other name than that of a Christian.' My father looked as if he could have plucked my eyes out; but he only harassed me, and departed, persuaded by the arguments of

* Milman.

the devil. Then after being a few days without seeing my father, I was enabled to give thanks to God, and his absence was tempered to my spirit. After a few days we were baptized, and the waters of baptism seemed to give power of endurance to my body. Again a few days and we were cast into prison. I was terrified, for I had never before seen such total darkness. O miserable day! from the dreadful heat of the prisoners crowded together and the insults of the soldiers. But I was wrung with solicitude for my infant. Two of our deacons however, by the payment of money, obtained our removal for some hours in the day to a more open part of the prison. Each of the captives there pursued his usual occupation; but I suckled my infant, who was wasting away with hunger. In my anxiety I addressed and consoled my mother, and commended my child to my brother; and I began to pine away at seeing them pine away on my account. And for many days I suffered this anxiety, and accustomed my child to remain in the prison with me, and I immediately recovered my strength, and was relieved from my toil and trouble for my infant, and the prison became to me like a palace; and I was happier there than I should have been anywhere else.

"My brother then said to me, 'Perpetua, you are exalted to such dignity that you may pray for a vision, and it shall be shown you whether our doom is martyrdom or release.' And accordingly I had a vision. I saw a lofty ladder of gold ascending to heaven; around it were swords, lances, hooks, and a great dragon lay at its foot to seize those who would ascend. Saturus, a distinguished Christian, went up first, beckoned me to follow, and controlled the dragon by the name of Jesus Christ. I ascended, and found myself in a spacious garden, in which sat a man with white hair, in the garb of a shepherd, milking his sheep, with many myriads round him. He welcomed me, and gave me a morsel of cheese; and I received it with folded hands, and ate it; and all the saints around exclaimed, 'Amen.' I awoke at the sound, with the sweet taste in my mouth, and I related it to my brother; and we knew that our martyrdom was at hand, and we began to have no hope in this world.

"After a few days there was a rumour that we were to be heard. And my father came from the city, wasted away with anxiety, to pervert me. And he said, 'Have compassion, O my daughter! on my grey hairs; have compassion on thy father, if he is worthy of the name of father. If I have thus brought thee up to the flower of thine age, if I have preferred thee to all thy brothers, do not expose me to this disgrace. Look on thy brother; look on thy mother and thy aunt; look on thy child, who cannot live without thee. Do not destroy us all!' Thus spake my father, kissing my hands in his fondness, and throwing himself at my feet; and in his tears he called me not his daughter, but his mistress (*domina*). And I was grieved for the grey hairs of my father, because he alone of all my family did not rejoice in my martyrdom; and I consoled him, saying, 'In this trial what God wills will take place. Know that we are not in our own power, but in that of God.' And he went away sorrowing. Another day, while we were at dinner, we were suddenly seized and carried off to trial, and we came to the town. The report spread rapidly, and an immense multitude was assembled. We were placed at the bar; the rest were interrogated and made their confession. And it came to my turn; and my father at that moment appeared with my child, and he drew me down the step, and said in a beseeching tone, 'Have compassion on your infant'; and Hilarianus the Procurator, who exercised the power of life and death in place of the Proconsul Timinianus; who had died, said, 'Spare the grey hairs of your parent; spare your infant; offer sacrifice for the welfare of the emperor.' And I answered, 'I will not sacrifice.' 'Art thou a Christian?' said Hilarianus. I answered, 'I am a Christian'; and while my father stood there to persuade me, Hilarianus ordered him to be thrust down and beaten with rods. And the misfortune of my father grieved me, and I was as much grieved for his old age as if I had been scourged myself. He then passed sentence on us all, and condemned us to the wild beasts; and we went back in cheerfulness to the prison. And because I was accustomed to suckle my infant, and to keep it with me in the prison, I sent Pomponius the deacon to seek it from my father; but my father would not send it. But by the will of God the child no longer desired the breast, and I suffered no uneasiness, that at such a time I should not be afflicted by the sufferings of my child or by pains in my breasts.

"Again a few days, and the keeper of the prison, profoundly impressed by their conduct, and beginning to discern 'the power of God within them,' admitted many of the brethren to visit them, for mutual consolation.

"And as the day of the games approached, my father entered, worn out with affliction, and began to pluck his beard and to throw himself down with his face upon the ground, and to wish that he could hasten his death, and to speak words which might have moved any living creature. And I was grieved for the sorrows of his old age." The night before they were to be exposed in the arena she dreamed that she was changed to a man; fought and triumphed over a huge and terrible Egyptian gladiator, that she put her foot upon his head, she received the crown, passed out of the Vivarian Gate, and knew that she had triumphed not over man, but over the devil. The vision of Saturnius, which he related for their consolation, was more splendid. He ascended into the Realms of Light, into a beautiful garden and to a palace, the walls of which were light, and there he was welcomed, not only by the angels, but by all the friends who had preceded him in the glorious career. Among the rest he saw a bishop and a priest, between whom there had been some dissensions; and while Perpetua was conversing with them the angels interfered, and insisted on their perfect reconciliation.

The narrative then proceeds to another instance of the triumph of faith over the strongest of human feelings—the love of a young mother for her offspring. Felicitas was in the eighth month of her pregnancy. She feared, and her friends shared in her apprehension, that on that account her martyrdom might be delayed. They prayed together, and her travail came on. In her agony she gave way to expressions of her suffering. "How then," said one of the servants of the prison, "if you cannot endure these pains, will you endure exposure to the wild beasts?" She replied, "I bear now my own sufferings; then there will be One within me who will bear my sufferings for me, because I shall suffer for His sake." She brought forth a girl, of whom a Christian sister took charge.

Perpetua maintained her calmness to the end. While they were treated with severity by a tribune, who feared lest they should be delivered from the prison by enchantment, Perpetua remonstrated with a kind of mournful pleasantry, and said that if ill-used they would do no credit to the birthday of Cæsar; the victims ought to be fattened for the sacrifice. But their language and demeanour were not always so calm and gentle; the words of some became words of defiance, almost of insult, and this is related with as much admiration as the more tranquil sublimity of the former incidents. To the people who gazed on them in their importunate curiosity at their Agape, they said, "Is not to-morrow's spectacle enough to satiate your hate? To-day you look on us with friendly faces, to-morrow you will be our deadly enemies. Mark well our countenances, that you may know them again on the day of judgment." And to Hilarianus on his tribunal they said, "Thou judgest us, but God will judge thee." At this language the exasperated people demanded that they should be scourged. When taken out to the execution they declined, and were permitted to decline, to wear the profane dress in which they were to be clad—the men that of priests of Saturn, the women that of priestesses of Ceres. They came forward in their simple attire, Perpetua singing psalms. The men were exposed to leopards and bears; the women were hung up naked in nets, to be gored by a furious cow. But even the excited populace shrank with horror at the spectacle of two young and delicate women in this state. They were recalled by acclamation, and in mercy brought forward again clad in loose robes. Perpetua was tossed, her garment was rent, and more conscious of her wounded modesty than of pain, she drew the robe over her person. She then calmly clasped up her hair, because it did not become a martyr to suffer with dishevelled locks—the sign of sorrow. She then raised up the fainting and mortally wounded Felicitas, and the cruelty of the populace being for a time appeased, they were permitted to retire. Perpetua seemed rapt in ecstasy, and, as if awaking from sleep, inquired when she was to be exposed to the beast. She could scarcely be made to believe what had taken place. Her last words tenderly admonished her brother to be steadfast in the faith. They were all speedily released; Perpetua guided with her own hand the merciful sword of the gladiator which terminated her sufferings.*

* Milman, "History of Christianity."

## CHAPTER XII.

### PROGRESS OF THE CHURCH—MARTYRDOM OF CYPRIAN.

FROM the close of the African persecution, which lasted till the second year of Caracalla (212 A.D.), the Church enjoyed uninterrupted peace till the reign of Decius.

In the reign of Alexander Severus it was even protected and encouraged. His mother, Mammæa, had at least taken so much interest in Christianity as to seek an interview with Origen when he was living at Cæsarea, and to converse with him on the subject. The emperor was acquainted with its doctrines, and had a favourable opinion of them, but he was not a Christian. He seems to have been in the state of mind in which many educated and inquiring minds were at the time. He had a good deal of religious sentiment; his first daily duty was to offer adoration to the Deity; but he believed all religions to be worthy of respect. He paid the customary honours to the ancient gods of Rome, and at the same time he held the Egyptian worship in respect, and enlarged the temples of Isis and Serapis. In his own chamber he had statues of those whom he specially honoured as the great religious teachers of mankind—viz., Orpheus and Abraham, Christ and Apollonius of Tyana. In his reign the Church assumed a position in the face of the world. Christian bishops were received at the imperial court in a recognised official character. Churches were built in different parts of the empire. In the case of a disputed title to a piece of ground in Rome, which was claimed by the Christians as the site of a church, and claimed also by the guild of victuallers, the emperor himself gave his decision in favour of the Christians, upon the principle that it was better that the land should be devoted to the worship of God in any form than applied to an unworthy use. We are told also that he adopted in the appointments to civil offices the same method which the Christians followed in the appointment of their clergy. It is clear, therefore, that the Church transacted her affairs in the light of day.

Indeed a striking, though indirect, indication of the spread of Christian doctrine is the change which was coming over the tone of the prevalent paganism and its whole attitude towards Christianity. The old speculative philosophy has become more than a philosophy; it has become a religion. It has come to acknowledge the being of one Supreme God, and either to look upon the gods of the nations as created beings, or emanations, employed by the Supreme Deity in the affairs of the world, or to explain them away as myths and symbols. It has joined philosophy with morality. It has begun to preach its belief as a means of ameliorating the condition of mankind. It no longer despises Christianity, but seriously argues against it, and defends itself against the Christian attack.

The persecution under Decius was deliberate and general. That able sovereign desired to revive the ancient virtue of the Roman character. He procured the revival in Valerian of the long obsolete office of censor, and his measures against Christianity were a part of his design to restore the ancient religion and manners of Rome. Fabian, the Bishop of Rome, was one of the first of the victims. Origen suffered cruel torments, but escaped with life. Antioch saw the martyrdom of its bishop, Babylas. Cyprian, Bishop of Carthage, escaped the same fate by a timely retreat. The persecution was general, and its effect upon the Church was great. The prosperity of the Church for many years past had made it easy to embrace the faith. With many it was an hereditary faith, not one which they had adopted with mature convictions, and many were found who shrank from the painful honour of martyrdom. In the African Church especially many lapsed; among them some of the bishops and other clergy. Many obtained from the officers, by bribes, certificates (*libelli*) that they had complied with the required tests when they had not. The former were called Lapsi, the latter Libellatici; and the question of their subsequent treatment by the Church raised a great controversy as soon as the persecution was over. The death of Decius, after two years' reign, put an end to the persecution. Valerian, in the early part of his reign, was favourable to the Christians. In the latter part of his reign, however, he issued an edict, in which all the bishops who refused to conform were subjected to the penalty of death, and the endowments of the churches were confiscated. Under this edict died Cyprian, Bishop of Carthage, whose life is so bound up with the history of the Church that it is desirable to introduce him at some length into our pages.

Cyprian was a teacher of rhetoric at Carthage, a man of eminence for his talent and a man of wealth, when in mature age he embraced the faith of Christ. He passed rapidly through the steps of initiation, almost as rapidly through the first orders of the Christian ministry; and on the occurrence of a vacancy in the bishopric the people of the city surrounded his house, and by their acclamations forced on him the honourable office of their bishop. At the time of the Decian persecution he acted on the prudent policy which was considered to be right for the rulers of the Church at such crises—he retreated from the city, and took refuge among the recluses of the desert, whence, by frequent letters, he directed the affairs of his Church, and animated and consoled the sufferers. His letters afford an authentic contemporary authority for the cruelty of the tortures to which the unhappy Christians were put, and the number of the sufferers in this persecution.

We must not suppress here the picture, which will hang so well between our previous and subsequent pictures of martyrdom, of the plague of Carthage. At the commencement of Valerian's reign a plague, which the armies brought back from the East, ravaged the whole western world. It was specially destructive in Carthage. It spread gradually from house to house. The usual panic seized the inhabitants, and the usual paralysis of all natural affection was exhibited. The sick were left untended or thrust out of doors; the dead were left unburied in the houses and the streets. Cyprian called his flock together, and exhorted them to show the sincerity of their belief in the doctrines of their Master, not by confining their acts of Christian charity to their own relations, or to the Christian brotherhood, but to show like love to their enemies. The city was divided into districts; different offices were assigned to different individuals; the rich gave their money and the poor gave their labour; the dead were buried, the sick were nursed. The confessors,* just released from the prisons and the mines, with the scars of their tortures yet upon them, might probably have been seen risking their lives anew in these acts of love to their enemies.

When the Valerian edict appeared Cyprian declined again to seek safety in concealment. He was arrested and carried to a place about four miles from the city, where the proconsul was residing. Here he was treated with great respect, and allowed to enjoy the society of his friends at supper. The news of his arrest drew the whole population of the city together; many spent the night in the

* A Confessor was one who, during a persecution, risked his life by confessing Christ before the Magistrate.

open air around the house. A great multitude crowded the place of judgment the next day when the bishop was brought to trial. There is a notable difference between the passionate fury with which the magistrates and the mob tore and burned the martyrs of Vienne, and the state of spiritual exaltation in which they triumphed over their sufferings; and the respect and courtesy with which the proprætor treats Cyprian, the reluctance with which he sentences him, the calmness with which the bishop accepts his death, and the orderly sympathy of the people. The examination was brief. The report of it is from the pen of one of Cyprian's clergy: "Art thou Thascius Cyprian, the bishop of so many impious men? The most sacred emperor commands thee to sacrifice." "I will not sacrifice." "Consider well what thou dost." "There is no need of consideration; do as thou art commanded." The proconsul consulted with his council, and reluctantly delivered the inevitable sentence of condemnation: "Thascius Cyprian, thou hast lived long in thy impiety, and assembled around thee many men involved in the same wicked conspiracy. Thou hast shown thyself an enemy alike to the gods and the laws of the empire; the pious and sacred emperors have in vain endeavoured to recall thee to the worship of thy ancestors. Since, then, thou hast been the chief author and leader of these most guilty practices, thou shalt be an example to those whom thou hast deluded to thy unlawful assemblies. Thou must expiate thy crime with thy blood." Cyprian replied: "God be thanked." The multitude of Christians cried: "Let us go and be beheaded with him." He was removed at once to a neighbouring field, surrounded by trees, whose branches were soon crowded with spectators. He spent a short time in prayer, bound his own eyes, ordered a considerable present to be given to the executioner, and submitted to the stroke. His blood was caught by the Christians in cloths and handkerchiefs to be preserved as relics. His body was buried close by, but was afterwards removed by torchlight with great solemnity and honourably sepultured.

Gallienus, when left sole emperor by the captivity of Valerian, rescinded the persecuting edict. The bishops were allowed to return to their sees, the churches and cemeteries and their endowments were restored, and the free exercise of their religion was for the first time expressly granted to the Christians.

## CHAPTER XIII.

### THE DIOCLETIAN PERSECUTION—THE CONVERSION OF CONSTANTINE.

FROM the conclusion of the Valerian persecution to the latter years of Diocletian (A.D. 260 to 302) the Church had enjoyed half a century of uninterrupted prosperity. The Christians had become a numerous and influential body. Eusebius says: "The number of Christians so grew and multiplied in these fifty years that their ancient churches were not large enough to receive them, and therefore they erected from the foundations more ample and spacious ones in every city." In the larger cities there were more churches than one.* Some of these edifices displayed a degree of architectural splendour, and were furnished with chalices, lamps, and chandeliers of gold and silver. Christians were found in the highest ranks of society, and the highest offices of the army and the State. Prisca the wife of Diocletian, and Valeria his daughter, who was married to the Cæsar Galerius, were believed to be Christians, as were some of the chief officials of the imperial household. Provincial governments were conferred on Christians, with a privilege of exemption from all duties which might interfere with their religion. The two emperors—Diocletian and Maximian—tolerated Christianity; of the two Cæsars, Constantius favoured and protected it, Galerius was bitterly opposed to it. In the years 302 and 303 Diocletian was induced by

* There were more than forty churches in Rome at the time of the Diocletian persecution.

Galerius, his colleague in the eastern half of the empire, to adopt a different policy, and to endeavour to suppress the Christian religion.

A series of edicts was issued. The first ordered that all who refused to sacrifice should lose their offices, property, rank, and civil privileges; that all ranks of Christians should be liable to torture; that churches should be razed to the ground, the sacred books burned, the endowments confiscated. A second edict ordered the arrest of the clergy. A third edict required them to sacrifice or be tortured. A fourth edict in the following year extended this order to Christians of every class. And since the constancy of Christians under torture was well known, the judges were charged to invent new and more exquisite torments. None of the edicts expressly enacted the punishment of death, but it must often have resulted from the torture, and was in many cases actually inflicted.

Constantius, in the provinces specially under his government, gave orders for the destruction of the churches, but as far as possible discountenanced violence against the persons of the Christians;* and on his death Constantine still more avowedly favoured Christianity, and promoted Christians to office. In the rest of the empire the persecution was conducted with great severity. Thousands were tortured, imprisoned, sent to the mines, mutilated, killed.

After the first two years the persecuting edicts were not pressed in the western provinces of the empire, but Galerius continued his endeavours to root out the existence of Christianity in the East until the year 311. In that year, sinking under a horrible disease, and impressed probably with the idea that it was a punishment for his persecution of the Christians, he published, in his own name and those of

* To the first year of this persecution must be assigned the story of St. Alban, the protomartyr of Britain.

Licinius and Constantine, an edict of toleration. He allowed Christians to rebuild their churches and freely exercise their religion; and he made so much admission of the truth of their religion as is implied in his asking for their prayers for his own health and safety. On the cessation of the long persecution, the prisons and mines released their victims. Everywhere long trains of Christians were seen hastening to the ruined churches; the public roads, streets, and market-places were crowded with long processions singing psalms of thanksgiving. The confessors were received with honour; the lapsed hastened to reconcile themselves to the Church.

Maximin's name had not been appended to the edict of toleration, but he so far acceded to the wish of the other emperors as to desist from open persecution. He continued, however, to oppose Christianity by other weapons. The old stories to the prejudice of the faith were revived, and new ones were invented and disseminated. Paganism was reorganised as a rival religion; a complete hierarchy was established after the model of the Christian episcopacy. Men of rank and wealth in the different towns were appointed pontiffs, the sacrifices were performed with great splendour, the people were required to attend them; the Christians were forbidden to meet for worship, and were harassed by all kinds of petty persecution, which sometimes rose to the dignity of torture and death.

As Constantine extended his power first over one then over another part of the empire, the cause of Christianity triumphed with him. In his contest with Maxentius the strife for empire assumed also the aspect of a religious war. Maxentius at Rome had ostentatiously displayed his belief in the ancient gods, and promised, if victorious, to restore their worship throughout the empire. Constantine, on his march against him, had seen the famous vision of the cross in the sky with the words, "IN THIS CONQUER," and had definitively embraced Christianity, and resolved to establish it as the religion of the empire, should God give him the victory. After his victory over Maxentius, in October 312, he at once published an edict in favour of the Christians. In June of the following year, after the overthrow of Maximin by Licinius, another edict was issued from Milan, in the joint names of Constantine and Licinius, giving complete religious toleration to the Christians, ordering that the churches and other property should be restored to them, giving compensation out of the public purse to those who might be losers by the restitution, and ordering the prefects to see the restitution carried into effect without delay and without chicanery. It was the great charter of the liberties of Christianity.

Besides restoring their ancient property the emperor made a considerable donation to the churches of Africa to help them to rebuild their destroyed churches. He also gave the Church the right to hold property and to receive it by bequest. This right had apparently been admitted by Alexander Severus, annulled by Diocletian, but was now conceded in the most explicit terms, and was the legal ground of the vast property afterwards acquired by the Church.

When the rivalry between Constantine and Licinius sprang up, the favour which was shown by one to Christianity seems to have thrown the other, as a matter of policy, into the opposite interest, and Licinius began to favour the pagan and to discountenance the Christian party. He would retain none in the ranks of his household troops who would not sacrifice. He confined the bishops to the care of their own dioceses, and forbad the holding of synods. At length he closed the churches in Pontus, and began to harass the Christians, and there was a widespread apprehension of a general persecution, when Constantine again took up arms against Licinius. The defeat of Licinius (A.D. 323) made Constantine sole emperor, and assured the triumph of Christianity. Among his first acts was the repeal of all the acts of Licinius against the Christians, and the extension to the East of the favours which had been accorded them in the West. In an edict addressed to all his subjects he exhorted them to embrace the Christian religion, but professed to wish that it should be advanced by persuasion only. He ordered that churches should be built everywhere of a size to contain the whole population. He withdrew the State sanction of paganism by discontinuing all sacrifices hitherto celebrated at the expense of the State, but allowed other sacrifices to continue. For himself, though he continued only a catechumen, according to a custom unhappily prevalent then and long subsequently, he regularly attended the services of the Church, read the Scriptures, heard sermons, in his journeys was attended by a travelling chaplain, and received bishops among his chosen associates. At first his support of Christianity had perhaps been only out of a tolerant spirit; then a piece of policy; later, though he may have been an imperfect believer and an inconsistent Christian, there seems no reasonable ground to doubt the sincerity of his ultimate adoption of Christianity, and that his real desire was to use his power fairly for the promotion of the religion which he had embraced.

The foundation of a new capital on the Bosphorus marked the completion of the revolution which had gradually changed the Roman republic into an absolute monarchy. It marked also the establishment of Christianity as the religion of the empire. The genius of paganism continued for many years to influence the men who were born and lived beneath the shadow of the ancient temples and the great prestige of Rome; but from the first Constantinople was a Christian city. There were, indeed, several temples of the ancient Byzantine town which were allowed to remain, but the new temples which rose in it were Christian churches.

Next to the adoption of the Labarum as the standard of his armies, and placing it on the coinage of the empire, the numerous and magnificent churches which he built were perhaps the most conspicuous evidences to the world that the emperor had embraced the Christian religion. He built a grand church at Jerusalem, near what was believed to be the site of the holy sepulchre; the emperor himself was present with a great concourse of bishops at the dedication of it. He built another at Antioch, which was called the Golden Church for its splendour. He built others at Mamre and Bethlehem, at Heliopolis in Phœnicia, and at Nicomedia. Especially in his new capital at Constantinople he built the noble church called, after his name, *Ecclesia Constantiniana*, to the memory of the twelve apostles, which, as Eusebius describes it, "was vastly high, and yet had all its walls covered with marble, its roof overlaid with gold, and the outside, instead of tiles, covered with gilded brass." He also laid the foundations of a second church in the capital dedicated to the Holy Wisdom, *Sancta Sophia*, which was finished by Constantius, and, after its destruction by fire, was rebuilt by Justinian as it stands to this day.

The emperor's mother, Helena, was also a great encourager of devotion. Our early historians used to tell us that Helena was a Christian princess, the daughter of a British king, who was married by Constantius, and that their son Constantine was born in Britain. But we must be content to abandon the distinction. There is no trace of Constantius having been in Britain at all before the year A.D. 296, at which time his son was twenty-four years old; and the most credible writers assert that his consort was not a Briton but a Bithynian. There is also express testimony that Constantine was born at Naissus in Upper Mœsia; and there is no evidence

that Helena was a Christian before the conversion of her son. She was, however, a devout Christian and a liberal benefactress to the Church, building churches and monasteries in many places. She took special interest in the holy places of Palestine; and probably the passion for pilgrimages, which sprang up in that age, is in great measure due to her example. She endeavoured to identify the scenes of the great events of our Lord's life, and to recover relics of the Gospel age. The supposed finding of the cross upon which our Lord suffered, buried in the place of execution, was done under her auspices; and many other of the relics venerated in the middle ages are due to her zeal and munificence.

## CHAPTER XIV.

### THE CONSTITUTION OF THE CHURCH.

THERE are in these days three theories of Church constitution, each of which claims to be primitive—the Congregational, the Presbyterian, and the Episcopal. Before we proceed to describe the actual Episcopal constitution of the early Church, which we assume to be a continuation of its primitive constitution as described in chapter III., it may be well to say a few words on these rival theories.

The Congregational theory is that any number of Christian people agreeing to form themselves into an organised congregation constitute a Church; that they have the right to elect their own ministers; that every such Church is complete and independent; that no one has a right to interfere with it in doctrine or discipline; and that it has a right to claim recognition and be received into full communion by all other churches.

We say that our Lord nominated the apostles; the apostles ordained elders in every church, and they also ordained the deacons of the Church of Jerusalem; Saint Paul says he left Titus in Crete to ordain elders in every city, and he gave Timothy directions to ordain elders in Ephesus; and he instructed them both what sort of men they were to ordain as deacons. We find this the custom in all the churches in the world for one thousand five hundred years. On the other hand, there is no example in the New Testament of any community of Christians organising itself and electing its ministers; no example of it in the whole Catholic Church until the sixteenth century of the Christian era.

The Congregationalists point to two facts in the history of the Apostolic Church—the election of Matthias to the apostolate, and the election by the people of the deacons of Jerusalem—as being in favour of their theory. And they refer also to the popular nomination of bishops—as of Cyprian, Ambrose, and others—as illustrations of their theory in the later history of the Church. The reply is easy, that however the designation of men to be raised to the sacred ministry may have been effected, yet their ordination—the actual conferring on them of the ministerial character and office—has always been by the laying on of hands of the bishop and presbytery.

When the Congregationalists abandon the argument from primitive practice, and boldly urge that though the constitution of the Church in primitive times may have been monarchical or aristocratical, yet this is not of Divine obligation, and that Christian men are at liberty to adopt the democratic form of Church constitution and government; that the clergy have no Divine right to rule, or teach, or administer sacraments; we reply that Christ, by His apostles, organised the Church, and he who revolutionises that constitution must answer to Christ for it; that for our part we cannot recognise the revolution; that the ministry of Christ's Church is Christ's ministry, their character and authority are derived from Him, and that no body of men can give one of their number the character and authority of one of Christ's ministers independently of Christ's appointment.

When a man claims to exercise this office on the ground of an inward call, those whose duty in the Church it is must examine his call, and, if it appear to be real, confer ordination upon him; but we decline to accept his assertion of an inward call as a valid title to assume the office, independently of Christ's ordinary appointment and regular ordination; unless he can establish this independent and special call by sufficient evidence, and the only sufficient evidence of such a special call would be that of miracles.

Another theory of Church government is the Presbyterian. It admits that the ministry is of Divine appointment, and has a Divine right to rule and teach and administer sacraments; but it asserts that the ministry is of only one order—the presbyterate—that deacons are only lay assistants, and that bishops are an usurpation. They point out that the elders were also called bishops in primitive times. They grant that the apostles exercised an authority over these elders, but they assert that this authority was exceptional, and that when the apostles died the elders remained the sole order of the ministry, without any superior under Christ. They admit that at a very early period the churches were governed by bishops, and they account for it in this way, that the affairs of each church were at first ruled by a college of presbyters, but, that one of these, ordinarily presiding at their meetings, and acting as their moderator, gradually assumed a superior function and authority.

We admit that the names of the various orders of the clergy were not at first settled, and that during the days of the apostles the title bishop was often applied to the second order. Theodoret, in the beginning of the fifth century, explains this point so clearly that we need not add a word to it: "The same persons," he says, "were anciently called bishops and presbyters; they whom we now call bishops were then called apostles. But in process of time the name of apostles was appropriated to those who were apostles in the strict sense; and the rest, who had formerly the name of apostles, were styled bishops. In this sense Epaphroditus is called the Apostle of the Philippians; Titus was the Apostle of the Cretans; and Timothy of Asia." But we assert that the apostles ordained an order superior to that of the elders, to whom they committed the supreme rule of the several churches and the power of ordination.

For the assumption that a presiding presbyter gradually usurped authority over his brother presbyters there is no evidence in the history of the primitive Church. It is impossible to believe that this usurpation should have taken place universally in all the churches of the world, without an exception here and there, and without any trace or tradition left of such a revolution.

On the other hand we have the scriptural examples of Episcopal constitution in Ephesus and Crete, and in the seven churches of Asia. A study of the method of the New Testament leads us to the conclusion that these are given as instances of the course which was universally taken in giving the churches their permanent organisation. We have already seen, in chapter III., other examples of bishops appointed in the lifetime of the apostles. We are about to see, in the present chapter, that when the Church emerged out of the obscurity which enveloped it, for thirty years or thereabouts, in the latter part of the first century, the Episcopal constitution was absolutely universal throughout its length and breadth. The inference seems to us irresistible that this universal existence of episcopacy is the result of apostolic direction, and according to the mind of Christ. When we come from the apostolic times to the most early records of the succeeding age, we find that the succession of bishops was preserved in all churches of which we have any account. Ignatius suffered martyrdom about the tenth year of Trajan, which was only about four years after the death of St. John, at which time he had been forty years bishop of that Church. He is said by Theodoret to have immediately succeeded Evodius, the first bishop, and to have been appointed by St. Peter's own hand. The epistles of Ignatius to the various churches are full of exhortations to private Christians to be obedient to the clergy, and to the lower orders of the clergy—viz., presbyters and deacons—to be obedient to their bishops. In the beginning of his epistle to the Magnesians he speaks of Damas their bishop, Bassus and Apollonius their presbyters, and of Solion their deacon ; * the last of them he praises because he was subject to the bishop and presbyters, and he exhorts all of them to reverence their bishop, and to do all things in godly peace and concord, "their bishop presiding in the place of God, the presbyters as the council of apostles, and the deacons as the ministers of Christ."† In the epistle to the Trallians he names their bishop, Polybius.‡ He says : " Let nothing by any means be done without the bishop, even as ye now practise ; subject yourselves to the college of presbyters, as to the apostles of Jesus Christ . . . . and let the deacons study to please all men ; without them a Church is not named " §— *i.e.*, an organisation of men is not a Church without these. Again, having cautioned them to beware of heresies and heretics, he adds, "And so ye will, whilst ye are not puffed up, and are not separated from God, Jesus Christ, nor from the bishop, nor from the precepts of the apostles. He that is within the altar is pure, but whoever doeth anything without the bishop, the college of presbyters, and the deacon, his conscience is defiled." ‖ To the Ephesians he says: " Let no man be deceived; whoever is without the altar is deprived of the bread of God. . . . Let us have a care of opposing the bishop, that we may be subject to God." ¶ In the same epistle he speaks of bishops settled to the end of the world, " who are after the mind of Jesus Christ, even as Christ is the mind of the Father." ** In the epistle to the Philadelphians : †† " Be not deceived, my brethren; if any man follows one who divides the Church he shall not inherit the kingdom of God. . . . Endeavour, therefore, to partake of one and the same Eucharist; for there is but one flesh of Christ,

* Chap. II.  † Chap. VII.  ‡ Chap. I.  § Chap, II. III.  ‖ Chap. VII.
¶ Chap V.  ** Chap. III.  †† Chap. III. IV.

and one cup in the union of His blood, and one altar, as there is one bishop with the college of presbyters and my fellow-servants the deacons; that whatever ye do may be done according to God."* To the Church of Smyrna† he writes: "Let all of you follow the bishop, as Jesus Christ doth the Father; and the college of presbyters as the apostles; and reverence the deacons as the commandment of God. Let no man do anything which concerns the Church without the bishop. Let that Eucharist be accounted valid which is ordered by the bishop, or one whom he appoints. Where the bishop appears there let the people be, even as where Christ is there is the Catholic Church. Without the bishop it is neither lawful to baptize nor to celebrate the feast of charity, but that which he approves is well-pleasing to God."

Irenæus, the disciple of Polycarp the disciple of St. John, was first a presbyter and afterwards Bishop of Lyons, succeeding the venerable Bishop Pothinus, whose martyrdom has been related. He makes the appointment of bishops in all the churches by the apostles and their regular succession an argument against the heretics who had crept into the Church in his days.‡ "We," says he, "can reckon up those whom the apostles ordained to be bishops in the several churches, and who they were that succeeded them down to our own times. And had the apostles known any hidden mysteries (as the heretics pretend) they would have committed them to those men to whom they committed the churches themselves; for they desired to have them in all things perfect and unreprovable whom they left to be their successors, and to whom they committed their own apostolic authority." He adds, "Because it would be endless to enumerate the successions of bishops in all the churches he would instance in that of Rome." So that Irenæus, one of the most learned men of his time, asserts

* Chap. III. and IV.   † Chap. VIII.   ‡ About 195 A.D.

that bishops had been appointed by the apostles in all the churches, and the succession kept up in them, and the names were still to be read in the archives of the churches.

About the same time (A.D. 170) lived Hegesippus, who travelled through a great part of the world on purpose to learn the doctrine and traditions left by the apostles in the churches which they founded. And after this inquiry he uses against the heretics the same argument which Irenæus makes use of. He says he had conversed with many bishops, and received the same doctrine from them all :—" In every succession" (of bishops), he says, "and in every city, the same doctrine is received which was taught by the Law, the Prophets, and the Lord." Polycrates, Bishop of Ephesus, writing A.D. 196, says that at that time he himself had been sixty-five years a Christian. He was therefore born about thirty years after the death of St. John, and was contemporary with Simeon of Jerusalem, Ignatius, Polycarp, and others, disciples of the apostles. He, writing about the time of keeping Easter, appeals to the tradition of former bishops and martyrs, and the practice of those who lived in his own time. Among others he mentions Polycarp, Bishop of Smyrna and martyr; Thraseas, Bishop of Eumenia and martyr; Sagaris, Bishop of Laodicea and martyr; seven bishops of his own kindred, and great multitudes of bishops who assembled with him to consult about the Easter question.

Clement of Alexandria (A.D. 192), the greatest scholar of his age, the man who made the Catechetical school of Alexandria the most famous school of Christian learning of that and succeeding times, speaks of the gradual promotion of bishops, presbyters, and deacons, which he likens to the orders of angels.

Origen, in the beginning of the third century, the more illustrious scholar of the illustrious Clement, also, speaking of the "debts" in the Lord's Prayer, first insists on the debts or duties common to all Christians, and then adds : "Besides these general debts, there is a debt peculiar to widows who are maintained by the Church, another to deacons, another to presbyters, and another to bishops, which is the greatest of all, and exacted by the Saviour of the whole Church, who will severely punish the non-payment of it." In another place he gives the same rule for maintaining orthodoxy which has already been quoted from Ignatius, Irenæus, and Hegesippus, to adhere to the rule of the celestial Church of Christ according to the succession of the apostles.

Cyprian (248) was Tertullian's scholar, and Bishop of Carthage. His epistles and tracts contain a most full account of the Church officers, and the method of transacting all ecclesiastical affairs which was then observed, both in his own and in other churches. He says, writing to Cornelius, Bishop of Rome: "This is and ought to be our chief care and study, that we maintain the unity which was delivered by our Lord and His apostles to us their successors." In another place he says that there being only one Church and one Episcopacy all the world over, and orthodox and pious bishops being already regularly ordained through all the provinces of the Roman empire and in every city, he must needs be a schismatic who laboured to set up false bishops in opposition to them."

Firmilian, Bishop of Cæsarea in Cappadocia (A.D. 233), contemporary with Cyprian, also calls the bishops the successors of the apostles, and affirms "that the power of remitting sins, which our Lord conferred on His apostles, was derived from them to the bishops who succeeded in their places."

Eusebius, the historian of the early Church, who lived in the latter part of the third and early part of the fourth centuries, derives the bishops of all churches from the apostles. He gives exact and authentic catalogues of the bishops who presided in all the principal cities of the Roman empire from the apostles down to his own time.

"There is such a multitude of unexceptionable witnesses for this fact," says Archbishop Potter, "as can scarce be produced for any other matter of fact, except the rise and progress of Christianity; so that whoever shall deny this may with better reason reject all histories whatever." "It is as impossible for an impartial man to doubt whether there was a succession of bishops from the apostles, as it would be to call in question the succession of Roman emperors from Julius Cæsar, or the succession of kings in any other country."

All bishops all the world over were accounted equal as to their spiritual authority. To use St. Jerome's words: "Wherever a bishop is, whether at Rome or Eugubium, at Constantinople or at Rhegium, at Alexandria or at Tani, he is of the same worth and the same priesthood; neither the power of riches nor the humility of poverty makes a bishop higher or lower; all are successors of the apostles."* St. Cyprian's way of putting the matter† is that there is but one episcopacy, which is shared by the whole college of bishops. He distinctly affirms that every apostle was invested with the same dignity and power which was given to St. Peter, and every bishop in the world is a successor of Peter as well as of the rest of the apostles, and has the same station and authority within his own diocese which our Lord conferred upon Peter. For the sake of order, however, every bishop limited the exercise of his episcopate to his own Church only. In theory every bishop was without superior, and every Church—*i.e.*, every several community of Christians with its bishop and clergy—was independent; but in fact, at a very early period, the churches were organised in groups. Of the growth of this organisation we have very little historical evidence, but it is

* Ep. 146 ad Evagrium.    † Ep. IV.

easy to conjecture how it came about when we call to mind the history of the Church's growth. Its growth naturally suggested such an organisation. One Church, usually the Church of the principal city, was historically the mother Church of the whole district, and this fact would in itself tend to make the daughter churches regard one another as specially united, and would make them all look up to the mother Church as their natural head. Even when this bond of union did not exercise any strong influence, it was natural that churches which were connected by ties of race, or language, or civil organisation, should acknowledge a special bond of brotherhood; it was almost inevitable that their bishops should meet occasionally to discuss the common interests of their churches, and make arrangements for the general advantage. It was natural that these meetings should take place at the principal city of the district, and that the bishop of that city should preside.

In the early part of the third century we find this provincial organisation already thoroughly established, and spoken of as an ancient recognised system. The "Apostolical Constitutions"* lay down as a custom of the Church "that the bishops of every nation should have a regard to the first among them, and account him their head, and attempt nothing without him besides what concerns their own particular dioceses, and that he should do nothing but by consent of the rest."

This ecclesiastical organisation usually coincided with the civil divisions of the empire. The words Diocese and Parish originally expressed civil divisions of the empire, the parish a territorial division which formed a bishopric, the diocese a still larger district of country which constituted a Province.

The dignity of chief bishop of a district was usually

* The date of this work is the third century; but the first part of it is believed to be a collection of the rules and the customs observed during the previous ages of the Church.

assigned to the bishop of the chief city, the metropolis of the district, and so the chief bishop came to be styled Metropolitan. But this was not always the case, for in Proconsular Africa the chief bishop of the province was elected; at one time Cyprian of Carthage, at another Augustine of Hippo, was chief bishop.

When any change in the civil organisation occurred, it was often found convenient to make corresponding re-adjustments of the ecclesiastical organisation. For example, if a provincial town became so populous or important as to have a separate civil government established in it, it was sometimes thereupon raised into a separate see; if a civil province were divided into two, this was followed by a corresponding ecclesiastical division into two provinces, each with its metropolitan.

We have an interesting example of these adaptations of ecclesiastical organisation to the political facts in the case of Judea. Jerusalem was the mother Church of Judea and of all the Churches; but Cæsarea was the ecclesiastical metropolis of the province, because Cæsarea was the civil capital; and it was not until the fourth general Council,* when the veneration for the holy places, and the fashion of pilgrimages, had directed the eyes of Christendom to the Holy City, that it was raised to the dignity of a patriarchate *causâ honoris*.

A still more important example is that of Byzantium. The little town on the Bosphorus had been subject to the primate of Heraclea, in Thrace; but when Constantine made it the seat of empire the Bishop of "new Rome" was speedily raised to patriarchal dignity. From ancient times the bishops of Rome, Alexandria, and Antioch held a pre-eminent position, because those cities were the capitals of the three great divisions of the empire, and Rome held the first place of honour because of the dignity of the imperial city. The western

* Page 235.

empire had been destroyed by the barbarians, and Rome depopulated and despoiled, while "new Rome" had grown into the most populous and magnificent city in the world, and the capital of the empire. The patriarchs of Constantinople from time to time attempted to take precedence of the popes of Rome; but Rome was still a great name, and the eastern bishops assembled at the general Council of Chalcedon, still allowed its precedence of honour to Rome, while it placed Constantinople next in order after it.

Each bishop was still chief ruler of his own Church. A metropolitan had no right of interference in the internal affairs of another diocese; his chief duties were to preside in the synods of his province, and to see that the canons there passed were generally observed. He had the supervision of the consecration of all bishops within his province; he represented his province in communications with other provinces of the Church. The rights of a patriarch were of a similar kind. He presided in the occasional greater synods of his patriarchate, saw that its canons were promulgated and observed, exercised the office of a kind of visitor over the metropolitans of his patriarchate, without any right of interference in the internal affairs of their provinces, and he represented the great branch of the Church of which he was the head.

This ancient organisation into provinces and the customary rights of metropolitans were recognised and sanctioned by the first general Council of Nicæa (A.D. 325). It was found then that there were some individual churches which never had been included in any province, and whose bishops had never been subject to any metropolitan, and it was decreed that these *autocephalous* churches should not be reduced under the obedience of any metropolitan, but should retain their ancient freedom.

## CHAPTER XV.

### THE RELATIONS BETWEEN CHURCH AND STATE.

WHEN the emperor embraced Christianity it was inevitable that the civil power should enter into new relations with the Church. The constitution of the empire, ever since the time of Augustus, made the emperor the source of all power and authority, legislative and executive, civil, military, and religious. The emperor held the title of Pontifex Maximus, and Constantine on his accession had been solemnly inaugurated into the office of chief pontiff of the ancient religion of Rome. The imperial exchequer had been accustomed to make grants for the support of temples and the celebration of religious ceremonials; the laws had allowed immunities and privileges to the priests and sacred persons. When the emperor became Christian it was inevitable that he should cease to support heathenism, and it was right that as a Christian he should use his authority and wealth to support and propagate the Gospel. As legislator it was right that he should make the laws of the empire conform to the laws of God; that he should give to the Church such immunities and privileges as would tend to the well-being of the people. As chief magistrate, it was right that he should restrain his subjects from actions which were contrary to God's law.

Accordingly the emperor naturally assumed towards the Church an attitude of protection and support and control, which the Church welcomed, without any formal preliminary definition on either side of the proper limitation of the relations between Church and State. These limitations were gradually worked out as occasion arose. The limitations of the civil and the spiritual power were from the first seen clearly in principle, whatever difficulties of detail might occur, and they were worked out more speedily and easily than might have been expected. Hosius, Bishop of Cordova, was Constantine's most trusted adviser in religious matters; his view of the right relations of Church and State we gather from words subsequently addressed by him to Constantius: "Intrude not yourself into ecclesiastical matters, neither give commands unto us concerning them; but learn them from us. God hath put into your hands the kingdom, to us He hath entrusted the affairs of His Church; and as he who should steal the empire from you would resist the ordinance of God, so likewise fear on your part, lest by taking upon yourself the government of the Church you become guilty of a great offence. It is written, 'Render unto Cæsar the things that are Cæsar's, and unto God the things that are God's.' Neither, therefore, is it permitted to us to exercise an earthly rule; neither have you, sire, any authority to burn incense."

The emperor, as we have seen, tolerated all religions, but he invited all his subjects to embrace Christianity; and he formally recognised Christianity as the religion of the State. This he did in the most significant manner when he associated the symbols of the faith with the chief insignia of empire, putting the sacred monogram on the standard of the army and on the coinage of the empire. He did not endow the Church throughout the empire, but he repealed the edicts which prohibited it from holding property, and he set the example of building and endowing churches out of his own possessions; he recognised the validity of ecclesiastical legislation within its own sphere, and used his authority to secure obedience to canonical decisions.

Whether we regard it from a religious or a political point

of view we pronounce this union of Church and State to have been right and wise. It was our Lord's intention that His kingdom should spread till it became co-extensive with human society, and that kings should be its nursing fathers. When it has so spread, Church and State become co-ordinate powers. They occupy the same field of human society, but fulfil different functions, and each is incomplete without the other. The Church has nothing to do with civil government: "My kingdom is not of this world." The defence of the commonwealth from foreign enemies, the maintenance of internal security and order, the promotion of commerce and the arts, the punishment of crime, all this belongs to Cæsar. But where the power of the State fails, there the power of the Church begins. Cæsar can only maintain external obedience by the sword; the Church bids the citizen render a willing obedience, not only for wrath, but also for conscience sake. The civil power can punish crime, but it fails to repress vice, and it cannot touch sin. The Church especially deals with sin, which is the root of all social and civil disorder. In short, the State can deal only with the material interests and the external life and order of society; the Church deals with the internal life—the beliefs and hopes and aims of the soul, which are the inner springs and regulators of the external life of man. Only religion can make a man a good citizen.

The Roman empire had found out long ago that civil government was inefficient without religion, and we have seen that some of the bitterest persecutions of the Church were a part of the efforts of the best emperors to revive the ancient religion and manners of Rome. The union of Church and State under Constantine was the true fulfilment of these aspirations after the revival of the religious element in civil society.

## CHAPTER XVI.

### THE CHURCH BUILDINGS. THE CATACOMBS.

THE first ordinary place of Christian assembly for public worship was that upper room in Jerusalem, probably in the house of Mary the mother of Mark, in which the Holy Communion was instituted; in which the apostles were gathered together when the risen Lord appeared in the midst of them, saying, "Peace be unto you," on the first day of the week after the resurrection, and again on the first day of the week following; in which the hundred and twenty disciples were assembled on the day of Pentecost, when the Holy Spirit descended upon them, and the Church of Christ began to be; and in which the disciples assembled daily for the breaking of the bread.

There is evidence that in other towns also either the upper room, or the atrium of the house, of some convert in all probability, afforded a meeting-place for the brethren. Lucian, or whoever was the author of the Dialogue called "Philopater," about the time of Trajan, brings in one Critias, telling how the Christians had carried him into an hyperoon (upper room), the place of their assembly, with a design to make him a proselyte to their religion.

The first church opened for public worship is said to have been in Rome. The Pudens saluted by St. Paul (2 Tim. iv. 21) is said to have been the distinguished senator of that name, in whose house St. Paul is said to have lived; and the grandson of this Pudens, Pius I., who was Bishop of Rome from 142 to 157 A.D., is said to have converted a part of the family mansion into a church. The present church of Sta. Pudenziana occupies the same site. Beneath the church, portions of the Roman house have recently been discovered, and three halls which have been thrown into one may very possibly have been this first public church. It was not unusual for wealthy Christians to give to the Church the houses which had thus been hallowed by the Christian assemblies, that they might be converted to the permanent use of the community. The same Bishop Pius, writing to Justus of Vienne, says that a pious matron, Euprepia, had given her house to the poor, "where now, dwelling with the poor, we celebrate the Divine offices." The early Christian Romance, called the "Clementines," already described, in saying that Theophilus (to whom St. Luke dedicated his Gospel and Acts) converted his house at Antioch into a church, shows what was customary at that period.

The popular idea that the Church was in hiding all through the first three centuries, and that it was only "when the persecuted Church emerged from the catacombs to bask in the sunshine of imperial favour" that they ventured to build churches for public worship, is a popular error. The history of the period in former chapters has shown that the Christians were not so continuously harassed by persecution, and were not compelled to keep their religion so secret, as is popularly imagined. It was only now and then that there was an outbreak of persecution, and Christians, especially the leaders of them, were compelled to hide; but we have seen that there were intervals of peace which lasted for whole generations, during which Christians made no secret of their religion; and probably they began to build churches almost as soon as the congregations were numerous enough to make it necessary. It is an historical fact that there were twenty-five public churches in Rome, and fifteen suburban basilicas connected with the different catacombs, before the Diocletian persecution in 303; and other churches had been built all over the empire. The persecuting edict of Diocletian condemned these churches to destruction, and he set the example by sending a body of troops with pioneers to wreck the Church of Nicomedia, which was a large and conspicuous building on a hill in full sight from his own palace.

Another popular error is that the two basilicas which Constantine assigned to the Christians at Rome for their public worship were the first examples of the use of buildings of this plan for churches, and that the later basilican churches were copies of these. The basilican plan had been adopted for churches long before the time of Constantine.

Some of these churches still remain, little injured, to show us what the plan and arrangement of the early churches were. One of the earliest is at Djemla, in Algeria. It is a rectangular hall, 92 feet long by 52 feet wide, divided by pillars into a body and two aisles, with a lofty square enclosure at the upper end on the usual site of the chancel. Its floor is covered with a fine mosaic pavement, so purely classical in design as to leave no doubt of its early date. Another very early church at Announa, also in Algeria, is of the common basilican plan—a body and two aisles, with a semicircular apse at the upper end; this is about 45 feet square. A basilica at Orleansville, the ancient Castellum Tingitanum, erected, according to an existing inscription, in the year 252,* is 80 feet long by 52 feet wide, divided by four rows of pillars into a body and double aisles, with an apse at the lower as well as the upper end. Another very similar example at Ermet, the ancient Hermonthis, in Egypt, is 150 feet long by 90 feet wide.

As soon as the edict of toleration of the dying Galerius

* 252 probably of a local era, corresponding to 325 A.D.

was issued, the Christians began to rebuild their churches; and to accommodate the increasing number of converts they often rebuilt them on a larger scale, and the increasing adhesion of the wealthier classes naturally enabled them to erect more handsome buildings.

The basilicas which Constantine gave at Rome for churches were, St. Peter's—which was a very large building, 380 feet long by 212 feet wide, as large as most mediæval cathedrals, with a very lofty body and double aisles—and St. John Lateran. He also built a circular baptistry, adjoining the latter church, which was used as a place of sepulture for his daughter Constantia. He built churches also in several cities. At Jerusalem he adorned the rock-tomb, which was believed to be the site of the holy sepulchre, with costly marbles, and paved the surrounding area, and enclosed it with a colonnade. At the eastern side of this area he erected a basilica in honour of the resurrection, with an atrium at its east end; and he ordered that these buildings should be such that they should not be exceeded in magnificence by any church in his dominions. He also built a fine octagonal church at Antioch, at whose dedication a synod of bishops famous in the history of the Church was convened. He built also a large church dedicated to the twelve apostles; and another to Sta. Sophia, at Constantinople, and others in other cities. The empress-mother Helena built a fine basilica at Bethlehem, over against the Grotto of the Nativity, which, with additions by Justinian, still remains.

There are a considerable number of other churches of early date remaining in many different countries. In Northern Syria are numerous basilicas of the fourth, fifth, and sixth centuries, so perfect that they need little more than roofing in to make them at once available for use. Thessalonica has basilicas of the fifth and sixth centuries. The Cathedral of Ravenna, built A.D. 400, has unfortunately been destroyed, but the Church of St. Apollinare Nuovo, built by Theodoric the Goth (A.D. 493—525), remains, 315 feet long; and the Church of St. Apollinare in Classe, begun A.D. 538, and dedicated 549, a very fine church, 216 feet long. At Parenzo, in Istria, is a basilica, built A.D. 542, with a very complete plan—a body and two aisles, each terminated with an apse, a western narthex (or porch), an atrium (court), westward of the church, a circular baptistry on the west side of the atrium, and a more modern addition of a circular tower west of the baptistry. Another basilica remains at Hierapolis, on the border of Phrygia.

It will be seen that we have in this long and uninterrupted series of buildings abundant evidence as to the early churches. The earliest examples are in all probability earlier than the time of Constantine's conversion. The probability is that the earliest examples which happen to have survived are not the earliest which were built, and there is no reason to think that the earlier and lost examples were of a different plan or character from those which remain. Again, we have seen that there was no change of plan in the time of Constantine. There were occasional varieties of plan; especially churches built for baptisteries or tombs were circular; but the normal plan of a church, from the third century certainly, and probably from the first, down to the twelfth, was that which is called the basilican plan, which is best illustrated by examples. The Basilica of St. Clement, Rome, is the best remaining illustration of the general arrangement and furnishing of a basilica, and is so exact a reproduction of a church of the earliest type that it was always believed to be the original erection of Constantine, until a few years ago a still earlier church was discovered immediately beneath the present one. On the chord of the apse stood the altar; the bishop's throne was elevated on steps at the end of the apse, facing down the church, and there were elevated stone benches round the apse for the presbyters. A space was railed off westward of the altar by cancelli for the choir; on each side of this choir were the raised pulpits (*ambones*), from which the epistle and gospel were read, and some other services sung, and occasionally the sermon delivered. The nave was the place of the faithful; the catechumens stood in the narthex. In the middle of the atrium was commonly a fountain. The floor had always a mosaic pavement, usually specially designed; the walls of the apse and the sacrarium were usually ornamented with mosaics, a colossal figure of our Lord attended by angels or saints usually occupying the semi-dome of the apse.

It is remarkable that the exterior of the church was nearly always studiously plain, all the architectural decoration being reserved for the interior—a feature in which the churches differed from the heathen temples, where the people stood outside to worship at an altar placed in front of the building, and it was the exterior of the building which was adorned with colonnades, and its cornices and pediments with sculpture. In the interior of the churches, however, there was never any abstinence from the use of costly material and the highest art. The architect made as finely proportioned an interior as his skill and circumstances allowed; he used marbles and bronze, sculpture, mosaic, and mural painting, freely, and in the furniture of the churches there was no affectation of poverty or plainness; they had gold and silver vessels for the Communion, silver lamps, and silken hangings.

Eusebius of Cæsarea, the historian of the Church, gives us an account of the new church which was built at Tyre, after the death of Maximin, in which he himself delivered the inaugural discourse on its reconstruction. It illustrates the power and opulence of the Church even in a city which had just taken a leading part in the attempted revival of paganism. The new church was built on the old site; for though a more convenient and imposing place might have been found, the piety of the Christians clung with reverence to a spot consecrated by the most holy associations. The whole site was surrounded by a wall; a lofty propylæon,* which faced the rising sun, commanded the attention of the passers-by, and afforded an imposing glimpse of the magnificence within. The intermediate space between the propylæon and the church was laid out as a cloister, with four colonnades, enclosed with a palisade of wood. The central square was open to the sun and air, and two fountains sparkled in the midst and reminded the worshipper, with their emblematic purity, of the necessity of sanctification. The uninitiated proceeded no farther than the cloister, but might behold at this modest distance the mysteries of the sanctuary. Several other vestibules, or propylæa, intervened between the cloister and the main building. The three gates of the church fronted the east, of which the central was the loftiest and most costly, "like a queen between her attendants"; it was adorned with plates of brass and richly sculptured reliefs. Two colonnades, or aisles, ran along the main building, above which were windows which lighted the edifice; other buildings for the use of the ministers adjoined. Eusebius does not give the actual dimensions, but speaks in general terms of eulogy of the spaciousness and loftiness and splendour of the interior. The roof was of beams of cedar, the floor inlaid with marble. In the centre rose the altar, which had already obtained the name of the place of sacrifice; it was guarded from approach by a trellis of the most slender and graceful workmanship. Lofty seats were placed for those of the higher orders, and benches for those of lower rank were

* Ornamental entrance gate.

arranged with regularity throughout the building. Tyre, no doubt, did not stand alone in this splendid restoration of her Christian worship; and Christianity, even before her final triumph under Constantine, before the restitution of her endowments and the munificent imperial gifts, possessed in many places sufficient wealth for these costly undertakings.

When we contradict the popular idea that the Church was hiding in the catacombs during the first three centuries, we ought, perhaps, to say a few words on the origin and use of those ancient and interesting excavations. The Romans made excavations in some of the hills at a little distance outside the city for sand and other building materials, and these excavations were in the shape of wide rude galleries. In one or more instances these arenaria* have been converted into burial places by the erection of brick walls on each side of their wide galleries. But the catacombs differ from these arenaria in that the galleries are much narrower and more regularly planned; they were not excavated for building material, but expressly for burial places. It has been suggested that the Jewish colony in Rome first made catacombs for the interment of their dead, and that the Christians adopted this custom of their spiritual ancestors. Two Jewish catacombs have been discovered—one in 1843 at Venosa, in the Basilicata; the other in 1862 outside Rome, near the Porta Capena. It has also been suggested that some of the great Roman families who practised the mode of interment instead of the national custom of cremation used catacombs. All but two of the existing catacombs of the first three centuries seem to be Christian. They are forty-two in number, distributed all round the city, and contain 350 miles of galleries two to four feet wide, with both sides pierced for graves, and seventy-six chambers, the sides of which are also pierced for graves, with

* Sand quarries.

occasionally a larger chamber which served for a chapel. Originally they belonged to private families who had embraced the Christian faith; the entrances were not originally secret, and some were ornamented with architectural façades; one, that of Calixtus, belonged to the Christian community, and all the Roman bishops of the third century were buried in it. The graves in the sides of the galleries, when occupied, had their openings closed by a stone, on which there is often an inscription. The chambers and chapels were often ornamented with paintings of the same character as those which decorated the Roman tombs and baths; and these paintings are the earliest remaining examples of Christian art. A glance at them is enough to dispel the notion that the earliest Christians had any objection to the use of art in the decoration of their places of assembly. Much of the painting is merely decorative, in the style which was used in the secular public buildings at the time, but paintings of Scripture subjects are freely and largely introduced. For example, in the catacomb of Calixtus is a lofty vaulted hall, built in the fine brickwork of the second century, whose walls and vaults are adorned with decorative painting of classical character; winged genii (representing the four seasons) are sporting among gracefully intertwined branches of trees, foliage, and vines; at the back of an arched recess is a picture of the Good Shepherd.

The figure subjects were chiefly allegorical, and conveyed to the initiated a meaning which would not be at all obvious to a pagan spectator. Orpheus charming the wild beasts with his lyre was a familiar subject to the pagan; to the believer it was typical of Christ by His doctrine taming the wild hearts of men. A shepherd carrying a lamb on his shoulders was to the one a pastoral incident, to the other an allegory of the Good Shepherd who came to seek and save that which was lost. When scriptural subjects were used it was usually with an allegorical meaning. Jonah cast into the sea, swallowed by the sea monster, and issuing forth again from his three days' imprisonment, was a type of our Lord's resurrection. Daniel in the lions' den and the raising of Lazarus appear with the same meaning. Noah in the ark was a type of baptism. A company of persons reclining at a feast, or a representation of the turning of the water into wine, serve for a type of the other sacrament of the Gospel. Most of the figure subjects sculptured or painted on the walls and vaultings of the catacomb chambers are of this kind. Though the product of days of persecution they breathe a sweet, calm, pastoral tone. The Good Shepherd is the oft-recurring and characteristic figure, as the Lord in glory was in the next period of the mosaics of the basilicas.

In times of persecution the clergy and others who were specially sought after took temporary refuge in the intricacies of these subterranean galleries, and Divine service was conducted in the greater chambers. At all times Divine service was performed in these chapels on the festivals of noted martyrs interred within them, or in the neighbouring galleries. Interments continued to take place in the catacombs till the close of the fifth century; and long after—till the thirteenth century—the martyrs' graves in them were visited by pilgrims to Rome. It is possible that the recollection of these subterranean galleries and chapels gave rise to the construction of crypts under great churches, and to the side chapels of the mediæval churches.

The Roman catacombs are those best known to the world, but similar catacombs exist at Naples and other places in Italy, and also at Alexandria, which are similarly adorned with early decorative and scriptural paintings.

## CHAPTER XVII.

#### THE WORSHIP OF THE PRIMITIVE CHURCH.

WHAT kind of service was it which was performed in the churches which we have described in the preceding chapter? Justin Martyr, who died about sixty years after St. John (about A.D. 140), in his Apology, gives a sketch of the worship of the primitive Church : " Upon the day called Sunday we have an assembly of all who live in the town or in the country, who meet in an appointed place, and the records of the apostles, or the writings of the prophets, are read, according as the time will permit. When the reader has ended, then the president admonishes and exhorts us in a discourse that we should imitate such good examples. After that we all stand up and pray, and, as we said before, when that prayer is ended, bread is offered and wine and water. Then the president also, according to the authority given him, sends up prayers and thanksgivings ; and the people end the prayer with him, saying, Amen. After which distribution is made of the Eucharistic elements, which are also sent by the hands of the deacons to those who are absent." Justin is giving the merest outline, in order to show to a heathen that the Christian worship consisted of prayers and addresses, and that, in place of bloody rites or elaborate mysteries, the only ceremonial consisted in the blessing, breaking, and partaking of bread and wine.

We are able, to some extent, to fill up the outline which Justin thus sketches. There are many ancient liturgies in existence which can be traced back to four or five originals of very early date known by the names of certain of the apostles.* The Liturgy of St. James, or of Jerusalem, was that used in Palestine and Mesopotamia. It seems to be the same with a synopsis of a liturgy, called the Liturgy of St. Clement, contained in the "Apostolical Constitutions," a work written probably in the third century, but embodying matter of much earlier date. It agrees with Justin's description above given, and it is almost certain that the Liturgy of St. James, as still used by the monophysite churches of the East, and that which is used by the orthodox Church of Jerusalem on the Feast of St. James, are versions of the primitive liturgy which was used by the churches of Judea and the surrounding countries in the age which immediately followed that of the apostles. The Liturgy of St. Mark, or of Alexandria, is similarly traceable to the second century, to which it is assigned by Bunsen. Palmer says, "There is nothing unreasonable in supposing that the main order and substance of the Alexandrian Liturgy, as used in the fifth century, may have been as old as the apostolic age, and derived originally from the instructions and appointments of the blessed evangelist." The Liturgy of St. Peter, or of Rome, may also "reasonably be assigned to the age succeeding the apostles." The Liturgy of St. John, or of the Church of Ephesus, is the original of that which was used in Britain during the earlier ages of Christianity. It was disused in the Ephesian dioceses as early as the fourth century, but meantime it had been carried by missionaries from that Church into Gaul, Spain, and Britain, probably about the middle of the second century, and continued in use in those countries—in France till the time of Charlemagne (eighth century); in Spain till the tenth century; in England till the time of Archbishop Theodore.

But, further, these four ancient liturgies have so much in common that they must have had a common origin, or have

* The word Liturgy in early times was restricted to the office for the holy Eucharist.

been constructed on the same principles. This is most conveniently shown by putting the different parts of the four liturgies side by side in the order in which they occur:—

**TABLE—SHOWING THE ORDER IN WHICH THE PRINCIPAL FEATURES OF THE PRIMITIVE LITURGIES OCCUR.**

| ST. JAMES. | ST. MARK. | ST. PETER. | ST. JOHN. |
|---|---|---|---|
| 1. Kiss of Peace | 1. Kiss of Peace | 2. Lift up your hearts | 7. Prayer for the living |
| 2. Lift up your hearts | 2. Lift up your hearts | 3. Tersanctus | 8. Prayer for the departed |
| 3. Tersanctus | 7. Prayer for the living | 7. Prayer for the living | 1. Kiss of Peace |
| 4. Commemoration of Institution | 8. Prayer for the departed | 6. Prayer for the descent of the Holy Ghost | 2. Lift up your hearts |
| 5. The Oblation | 3. Tersanctus | 4. Commemoration of Institution | 3. Tersanctus |
| 6. Prayer for descent of the Holy Ghost | 4. Commemoration of Institution | 5. The Oblation | 4. Commemoration of Institution |
| 7. Prayer for the living | 5. The Oblation | 8. Prayer for the departed | 5. The Oblation |
| 8. Prayer for the departed | 6. Prayer for the descent of the Holy Ghost | 10. Union of the Consecrated Elements | 6. Prayer for the descent of the Holy Ghost |
| 9. The Lord's Prayer | 10. Union of the Consecrated Elements | 9. The Lord's Prayer | 10. Union of the Consecrated Elements |
| 10. Union of the Consecrated Elements | 9. The Lord's Prayer | 1. Kiss of Peace | 9. The Lord's Prayer |
| 11. Communion | 11. Communion | 11. Communion | 11. Communion |
| 12. Thanksgiving | 12. Thanksgiving | 12. Thanksgiving | 12. Thanksgiving |

The explanation of this striking similarity is probably this, that the apostles used an unwritten liturgical form, always retaining the same elements, but presenting them with a certain amount of freedom. That since, as we know, liturgies were not committed to writing till the second century, the tradition of the apostolic liturgy had by that time in different churches assumed the different forms which were then perpetuated. These liturgies afterwards received modifications and considerable additions, as one great patriarch in one Church, and another in another, saw fit to adapt them to the requirements of his time.

We may, then, feel quite sure that the principal Sunday service in any one of these primitive churches was performed according to this ancient liturgical model. In order to complete the scene of a primitive Church and its worship, which is thus gradually growing up before our mind's-eye, let us ask next, What were the official vestments of the clergy?

At the beginning of the Christian era, and for some centuries afterwards, all people of a certain position in the social scale, in all civilised countries, wore the same costume—viz., a tunic and pallium. The tunic was ordinarily worn by men short and with short sleeves; on occasions of state and ceremony men wore a long tunic down to the ankles. The tunics of people of the senatorial order were distinguished by a broad purple stripe (*clavus latus*) down the front of the tunic; people of the equestrian order had their tunics marked with two narrow purple stripes (*clavus angustus*), reaching from the shoulders straight down the front. The pallium was a large square, or nearly square, woollen robe; it was worn in various ways. One of the commonest ways was thus: passed over the left shoulder, drawn behind the back under the right arm, leaving it free, and thrown again over the left shoulder, covering the left arm. Great dignitaries had a broad ornamental border to the pallium, and sometimes the whole robe was embroidered. A heathen offering sacrifice or attending a religious ceremony wore an orarium, a square of cloth laid like a veil over the head; the orarium was reduced in the first century to a narrow strip of cloth laid over the shoulders. A Roman, or Greek, or Syrian, offering sacrifice at his temple or taking part in any high religious ceremonial would wear a long tunic with sleeves, and a pallium, and an orarium over his shoulders, and the colour of all these would be white. Our Lord and His apostles are always, from the earliest representations of them in the second century to the present day, represented in tunic and pallium, which, no doubt, they actually were accustomed to wear. The early bishops and saints in the paintings of the sixth century are also represented in tunic and pallium; and it is highly probable that the clergy of the early Church in their ministrations wore this customary dress of religious ceremonial. The bishop and priest wore the full dress, the deacon wore the tunic only.

It is not till the fourth century that we find any clear mention of the vestments of the clergy. Athanasius was accused by his enemies of laying a tax on the Egyptians to raise a fund for the linen tunics of the clergy. Jerome says: "What harm is it if a bishop, presbyter, or deacon come forth in a white vestment when they administer the sacraments?" Chrysostom speaks of "the deacons walking about the church in their white tunics." Severianus, Bishop of Gabala, contemporary with St. Chrysostom, speaks of the deacons ministering at the sacred mysteries "with their veils on their left shoulders"; this veil was doubtless the orarium. The Council of Laodicea (A.D. 370) has two canons on the use of the orarium—allowing it to bishops, priests, and deacons, and forbidding its use by sub-deacons, singers, and readers.

There is no difficulty, therefore, in presenting before our

minds with considerable fulness and accuracy a church and its services of these first ages. Passing down the busy street of a city of Italy, or Africa, or the East, we approach a rather large public building of plain exterior. We enter from the bustle and glare of the street into an open court, with a fountain throwing up its grateful waters in the midst, at which some are washing their hands before they enter the church. Its plain façade is opposite; we lift up the door-curtain and enter. We are in a vestibule (the narthex), opening by three arches into the church; this is the place specially appointed for the catechumens; we press forward with others into the main body of the building. It is a large and lofty hall, shady and cool and quiet after the glare and bustle of the streets, divided into a body and aisles by rows of columns of classical architecture, which support the horizontal beams on which the upper wall is carried. The floor has a handsome tesselated pavement; the columns are of marble, some of them clearly taken from older buildings of earlier and purer art; the walls are divided into panels by painted borders, and the panels are filled with subjects from Scripture. The church is already filling with people, the men taking their places on one side and the women on the other. We observe an unusual mixture of classes—the high-born Roman lady, the citizen's wife, and the slave girl side by side; patricians of the city with embroidered pallium thrown over the shoulder, and a soldier of the garrison here and there, in his breast-plate and sword, amidst a mixed crowd of burghers and slaves. The double row of singers in white tunics, within the cancelli, are conspicuous above the heads of the people; and beyond all is the bishop in his white robes, seated aloft in his raised stone chair, looking over the whole church; and his presbyters in the same costume on their raised bench form a semicircle on either side of their chief; the deacons, in their white tunics, stand beneath, and the deaconesses and Church virgins also have their special place. The service begins, and the people stand; there are no seats, and Christians do not kneel at public worship on Sundays. The priest recites the prayers in a sustained and measured tone, the people responding with a loud AMEN, which rolls along the aisles like a peal of thunder; then they take part with the singers in the responsive chanting of the psalms—now the deep voices of the men, now the soprano voices of the women, with the grand effect of the union of many voices. The bishop delivers his address, still seated in his lofty sedile; then a deacon comes down the church and gives the signal that the service of the catechumens is over. If it be an assembly of the first century at which we are assisting, comparatively few will depart; if it be one of the fourth or later age, many, alas! will leave—as large a proportion, perhaps, as in a modern English congregation. Then the sacred liturgy proceeds, the bishop himself officiating with solemn reverence, standing behind the altar and looking towards the people. The prayers are said, the memorial is made, the deacons come down among the people, kneeling in their ranks, and give them the sacred elements, saying to each as he delivers into his hands bread or cup—τὸ σῶμα τοῦ κυρίου, τὸ αἷμα τοῦ κυρίου—" The Body of the Lord;" "The Blood of the Lord." The Bishop concludes by blessing the kneeling flock. And in a few minutes the clergy have defiled in procession into their sacristy, and the crowd of worshippers have crossed the great court, and are again jostling among the crowds in the busy sunlit streets of the city.

## CHAPTER XVIII.

#### EARLY HERESIES AND SCHISMS.

OF the faith held by the primitive Church we have no lack of evidences. The disciples had been exhorted to hold fast the faith once for all delivered to the saints by the preaching of the apostles and apostolic men, of which they had the permanent record in the Gospels and Acts and Epistles. That they did so we have the evidence of the early writers of the Church—1. In their Apologies (or defences) of Christianity; 2. In their controversial books, in which they maintain the several truths of Christianity against the Jews on one side, the heathen on the other, and the heretics on the third side; 3. In their expositions of the Scriptures, in homilies, essays, and letters addressed to the faithful. These evidences enable us to say that, for six centuries at least, the sacred deposit of the faith and discipline of Christ was kept whole and undefiled by the churches of Christ all over the world.

From the earliest times, however, there were heresies and schisms, and their history forms an important branch of the Church history of the first six centuries. It is to be remarked that all the heresies (except the last, Pelagianism) sprang up in, and were almost entirely limited to, the churches of the East. They were the results of Oriental mysticism or of Greek speculation. The earlier heresies, as Gnosticism and Manicheism, were not so much erroneous doctrines, springing up in the bosom of the Church, as wild theories of men studying the Church of Christ from without, and endeavouring to combine their previous religions and philosophies, with what they chose to select out of Christianity, into new eclectic religious systems of their own. They were transitional phases of the mind in its passage from Pagan philosophy to the Christian religion. The later heresies—Arianism and the series of heresies which sprang out of it—all relate to the mystery of the Being of the undivided Trinity; they were the erroneus speculations of Christian theologians who missed their way, one on this side and another on that, in the process, which occupied the mind of the fourth, fifth, and sixth centuries, of casting the truths contained in Revelation into philosophic modes of thought and expression. The last of the early heresies, Pelagianism, which sprang up in the West, turned on the relations of grace and free-will, and belongs to the practical sphere of human conduct.

As Gnosticism and Manicheism were the result of the combination of the Oriental religions with Christianity, so Neo-Platonism was the corresponding result of the attempt to take up into Greek philosophy those elements of Christianity which commended themselves to the Greek mind.

The two great systems of error, in this early period with which we are now concerned, which were widespread and important enough to require a few words of notice here, were those which have already been named, Gnosticism and Manicheism.

There were varieties of Gnosticism which we need not minutely describe. They all agreed in claiming a degree of enlightenment superior to that of the vulgar. As the philosophers professed the old paganism, but claimed to explain the vulgar mythology on their intellectual theories, so the Gnostics professed Christianity, but claimed to soar as much above the vulgar Christianity as the philosophers did above the vulgar paganism. They all started from the doctrine which exists in all the Oriental religions, of the eternity of matter, and busied themselves with the speculation which underlies all Oriental philosophies, the origin of evil. We find as common to all the GNOSTIC systems a belief in one Supreme God, dwelling from eternity in the *pleroma*, the fulness of light. From him proceed forth successive *Æons*, or spiritual beings, the chief of which appear, from their names, to be impersonated attributes of the Deity. Matter is regarded as eternal and essentially evil. Out of matter the world and the bodies of men were formed by the *Demiurge*, a being represented by some as a subordinate agent of the Divine will, by others as a hostile and malignant being. The soul of man is imprisoned in his body. Christ was also an emanation from God, and was sent into the world to free man from the tyranny of the Demiurge. Since they believed the body to be evil, they did not believe that Christ had a true body, or that man when delivered would have a body— *i.e.*, they denied the divinity of our Lord and His incarnation, and the resurrection of the dead. In practice, some of the Gnostics sought the victory over their evil nature in an ascetic life, others taught the moral indifference of our actions, and wallowed in sensuality.

Simon Magus is regarded as the precursor of Gnosticism. After the incident mentioned in the Acts of the Apostles, he soon abandoned the apostles' fellowship, and mixing up Christianity with his system continued to teach it; and Justin Martyr says that, in his day (about A.D. 140), Simon was worshipped as the chief god by almost all the Samaritans, and had adherents in other countries.

Cerinthus is the next great leader of this school. He taught in Ephesus at the time that St. John was living there, and both in his gospel and epistles the apostle refers to the errors of a teaching like to that of Cerinthus.

The system was at its height from about A.D. 120 to A.D. 140. In all the great cities of the East in which Christianity had established its most flourishing communities this rival sprang up beside it. After Cerinthus, Saturninus taught in Ephesus. Basilides and Saturninus taught in Alexandria, and the latter for a time in Rome. Bardesanes was another teacher, whose hymns for a long time were popular even among orthodox Syrian Christians.

The other great system of false Philosophy of this period was introduced towards the close of the third century by Mani, a native of Persia, deeply skilled in the learning of his age. It consisted of an eclectic system of doctrines, having the Zoroastrian religion of his native country for its basis, combined with doctrines gathered out of the Christianity of the Roman empire on the one hand, and out of the Buddhism of India on the other. Mani gave himself out to be the promised Paraclete, by which he does not seem to have intended to claim to be the Holy Spirit, but a man invested with a Divine mission, whose office it was to complete the revelation and work commenced but unfulfilled by Christ. He put forth a gospel, in a written and illuminated volume, which was to supersede the orthodox gospels. His community was organised on the Christian model, and at his death he left twelve apostles, seventy-two bishops, and a priesthood. His doctrines met the eclectic philosophical taste of the times and spread with great rapidity, were embraced with zealous fervour, and lasted for a considerable period. St. Augustine, though brought up in Christian doctrine, for several years of his early manhood embraced the Manichean heresy.

The above were rather false religions than Christian heresies. Other variations from the truth, which are commonly called heresies, as Montanism, Novatianism, and Donatism, were rather schisms based on disciplinary than doctrinal differences, though a certain amount of erroneous doctrine entered into them.

MONTANUS was a native of Phrygia, and had been, it is said, a priest of Cybele. Soon after his conversion to Christianity, which happened about the middle of the second century, he began to fall into fits of ecstasy, and to utter ravings which were dignified with the name of prophecies, and he declared himself to be the Paraclete, meaning, perhaps, no more than that he was the special organ of the Holy Ghost for completing Christianity by a new revelation. This revelation, however, did not pretend to alter the received theology, but dealt with questions of discipline. The chief characteristic of Montanism was, that it aimed at the introduction of a more rigid system of morals into the Church. It added to the established fasts, proscribed second marriages, denounced profane learning, the military service, amusements of every kind; declared that the Church had no power to remit sin committed after baptism, and cut off such sinners from the communion of the Church on earth, though it admitted that the mercy of God might nevertheless be extended to them. These doctrines appealed to that stern, enthusiastic class of minds which are always to be found, and had many followers. The most distinguished of these was Tertullian, who, though a presbyter of Carthage, and one of the most able and eloquent men of his time, in middle life fell away into Montanism.

About a century later NOVATIAN, a presbyter of Carthage, started a schism on a point of discipline. After the persecution of Decius some of the severer spirits denied to those who had lapsed re-admission to the communion of the Church. Novatian, who was one of these precisians, and eminent for his learning and eloquence, was at Rome during the vacancy of that see, and procured himself to be elected by three obscure bishops in an irregular way, and made himself the head of a schismatical sect. The sentence of exclusion from communion of those who had denied the faith was extended to those who had committed deadly sin after baptism. They also adopted the practice (which many orthodox churches for a time fell in with) of refusing to recognise the baptism of those who had been baptized by heretics or schismatics. The sect, though not very powerful, long continued to exist.

The greatest schism of the primitive Church was that of the DONATISTS, which arose out of similar questions. The rigid, enthusiastic spirit which existed so largely in African Christianity, and which had broken out in the sects of the Montanists and Novatians, showed itself in the Diocletian persecution. Many thought it wrong to do anything to avoid persecution—either to give up the sacred books, or to flee from the persecution, or to evade it in any way; rather many of them courted and provoked martyrdom; in some cases, it is said, impelled by weariness of the hardships of their lot, and the hope of washing away at once in the blood of martyrdom the sins of a lifetime.

Mensurius, the Bishop of Carthage, strongly discountenanced this ill-regulated fanaticism. He refused to acknowledge as martyrs those who had voluntarily courted their fate; and forbade that they should receive the attentions in prison, and the respect from their fellow-Christians, with which those who were really confessors were treated. He himself, on being required to give up the sacred books, had adopted the common evasion of giving up some heretical writings to be burnt instead. His archdeacon, Cæcilian, had been his chief instrument in all this business. On the death of Mensurius (A.D. 311) Cæcilian was elected bishop; but the severer party opposed him, ostensibly because he had been consecrated by Felix, Bishop of Aptunga, who, they said, was a traditor;* they excommunicated Cæcilian and his adherents, and elected another of the clergy, Majorinus, to the bishopric.

It was at this time that Constantine, after his victory over Maxentius, sent large donations to the African churches; and hearing of the dispute which had arisen, he directed that the gifts should be confined to those who were in communion with Cæcilian. The Donatist party petitioned that their cause might be tried by the bishops of Gaul, who had themselves been exempt from the persecution and its trials. Constantine complied with their request, and issued a commission to twenty bishops, who after due inquiry gave their decision in favour of Cæcilian, and suggested, as a way of healing the schism, that both parties should reunite in communion, and that where rival bishops laid claim to a see the bishop first consecrated should be acknowledged. The Donatists appealed against this decision, whereupon Constantine summoned the Council of Arles, consisting of about two hundred bishops, from all parts of the Western empire.†

The council also decided in favour of Cæcilian, and made some canons on the questions which had so much disturbed the African Church. It was enacted that a clerical traditor should be deposed; that the ordination of a cleric by a traditor was valid; that the baptism of heretics in the name of the Holy Trinity should not be repeated, but the person so baptized should be admitted into the Church by the imposition of hands. The Donatists appealed again

---

\* One who had given up the sacred books.

† At this council, held Aug., A.D. 314, were present three bishops from Britain—Eborius, Bishop of York; Restitutus, Bishop of London; and Adelfius, Bishop of Civitas Colonia Lodinensium, which has been conjectured to be either Camulodunum (Colchester), or Carleon; with Sacerdos, a priest, and a deacon.

from the decision of the council and begged the emperor to take the cause into his own hands. He did so, reheard the case, and decided as the council had done, and issued severe edicts for the deposition and punishment of the schismatics, which, however, were not enforced. The sect continued to exist in Africa, and being condemned by all the rest of the Church, they held that the true Church existed only in their own communion. It gradually spread in Africa until the Donatists became more powerful than the Catholics; the number of their bishops is said at one time to have amounted to four hundred. In nearly every city of Africa were rival bishops and rival churches.

The whole history of the schism is very interesting in the light which it reflects on the history of modern schisms. We can only very briefly sketch the sequel. The Donatists having been driven out of their churches by Constantine, and restored by Julian, continued to flourish down to the time of Augustine, in the beginning of the fifth century. In his time they were guilty of violence against Augustine himself, and others of the Catholic bishops and clergy, and the emperor was petitioned to revive the old edicts against them. At length, in 411, at the request of the Catholics, an imperial commissioner was sent to conduct a conference between the two parties. The bishops of each side assembled in great numbers. A debate of several days ensued; Augustine was the chief advocate on the side of the Catholics. They offered that, if it were proved that the Church had failed except in the Donatist communion, they would submit and enter that communion; and on the other hand they promised that if they should be able to convince the Donatists, they would receive them into communion, acknowledge their bishops and clergy, and agree to an arrangement for the joint government of the churches. The imperial commissioner gave his judgment against the Donatists; they appealed to the Emperor Honorius, who confirmed the decision, and enacted penalties against them. Little is known of the history of the sect after this time; it gradually dwindled into insignificance; but it is supposed not to have been entirely extinguished till the Saracenic invasion of Africa in the seventh century swept Catholic and Donatist together into a common ruin.

## CHAPTER XIX.

### THE EMPIRE FROM THE DEATH OF CONSTANTINE TO THAT OF THEODOSIUS.

CONSTANTINE, on the death of Licinius, had reunited the empire (A.D. 324), and continued to rule it with sole and absolute authority during the remaining thirteen years of his life. But he continued in a modified form the subdivision of the government which Diocletian had introduced, by according to his three sons and two nephews the title of Cæsar, and appointing them to nominal governments, while he surrounded them with ministers and generals whom he trusted, and who guided the councils of the youthful princes. Constantine, his eldest son, he appointed to the government of Gaul; Constantius to the East; Constans to Italy and Africa; Dalmatius, to Thrace, Macedonia, and Greece; Hannibalanus to Pontus, Cappadocia, and Lesser Armenia.

On the death of Constantine (A.D. 337) a conspiracy, of whose real motives we are ignorant, headed by his ministers and generals, and backed by the army, declared against the brothers and nephews of the late emperor. His two brothers, the husband of his sister, seven of his nephews, and Ablavius, his chief favourite and minister, were massacred. Gallus and Julian, two of his nephews, escaped death. His three sons—Constantine, Constans, and Constantius—redivided the empire among them, Constantine retaining the new capital, with a certain pre-eminence of rank. After three years, however, Constantine complained that he had not received a just proportion of the empire, and demanded of Constans the cession of several of his provinces. Following up this demand by an invasion, he was led into an ambuscade and slain (A.D. 340). Constans refused to yield to his surviving brother any share in his new acquisitions. Ten years after (A.D. 350) Constans fell a victim to a rebellion, which raised Magnentius to the purple. War ensued between the surviving son of Constantine and the usurper, which after various fortunes was determined in favour of the former, in the great battle of Mursa (A.D. 353), in which the victors lost more men than the vanquished. Upon a further defeat at Lyons, Magnentius fell on his sword, and left the empire once more united in the hands of Constantius (A.D. 353). This emperor was of strict morals, but vain and weak, and in the latter part of his reign he became suspicious and cruel. His weakness allowed the eunuchs, who, after the fashion of the Eastern kings, filled the chief offices of the imperial household, to exercise an unworthy influence in his government. In religious matters he was under the influence of the Arian party, and his power contributed very largely to the temporary predominence which that heresy attained in the Eastern Church. His unsuccessful endeavours to force it on the Western Church also, when he succeeded to the sovereignty of the West, will be spoken of hereafter.

Constantius appointed his cousin Gallus to the rank of Cæsar and to a share in the government; but in consequence of his misconduct deposed and beheaded him, and appointed his other surviving cousin, Julian, to the dangerous honour. Julian developed unexpected capacity, and fought three successful campaigns against the Alemanni, who were threatening the frontiers of the empire. This made the Cæsar a favourite with his legions, and consequently an object of jealousy and suspicion to Constantius. To diminish his power the emperor ordered the legions of the West

to march to the defence of the Eastern provinces. The
soldiers, unwilling to leave their homes and families, and
resenting the treatment of their general, proclaimed Julian,
Augustus. Both sides were preparing for civil war, when
the death of Constantius left Julian sole and undisputed
possessor of the empire.

JULIAN (A.D. 361) is a remarkable person in Church
history. He, like all the family of Constantine, had been
educated as a Christian, and his life is said to have been
saved, when so many of his relatives were massacred, by
Mark the Bishop of Arethusa. But in his youth he had
showed an inclination for the heathen philosophy, and
sought the society of the leading philosophers of his time,
who diligently courted him as the hope of their party. On
his accession to empire he at once declared against Christianity, and took steps for the revival of the ancient religion.
But Christianity was now too strong to be assailed with open
violence, nor did the temper of Julian incline him to the
resolute cruelty which such a policy would have necessitated.
He withdrew the State support from it; he wrote against it,
ridiculed it, harassed it with legal persecutions, which in
some cases affected the property, and in a few cases the
lives, of Christians. On the other hand he invited the re-
opening of the deserted temples, and encouraged the re-esta-
blishment of the ancient worship. The condition to which
heathenism had fallen is illustrated by a story which is related
by Julian himself, that when he was in Antioch, having
restored the Temple of Daphne, near the city, he went
thither on the day of a great local festival to join in the
worship; but instead of the splendid ceremonial and the
crowd of worshippers which he had expected, only one poor
old priest was in attendance, with no better sacrifice than a
goose, which the priest had been obliged to provide at his
own cost.

Another enterprise which the emperor undertook in opposition to Christianity was the rebuilding of the Temple of Jerusalem, and the restoration of the Jewish worship and nationality. The destruction of the Temple, the cessation of its worship, and the dispersion of the Jews, were looked upon then, as now, as evidences of the truth of Christianity. The rebuilding of the Temple, the resumption of the daily sacrifice, the restoration of the Jewish nationality in its own land, would, therefore, have been considered by unbelievers as a heavy blow to Christianity. Julian undertook the enterprise; he devoted large sums to it, and invited the co-operation of the Jews. He entrusted the special oversight of the work to his friend Alypius of Antioch, who had before that been Lieutenant of Britain, and he was backed by the governor of the province. Workmen were assembled. The Jews naturally embraced the project with religious enthusiasm; men and women of wealth came to the inauguration of the work—the men wielded tools of gold and silver, as we do at the laying of the foundation stone of a great undertaking, the women carried stones in the laps of their silken robes. But the undertaking was wonderfully frustrated. We have the testimony of Ammianus Marcellinus, a contemporary heathen historian, for this fact, and the admission of Julian himself. The former says that "fearful balls of fire, breaking out from the foundations, continued their attacks till the workmen, after repeated scorchings, would approach no more, and thus the fierce element obstinately repelling them, he gave over the attempt." The Church historians of the next age add other particulars, as that there was a whirlwind which scattered the building materials; lightning which melted the tools of the workmen and slew some of the workers; an earthquake which destroyed neighbouring buildings, and disclosed the recesses of the foundations out of which the balls of fire were cast forth.

To check the aggressive spirit of a dangerous neighbour, Julian undertook an invasion of the Persian kingdom, and was killed in a nocturnal skirmish, after a vigorous reign of one year and eight months.

Being the last of the family of Constantine, and not having associated any Cæsar with himself in the government, or nominated any successor, the generals met in council, and avoided the danger of rivalries among themselves by the unanimous election of JOVIAN (A.D. 363), one of the civil officials of the household.

Jovian at once repealed all his predecessor's edicts against Christianity, and restored to the Church its property and its immunities. The imperial support was again withdrawn from paganism; the pagan priests and philosophers, who had abused their temporary triumph, sank into neglect, and the Church was more firmly established than ever.

When Jovian died, after a short and inglorious reign, the able VALENTINIAN (A.D. 364), who had commanded in Britain, was unanimously elected his successor. He associated his brother VALENS with himself in the empire, assigning the eastern half to his brother, and taking the western half as his own province. Valentinian was a constant and firm supporter of the Church and of the orthodox party in it. Under Valentinian the pagans suffered some of the evils which they had inflicted upon Christianity in its earlier period. They fell under the suspicion of magical incantations and immoral rites, and on this ground a terrible persecution was directed against them, especially in Rome itself, which spared neither rank, age, nor sex. Valens put himself into the hands of the dominant Arian party in Constantinople, and continued to support it, though showing personal respect for Athanasius, Basil, and others of the great men of the Catholic minority. The election of Damasus as Bishop of Rome during Valentinian's reign marks an era in the external history of the Church. The position of Bishop of Rome had become one of such great wealth and influence as to be an object of ambition. On the death of Liberius (A.D. 366) there were two rival candidates for the office, each supported by a numerous and excited following, who filled the city with riot and bloodshed. Damasus was the successful competitor.

Valentinian died a natural death in A.D. 375, and was succeeded by his son GRATIAN, who had long been graced with the rank of Augustus, and designated as his successor; with him was associated his infant half-brother, Valentinian II.

Three years afterwards (Aug. 9, A.D. 378) Valens perished with great part of his army in the fatal battle of Hadrianople against the invading Goths. Gratian conferred the purple and the government of the East upon THEODOSIUS, the son of a general of the same name, whose exploits in the rescue of Britain from an invasion of the Picts and Scots, and subsequently in Africa, had been among the most splendid achievements of the reign of Valentinian. Theodosius, by his conduct and valour, restored the peace and prosperity of the Eastern empire; his private character adorned the purple; under his legislation paganism was finally supplanted, the Catholic faith triumphed over Arianism, and the Church was established as the sole religion of the whole empire. At his death commenced a new era of history—the era of the disruption of the empire and the construction out of its fragments of the nations of Western Europe.

## CHAPTER XX.

#### THE ARIAN CONTROVERSY.

THE history of the Church during the reign of Constantine and his successors down to the time of Theodosius is chiefly a history of the Arian controversy. The gradual absorption of the pagan population into the ranks of Christianity went on, the building up of converts into saints went on; but the energies of Eastern Christianity were chiefly expended upon this great and critical controversy. The great Churchmen of the time appear as the heroes in this struggle; the interest of this period of Church history hangs upon the great peril and the ultimate triumph of the truth. The heresy began in Alexandria, that fruitful seat of philosophical speculation. Arius, a presbyter of that Church, taught and maintained a view of the relations in the Godhead of the Son to the Father which was inconsistent with the doctrine of the true Deity of the Son. According to his teaching "there was a time before the commencement of the ages when the parent Deity dwelt alone, in undeveloped, undivided unity. At a time, immeasurably, incalculably, inconceivably remote, the majestic solitude ceased, the Divine unity was broken by an act of the sovereign will; and the only-begotten Son, the image of the Father, the vicegerent of all the Divine power, the intermediate agent in all the long subsequent work of creation, began to be."* He further held, as to the incarnation, that in it the Son assumed a human body, His nature supplying the place of a human soul.† The Church at large held that this was a novel

\* Milmar's "Hist. Christ.," ii. 358.   † Robertson, i. 208.

doctrine and a false one. It was argued that if the Son was not coeval in existence with the Father, He must have been created, and created out of that which was not pre-existent.

Arius, persisting in his doctrine, was condemned by his bishop. The condemnation was ratified by a synod of Egyptian and Libyan bishops; the heresiarch was excommunicated with his adherents, among whom were two bishops, about twelve presbyters, and as many deacons, and a great number of Church virgins. Arius took refuge in Palestine, and industriously propagated his opinions. Eusebius, Bishop of Nicomedia, and a synod of Bithynian bishops, accepted him as orthodox. The controversy attracted attention, and began to disturb the Church far and wide.

Constantine, on becoming master of the East, found this controversy troubling the Church, and addressed a letter to Alexander and Arius, treating the controversy as unimportant, and urging them to peace and unity; he sent the letter by the hands of Hosius, Bishop of Cordova, the prelate in whom at that time he specially confided, that he might compose the strife. The emperor, however, soon found that the doctrine was considered of vital importance, and he took the important step of summoning a general council of bishops of the whole Church to determine it.

There had been continual councils of larger or smaller portions of the Church, but this was the first time that a general council had been held since the apostolic council at Jerusalem. It met at Nicæa in Bithynia, in June, 325, and consisted of about 300 bishops and many of the lower clergy; some heathen philosophers also were attracted to the assembly, and held separate conferences and disputes with the bishops. Hosius, Bishop of Cordova, presided.

In the earlier sessions, which were held in one of the churches of the city, Arius was repeatedly heard in explanation and defence of his opinions. His chief opponents were

Marcellus, Bishop of Ancyra, and Athanasius, Archdeacon of Alexandria, then about thirty years of age, who was in attendance on his bishop, Alexander. About a fortnight after the opening of the council Constantine arrived at Nicæa, and the future sittings were held in his palace, the emperor himself attending them and acting as moderator.

The work of the council was not to settle by argument whether this or that doctrine most approved itself to the reason of the bishops present, but to gather the testimony of the bishops whether the doctrine of Arius was in accordance with the doctrines which had always been received and taught in the several churches. The result was not for a moment doubtful. When the assembled clergy heard Arius' plain statement of his teaching they stopped their ears as at the hearing of blasphemy, and the decrees of the council were ultimately signed by all but fifteen or twenty of the whole 300 bishops.

The famous Creed of Nicæa was not then drawn up for the first time. All the churches already possessed creeds, the same in substance, though some more or less full in their summary of the common faith. The ancient creed of the Church of Cæsarea was adopted by the council as a basis, and the discussion turned upon the modification of its statements about the Son which should serve to exclude the Arian heresy, and to express clearly the Catholic doctrine of His co-equal Deity. The word homoousion—of one substance or essence—was at length adopted, and inserted in the creed as an expression of that co-equal Deity which was recognised as the ancient faith of the Church. A long protracted strife continued to rage about this word through many years; it still stands in the Nicene Creed, the monument of the ultimate victory of the true faith.

The decree of the council entirely failed to terminate the strife. Arianism continued to spread. It found favour at court. Constantia, the sister of Constantine and widow of Licinius, who had been under the influence of Eusebius, Bishop of Nicomedia, a leader of the Arian party, was persuaded that Arius had been unjustly condemned. On her death-bed she appealed to her brother on his behalf. The condemned Arians were recalled, and, by their influence at court, some of the leading Catholic bishops, assailed by false accusations, were banished from their sees; Athanasius himself, who had succeeded Alexander in the see of Alexandria, was exiled to Treves.

On the death of Constantine, not only the empire was divided into East and West, but the Church was divided into Catholic and Arian. Constantius, his empress, and the eunuchs who directed the government, adopted the Arian interest, and sustained it with all the power of the State. Valens, his successor, after the brief reigns of Julian and Jovian, was also an Arian, so that for forty years from the trial of Athanasius, under Constantine the Great, to the beginning of the reign of Theodosius, Arianism was predominant in the East. In every city of the East and of Egypt the Arian party filled the sees, held the churches, and formed the most numerous party. The Catholics were a despised and persecuted minority, and the most violent measures were adopted to compel them to conform.

In the western portion of the empire Constantine the younger was of the orthodox faith. The Western mind, moreover, then as always, was little exercised by the subtle speculations which engaged the Oriental mind; so that during the greater part of this period the Western Church held on its peaceful course, only hearing afar the noise of the distant controversy, and rousing occasionally to keener sympathy when Catholic bishops, expelled as fugitives from their own sees, sought refuge in Rome.

But when (in A.D. 353) the death of Constantine II. and

defeat of Magnentius had made Constantius sole emperor, the Arian persecution swept for seven years over the Western world. A council was convened at Milan, where the bishops of the West, overawed by Constantius and his soldiers, consented to join in the condemnation of Athanasius, and to communicate with the Arians. Let it be noted in their excuse that Athanasius was condemned ostensibly on other grounds than those of his orthodoxy; and that, in admitting the Arians to communion, they were not admitting that the doctrine of Arius was right, and that of Athanasius wrong, but only that the Arian doctrine did not disqualify its holder for recognition as a member of the Catholic Church. The bishops who refused to assent to this decision were exiled, and others more compliant put in their places, and a general persecution was carried on against the orthodox, who complained that the days of Nero and Decius had returned. The two leading bishops of the West still held out—Hosius of Cordova, illustrious for his age and character, and the prominent part he had so long played in the affairs of the Church; and Liberius of Rome, the bishop of the premier see of the West. The conduct of Liberius was at first not unworthy of his great position. Eusebius, the powerful chief of the eunuchs, visited him in Rome, and in vain assailed him with promises and with threats. He declined to go to Milan to wait on the emperor, and was forcibly carried off from Rome by night. But at Milan he withstood the personal flatteries and threats of the emperor with equal firmness, and was condemned to banishment. Eusebius again waited on him with large presents of money from the emperor and empress, ostensibly for the expenses of his journey, but the bishop indignantly refused them. Hosius also withstood all endeavours to induce him to yield, and, after being a year under restraint, he too was banished. The emperor then proceeded to remove Athanasius from

Alexandria by force. The power which the bishops at this time exercised in their sees, derived from the attachment of their flocks, is illustrated in these two facts, that Liberius was abstracted from Rome, for fear of a rising of the people, by stratagem in the night; and that in surprising Athanasius, also by night, it was thought necessary to surround the Cathedral Church of Alexandria with a force of five thousand troops, and even then the people in the church resisted, a scene of tumult and bloodshed followed, and Athanasius was carried safely away by his friends in the confusion.

At length Hosius, now 100 years old, gave way and signed a heterodox creed, and a few months after was followed in his defection by Liberius, and Arianism seemed to be triumphant. Its triumph appeared to be sealed by the acceptance of the Creed of Rimini (A.D. 359). A council of the whole Church was convened by the emperor, and, ostensibly for the convenience of its members, the Western bishops were to meet at Rimini, the Eastern at Nicæa. Each party was dealt with separately. The Western bishops signed an ambiguous creed in ignorance of the meaning which its propounders put upon it; the Eastern bishops also were talked into signing the same formula; and "the whole world," says St. Jerome, "groaned, and was astonished to find itself Arian." Many of the bishops, however, as soon as they understood the meaning put upon the words they had accepted, repudiated the new creed.

But the end of the long struggle was at hand. On November 3, 361, at the age of 44, in the twenty-fifth year of his reign, Constantius died, having only shortly before his death been baptized by the Arian Bishop of Antioch. Julian recalled all exiles, and the orthodox bishops returned to their sees under favour of the general amnesty.

The success of Arianism was chiefly owing to two things: it was supported by the power of the emperor, a power made the more difficult to resist because it was exercised under cover of the forms of ecclesiastical law:—if the emperor employed five thousand troops to turn Athanasius out of his church, the patriarch had first been deposed by a council; if he banished Liberius, Hosius, and other Western bishops, it was because they declined to recognise the decisions of the Council of Milan.

The other cause of Arian success was, that it was careful to do as little violence as possible to the belief of the people. Until it had gained the victory it was careful to make the difference between itself and the Catholic faith look as small as possible. It used language, both in formal creeds and in popular sermons, which was orthodox as far as it went, or which was ambiguous and would naturally be taken by orthodox minds in an orthodox sense. So that numbers of unpolemical pious souls might wonder what all the dispute was about, and attend the services, hear the sermons, recite the creeds, and use the prayers in an Arian church, and grow in faith and holiness—"the ears of the people, uninjured by the subtle heresy, were purer than the lips of the preachers." Moreover, their cause enlisted the natural sympathies of men. Throughout the early part of the struggle they were fighting for mere toleration. All they asked was to be recognised as Catholic Christians. We shall lose the lesson this great crisis in the history of the Christian religion ought to teach us if we fail to meet the natural question, This being so, was the matter worth all the widespread and long-continued strife? Is not Gibbon justified when he sneers at all this strife and bloodshed over the difference of a diphthong? (hom*o*ousion and hom*oi*ousion.) But it was not merely a subtle disputation as to the nature of the Deity, which had no practical importance. The question at issue was really this, Who was Jesus of Nazareth? The answer given by the Catholics was, that He was very and eternal God. The answer of the Arians, however high they might place Him, amounted to this, that He was a creature. The difference between the two answers is immeasurably great. If the Catholics were right, it was sin not to worship Him; if the Arians were right, to worship Him was idolatry. If Jesus must be brought down from the Catholic altitude of God to the Arian level of a creature, the whole Christian scheme must undergo a corresponding degradation. The notion of the sinfulness of sin; of the value of the atonement; of the love of God in giving the Son to die for us; of the exaltation of our humanity in Jesus; of the power of Jesus to aid us; must all be brought down from the height at which the Deity of Jesus places them, to a level immeasurably lower. Moreover, it was not merely the specious, cautious, refined doctrine, which was put forward by Arianism when seeking recognition from Catholics, which the Church had to consider; it was the grosser doctrines which lay beneath, and which came to light as soon as Arianism appeared triumphant; and it was, further, the logical conclusions to which Arianism led— Theism first, perhaps Atheism in the end. It is a great lesson which we learn from the spectacle of *Athanasius contra mundum*—the lesson that the minority may be right, and that if it is right, though only one against the world, it will in the end prevail.

## CHAPTER XXI.

#### THE TRIUMPH OF THE CHURCH.

WHEN Theodosius was elevated to the purple he not only took the rule of the eastern half of the empire, but also guided the counsels of his youthful colleagues in the West. In religious matters he at once threw the whole weight of his power and influence on the side of orthodoxy as against the Arian and subsequent heresies, and on the side of the Church as against paganism. In the first year of his reign he was baptized* (February, 380), and immediately issued an edict in the names of the three emperors, declaring their will that their subjects should embrace the Catholic faith, branding the other parties as heretics, and uttering vague threatenings against them. In the following year, having concluded a successful campaign against the Goths, he made his entry into Constantinople, and at once gave Damophilus, the bishop, the choice of subscribing the Nicene Creed or resigning. The Arian bishop resigned, and the emperor placed all the churches of the capital in the hands of the Catholics, and proceeded to take the same step throughout his dominions.

The Arian heresy seems to have been "played out." While under difficulties its advocates had minimised their difference from the orthodox creed; when triumphant their real belief had been more plainly expressed, and the

---

\* He had previously been only a catechumen. It seems to have been very usual for men to make a profession of Christianity, but to abstain from baptism, for some such reason as in these days influences so many men making a profession of Christianity to abstain from Holy Communion.

tendencies of that belief had been illustrated in the grosser errors of Aëtius. The violence and cruelty of the party when in power had also alienated men's minds, and people generally were not indisposed to receive the orthodox creed. On the whole, the Catholics were re-established throughout the East with little disturbance and opposition.

In 391 the emperor issued an edict forbidding the people to offer sacrifices, and even to enter into the pagan temples. No edict for their destruction was issued, but the zeal of Christians moved them in many places to destroy the temples; the monks especially were active in destroying the fanes and shrines and altars.

Paganism now in turn began to plead for toleration. Libanius, the most famous philosopher of his time, addressed an elaborate oration to the emperor "For the temples," pleading against their destruction. In some places the people rose in defence of their famous local temples, and their worship continued in spite of the imperial edicts. The destruction of the temple of Serapis at Alexandria is an illustrious example of what took place. Next to the temple of Jupiter in the Capitol the temple of Serapis was the proudest monument of pagan religious architecture. Built on an artificial mount in the old quarter of the city, it comprehended a vast mass of buildings, forming a little city in itself, and was one of the wonders of the world. The apartments of the priests and ascetics devoted to the god, stately halls adorned with statues, a great library, and other subsidiary buildings, surrounded the temple. The temple was ascended by 100 steps; it stood in the centre of a vast square, surrounded by a portico of enormous magnitude and beautiful proportion, supported by 400 pillars, the work either of Alexander the Great or of the first of the Ptolemies.* The god was believed to influence the rise and fall of the

* Pompey's Pillar is one of them.

Nile, which influenced the harvests of Egypt, the granary of the empire. A religious riot in Alexandria, in which the pagans had used the Serapion as a fortress, and had immolated Christians whom they captured as victims on the altar, called forth a rescript from the emperor ordering the destruction of the temple. The Prefect of Egypt, with the Bishop of Alexandria by his side, and a military guard, took possession of the temple, which had been abandoned. They ascended to the sanctuary. They stood in superstitious awe amidst the silence of the deserted temple. The huge image of the god, covered with plates of gold and silver and adorned with jewels, filled the sanctuary. The popular belief was that any injury to it would be the signal for the final crash of heaven and earth. The bishop bade a soldier strike; he struck it in the face, and no prodigy followed; another climbed up and struck off the head of the statue, and a colony of rats leaped out and ran about in all directions. Shouts of laughter hailed the incident, and the work of destruction went merrily on. The pagans threatened that the vengeance of the god would be shown in the cessation of the rise of the Nile; and, indeed, the inundation did delay long enough beyond the usual time to cause general anxiety; but at length it rose and began to exceed its usual height, and the heathen began to hope that the god would avenge himself by an inundation; but the waters subsided to their proper level, and put an end to all fears of the vengeance of the pagan gods. The example was followed, and others of the great Egyptian temples were speedily destroyed; and a similar work was carried on in the other provinces of the empire. The power and majesty of the ancient gods were, however, still predominant in Rome. The Capitol was still crowned with the temples and statues of her ancient gods. On the Palatine right opposite stood the vast palace of the Cæsars, surrounded by its marble porticoes. At the foot of the two hills was the old Forum, hedged in with pagan temples. There were no less than 152 temples and 180 smaller shrines scattered through the city, in which the sacrifices and solemnities were still maintained with splendour by ancient endowments, the noblest families of Rome counting the priesthoods among their honours. The ancient aristocratic families still for the most part retained the old religion; it was a part of their ancestral dignity. Only eight years before the accession of Gratian, Pretextatus, the flower and pride of the contemporary Roman nobility, in whom the wisdom of pagan philosophy was united with the serious piety of pagan religion, had publicly consecrated twelve statues in the Capitol to the *Dii Curantes*, the great guardian gods of Rome.

In 383 the emperor issued an edict which at one blow confiscated the property of all the heathen temples, and deprived the priesthoods of all their privileges and immunities. Symmachus, the Prefect of Rome, a man of a character which commanded universal respect, assembled the senate, and they presented a petition to the emperor, pleading for the toleration of the ancient religion of the empire. Ambrose, Bishop of Milan, replied to the petition of the senate, and the emperor did not relax in his suppression of idolatry. In the year 388, it is said, the emperor formally proposed for debate in the senate the question whether the worship of Jupiter or that of Christ should be the religion of the Romans, and by a large majority it was resolved to abandon the ancestral religion. Few of them really believed in it; many of the ladies of their families were already Christian; and it did not cost them much to yield to the authority of the emperor and embrace the established religion. Six hundred families inheriting the great names of the Republic are said to have passed over at once to Christianity.

But, though the temples were closed and the sacrifices forbidden, the pagans in many places evaded the laws. On the days of solemn festivals they assembled in some convenient place under the shade of the trees, under pretence of a convivial meeting; sheep and oxen were slain and roasted, and the feast was sanctified by the use of incense and of hymns in honour of the god. But a last edict of Theodosius, A.D. 390, prohibited any sacrifices, the use of luminaries, garlands, incense, and libations of wine, in any place whatever; the house or estate on which such ceremonies were performed was confiscated; or if performed on the estate of another, a heavy fine of twenty-five pounds of gold was imposed. It is said that there were few or no persecutions under these laws. Pagans, though forbidden to exercise their worship, were not molested, and paganism was left to die out slowly as a religion, though many of its superstitions retained their hold in the minds and customs of the people for centuries.

The changes which had taken place between the reign of Constantine and that of Theodosius may be thus described. Constantine, himself a new convert, first placed Christianity on the throne of an empire only half converted from paganism. Constantius and Valens had made half the empire Arian. Theodosius, an hereditary Christian, ruled over a Christian and orthodox empire, in which the lingering traces of paganism and heresy were barely tolerated.

## CHAPTER XXII.

THE EXTENSION OF THE CHURCH OUTSIDE THE EMPIRE—ARMENIAN, GOTHIC, ETHIOPIAN, AND IBERIAN CONVERSIONS.

THE Roman empire was not the first of the kingdoms of the world to accept the faith of Christ as its national religion ; that honour belongs to the kingdom of ARMENIA. Gregory, surnamed the Illuminator, was the apostle of the first Christian kingdom. Sapor, King of Persia, had procured the assassination of Kosrov, the powerful king of Armenia, and annexed his kingdom. Tiridates, a younger son of Kosrov, alone escaped to the Roman dominions and served with distinction in the Roman armies. Kosrov's assassin had also been put to death by the enraged soldiery, and only one of his children, the infant Gregory, was saved from their vengeance by a Christian nurse, who fled with him to Cæsarea.

Towards the end of the third century Tiridates reconquered his hereditary throne, and Gregory re-entered his native country in his train. When the king offered a thanksgiving sacrifice, Gregory refused to join in the idolatrous ceremony. It was made known to the king that the recusant was the son of his father's assassin; and Gregory was tortured and thrown into prison. A pestilence happened, and the king himself was seized. His sister, who was a Christian, advised the release of Gregory. The king was healed, the plague ceased ; the king, the nobles, and the people almost simultaneously submitted to Baptism, and

Armenia became the first Christian kingdom. Priests were invited from Greece and Syria, 400 bishops were consecrated, and Gregory was made archbishop. Churches and religious houses rose in every quarter; the Christian festivals and days of religious observance were established by law. Dara, however, the sacred province of the kingdom, resisted the introduction of the new religion in arms, and it was only by the sword that its resistance was overcome and Christianity established in the province.

After the Council of Chalcedon the Armenian Church unhappily embraced the Monophysite heresy, but it has continued to flourish to the present day, and is now the most important of all the Eastern churches except the Greek.

In the first inroads of the GOTHS into the Eastern empire in the reign of Gallienus, the invaders carried back with them numbers of slaves, among whom were many Christians. The slaves succeeded in converting their masters, and the families of the captives continued to supply a priesthood to the Goths. A Gothic bishop with a Greek name, Theophilus, was present at the Council of Nicæa (A.D. 325). In A.D. 348, Ulphilas came with an embassy from the Goths to the Emperor Constantius, and obtained consecration from the Bishop of Constantinople, probably as the immediate successor of the Theophilus above mentioned. Ulphilas is said to have first reduced the Gothic tongue to a written language, into which he translated the Bible for the use of his people. He held Arian tenets, and by his influence impressed them upon the Gothic Church; thence they spread to the kindred nations, the Vandals and Burgundians; so that while Arianism was dying out in the empire, it was gaining new force among the barbarians, and was by their subsequent conquests, as we shall see, planted in Italy, Spain, and Africa.

The ABYSSINIAN Church (in which the recent war gave us a special interest) was founded at this period. A scientific expedition made in the early part of the fourth century by Meropius, a philosopher of Tyre, calling, on its homeward voyage, at a place on the coast, in search of fresh water, was attacked, and all were massacred by the inhabitants except two Christian youths, the relatives and pupils of Meropius. They were carried as captives to the king, who made one of them, Ædesius, his cup-bearer, and the other, Frumentius, his secretary and treasurer. On the death of the king, his widowed queen begged the two strangers to act as regents of the kingdom until her son came of age. They introduced the Gospel among the people; and when at length they left the country, Frumentius, on arriving at Alexandria, told his story to Athanasius, and requested him to send a bishop to follow up the work thus begun. Athanasius thought no one so fit as Frumentius himself, and accordingly consecrated him and sent him back to Abyssinia. The Church thus founded continues, as we know, to this day. It still acknowledges obedience to the see of Alexandria, and its patriarch is always an Egyptian monk, chosen and consecrated by the Coptic patriarch.

The IBERIANS, or Georgians, about the same period received the Gospel, as the Goths did, by means of a Christian woman whom they had carried back a captive after an incursion into the empire. A child of the king was healed of sickness by her prayers, the queen soon after was healed in like manner, and other miracles are said to have been wrought. The king and queen were converted, many of the people followed their example; and the Iberians, on application to Constantine, were supplied with a bishop and clergy. In the fifth century, when so many of the Eastern churches adopted the Nestorian and Monophysite heresies, the Georgian Church adhered to the orthodox faith. After continuing under the patriarchate of Constantinople for 1,500 years, it fell by conquest, in 1801, into the power of Russia, and was transferred from the patriarchate of Constantinople to the rule of the Holy Synod of Moscow.

## CHAPTER XXIII.

#### THE FATHERS OF THE CHURCH.

GREAT men are scattered singly all down the roll of history, but every now and then the circumstances of a nation produce a cluster of great men. The great masters of the Greek tragedy were contemporaries, so were the great Greek philosophers, so were the great Latin poets.

So the great Fathers of the Christian Church are nearly all included within a century, and the greatest of them were contemporaries. The great Alexandrian and African writers, Clement, Origen, and Tertullian, belong to a rather earlier period; St. Gregory the Great and the Venerable Bede to a period rather later. Putting them aside, the Fathers, both Greek and Latin, may be said to begin with Athanasius and to end with Leo the Great, and are included between the dates 330 and 461. It was in the last year of Athanasius' long reign in Alexandria that the popular acclamation called Ambrose to the see of Milan. Ambrose was ruling the Church of Milan, and influencing the councils of the Western emperors, at the same time that Augustine was occupying the see of Hippo, and writing the works which have influenced the mind of Western Europe ever since; and at the same time Jerome, in his cell at Bethlehem, was studying Hebrew by stealth with his Jewish teacher, and writing the popular version of the Scriptures, which had still more influence on Western Christianity than all the writings of all the Fathers. While Jerome was yet a young man he travelled through Cæsarea, and made himself known to Basil, who had lately succeeded Eusebius in that great see;

thence he travelled on to Constantinople, where he heard Gregory of Nazianzum preach; and he witnessed the elevation of John Chrysostom to the throne of Constantinople, and outlived him by thirteen years. In this list of contemporaries is included all the four doctors of the Greek Church and all the four doctors of the Latin Church, except only Gregory the Great.

There are thousands of educated English Churchmen who would be ashamed to be thought ignorant of the great men and the great works of Greek and Latin literature, but who are contentedly ignorant almost of the very names of these great writers of the Christian Church.

It is the fashion to underrate them. It is popularly supposed that they were all ignorant and superstitious priests, who wrote ponderous tomes which have been long since superseded by the results of modern enlightenment. Let us glance at the men and their work. The men afford a curious illustration of the cosmopolitanism of their time, and the very various sources from which the clergy were drawn. To limit ourselves to the names already mentioned. Augustine was a Numidian, Jerome a Dalmatian, Basil and Gregory Cappadocians, Chrysostom a Greek of Antioch, Ambrose an Italian. Augustine, before his ordination, was a middle-aged professor of rhetoric; Basil and Gregory young men of family and fortune, who had finished their education in Athens; Jerome, a student, first at Aquileia then at Rome; Chrysostom began to practise at the bar; Ambrose was a middle-aged statesman and governor of a province when he was suddenly called to the bishop's chair. Another remarkable fact about these men is that, differing in so many respects, they are alike in this, that they all had some years of ascetic training before they entered upon their work, with the single exception of Ambrose, who, as we have said, was suddenly called from the office of magistrate to that of bishop.

What was their work? The Gospel had not only to give an answer to simple souls asking nothing more than a practical rule by which to live here and to win heaven hereafter; if it was to dominate the whole realm of human thought and life, as it claimed to do, then it must deal with the whole range of science and philosophy. It must not only refute and reject all that was false, but it must welcome and adopt and gather into itself all the true results of human thought which the great races—Egyptian, Indian, Greek, and Jewish—had been maturing for centuries; all the true conclusions which human reason had painfully wrung out of the facts of the universe; all the prophetic guesses of the heart and soul stretching out to the unseen and the future.

The Fathers of the Church were the men who, by God's grace, accomplished this great and noble task. Holding the faith once for all delivered to the Church by Christ and His apostles with a firm, unfaltering grasp, they, with a wonderful breadth and depth of learning, and a still more wonderful soundness and sobriety of judgment, gathered round the Gospel all that was true and valuable in the heterogeneous mass of ancient thought. Amidst the confusion which resulted from the break-up of the civil, social, and domestic system of the ancient world, and the inroad of the rude customs of barbarous tribes, they laid the foundations of the civil organisation, the social and domestic habits, and the philosophy and modes of thought, of the nations of the modern world.

Our plan and limits do not allow us to bring before the reader all these Fathers of the Church, but there are several of them so great in themselves, or so identified with the events of great periods of Church history, that we must not pass them by.

We have had occasion to speak of ATHANASIUS in our chapter on the Arian conflict. He was the central figure round which all the world-wide and long-continued battle raged. As archdeacon of Alexander he had not improbably been the first mover in the opposition to the new and dangerous teaching of Arius; though but archdeacon, and under thirty years of age, he had been the leading speaker on the orthodox side at the Council of Nicæa. Immediately after the council, Alexander dying, Athanasius was raised to the bishopric of Alexandria, and held this great and powerful see from the age of thirty to the age of seventy-six. " He displays in his writings a manly and direct eloquence; a remarkable and unusual combination of subtlety with breadth of mind; extreme acuteness in argument, yet at the same time a superiority to mere contentiousness about words. His unbending steadiness of purpose was combined with a rare skill in dealing with men; he knew when to give way as well as when to make a show of resistance. His activity, his readiness, his foresight, his wonderful escapes and adventures, gave countenance to the stories of magical art which circulated among his enemies, and to the belief of his admirers that he possessed the gifts of miracles and prophecy; throughout all his troubles he was supported by the attachment of his people and of the hundred bishops who swore allegiance to the see of Alexandria."*

In the latter part of Constantine's lifetime the Arian party gained the ear of the court. The emperor himself was induced to write to Athanasius, requiring him to receive Arius and his followers into communion. An imperial command in those days, whatever it bade, was looked upon as irresistible throughout the whole empire; but the undaunted Athanasius replied that he could not acknowledge persons who had been condemned by the whole Church, and the emperor desisted from urging the matter.

The Arians, however, besieged the emperor with all kinds

* Canon Robertson.

of complaints against Athanasius; he was summoned to appear before a council at Tyre, and finding that force would be employed if he did not obey the summons, he appeared at the head of 50 out of his 100 Egyptian bishops. When Athanasius was about to take his seat, Eusebius of Cæsarea, who presided, bade Athanasius stand, as became a person accused. On this one of the Egyptian bishops, Potammon, a man of high repute for sanctity, is said to have addressed Eusebius: "Do you sit while the innocent Athanasius is tried before you? Remember how you were my fellow-prisoner in the persecution. I lost an eye for the truth; by what compliances was it that you came off unhurt?" The ecclesiastical charges against Athanasius were fortified by others of a criminal kind. A bishop named Arsenius had disappeared; he was hiding in consequence of some irregularity. Athanasius was accused of having killed him, and moreover with having cut off his hand and used it for magical purposes; the accusation of magic was one of the popular charges of the period. The charge was triumphantly answered by the production of Arsenius before the council safe and sound. The accusers were silenced by this failure. The council adjourned, appointing, however, a commission to collect fresh evidence. Athanasius at once embarked for Constantinople, sought an opportunity of meeting the emperor, and appealed to have his case tried by himself. The council meantime met again, condemned him in his absence, excommunicated him, and decreed his deposition. The Arian members of the Council of Tyre then adjourned to Jerusalem, and there brought a new accusation against him. They asserted that he had threatened to stop the sailing of the Egyptian fleet, on which the capital depended for its supply of corn. The mere suggestion was full of danger. For a similar suspicion Constantine had some years before put to death Sopater, a man who had been his friend.  Athanasius had, perhaps, power enough in Alexandria to have done it.  The possibility was enough to alarm the emperor, and Athanasius was banished to Trèves, where, however, he was honourably entertained at the court of the younger Constantine, and the emperor refused to allow his see to be filled up.  On the death of Constantine (A.D. 338) Athanasius returned to his see after two and a half years' absence, with a recommendatory letter from Constantius, and was joyfully welcomed by his flock.

At a council held at Antioch two years afterwards, the enemies of Athanasius procured the passing of a canon, that if any bishop deposed by a council should appeal to the temporal power, instead of seeking redress from a higher council, he should forfeit all hope of restoration.  The canon was perhaps unexceptionable in itself, but as soon as it was passed it was applied, *ex post facto*, to the case of Athanasius, who had appealed from the Council of Tyre to the emperor.  He was condemned under it, and Gregory of Cappadocia, an Arian, was consecrated to the see of Alexandria in his stead.  Gregory was escorted to his see by a military force under the command of the Prefect of Egypt.

When the prefect announced that Athanasius was deposed, and Gregory of Cappadocia was their bishop, Athanasius tells us what ensued : "'l'he people were very indignant, and flocked to the churches when the news was spread about, determined that no Arian impiety should defile the faith of the Church.  Philagrius the prefect—the man who once before was known to have insulted the Church and the Church's consecrated virgins, a renegade from his faith, a fellow-countryman of Gregory, who owed his place to the court influence of the Eusebians, and was therefore, as may be supposed, a sorry friend to the Church—this Philagrius gathered together by promises—promises which he only too scrupulously fulfilled—the heathen mob, the Jews, and all the abandoned characters of the city, worked them up to a pitch of frenzy, and then hounded them in pell-mell on the people assembled in the churches. To give an idea of what ensued is out of my power; it is beyond language and expression; the memory cannot dwell upon it without sorrowful tears. What ancient tragedy has come up to it? In what war or dire persecution did such things happen? The churches and the sacred baptisteries were set on fire; at once the whole city was filled with the outcries, the wailings, and the grief of the outraged people, protesting against the prefect and the brute force employed against them. The sacred and undefiled virgins were horribly insulted, or nearly killed; the monks were trodden under foot and left to die; some were brained with the discus; some were killed with swords and bludgeons; others were wounded and beaten. The holy table was profaned with indescribable impiety and wickedness. They sacrificed birds and snails to the glory of their idols, and they burnt all the Holy Scriptures they could find, blaspheming our Lord and Saviour Jesus Christ, the Son of the living God. In the second baptistery (horrible to relate) the deicide Jews and unbelieving pagans, unrestrained by decency, committed such obscenities in word and deed that I am ashamed to relate them. Nay, some of the impious crew, imitating the bitterest of the persecutors, would seize the consecrated women and drag them about, forcing them to blaspheme the Lord, or if they refused, stabbing and kicking them. Gregory, who had promised pay and booty to the heathens, Jews, and other conquerors in this iniquity, now fulfilled his promise (for he was well pleased with what had been done), and gave them the church to sack. What followed was worse than the horrors of war and piracy. They fell to spoil and pillage; all the large stores of wine they drank, or wasted, or carried off; they appropriated the oil of olives; doors and railings were borne away as trophies; the wall lamps were pulled down, and the wax candles were taken to burn before idols; in a word, destruction and death filled the church. But they did not stop here. Priests and many of the people were torn with scourges; the holy virgins were stripped of their veils, dragged before the prefect's judgment-seat, and thrust into prison. Some were outlawed, some beaten with the slave's lash, and they attempted to starve out the colleges of ecclesiastics and consecrated women by intercepting their food. This happened in the Lenten time, when the brethren were fasting; nay, on the very day of Good Friday itself, Gregory induced the prefect to order to be publicly scourged, during one hour, no less than thirty-four virgins, besides married women, and men of gentle birth." (St. Athan. Epist. Encyc., 3, 4.)

Athanasius withdrew on the arrival of Gregory, and went to Rome, where a council of fifty bishops pronounced him innocent. Constans, the emperor of the West, requested his restoration to his see, and at length threatened to restore him by force of arms. Constantius, partly perhaps moved by the threats of his brother, partly disgusted with the revelation of some of the intrigues of the Arian party, partly desiring the support of the West in his meditated campaign against Persia, put a stop to the persecution, wrote himself to Athanasius inviting his return, and sent him back to Alexandria with a recommendatory letter. Gregory had died a little while before, and Athanasius was again received with universal rejoicing.

When the death of Constans and the defeat of Magnentius left Constantius sole master of the empire, the machinations against Athanasius recommenced. A council at Milan, overawed by the presence of the emperor, who pressed his condemnation as a question of personal interest, condemned him. Athanasius, however, declined to resign his see, or to leave the city. It was feared that the Alexandrians would oppose by force any forcible attempt to remove him, and the general in command of the province proceeded to obey the emperor's orders by a mixture of stratagem and force. In the night of February 9 (A.D. 346), while the bishop and a large congregation were keeping the vigil of St. Thomas, the general, with 5,000 soldiers and a mob of Arians, surrounded the church. The bishop, hearing the noise, calmly seated himself on his throne, and gave out the 136th Psalm to be sung, the whole congregation joining in the response, " For His mercy endureth for ever." The doors were forced, and a fearful confusion ensued. The soldiers pressed up towards the east end of the church to seize the bishop; many of the congregation were trodden under foot and crushed to death; some were pierced by the soldiers' javelins; the consecrated virgins were beaten. The bishop bade all escape, determined himself to be the last. But those about him at length carried him away by a side door, and he escaped from the city. In a few months another Arian bishop, George of Cappadocia, made his appearance, and behaved with still greater violence than his predecessor against the Catholics; bishops, clergy, monks, virgins, and laity were plundered, scourged, mutilated, banished, and committed to the hard labour of the mines. Some of the bishops died through their sufferings. George was driven away by the people, but, reinstated again by the civil power, made himself more detested than ever. On hearing the tidings of the death of Constantius, the heathen populace of Alexandria murdered the intrusive bishop George. Julian recalled all the banished, and Athanasius returned to Alexandria; the churches were surrendered to him and the Catholics restored. Julian, however, afterwards declared Athanasius excepted from the general recall, and banished him from all Egypt. Athanasius said, "Let us withdraw; this is a little cloud, which will soon pass over." He embarked on the Nile and sailed up the stream; a galley pursued him. At a turn of the stream he doubled back, evaded his pursuers, and returned to Alexandria; but soon after, to evade the search, he again left and took refuge among the monks of the desert. On the accession of Jovian, the emperor wrote to Athanasius and invited him to court, requesting his instruction and advice, and replaced him in his see. Valens issued a general sentence of banishment against the bishops who had been banished by Constantius and recalled by Julian, and Athanasius took refuge for a time in his family tomb; but on its being represented to the emperor that he did not fall under the letter of the edict, Valens permitted his return. He spent the remaining years of his life in quiet possession of his see, dying about the year 373, at the age of seventy-six.

CHRYSOSTOM leads us to the other great sees of the Eastern Church—Antioch and Constantinople. He was born at Antioch about A.D. 347, the son of a military officer of high rank, and was early left to the care of his widowed mother. He studied under Libanius, a heathen, but the most famous teacher of his day; and years afterwards Libanius declared that he would have been his own worthiest successor had not the Christians stolen him. He was destined to practise at the bar, but at the age of twenty he resolved to devote himself to a religious life. At his mother's entreaties he continued to live with her, but in the practice of an ascetic life, till her death set him at liberty to follow his intentions. He then lived four years in a monastery near Antioch, and spent two other years as a hermit in a cave, when ill-health, brought on by his austerities, led to his return to Antioch. Here he was ordained deacon, and in 386 Flavian, the Bishop of Antioch, appointed him as the chief preacher in the church of that great see. His eloquence won for him the name of Chrysostom—the golden mouth. A very great number of his sermons, taken down as they were preached, still remain, and justify his reputation as the Church's greatest preacher. His style is clear, flowing, and ornate; he uses abundant and apt illustrations, constantly introduces the topics of passing general interest, and is ready and happy in taking advantage of any little thing which may happen while he is speaking. His homilies extend over the greater part of the New Testament, with certain books of the Old; he adheres to the literal meaning of Scripture, and his exhortations are distinguished by good sense. He is always making practical applications, and appeals to the hearts of his hearers with a deep knowledge of the human heart.*

A remarkable opportunity occurred for the exercise of the influence of his popular eloquence. The weight of the taxes imposed by Theodosius excited great discontent at Antioch. The principal inhabitants presented a remonstrance to the prefect, and meantime an excited mob collected round his doors, and, being stimulated by designing persons, proceeded to acts of violence; the prefect's house was assaulted. Repulsed in this attempt the mob plundered the public baths; and, lastly, the statues of the emperor and his deceased empress, which stood in the public places, were overthrown, dragged through the streets, and assailed with insults. When the news of this riot was brought to the emperor, he gave way to a fit of fury, and gave orders for the destruction of the city which had thus outraged him. The bishop, Flavian, prevailed on the prefect to suspend the execution of the order, and to occupy himself in an inquiry into the affair, while he, old as he was, undertook a mission to the emperor in the hope of appeasing his anger,

* Canon Robertson.

and obtaining a reversal of the terrible sentence. The people of Antioch were panic-stricken. Day by day some of the principal people were arrested and carried before the prefect, and examined with tortures; the rest waited in terrified suspense to learn their doom. This was the great preacher's opportunity. Every day he preached in the principal church, which was every day crowded with hearers, and applied himself to lead the city to a general repentance of its sins, and an earnest preparation either on one hand for death, should the emperor's sentence be executed, or on the other for a new and holier life, should God hear their prayers and turn the emperor's heart. The emperor was touched by the appeal of the aged bishop, and granted the pardon which he asked in the name of Christ.

After he had been thus engaged for nearly twelve years the see of Constantinople fell vacant, and there were disputes about the succession; the Emperor Arcadius, being requested to put an end to the difficulty, nominated Chrysostom, and he was consecrated in A.D. 398. At the capital his preaching and his virtues made him popular and influential; but an ascetic mode of life, and the severe discipline he endeavoured to force upon the clergy, made him many enemies among them; while his severe condemnation of the vices of the court, and his personal and public strictures on the Empress Eudoxia, made the emperor and the empress his enemies. The latter part of his life was spent under persecution. Theophilus, Bishop of Alexandria, instigated by the empress, headed a party against him. He was summoned before an irregular synod, called "of the oak," to answer certain charges; and refusing to acknowledge the jurisdiction of the synod, was condemned in his absence. He was sent out of the city and across the Bosphorus on his way to exile; but the people beset the imperial palace with cries for their bishop; an earthquake added superstitious fears to the natural apprehension of popular disturbances, and Chrysostom was recalled. A few months afterwards, when the court had recovered from its terrors, he was again banished to Cucusus, a town among the ridges of Mount Taurus, where he spent three years, exercising a great influence by means of correspondence with churches in all quarters, and receiving visitors, who came to see and consult him, amply supplied with funds by his friends, and distributing them bountifully in alms. His enemies, provoked by all this, procured that his place of exile should be changed; and he was ordered to Pityus, a town on the extreme north-eastern frontier of the empire. On his way thither he died of the hardships of the journey. His body was afterwards brought to Constantinople, and the emperor, Theodosius II., met the procession, and asked pardon of the saint for his persecution by his parents.

AMBROSE, Archbishop of Milan, was the greatest Churchman who had as yet appeared in the Western Church. On the death of the Arian Archbishop Auxentius, in 374, the Emperor Valentinian was invited to nominate his successor, but he referred the choice to the people of the city. They assembled in the principal church for the election; but there were rival nominations, and party spirit ran high, and there were symptoms of a riot in the church. Then Ambrose, the Prefect of Liguria, who presided, made a speech exhorting the people to peace and unity. When he concluded a voice as of a little child was heard to say, "Ambrose for Bishop," and the cry was caught up by the whole people. Ambrose, the son of a Prætorian prefect of Gaul, had been educated for State employments, and had attained to the office of Prefect of Liguria. He was now thirty-four years old; but after the bad custom of the time, which we have had to notice before, was only a catechumen. He did not desire the office of bishop, and was with difficulty induced to accept it. Milan was at this time the chief residence of the Emperors of the West, and the position of its bishop afforded great opportunities to a great man. Ambrose set himself diligently to theological study and to the administration of the affairs of his see, and his strong practical sense and statesman's experience and lofty character gave him great influence both with the court and the people.

On the death of Valentinian, Ambrose acquired a great influence over the mind of the young Gratian, though in the empress-widow Justina, who was an Arian, he had a bitter and persevering enemy. Nevertheless, when Gratian was murdered at Lyons by the partisans of the rebel Maximus, the empress-mother placed her younger son Valentinian II. in the Archbishop's arms and entreated him to become his protector. Ambrose accepted the charge, proceeded to Trèves, where Maximus had fixed his court, and negotiated a division of the empire, which ceded to Maximus, Britain, Gaul, and Spain, and secured Valentinian in the possession of the remainder.

Ambrose succeeded in extinguishing Arianism in Milan, which had been kept alive by the influence of his predecessor; but the empress-mother, with some of the courtiers, and the Gothic body-guard, still adhered to the heresy. For their use the empress demanded of Ambrose a church without the walls, and subsequently a large church which had just been built and was not yet consecrated. Ambrose was twice summoned before the imperial council, who told him he must yield to the imperial will, but he refused; the people surrounded the palace, the troops sympathised with the archbishop, and the demand was withdrawn for the time. A year after it was again renewed, and on his refusal the archbishop was ordered to quit the city. He refused to quit his flock unless compelled by force, and for several nights the people filled the church and its adjoining buildings as a guard, and again the archbishop's firmness prevailed. It was on this occasion that Ambrose, it is said, introduced into the Western Church the custom already then in use in the East—that the psalms, instead of being left to the choristers, should be sung by the congregation also, antiphonally.

When Maximus, in violation of the treaty, invaded the territories of Valentinian, Theodosius marched against the invader, defeated him, and for a time fixed his residence in Milan. The archbishop acquired as strong an influence over the mind of the great emperor as he had done over the younger princes. The most remarkable exhibition of the bishop's firmness and of the emperor's respect was on an occasion similar to that which has already been narrated in the sketch of St. Chrysostom. The people of Thessalonica, on the occasion of a chariot race, had raised a popular cry for the release of a favourite charioteer who had been imprisoned for a shameful crime. The military prefect refused to yield to their demand, upon which they broke out into a riot, and murdered him, with many of his soldiers and others. Ambrose interceded for the Thessalonians, and obtained the emperor's promise of a pardon; but others of his advisers urged the impolicy of passing over such an outbreak against the imperial authority, and obtained an order for their punishment, which was kept secret from Ambrose. The people of Thessalonica were invited to a performance in the circus, and, while assembled there, were surrounded and attacked by troops, who put all of them to death, to the number of 7,000 men, women, and children. The archbishop at once wrote to the emperor, giving expression to his horror at this great crime, and refusing to allow his presence at the Holy Communion until he should have given proof of repentance. And as Theodosius was about to enter the principal church, the archbishop met him in the porch, and desired him to withdraw. The emperor spoke of his contrition; the archbishop told him that public evidence of his contrition ought to be given for so public a crime. The emperor submitted, and withdrew, and for eight months remained in seclusion, laying aside his imperial ornaments; he consented to pass a law, intended to guard against like effects of sudden anger on the part of the emperors, that an interval of thirty days should come between a capital sentence and its execution; and so at length on Christmas Day he was formally received back into the communion of the Church. When Theodosius returned to the East the young emperor of the West was entirely under the guidance of Ambrose until his violent death. The great statesman bishop died on Easter Eve, A.D. 397.

A glance at the lives of Jerome and Augustine will come more appropriately in later chapters in connection with their own special surroundings.

## CHAPTER XXIV.

#### MONASTICISM. ANTONY. HILARION. BASIL. JEROME. MARTIN OF TOURS.

THERE have always been men who have felt keenly the awfulness of life and the vanity of the ordinary ways of men, and have had the courage to break the chains of custom, and live a life apart. The Christian faith gave a new meaning and dignity and sacredness to the common life of man, but it also revealed more certainly and vividly the grandeur of the Unseen and the Eternal, and gave food and encouragement to the contemplative and ascetic class of minds.

From time to time this ascetic spirit has exercised a wide and deep influence on the minds of Christian people, due partly, perhaps, to the external circumstances of the time, partly to the example of some illustrious man, or perhaps to one of those waves of feeling which sweep across the sea of human society for which we can find no natural cause, such as that which filled the deserts of Egypt and Syria with hermits in the fourth, fifth, and sixth centuries, and the forests of Germany with monks in the eighth, and revived the monastic spirit throughout Europe in the eleventh, and gave rise in the thirteenth to the mendicant orders.

ANTONY was not the first who led a solitary life, but he was the first who attained to any great reputation; for his life was written by St. Athanasius, his contemporary, and he is regarded as the father of the Hermits. He was born A.D. 251 in a village in the Thebaid, of wealthy Egyptian parents; he was brought up by them as a Christian, and was a thoughtful and religious boy. Before the age of twenty he lost both parents and came into possession of considerable property. One day in church hearing read the Gospel of the rich young man who was bidden by our Lord, if he would be perfect, to go, sell all that he had, and give to the poor, and come and follow Him, he accepted the words as addressed to himself, to be literally obeyed. He gave his land to the inhabitants of his village, turned the rest of his possessions into money and distributed it to the poor, and embraced the ascetic life. At first he lived near his own village, supplying his frugal wants by the labour of his own hands, and giving to the poor what he could spare. He visited all the most famous solitaries he could hear of, and endeavoured to learn from each his special virtue, and to combine them all in his own character. After a time he left his village and afterwards shut himself up in a tomb, where he continued to live a solitary life for ten years. We may picture him sitting in the shaded entrance to his cell—one of the painted tombs with which the hill-sides are honeycombed—with the silence and solitude of the desert around him, and at his feet the green and fertile valley of Egypt, teeming with a busy population and dignified by the grand monuments of the most ancient civilisation of the world. He sits there by night and gazes at the stars glowing in the pure cloudless sky. He watches the sun rise rapidly over the chain of hills on the other side the valley. The hum of awakening life rises faintly up towards him; he can catch the gleam of the Nile, and see the sails of the boats passing up and down on its great highway; he says his prayers, and sings his psalms, and reads his book; and then busies himself in his little garden in the hollow dell through which the spring trickles down towards the Nile; in the evening he sits again in the door of his cell and listens to the hum of the busy world beneath, and watches the day fade out of the sky, and the stars come out; and says his prayers and sings his psalms; and lies down to sleep in peace. Who has not felt, amid the bustle of a life full of petty occupations and petty cares, what a relief it would be to sit down in such a solitude, with leisure to think and pray:—" O that I had wings like a dove, for then would I flee away and be at rest"? What better place could one choose than the edge of the boundless desert, yet overlooking the beautiful valley? what better solitude than the serene hill-top, yet looking down upon a busy world? what better cell than a tomb amid the tombs?

His reputation spread abroad, and people imitated his example, Antony consenting to receive them as disciples, and the neighbouring desert began to be peopled with their cells. Multitudes of people also came to seek his spiritual counsel; the Emperor Constantine and his sons corresponded with him and sought his advice. Twice he visited Alexandria: once during the persecution of Maximin, when he went to give courage to the sufferers, and to seek, if it should be God's will, the crown of martyrdom for himself; but the heathen, moved, no doubt, by superstitious fear, did not venture to molest him. When he returned to the desert he sought out a remoter solitude and dwelt in a cave in the side of a lofty mountain, with a spring of water near, and a few palm-trees fed by its waters, and a little patch of fertile land, which he cultivated, and reaped enough corn and vegetables to supply his own wants and to furnish refreshment to his visitors. His second visit to the city was during the Arian controversy, in which he and his disciples were steady and influential supporters of the orthodox belief.

A notable feature in the life of Antony, to be found also in the lives of many others of the solitaries, is his believing himself to be assailed by temptations in visible shapes—demons trying to disturb his meditations by noises and antics, or in the form of beautiful women trying to seduce him into lustful desires, or Satan in person trying to tempt him to despair. Jerome describes his own similar experiences in striking language. The reader will call to mind that Luther, in the solitude of the Wartzburg, had visions of the same kind. It would seem as if a condition of mind was induced by solitude, fasting, and meditation, in which the subjects of intense and long-continued thought assumed the vividness of reality. He died in 356, at the age of 105 (a few days before Athanasius sought refuge from the violence of the Prefect of Egypt among the solitaries), and charged his disciples to bury him in secret, to avoid the honours which would have been paid to his body.

PACHOMIUS modified the ascetic life by gathering together a number of religious persons into one of the islands of the Nile called Tabenne, where they lived together under a rule of life which he laid down for them. Their dress was, after the fashion of the country, a long linen tunic with a woollen girdle, a black frock, and over it a sheepskin cloak. They usually went barefooted. Their food was bread and water, herbs and vegetables, oil, and a little fruit. Each had his own little cell, furnished with a mat of palm leaves for a bed, and a bundle of papyrus reeds served for a pillow by night and seat by day. A group of such cells was called a Laura. Every morning early, and every evening, the boats which glided down the river heard the sound of the horn which summoned the brethren to the worship of God. The service consisted chiefly of the chanting of psalms, twelve at each service; at the close of each psalm the whole assembly prostrated themselves in adoration. On certain days lessons from the Scriptures were read.

The institution, both of solitaries and of monks living in community, spread rapidly. The rocky hills which on each side border the long narrow green Nile valley, and divide it from the enclosing deserts, were peopled with hermits. Ammon established a great colony of them in the hilly desert called Nitria. Macarius founded another in the vast solitude of Scetis. Tabenne was a town entirely peopled by monks. In the fifth century the monks were said to be as numerous as all the rest of the population of Egypt. But as asceticism grew into an institution—it is the inevitable fate of ascetic institutions—the character of its professors deteriorated. Men of the lowest class sought the Laura as an escape from poverty and toil. Some carried their mortification to fanatical excesses—wore iron chains, lived half naked, and fed on grass; some fell into excesses of spiritual pride, accounted themselves already saints, no longer needing prayer or sacraments. Some even made the monk's black gown a cloak for religious vagabondage and secret sensuality. They played an important part in the religious history of Egypt. In the frequent religious disturbances of Alexandria, some hundreds of fanatical Nitrian monks would flock into the city, and, unarmed as they were, their fierce enthusiasm and contempt of death made them formidable not only to the townspeople, but even to the troops who were called out to restore order.

From Egypt the fashion spread to other lands. HILARION introduced it into Syria. We have his life written by St. Jerome. Born of heathen parents at a village near Gaza, he was sent by his parents for education to Alexandria; there he learnt not only rhetoric and philosophy, but Christianity also, and lived a well-conducted life. Hearing of Antony, though a mere boy he left Alexandria and went to him, and stayed two months, a dil'gent listener and close observer. Disliking the concourse of people who visited Antony and disturbed the solitude of the place, he returned with some monks to his own country, being then only fifteen years old; he found his parents dead, and abandoning his home he assumed the linen tunic, black gown, and coat of skin, and took up his abode in the desert near Gaza, in a desolate place, between a marsh on one side and the sea on the other. Here he first made himself a little cabin, woven of rush and sedge, for shelter; after four years he built himself a little hut, four feet wide by five feet high, and a little longer than his own length. Here he learned the Scriptures by heart; had his visions and temptations like other solitaries; was said to work miracles; gradually became known; and people flocked to him from Syria on one side and Egypt on the other. Others followed his example; and solitaries and monks multiplied in Syria. Mar Saba, founded by Sabas, half-way between Jerusalem and the Dead Sea in the valley of the Kidron, is the oldest monastery in Palestine. All round for miles and miles the hills are honeycombed with rocky chambers, the deserted dwellings of the thousands of monks who peopled this part of the wilderness. Two, three, sometimes four stories of cells pierce the sides of the valleys, overhang the precipices, or bury themselves below the level of the ground. Some of the monastic buildings still stand—the domed church, the libraries, the hospice—and twenty or thirty monks still inhabit it. The mountain of Quarantania, behind Jericho, which was believed to be the scene of our Lord's temptation, is also honeycombed from top to bottom with the cells of hermits; they still contain many frescoes and inscriptions dating back to the fourth and fifth centuries. Another colony peopled the wilderness adjoining the Red Sea, others the mountains of Sinai.

The spirit of Hilarion was grieved by the multitudes who came to consult him; he had fled from the world, and the world had found him out and come to him. So he left his cell, and travelled to the desert where Antony had dwelt; and two ancient solitaries, who had dwelt near him and had buried him in a secret place as he desired, showed Hilarion his cell, and took him to his grave, and told him stories of his life; and Hilarion took up his abode with two monks in that neighbourhood. But in a little while the world found out his retreat, and crowds again began to invade his solitude; to escape them he embarked on the Nile, sailed down to Alexandria, and thence up to the other oasis. But there also his fame followed him, and once more he fled in search of solitude. He went down to the sea-coast with one companion, and, finding a vessel sailing to Sicily, he went on board. He offered to pay his passage with his book of the Gospels, his only possession besides his black gown and his sheepskin cloak; the captain, however, would not receive payment, but gave him his passage for the love of God. In Sicily again he could not be hid; his ascetic virtues and his miracles betrayed him, and he fled to Cyprus, where, in the course of a two-years' stay, he had again attracted the notice which he shunned, and meditated a last flight, when, at his companion's suggestion, he moved into the solitary interior of the island, where he stayed five years, and died at the age of eighty.

BASIL of Cappadocia introduced the monkish life into Asia Minor. He was born about the year 329, of noble and Christian parents, and was sent for education, first to Cæsarea, the principal place of his native province, and then to Athens, where his brother Gregory, afterwards Bishop of Nyssa, Gregory, afterwards Bishop of Nazianzum, and the young prince Julian (the Apostate), the nephew of Constantine, were among his fellow-students. Basil and his friend Gregory both determined to renounce their prospects of secular eminence, and to embrace a religious life. Basil was baptized after leaving Athens, travelled in Egypt and elsewhere, returned to his country, and was ordained as one of the clergy of Cæsarea. Then he withdrew for five years into Pontus, and founded monastic establishments. Mr. Kingsley gives us a picturesque sketch of him at this period: "On the south side of the Black Sea, at the mouth of the river Iris, beside a roaring waterfall surrounded by deep glens and dark forests, with distant glimpses of a stormy sea, lived as a hermit, on bread and water, a graceful young gentleman, handsome, a scholar, heir to great estates; the glens and forests around were all his own. On the other side of the torrent his mother and his sister, a maiden of wondrous beauty, also lived as hermits, with their female slaves, and other women who had joined them." But the community life was Basil's ideal of the ascetic life: "God," he said, "has made us, even like the bodily members, to need one another's help. For what discipline of humility, of pity, and of patience can there be if there be no one towards whom these can be practised? Whose feet wilt thou wash, whom wilt thou serve, how canst thou be last of all, if thou art alone?"

Basil's rule continues to be the rule of the monks of the Eastern Church. But Basil himself returned to the city, was ordained a presbyter of the Church of Cæsarea, and on the death of Eusebius (the Church historian) in 370 or 371 was elected to the see; he enjoyed the confidence of Athanasius, and on the death of that great prelate became the leader of the orthodox of the East.

JEROME introduced the ascetic profession into the Western Church. Jerome was born at Strido, near Aquileia, and was probably of Dalmatian race; he was brought up a Catholic Christian, educated at Aquileia, and sent at seventeen years of age to complete his education in Rome. There, besides going through his courses of rhetoric and dialectics, he tells us that he fell into some of the sins which beset the students of those days, as of these. At the age of twenty he was baptized, and soon after returned home. About that time the Syrian Evagrius visited Aquileia. His description of Syrian monasticism fired the imaginations of the young men, and Jerome and some others set out for the East. Passing through Cæsarea he visited Basil. At length he adopted the solitary life in the desert of Chalcis, where he spent three years. He writes of the solitary life to his friend Heliodorus thus: "O desert, blooming with the flowers of God! O wilderness, in which are found the stones of the city of the great King! O solitude, familiar haunt of God Himself! Brother, brother, what dost thou among secular men, thou who art greater than all this world? How long shall the weight of a roof press upon thy head? How long dost thou hold thyself a prisoner in the smoke of cities? What dost thou fear? Poverty? But Christ calls the poor blessed. Labour? But no one that striveth is crowned without hard work. Dost thou dread to lay thy fasting body on the bare ground? But thy Lord lieth beside thee. Does the infinite vastness of the wilderness frighten thee? Walk in spirit through the land of Paradise, with thy thoughts up in heaven, and thou shalt never heed the desert." He had the usual visions and temptations of the solitary seeker after perfection.

After three years, his health suffering from his austerities, and being plagued by the neighbouring solitaries, he returned to Antioch. Thence he went to Constantinople, where he listened with delight to the preaching of Gregory Nazianzen. Thence he accompanied Epiphanius and Paulinus of Antioch to the synod held at Rome in 381, under Bishop Damasus. Jerome was appointed secretary to the council, and when it was ended the Pope appointed him to the important and confidential position of his own secretary. He was the foremost priest in Rome, and many regarded him as the probable successor to the see. Jerome had retained all his admiration of the ascetic life, and preached it so effectually in Rome that a group of noble Roman ladies embraced it, and put themselves under his direction :—Albina and her daughter, the learned Marcella; Asella, another patrician dame; the wealthy widow Paula and her three daughters, Blessilla, Paulina, and Eustochium. The Pope died in 385, and Jerome left Rome and returned to Antioch; Paula and Eustochium followed him, and together they made a pilgrimage to Jerusalem, thence to Egypt, penetrated Nitria, and witnessed the monastic life there, tarried at Alexandria and listened to Didymus the Bishop, and so back to Jerusalem. Finally they settled at Bethlehem, where Jerome spent the remaining thirty-one or thirty-two years of his life. The Church of the Nativity, built by Constantine, protected the grotto in which tradition said our Lord was born. Paula and Eustochium describe it in a letter to their friend Marcella : " How shall we tell you of Christ's own little city, of Mary's guest chamber, of our Saviour's grotto? These are our own, and our hearts would fain speak their praises; but the crib and the weeping infant are better praised in silence than by weak words. No broad pictures here, no gilded ceilings, no apparelling and furniture that slaves and convicts have painfully toiled over, no palaces that a man builds with his money to enable his vile body to step on a precious pavement, and to give his eyes the privilege to look up to his own roof-tree instead of to God's beautiful heavens. So in this little hole of the earth the Maker of men was born. Come out of Babylon, and let each one save his soul; so speaks the Scripture. At Rome you have a holy church, you have the trophies of the apostles and the martyrs, you have paganism crushed at your feet, and the Christian name daily growing into greater majesty; but you have ambition, pomp, a huge city, noise, vanity, and pride. Come to Bethlehem, come to Christ's little city, and see our rural solitude, and share our silence that nothing but the chanted psalm ever breaks; where the tiller of the soil sings 'Alleluia' as he guides his plough; where the hot reaper at his rest in the noontide, and the vine-dresser busy with his curved knife among the vines, refresh themselves with verses from the songs of David."

Paula built two monasteries at Bethlehem, one for men, the other for women. Jerome sold his little patrimony and contributed it towards the cost. Jerome lived in a little cell in the limestone rock near the Grotto of the Nativity, and there he carried on a large correspondence, wrote treatises, took a part in the theological controversies of his time; but especially there he studied Hebrew, and accomplished his great work, a new Latin translation of the whole of the Old and New Testaments from the original languages, which, under the name of the Vulgate version, continued to be the authorised version of the whole Western Church till the sixteenth century, and still continues to be that of the Roman communion. He was a man of great learning and vigorous mind, irascible, contentious, intemperate in language, but a sincere Christian and a great man.

ST. MARTIN OF TOURS introduced the monastic institution into Gaul about the year 360 A.D. A man of noble birth, and a soldier of the empire, he abandoned the world and lived as a monk in the island of Gallinaria. Thence he was led to undertake the preaching of the Gospel in Gaul, great part of which province was still heathen. He gained converts, destroyed the temples and statues, erected churches, founded monasteries at Poitiers and Tours, and by his evangelical labours earned the title of the Apostle oi Gaul. He still retained his preference for the monastic life; and when he was consecrated bishop, fixed his see in his monastery at Tours, and continued to be both abbot and bishop. At his death he was followed to the grave by 2,000 of his monks, and his shrine continued to be the chief place of pilgrimage of the French Church. The Church of Christ was probably first introduced from Gaul into Britain; and the Gallic Church as our nearest neighbour, through whom all foreign influences flowed to us, for many centuries exercised an influence here. The monasteries of Gaul were famous schools of learning, to which students from these islands resorted, and it is probable that from this precedent of the abbot-bishop St. Martin may be derived the fact that most of the sees of the Celtic churches were founded in monasteries, instead of in the great towns, according to the earlier custom of the Christian Church.

The lives of some of these leading ascetics show that the solitaries and monks were not all poor ignorant half-crazed enthusiasts, but men of birth, and wealth, of education, and genius. Indeed, the striking thing in the asceticism of these ages is not so much that there were many ascetics in the Church, but that asceticism had leavened the Church; so that, as we have seen, all the leading men in it of this period had been trained by some years at least of the ascetic life.

It was not only among the men that this spirit of asceticism existed; women embraced it with equal ardour. Besides a number of deaconesses attached to every great church in the East (in Chrysostom's time the Church of Constantinople had 100) and a number of poor widows, the pensioners of its charity, there were also a number of unmarried women and widows who consecrated themselves to perpetual chastity and a life of ascetic devotion, many of them continuing still to live in their own homes. Some letters of Cyprian to the Church virgins of Carthage show us their outward observances and their inner spirit. St. Ambrose, the one great man of his time who had not himself received an ascetic training, yet preached asceticism so persuasively that we read of mothers of Milan forbidding their daughters to attend his preaching, lest they should be induced to take vows of virginity.

## CHAPTER XXV.

**THE DISRUPTION OF THE WESTERN EMPIRE AND CONVER-
SION OF THE BARBARIANS.**

TAKE a line from the Frith of Forth down the east coast of England across to the mouth of the Rhine, strike across Europe to the mouth of the Danube, and right across the Black Sea till it touches the Caspian; then start again from the south-west corner of the Caspian and draw another line to the top of the Gulf of Suez. Everything south-west of these two lines in Europe and Asia was in the Roman Empire. Add, from the continent of Africa, Egypt to the Cataracts of Syene, and the whole fertile strip of country which forms the southern shore of the Mediterranean, and we have before us on the map the whole of the Roman Empire. On the death of Theodosius (A.D. 395) this empire was again divided, according to the Diocletian constitution, between his two youthful sons—ARCADIUS taking the eastern, and HONORIUS the western division. Their accession marks two great eras in history, the final division of the empire—for the two divisions were never brought together again into one hand, and the beginning of the disruption of the empire by the invasion of the barbarians. It was a mighty fabric, which had been gradually consolidated during 400 years. In the space of 100 years more, the western empire had been broken into pieces and ravaged again and again by successive hordes of barbarous tribes, and finally partitioned out into independent sovereignties, which are represented by the modern nations of Europe. In the space of another half-century, the Eastern empire had been stripped of provinces east, west, north, and south, but retained with a diminished territory its imperial city, its constitution, civilisation, and religion, down to the fifteenth century. It is this revolution—the last great reorganisation of the society of the Western world—which we have next to sketch.

The rapidity of this revolution fills us at first with amazement, and it needs a careful consideration of the state of Roman society before we recognise its causes. The population of the cities consisted of the wealthy proprietors whose estates were scattered over the adjoining provinces; their households were very numerous, and consisted of slaves, with two or three freedmen as upper servants. The manufacturing and trading class was small, and the actual handiwork of all the crafts and trades was done by slaves. The rural districts were chiefly divided into great estates, cultivated by slaves under the supervision of the steward of an absent master. The legions for many years past had been recruited chiefly from among the warlike barbarians on the frontiers of the empire. When the barbarians burst upon the empire there was nothing but the legions to oppose to them, and when the legions were weakened by partial engagements, or crushed in some great defeat, there was neither a sturdy peasantry nor a spirited town population out of which to recruit them. The country could offer no resistance to an invader; the slave cultivators would be more likely to effect their escape, or even to join the ranks of the enemy, than to stay his march. The fortified towns might muster enough of soldiers and citizens to man the walls and resist an assault, but they could do little to arrest the progress of the invasion.

In the fourth century some great movement in Eastern

P

Asia impelled the Tartar population, which inhabited the vast central steppes, in a westerly direction. One wave of emigration pushed another before it, until at last the Goths, who touched the eastern border of the Roman empire, unable to resist the pressure behind them, asked leave of the Emperor Valens to cross the boundary of the Danube and take refuge within the empire (A.D. 376). The Roman officers who superintended the immigration computed the Gothic warriors at 200,000 men—the whole people probably numbered a million. Shortly after the Ostrogoths also, in spite of the imperial prohibition, crossed the Danube and sought shelter within the empire. The imperial officers plundered and oppressed the refugees, who sought redress by force of arms. They overran Thrace, defeated the army sent against them in the great battle of Hadrianople, and ravaged the country from the walls of Constantinople to the foot of the Julian Alps. The great Theodosius at length defeated them, and reduced them to obedience. They were permitted to settle as subjects of the empire—the Visigoths in Thrace, the Ostrogoths in Asia Minor—and were required to furnish 40,000 troops for the service of the empire.

On the death of Theodosius (A.D. 395) this Gothic contingent revolted. Alaric, a prince of the nation, had been their commander. In this situation he had frequented the court and entered into its ambitions, and on the accession of Arcadius aspired to the command of the armies of the East. Being disappointed, he raised the standard of revolt. The Goths of the empire and the kindred tribes on the other side the Danube flocked to his camp. He ravaged Greece, invaded Italy, and approached Rome. The Emperor Honorius was compelled to flee from Milan and seek shelter at Ravenna, which lay secure amidst its marshes from any approach by land; and thus Ravenna for 350 years afterwards came to be the capital of the Western empire. But Stilicho, the able minister of Honorius, had by this time collected the scattered garrisons from all quarters, and gave battle at Pollentia, in Liguria, and inflicted a defeat on the invaders.

After three years of peace a vast mixed host of Suevi, Vandals, Burgundians, and Alani, under Radagaisus, burst upon the empire (A.D. 405), and marched unopposed from the northern extremity of Germany almost to the gates of Rome, leaving the emperor shut up in Ravenna, and Stilicho in his camp at Pavia, painfully endeavouring, by enlisting slaves and barbarians, to raise an army to meet them. Florence at length, animated by Ambrose, detained the invaders before its walls till Stilicho was able to act. He did not give battle, but with great strategical skill enclosed the besiegers within intrenchments, and at last reduced them by famine to surrender.

In 408, 409, and 410, Alaric once, twice, and thrice besieged Rome. The first time he accepted a ransom; the second time the city surrendered, and he placed a puppet emperor on the throne, and marched to Ravenna to demand the confirmation of his power. Being refused, he retraced his steps, forced his way into the city, and the world heard with amazement and horror that the eternal city, the mistress of the world, had been given up to sack and plunder by the barbarous Goths.

But Alaric had been so far influenced by the religion which he professed that he bade that life should be spared, and he commanded that the churches of the apostles, with all they might contain, should be inviolate. An incident related by Orosius will illustrate the force of this Christian feeling. A soldier entered the dwelling of an aged Christian virgin in search of plunder, and demanded in courteous terms the surrender of her treasures. The vessels and ornaments of the principal church had been placed under her care. She calmly showed them to the astonished soldier— vessels of gold of great size and beautiful workmanship. "These," she said, "belong to St. Peter; I, a defenceless woman, cannot protect them; my soul is free from sin, if you dare, take them, and answer to God for it." The soldier sent a message to Alaric. He ordered that the virgin and her charge should be safely conducted to the Church of the Apostle. The virgin, and the vessels under her charge, with an escort of troops, wound through the streets, while the people broke out into hymns of thanksgiving at the sight.

But the palaces and temples were plundered of their riches, the spoils of ages of conquest; many of the noblest families were reduced to slavery; many more had fled before the conquerors; and the cities of Africa, Egypt, and even of the East, swarmed with the unfortunate exiles.

Innocent, the bishop, was absent at Ravenna, seeking in vain for aid from the emperor. When he returned he found ancient Rome ruined, and the ancient Roman society dispersed. But though palaces and temples had been emptied, the churches and houses of the people remained. Pagan Rome was destroyed, but Christian Rome rose out of its ruins. Henceforward the bishop was beyond question the greatest man in Rome, and his power continually increased. The imperial prefect represented the distant and waning authority of the emperor, but the bishop was the elect of the people; he had large revenues, and the ecclesiastical organisation easily supplied the machinery of a constituted government.

Alaric ravaged all Italy and Sicily, and was embarking for the conquest of Africa when death arrested his career. Adolph his brother-in-law was elected King of the Goths in his place. He made peace with the emperor, married

Placidia, the emperor's sister, who had fallen into the hands of the Goths, and resumed the attitude of a general of the Roman armies.

Then came the invasion of Spain by the Suevi, Vandals, and Alani, kindred tribes from beyond the Rhine, who, after some alternations of fortune, finally made good their occupation of Spain and Aquitania.

About the same time the Burgundians and Franks obtained settlements in the distracted province of Gaul. But another horde, which had hitherto been pressing forward the Goths and Germans, now reached the empire, which lay like a huge monster in his dying throes at the mercy of all the beasts of prey. The Huns made their appearance in Gaul in A.D. 451, and next year invaded Italy. They were Tartars by race, heathens in religion, savages in manners; travelling on little active horses, with their families in waggons; living in the open air, feeding on flesh only; a nomad race, they did not spare the towns because they did not propose to occupy them, or the vineyards and fruit-trees because they did not intend to cultivate them; and calmly slaughtered tens of thousands in cold blood as the natural usage of warfare; they were led by Attila, the sublime savage, with genius, and a consciousness of a Divine mission, calling himself the "Scourge of God." Rome had to care for her own safety. The bishop was looked up to by the whole city as their leader, and Leo was not unequal to the crisis. One of the most wonderful pictures of this wonderful time is that presented by the embassy of Leo, the Bishop of Rome, in the vestments of his office, with a procession of his clergy singing psalms, proceeding to the camp of the Tartar horde pitched a few miles from the gates of Rome. The "Scourge of God" listened to the Bishop of Rome, accepted an immense ransom, and spared the city.

Meantime the Vandals, under their king, Genseric, had established themselves in the African province, A.D. 439 (St. Augustine died (A.D. 431) in his see of Hippo, while the city was besieged by the barbarians); and on the murder of Valentinian III. (A.D. 455) they sailed for the Tiber, and marched on Rome. Again Leo went out to meet the conqueror, and obtained a promise that the city should not be fired nor the captives tortured; but Rome was given up for fourteen days to pillage. In this sack the spoils of the Temple of Jerusalem, brought by Titus to Rome, were carried off to Carthage, with all the valuables of the city and a host of captives.

While these great provinces were one by one torn away, a shadow of the empire still remained, the nominal emperor being usually the puppet of some successful soldier, who wielded the real power behind this purpled representative. We need do no more than mention the succession of names. After Honorius, Valentinian III., A.D. 425; Maximus, A.D. 455; Avitus, A.D. 455; Majorian, 457; Severus, 461; Anthemius, 467; Olybrius, 472; Glycerius and Nepos, 472; ending with Augustulus, 475. This last in a few months resigned his nominal dignity; the senate signified their intention not to elect another emperor, and sent the imperial ensigns and sacred ornaments of the throne and palace to Constantinople. The Western empire was entirely extinct, and Odoacer openly ruled Italy. He, after a vigorous administration of fourteen years, was superseded by Theodoric, King of the Ostrogoths, with whom the modern history of Italy begins.

In the year 410 Honorius had withdrawn the legions and the civil administration from the distant province of Britain, and left its inhabitants to form a government of their own and provide for their own safety. The helpless state of the abandoned province invited the incursions of the piratical people from the opposite coast of Germany. Saxons, Jutes, and Angles came in different expeditions under different leaders, and gradually forcing the Britons back into the western extremities of the island, Cornwall and Wales, and into the north, established eight small independent kingdoms.

Thus the empire of the West was divided among the Franks in Northern Gaul; the Burgundians in the country watered by the Saone and the Rhone; the Visigoths in Spain and Gaul south of the Loire; the Suevi in the north-west corner of the peninsula; the Ostrogoths in Italy and Dalmatia up to the Alps and the Upper Danube; the Vandals in Africa; and the Saxons in Britain.

Of these nations the Goths, we have seen, had long since embraced Christianity, but in its Arian form; the rest of the tribes who permanently settled in the empire had received Christianity during the course of these events which we have related, but received it from the Goths, and therefore were also Arians; all except the Franks, who embraced Catholic Christianity, as we shall relate, and the Saxons, who were and continued heathens for the next two hundred years.

The history of the Frankish conversion is an important event in the history of modern Christendom. Clovis, King of the Franks, had married Clotilda, the niece of the Burgundian king. Clotilda, though brought up in the midst of an Arian court, had imbibed the Catholic faith, and used her influence to induce her husband to embrace her own creed. He allowed his children to be baptized, but for himself retained his ancestral religion. In the crisis of the great battle of Tolbiac, near Cologne, against the invading Alemanni, he invoked the God of Clotilda, and on his subsequent victory acknowledged the God who, he believed, had responded to his call. His subjects were willing to follow the example of their chief; and in the Cathedral of Rheims, together with three thousand of his warlike followers, Clovis was baptized into the Catholic Church (A.D. 496).*

The dominions of Clovis increased. The Catholic bishops were powerful in the cities of Gaul, and were well disposed towards the Catholic king; and Clovis, partly by treaty and partly by force, gradually acquired the whole of Gaul, and established the Catholic religion in it. Burgundy also yielded to the valour of Clovis and his sons.

In 510 the emperor of the East acknowledged the conquests of Clovis by bestowing on him the title of Consul. It added nothing to the power of the conqueror, but this recognition by the representative of the imperial power gave an appearance of legitimacy to his reign, while his acceptance of it gave a pledge of good government to the conquered. Clovis therefore accepted the honour, rode to the Church of St. Martin and thence to the Cathedral at Tours, wearing the purple tunic and mantle and diadem, and scattering a royal donative with his own hands among the people, who hailed him with the titles Cæsar and Augustus. He was at that time the only Catholic sovereign in the world, and the Church added to his honours the title of Eldest Son of the Church, which his successors on the throne of France have ever since retained.

The Goths, as we have said, had adopted the Arian form of Christianity from their teachers in good faith, believing it to be the true form of the religion; and their allies, the Visigoths, the Burgundians, the Gepidæ, and the Vandals, had received Christianity from them in the

---

* These phenomena of a barbarian king converted through the influence of a Christian wife, and of his people consenting to change their religion with him in a mass, are repeated several times over in the history of the conversions of these northern races.

period of their conquests. We know absolutely nothing of the details of their rapid conversion; not a record, not even a legend of it remains. This may probably arise from the fact that they had as yet no historians of their own, and that the Roman historians were not solicitous to gather and record the story of the way in which the barbarians came by their heresy.

When these various tribes had completed their conquests, and came to settle down among the conquered people, they had to deal with the fact that the Catholic clergy and people of the land refused to recognise the religion of their Arian conquerors, or to enter into religious communion with them. Different courses of action were taken in different countries.

In Italy the Ostrogoths retained their own creed, but tolerated the creed and did not molest the clergy of the conquered race. And this condition of things continued till Arianism was extinguished, together with the Gothic monarchy of Italy, by the conquests of Belisarius (A.D. 537) and Narses.

In Africa a fierce and long-continued persecution of the orthodox was carried on by the Vandal conquerors, Genseric and his successors, Hunneric, Gundamund, Thrasimund, with a short interval of toleration under Hilderic, and a renewal of the persecution by Gelimer, extending in the whole over a miserable period of seventy-seven years, terminated at last by the overthrow of the Vandal dominion by Belisarius.

In Spain the Suevi, under Theodoric, returned to the Catholic faith in A.D. 569. The Visigothic portion of the peninsula was brought to orthodoxy by King Recared, who, on succeeding to the throne in A.D. 586, avowed himself a Catholic; and a synod of seventy bishops, held at Toledo in A.D. 589, established the true faith among his people. This synod is very remarkable from the fact that in it the

Nicene Creed was submitted to and adopted by the council, with the addition of the " Filioque," which afterwards became the chief point in dispute between the Eastern and Western divisions of the Church of Christ.*

* Who suggested this interpolation, and under what influences this obscure council of a race just emerging from Arianism took upon itself to alter the venerable Nicene symbol, received through all the churches of the world, is not known. The subsequent history of the clause is briefly this : Charlemagne patronised the addition, and got it formally recognised by a council of the bishops of his dominions, held at Friuli, A.D. 796. Then he tried to induce the Bishop of Rome, Leo III., to adopt it; but the Pope declined to do so, and, on the contrary, had the ancient creed engraved on two plates of silver, and hung up in his Church of St. Peter's, as monuments of the true form of the Catholic Creed. At last, without any formal act of the Church, the alteration was quietly adopted by the Popes. It is said that Pope Benedict VIII., at the suggestion of the Emperor Henry II., first introduced the singing of the Nicene Creed into the service of the mass, and that the form of the creed so introduced contained the " filioque." From Rome it gradually spread all over the Western Church

## CHAPTER XXVI.

THE EASTERN EMPIRE FROM THE DEATH OF THEODOSIUS TO THAT OF JUSTINIAN.

IN the last chapter we saw that on the death of Theodosius the Great (A.D. 395) the empire was divided between his sons—Arcadius taking the Eastern, Honorius the Western portion. We have traced the history of the Western empire, however briefly, through the invasion of the barbarians, and its partition among them into the modern nations of Europe. We now turn to give a glance, equally rapid, at the happier history of the Eastern empire down to the end of the great reign of Justinian.

The reign of the virtuous but weak Arcadius is chiefly interesting to us as the time in which Chrysostom lived. The writings of Claudian, and of Chrysostom himself, give us a vivid and complete picture of the age: the intrigues of the palace, directed by the young and beautiful and faithless Empress Eudoxia, the rapacity and cruelty of the favourite Rufinus, the still more open avarice and vanity of his successor, the aged eunuch Eutropius, the venality and corruption of the state, the luxury and frivolity of society, the worldliness and self-indulgence of the clergy, with the ascetic and eloquent bishop endeavouring in vain to stem the tide of ungodliness.

On the death of Arcadius, at the early age of thirty-one, he left three daughters and a son. PULCHERIA, the eldest, had inherited the talents of her grandfather, the great Theodosius. At the age of sixteen she received the title of Augusta, and began to reign as guardian of her brother, THEODOSIUS II., who was only two years younger than herself, but who appears to have inherited the feebler character of his father. Pulcheria and her two sisters, Arcadia and Marina, publicly took the profession of Church virgins; they formed their female attendants into a religious community, and turned their palace into a monastery; the usual religious exercises were diligently carried on; the princesses expended large sums in building and endowing churches, charitable institutions, and monasteries; yet out of the midst of this religious retirement the imperial nun firmly, wisely, and successfully administered the affairs of the Eastern empire for nearly forty years. The Empress Eudocia, the wife of the younger Theodosius, in her middle age, made a pilgrimage to Jerusalem, and afterwards retired thither, and spent her last sixteen years in devotion, her alms and pious foundations in the Holy Land exceeding even the munificence of the Empress Helena.

Pulcheria, towards the end of her life and reign, had found it prudent to call the military talents of MARCIAN (A.D. 450) to her assistance, and to give him the dignity of a nominal marriage with herself and the imperial title. On his death (A.D. 457) LEO OF THRACE, by favour of the powerful Aspar, the patrician and commander of the troops, was elected by the senate, and received his crown from the hands of the Patriarch of Constantinople, the first example of this symbolical representation of the truth that "the powers that be are ordained of God," and that kings are God's ministers.

On Leo's death his inheritance devolved on his infant grandson (A.D. 474) LEO II., and Zeno, his father, was associated with him in the empire. Leo II. died in his infancy, not without suspicion of foul play. ZENO reigned seventeen years, when his widow gave her hand and the imperial title to ANASTASIUS, an aged officer of the household of high character. On his death JUSTIN, a Dacian peasant, who had risen in the army to the command of the imperial guards, procured by intrigue his election (A.D. 518), and after a reign of nine years was succeeded by his nephew JUSTINIAN (A.D. 527), whose remarkable reign of thirty-seven years demands a longer notice.

The military genius of his great general, Belisarius, widely extended the dominions of Justinian. In a three months' campaign, in the year A.D. 534, he defeated the Vandals, and reconquered Africa, after it had been nearly 100 years severed from the empire. Next, turning his arms against the Ostrogoths, he conquered Sicily and Italy, and entered Rome, where he was welcomed as a deliverer; withstood a siege of Rome; followed the Goths to their last stronghold in Ravenna, which at length surrendered to him (A.D. 539), and all Italy was annexed to the Eastern empire. The civil achievements of the reign were as remarkable as its military conquests. The genius of Tribonian digested the laws of the empire since the time of Hadrian into three great works—the Code, the Pandects, and the Institutes of Justinian—which were established as the system of civil jurisprudence throughout the empire. Justinian encouraged commerce and manufactures; it was in his time that the silkworm was introduced from China into Greece. The empire was filled with magnificent works; the frontiers of the empire were strengthened by chains of fortifications; the provinces subject to inroads of the Scythian horse were furnished with castles and towers of refuge; the great cities were strengthened; Constantinople itself was made impregnable. The empire was adorned with magnificent public buildings. Almost every city obtained the solid advantages of bridges, hospitals, and aqueducts; innumerable churches were built with lavish expenditure. In Constantinople alone and the adjacent suburbs the emperor dedicated twenty-five churches in honour of Christ, the Virgin, and the saints. The greatest of all his works, the Church (now the mosque) of Santa Sophia, still stands, after twelve centuries, a monument of the munificence of the sovereign and the genius of his architects, Anthemius and Isidore. At its dedication the emperor exclaimed, "Glory be to God, who hath thought me worthy to accomplish so great a work!" and then, with an outburst of vanity, added, "I have vanquished thee, O Solomon!" Architecture and art had been in a state of transition ever since the time of Constantine. The palace of Diocletian at Spalatro is one of the great landmarks in the history of architecture, the Church of Sta. Sophia is another. Between the two periods the style which we know as Byzantine had grown into its full development and perfection; and Byzantine art continued to exercise an influence on the art of the world for many subsequent centuries. We must not, however, omit to say that Justinian allowed his subjects to be oppressed by a favourite minister; that the administration was incurably corrupt; that the empire, notwithstanding the victories of Belisarius in the West, was feeble and unwarlike, and that its home provinces were annually insulted and plundered by barbarians, and that the subjects of Justinian groaned under the weight of his taxes.

The latter part of his reign, too, was marked by increasing troubles. For twenty years a feeble but destructive war was waged with Chosroes, King of Persia. Rebellions broke out in Africa, and the successive wars almost depopulated that once fertile province. The Goths revolted in Italy under Totila, and twenty-eight years of war ensued under Belisarius and Narses. Rome was taken and retaken, and its senators ruined and dispersed, before the Gothic power in Italy was finally broken, and Italy once more annexed as a province to the Eastern empire, under an exarch seated at Ravenna.

## CHAPTER XXVII.

### THE SECOND, THIRD, FOURTH, FIFTH, AND SIXTH GENERAL COUNCILS.

WE have already had occasion to see that Theodosius the Great was an earnest orthodox Christian, who with one hand suppressed the paganism which lingered in the empire, and with the other the Arianism which had flourished in the East by the encouragement of his predecessors. He also, at an early period of his reign, took steps to obtain a settlement of several other questions of doctrine and discipline which were disturbing the peace of the Eastern Church.

The first of these was the rival claims of Gregory of Nazianzum and Maximus to the see of Constantinople. Gregory in bygone years had, contrary to his own wishes, been consecrated by his friend, Basil of Cæsarea, Bishop of the city of Lasima; but a dispute arising, he willingly resigned his pretensions to the see, and retiring to his father, who was Bishop of Nazianzum, and old and infirm, acted as what would now be called his coadjutor. After his father's death a vacancy occurred, during the earlier part of which Gregory continued to act as bishop, but at length withdrew to Seleucia, and passed some years in retirement.

On the death of Valens, which seemed to offer a new prospect to the orthodox, Gregory was induced by Basil, and others of their leaders, to go to Constantinople and endeavour to rally the orthodox and to uphold the true faith there. He commenced his work in the house of a friend, where his little church was called the Anastasia, the place of the resurrection of the true faith; it was afterwards enlarged into a splendid church. At first he encountered much opposition. The dominant Arians declared his views to be polytheistic; he was repeatedly assaulted by the populace; he was even stoned by the Arian monks and virgins; he was carried before the magistrates as a disturber of the peace. He met with opposition even from his own friends. One Maximus, an Egyptian, who had been in Gregory's confidence, allowed himself to be set up in opposition to Gregory. Some Egyptian bishops, who were at Constantinople acting under the direction of Peter of Alexandria, got access by night to the metropolitan church of Constantinople, and there consecrated and enthroned Maximus as its bishop.

When Theodosius arrived at Constantinople in 380 he summoned the Arian bishop, Demophilus, before him, and on his refusing to subscribe the Nicene Creed he ejected him and all the Arian clergy from the churches, and a few days afterwards formally put Gregory into possession of the principal church of the capital.

The other questions which needed the decisions of a council were the Macedonian and Apollinarian heresies. The Apollinarian heresy had sprung up in the latter part of the life of Athanasius out of the discussion of the nature of Christ. Apollinarius, Bishop of Laodicea, taking the Platonic analysis of man's being into body, animal soul, and rational soul, started the theory that the Son of God, in taking man's nature, took only the body and animal soul, and that the Divine Person supplied the place of the rational soul. Finding that his theory was not received, he formed a sect, setting up rival bishops at Antioch and elsewhere. The heresy known by the name of the Macedonian was also a remnant of the Arian heresy. Some of that party who had come to acknowledge the Godhead of the Son, continued to deny the personality and co-equal Godhead of the Holy Spirit.

The Second General Council, summoned by Theodosius at Constantinople to settle these questions, met May 2, 381. It was attended by one hundred and fifty orthodox prelates, entirely from the Eastern Church, among them being Meletius of Antioch, Gregory of Nyssa (whose brother, the great Basil, had died the previous year), and Cyril of Jerusalem; there were also thirty-six bishops of the Macedonian party.

The earlier sessions of the council were presided over by Meletius, and the first matter which engaged its attention was the pretensions of Maximus to the see of Constantinople. The council decided in favour of Gregory, and he was solemnly enthroned as Bishop of Constantinople. Meletius died while the council was still in session, and Gregory assumed the president's seat. Timothy, Bishop of Alexandria, who had just succeeded his brother Peter, then arrived with a train of Egyptian bishops, and was greatly offended that the council had been begun without him, and dissatisfied with its confirmation of Gregory to the throne of Constantinople. He revived the pretensions of Maximus, and argued against the appointment of Gregory, on the ground that he had been consecrated Bishop of Lasima and acted as Bishop of Nazianzum, and that the Nicene canon forbade translations. Gregory, with his usual spirit of self-denial, resigned the see; but Maximus was not accepted as his successor. A list of those who were considered eligible was presented to the emperor; among the names was that of Nectarius, an aged man of senatorial rank and excellent character, but who, after the bad custom of the time, was as yet only a catechumen. His, however, was the name selected by the emperor, and

Nectarius was at once baptized, and a few days after, being consecrated bishop, took his seat as president of the council, wearing the episcopal robes over his white baptismal dress.

The Apollinarian heresy was condemned; its founder, however, retained his bishopric till his death, some ten years after, and his peculiar tenets did not long survive him.

In dealing with the Macedonian heresy the council revised the Nicene Creed. First it seems to have added several clauses * to the statement of doctrine about the second person of the Trinity; and then it added all the clauses which follow "I believe in the Holy Ghost."

What, perhaps, throws light upon the dealing of this council with the creed is the fact that Epiphanius in his "Anchorate," written some time before this council, says that every catechumen repeated at his baptism, from the time of the General Council of Nicæa to the tenth year of Valentinian and Valens (A.D. 373), a creed in the following words—and he recites the Niceno-Constantinopolitan Creed almost exactly as we now have it. "We must infer, then, either that a larger as well as a shorter creed was put forth at Nicæa, such as Epiphanius has recorded; or that such a longer form had existed of old time, and that the council only specified those parts which bore particularly on the controversy of the day; or, lastly, that shortly after the Council of Nicæa the Nicene fathers, or some of them, or others who had high authority, enlarged and amplified the Nicene symbol, and that this enlarged form obtained extensively in the Church." †

---

* "Begotten of the Father before all worlds." "By the Holy Ghost of the Virgin Mary." "Was crucified also for us under Pontius Pilate." "Sitteth on the right hand of the Father." "Whose kingdom shall have no end."

† Bishop Harold Browne, Thirty-nine Articles, i. 296. See note P. in the *Library of the Fathers* Edition of *Tertullian*.

The creed thus enlarged was accepted by the whole Church everywhere, and formed the great symbol of the Church's unity of doctrine. The subsequent addition of the clause "filioque" has already been incidentally mentioned (page 218). That addition, accepted in the West and rejected in the East, is the basis of the division between the two great branches of the Church. The third canon of this council relates to the ecclesiastical rank of the Patriarchs of Constantinople, but it throws light on the views which were then entertained as to the primacy of the Roman see, and will hereafter be seen to be of great importance. The canon gives to the Bishop of Constantinople precedence among bishops next after the Bishop of Rome, and assigns as the reason, "forasmuch as it is a new Rome," implying that the Bishop of Rome obtained his precedency because of the political grandeur of his see in the ancient capital of the Christian world.

The events which led to the THIRD GENERAL COUNCIL, held by the Emperor Theodosius at Ephesus in A.D. 434, were as follows.

On the deposition and banishment of Chrysostom the see of Constantinople was filled by Arsacius, a man of eighty, brother to the former bishop, Nectarius. He having feebly held the see for a year, was succeeded by Atticus (A.D. 406). After Atticus came Sisinnius. On his death Nestorius, a presbyter of Antioch, was appointed. He had been a monk, was of blameless life, had some reputation for learning and eloquence, but is charged with vanity and love of popularity.

He signalised the beginning of his episcopate by severe measures against the Arian, Novatian, Macedonian, and other separatist bodies in the capital.

He himself, however, soon fell under suspicion of unsound doctrine. A presbyter who had accompanied Nestorius from Antioch, and was much in his confidence, preached a sermon, in which he attacked the use of the title *Theotokos*, as applied to the Virgin Mary. The word had been used by Athanasius, the two Gregories, of Nazianzum and of Nyssa, and other great orthodox fathers of the Church. It did not mean that the Virgin-mother communicated the Divine nature to the Saviour, but it expressed the truth that the conjunction of the Godhead with the humanity took place simultaneously with the miraculous conception of the humanity. Nestorius, in a series of sermons, supported the view of his presbyter. He was understood to teach that a man was born of the Virgin, and then the Divine Person entered into and united Himself with this man, which would imply that there were two persons in our Lord. The question roused a great excitement throughout the city. The bishop was frequently interrupted in his sermons by expressions of dissent from his excited audience. On the other hand, when a distinguished presbyter preached in Nestorius' presence in defence of the title Theotokos, Nestorius rose and objected to his doctrine as being a confusion of the two natures into one mixed nature. The clergy and the monks were against the bishop, the court supported him, and the majority of the people at first were in his favour.

Then Cyril, the Patriarch of Alexandria, took up the question. His uncle Theophilus had succeeded to the see of Alexandria very soon after the death of Athanasius, a strong-willed, hot-tempered, turbulent, unscrupulous prelate, who harassed the heathen and persecuted the heretics of his own province, and thrust himself into the affairs of Constantinople, and was the leader of the opposition to Chrysostom. After twenty-seven years' rule over the Alexandrian Church he was succeeded by his nephew. Cyril had, like so many of the eminent Churchmen of the period, spent some years of his early life in ascetic discipline among the Nitrian monks. He was the true nephew of Theophilus, strong-willed, eloquent, ambitious. By help of his army of Parabolani,* and his allies the fanatical Nitrian monks, and his wealth and popularity, he exercised a degree of power and authority in the great city of Alexandria such as no Churchman before him had wielded. On one occasion, the prefect failing to restrain outrages of the Jews against the Christians, he plundered the Jews' quarter and drove them (numerous as they were) out of the city. On another occasion the monks attacked the prefect himself and nearly killed him. The prefect executed one of the monks who had struck him with a stone; the bishop rescued his body, gave him sumptuous burial, and canonised him. Cyril had accompanied his uncle to Constantinople on the occasion of the Council of the Oak, when Chrysostom was deposed. And his action against Nestorius seems to have arisen partly out of the jealousy which Alexandria entertained of the precedence which had been given to the new see of Constantinople.

Cyril denounced the teaching of Nestorius in a pastoral letter to his church, and also entered into an angry correspondence with Nestorius himself. Nestorius threatened to bring Cyril before a council for alleged misdemeanours; Cyril retorted that he should rejoice in the opportunity of bringing Nestorius' heresies before a council. Both parties sought to gain the support of the great Western see. Celestine, the Bishop of Rome, held a synod, which condemned the opinions of Nestorius, and threatened him with deposition and excommunication. Cyril also held a synod, which condemned Nestorius, and he drew up twelve " ana-

* District visitors, first organised by Cyprian on the occasion of the plague mentioned p. 105; in the time of Cyril, a numerous organisation of Church servants, paid by the Bishop, and at his devotion.

themas," in which he stated what he held to be the true faith in opposition to Nestorius' errors, and called upon Nestorius to subscribe to them. The Eastern bishops, headed by the Patriarch of Antioch, and including Theodoret, the greatest theologian of the time, declared, on the other hand, that Cyril's anathemas involved the Apollinarian heresy.

The four great patriarchs were, therefore, divided—those of Rome and Alexandria on one side, those of Constantinople and Antioch on the other. Clearly a THIRD GENERAL COUNCIL, to which all appealed, was needed, and the Emperor Theodosius II. summoned the fathers of the Church to Ephesus, and sent Candidian, one of his chief officials, with a sufficient guard to regulate the proceedings. Nestorius came under the protection of Candidian. Cyril came with fifty bishops and a large train of monks and Alexandrian sailors. Memnon, Bishop of Ephesus, on the side of Cyril, had the support of the local clergy and mob. Celestine of Rome had deputed two bishops and a presbyter to represent him and the whole council of the West. John of Antioch and the Syrian bishops, delayed by local disturbances and by heavy floods, had not arrived. The 200 bishops assembled waited for a fortnight, then they received letters from the Syrian bishops apologising for their delay, and announcing their arrival within a few days. But the council would wait no longer. On the 21st June, 431, the council opened its session. Cyril, by right of the dignity of his see, presided. Nestorius was cited to appear, but refused till the Orientals should arrive. Theodoret and sixty-seven other bishops protested against proceeding to business without them. Candidian, in the name of the emperor, demanded delay. But on the morrow the council proceeded to its work and got through it that day, ending with a sentence of deposition against Nestorius.

On the 27th of June, John of Antioch and the Oriental

bishops arrived. On hearing what had been done they constituted themselves, with twenty-nine others who joined them, into a rival council, and proceeded to consider Cyril's conduct and the "anathemas" which he had put forth. They condemned him of turbulence, and of reviving the Apollinarian heresy, and condemned him and all the bishops who had adhered to him. The representatives of the Western Church did not arrive till all this had taken place. They recognised the Cryillan Council, and at a subsequent session of its members they too subscribed its decree.

Deputations from both councils appeared before the emperor; but in the meantime he had issued an order that Nestorius, agreeably to a request which he had formerly made, should resign his see and retire to his monastery. Maximian was consecrated in his place, and the Church was left to choose between the rival councils.

The history of this third council is not edifying, and we rise from the perusal with little sympathy for either Nestorius or Cyril—with a feeling that, perhaps, the statements of both were one-sided, and that each might have been led by patience and charity to have explained himself to the satisfaction of the other, and so a great and lamentable schism have been spared, which has lasted from that day to this.

The great body of the Church has ultimately accepted the condemnation of the doctrine attributed to Nestorius, and the Council of Ephesus counts as the third of the six general councils. Cyril subsequently gave an explanation of his anathemas, which was accepted as satisfactory, and John of Antioch, and Theodoret, and the rest of the Syrian bishops, accepted the decrees of the council, and the bishops who refused to accept them were persecuted.

The council had not, however, the success which the previous general councils had had in suppressing the errors against which they were directed. The Latins and Greeks generally received the decrees of the council; but the opinions of Nestorius were zealously propagated and widely adopted in the East. The teachers of the famous school of Christian learning which had long existed at Edessa adopted and taught them. The Catholicos, the head of the Church of Persia, avowed the opinions condemned at Ephesus. The Persian king was induced to recognise the Nestorian tenets as those of orthodox Christianity, and to expel from his dominions those who refused to adopt them. Nestorianism was thus confirmed in possession of the Ecclesiastical establishment of Persia, which it retained ever after. A famous school was founded at Nisibis, which became a great centre of missionary enterprise throughout the East, and spread Christianity and learning from the Euphrates to China, from the north of Tartary to Ceylon. The prosperity of this great Church of the further East culminated in the beginning of the 11th century, it may be doubted whether even Pope Innocent III. possessed more spiritual subjects than the Patriarch of the City of the Caliph. The see was moved successively from Ctesiphon to Bagdad, to Mosul, and to Kochanes. The descendants of this Church still exist in the mountains of Koordistan, about Mosul, and in the plain of Oroomiah in Persia.

The FOURTH GENERAL COUNCIL was preceded by a false council, whose history, though painful and disedifying, must be told.

Twenty years had passed since the Council of Ephesus. Dioscorus had succeeded Cyril in the see of Alexandria, Proclus had succeeded Maximian, and Flavian had succeeded Proclus at Constantinople, when Eutyches, abbot of one of the great monasteries of Constantinople, was accused of teaching a doctrine the opposite to that held by Nestorius, viz., that the Godhead and the manhood were not distinct in the person of Christ, but that the two natures were united in a third mixed nature, neither wholly God nor wholly man. Flavian tried to prevent the new dissension, but was obliged to proceed synodically against Eutyches and to condemn him. Eutyches appealed to a general council, and a council was summoned in the same church at Ephesus in which the third general council had been held. Dioscorus of Alexandria attended with a train of Parabolani and monks, Barsumas, a Syrian abbot, with a thousand monks. Leo of Rome, having in vain endeavoured to procure the holding of the council in Italy, excused himself from personal attendance on the ground that the Roman bishops were not accustomed to attend councils beyond the seas (in fact no Pope was present in person at any one of the six general councils), and sent three legates as his representatives, and by them a letter on the subject under discussion, which, under the name of his "Tome," became famous in the history of the controversy. Dioscorus presided. The proceedings were disorderly from the beginning. The orthodoxy of Eutyches was acknowledged and his opponents condemned amid cries of "Drive out, burn, tear, cut asunder, massacre all who hold two natures." At the demand of Dioscorus the imperial commissioners and their guard were called into the assembly, and all present were compelled by threats to sign the decrees, and Flavian suffered personal violence. Theodosius II., under the influence of his minister the eunuch Chrysaphius, confirmed the proceedings, and proceeded against the deposed bishops. Leo, however, disavowed the proceedings of his legates, held a synod at Rome, which declared the proceedings at Ephesus invalid, and gave to the council a name which has adhered to it ever since, the *Concilio latrocinium* (the council of robbers).

Theodosius died a few months afterwards; Chrysaphius

was put to death; and Marcian expressed his willingness to hold another council. Leo again tried to have it held in Italy, but the emperor persisted in summoning it at Chalcedon (A.D. 451), a place on the Asiatic shore of the Dardanelles, forming a suburb of Constantinople. The number of bishops assembled is traditionally said to have been 630, the council itself reckons 520, all from the East, except the two bishops who represented Leo of Rome and the Western Church, and two African bishops. The Roman legates and Anatolius of Constantinople sat as presidents of the clergy, but the real direction of the council was in the hands of the imperial commissioners, nineteen in number, and of the highest rank. The results of the council were: (1) the deposition of Dioscorus, and the restoration of the bishops deposed by the *Concilio latrocinium;* (2) a definition of the orthodox faith against the errors of Eutyches in these words, "That Christ is perfect alike in Godhead and in manhood; very God and very man, of a reasonable soul and human flesh; co-essential with the Father as to His Godhead, and co-essential with us as to His manhood; like to us in all things except sin . . . ; one and the same Christ, Son, Lord, only-begotten, to be acknowledged in two natures, without confusion, change, division, or separation; the difference of natures being in no wise taken away by reason of their union, but rather the properties of each nature being preserved, and concurring into one person and one hypostasis, not as it were divided or separated into two persons, but one and the same Son and only-begotten, God the Word."

Some decrees were also made as to ecclesiastical precedence and jurisdiction. The canon of the second general council had given honorary precedence to Constantinople after Rome, but had not given it any jurisdiction; its patriarchs had, however, claimed certain rights over Thrace, Asia, and Pontus—*e.g.,* that of nominating the metropolitans and bishops. The present council decreed a compromise on the subject, giving Constantinople the right to consecrate the metropolitans only, whose appointment was left to the election of their suffragans. The wording of this canon is important, since it declares still more explicitly than the second council did that the precedence of Rome rested on political grounds. "New Rome," it says, "ought to be magnified in ecclesiastical matters, even like the elder Imperial Rome, as being next to it." The see of Jerusalem had long been subject to the see of Cæsarea, the capital of the province; but Jerusalem, by reason of the vast confluence to it of pilgrims from all countries, had latterly assumed a much higher importance, and the claims of the see of the mother Church of the whole world to a special reverence were specially prominent in the minds of all Christians. The council therefore, on the application of Juvenal, Bishop of Jerusalem, raised his see to the dignity of a patriarchate, and gave it jurisdiction over Palestine, leaving to Cæsarea the honorary title of metropolitan.

Leo's representatives had opposed the canon on the see of Constantinople, and Leo himself when he heard of it challenged its assertion that the precedence of his see arose out of the political importance of his city; he declared the canon annulled by the authority of St. Peter, and threatened to excommunicate Anatolius. The emperor and the Eastern Church, however, held by the acts of the council; Anatolius said some conciliatory things to Leo, which he accepted as satisfactory, and the matter remained as the council had settled it, and its decrees have been accepted as those of a general council by the whole Church ever since.

The results of this fourth general council were very similar to those of the preceding Council of Ephesus. The opinions of Eutyches gradually died out of the Greek Church, but the general doctrine of one nature in Christ, under various modifications of detail, took permanent root and spread and flourished in the East and in Africa. The adherents of these sects were known by the general name of Monophysites (believers in One Nature). Just as the Nestorians had a second founder in Barsumas, so the Monophysite heresy seemed on the brink of extinction, when the genius and eloquence and industry of Jacob Baradæus restored it again to credit and prosperity, and propagated it far and wide beyond the limits of the empire. He died Bishop of Edessa, A.D. 588, leaving his sect in a very flourishing state in Syria, Mesopotamia, Armenia, Egypt, Western Abyssinia, and other countries, in some of which it has continued ever since to be the prevalent form of Christianity.

In Egypt the adherents of Dioscorus established a Monophysite Church, which flourished and still survives in the Coptic Church, the chief representative at the present day of the ancient Christianity of Egypt.

The FIFTH AND SIXTH GENERAL COUNCILS are of less theological importance than their predecessors, forming little more than supplements to the third and fourth; but they are of considerable historical importance in their bearing on the modern pretensions of the Roman see, and it is worth while to give a brief account of them so as to complete the sketch of the general councils of the undivided Church received by the Church of England.

We have seen that the Monophysite opinions were not silenced by the Council of Chalcedon, but prevailed in the eastern provinces of the empire, and were still held by many and influential persons within the patriarchate of Constantinople. The Emperor Anastasius (491—518) was a zealous Monophysite; he appointed Severus, a learned monk who held the same opinions, to the patriarchate of Antioch; and by his vehement action in favour of his co-religionists excited deplorable seditions and tumults in the Church. His successor, Justin I., laboured with equal zeal to restore the Catholic faith. Justinian was also a supporter of the decrees of the council, but Theodora was an avowed Monophysite and protected its professors. She invited Severus, who had been expelled from the see of Antioch, to take up his abode at the capital; she procured the appointment to the see of Constantinople of Anthimus, a secret enemy of the decrees of Chalcedon. Towards the latter part of their reign Justinian was induced, by the boundless influence which Theodora possessed over him, to enter into plans for promoting Christian unity by setting aside the decrees of Chalcedon.

Pope Agapetus, who had been sent by Theodahat, the Gothic King of Italy, on a mission to Constantinople, died there. Vigilius, his archdeacon, who had accompanied him, was urged by Theodora to become a candidate for the papacy, and Justinian promised to support him with influence and money, on condition that he would concur in setting aside the decrees of Chalcedon, and hold communion with the Monophysites. Before he reached Rome, however, an election had been made, and Sylverius consecrated as Pope. Here we have one of those transactions which blacken the page of history. In the following year Belisarius, who was at that time defending Rome from the besieging Goths, sent for Sylverius, accused him of treasonable correspondence with the enemy, and sent him off by sea into exile. Vigilius was then elected in his room, and paid Belisarius two hundred pounds of gold for his interest. Justinian sent Sylverius back to Italy for a fresh investigation of his case, but through the contrivance of Vigilius he was seized and carried off to the island of Palmaria, where he died of hunger.

Now commenced the controversy of the Three Chapters.

Theodore, Bishop of Cæsarea, persuaded Justinian that the opposition of the Monophysites to the Council of Chalcedon was not due so much to dislike of its definition of doctrines, as to its recognition of persons suspected of Nestorianism, such as Theodore of Mopsuestia, the reputed father of Nestorianism, Theodoret, and Ibas. The emperor published an edict (A.D. 544), in which he ordered the works of the above-named writers, known by the name of the three chapters, to be condemned, without prejudice, however, to the authority of the Council of Chalcedon. It was required that this edict should be signed by all bishops. The Eastern bishops in general subscribed, the few who refused were banished; the African bishops—who had learnt to oppose the civil power during the Vandal persecutions—resolutely opposed the edict. Vigilius of Rome was in a difficult position. He was under secret engagements to Theodora to concur in action against the council, but the Western clergy were opposed to the edict, and Vigilius refused to sign it. The emperor summoned him to Constantinople, where he was detained seven years, vacillating from side to side with pitiable weakness. At first he refused to hold communion with Mennas, the Patriarch of Constantinople; then he was persuaded to an agreement with him, and bound himself to the emperor, by a written engagement, to condemn the three chapters. A synod of seventy Western bishops was summoned to Constantinople, but they refused to concur in the condemnation. Vigilius next endeavoured to satisfy both parties by issuing a document, known as his *Judicatum*, in which he condemned the three chapters, but professed at the same time to uphold the Council of Chalcedon. His defection raised a great commotion. An African synod, under Reparatus of Carthage, excommunicated him. The Pope's own deacons who had accompanied him to the capital deserted him, and returned home to agitate the West against him. Vigilius appealed to a general council, and meantime withdrew his *Judicatum*. The emperor then issued a declaration of faith, which he required the Pope and other bishops to sign. He refused, and took sanctuary in a church. A guard was sent to seize him. The Pope laid himself under the altar, and when the soldiers tried to drag him away, laid hold of the pillars which supported the altar; these gave way, and the altar would have fallen upon him if some of the clergy present had not supported it. The spectators broke forth into loud denunciations of the violence, and the officer was shamed into putting an end to the scandal. Vigilius was induced by oaths to leave his sanctuary, but finding himself guarded in his lodging he effected his escape to the suburb of Chalcedon, and took refuge in the Church of the Deipara, the same in which the council had been held exactly a century before.

At length the FIFTH GENERAL COUNCIL met at Constantinople in May, 553. It was attended by 165 Eastern bishops, including all the Eastern patriarchs, but from the West there were only five African bishops. Reparatus had come to Constantinople for the purpose of attending the council, but as it was found that he would oppose the imperial designs he was banished on the charge of a crime against the State, and another was put in his place whose concurrence had been previously secured. Vigilius obstinately refused to attend the council. At last the emperor caused the secret engagements to which Vigilius had subscribed to be laid before the council, and demanded that he should be excluded from the communion of the Church. The council acted as the emperor desired. It confirmed the decrees of the four earlier councils, condemned the three chapters, and declared that they were not countenanced by the Council of Chalcedon. It condemned Theodore of Mopsuestia as a heretic, but spared the memory of Theodoret and Ibas.

Some months later Vigilius made a humiliating submission to the decrees of the council, in which he ascribed his past difference of opinion to the devil. The emperor then gave him leave to return to his see, but he died on his journey, having greatly damaged the prestige of his church. His archdeacon, Pelagius, was by Justinian's influence appointed to the vacant see, and accepted the decrees of the council; but the Western bishops were very slowly brought to concur. The metropolitan of Aquileia and the Istrian bishops remained in separation for a century and a half.

The Monothelite controversy was the last phase of the discussion, which had continued through so many centuries, as to the mode of the union of the Divine and human natures in our Lord Jesus Christ. Sergius, Patriarch of Constantinople, was the author of it. About A.D. 616 he started the notion that there was only one will and one operation in Christ—viz., the Divine will, which used the humanity as the agent of its operations. The Emperor Heraclius, in the course of his Persian wars,* had experienced the ill consequence of the alienation of the Nestorians from the empire, and desired to promote their reconciliation to the Catholic Church. He was led to believe that Sergius' new notion of one will might supply a middle term upon which such a reconciliation might be effected. The doctrine seemed to be undisputed among Catholics, and some of the Nestorians seemed willing to admit it. In the year 626 the emperor consulted Cyrus, the Bishop of Phasis, on the subject, who wrote to consult Sergius; and, convinced by his reply, encouraged the emperor's plan. Cyrus was soon after elevated to the patriarchate of Alexandria, and, acting on the emperor's design, succeeded in reconciling the Monophysite sect of the Theodosians by a compromise, in which it was admitted that our Lord wrought the acts per-

* See next Chapter.

taining both to God and man by one *theandric* (*i.e.*, divinely-human) operation.

Sophronius, a learned monk of Palestine, who was then at Alexandria, opposed the doctrine on which this compromise was based, but was induced by the authority of the two patriarchs to keep silence on the subject. In the following year, however, Sophronius became Patriarch of Jerusalem.[*] Sergius, in anticipation of his re-opening the question, wrote to Honorius of Rome. The Pope replied in a document, which continued for a century one of the main supports of the monothelite opinions. The Church was distracted with this new question. Heraclius thought to settle the controversy after the manner of Justinian, by the issue of an imperial edict called the *Ecthesis*, or Exposition of the Faith. He declared that "one will was to be confessed, agreeably to the doctrine of the holy fathers, forasmuch as the Saviour's manhood never produced any motion contrary to the inclination of His Godhead;" but he forbade a discussion of the question as to one or two operations. The Eastern patriarchate received the Ecthesis, but Honorius was dead, and his successor John IV., with a Roman council, refused it; whereupon Heraclius disowned the authorship, and threw the onus on Sergius. In 648 Constans II. put forth a new formulary called the Type, which was intended to supersede the Ecthesis. It betrayed no inclination to either party, but simply forbade the discussion of the subject and the use of the obnoxious terms on either side, under severe penalties. A Roman council under Martin, known as the first Lateran Council, refused to be silenced by the imperial decree, and declared that there are two natural wills and operations—the Divine and the human—the same one Lord Jesus Christ working our salvation both

[*] It was he who negotiated for the surrender of Jerusalem to the Caliph Omar. See page 253.

as God and as man, and the council anathematised Theodore, and Cyrus, and Sergius, and Pyrrhus, and Paul, and the most impious Ecthesis and the most impious Type, but spared the name of Honorius.

Three years after the Exarch of Ravenna arrived at Rome, and by the imperial orders seized the Pope and sent him off a prisoner to Constantinople, where he was treated with great cruelty, imprisoned six months, and at length banished. Other bishops who refused to receive the Type were similarly persecuted. The Emperor Constantine Pogonatus, the successor of Constans II., desirous of restoring peace to the Church and empire, summoned the SIXTH GENERAL COUNCIL at Constantinople, which lasted from November, 680, to December in the following year. The emperor presided, and the proceedings were conducted with ability, impartiality, and decorum. The result of their consultations was that the monothelite opinions were condemned as destroying the perfection of our Lord's humanity by denying it a will and operation.* In its anathemas the sixth council included the name of Honorius, with those of Sergius, Pyrrhus, and others of the leaders of the monothelite heresy, declaring that "in all things he had followed the opinions of Sergius, and sanctioned his impious doctrines."

The fifth and sixth councils had concerned themselves only with questions of doctrine. A supplementary council was held

---

* That is to say, in the one person of our Lord are united two whole and perfect natures. That He had two whole and perfect natures implies that He had two wills, and that both these wills were operating and active. There is no question about the existence and operation of the Divine will; the question is, 1. Whether there was a human will also; and 2. Whether, if there was a human will, it was not the mere instrument of the Divine will, so that it never operated or acted of itself. But our Lord's human nature would be imperfect without a human will, and the human will is a free will; therefore our Lord's human will wrought (operated) independently—*i.e.*, He had two wills and two operations.

in the same place ten years after to make some necessary canons on questions of discipline, called the Quinisext Council, because it was held to be an appendix to the fifth and sixth. The decrees of the council contain some canons contrary to Roman customs, and in two instances expressly call upon the Roman Church to adopt the new canons. They were signed by the two ordinary representatives of Rome at the capital, and by Basil, Bishop of Gortyna, in Crete, who professed to sign as representing the "whole synod of the Roman Church." In these canons we have one of the earliest open steps towards the breach between the Greek and Latin churches.

## TABLE OF THE FIRST SIX GENERAL COUNCILS.

| DATE. | PLACE WHERE HELD. | EMPEROR UNDER WHOM HELD. | HERESIARCH CONDEMNED. | HERETICAL TENETS CONDEMNED. | REMARKS. |
|---|---|---|---|---|---|
| A.D. 325 | Nicæa | Constantine the Great | Arius (Presbyter of Alexandria) | Denial of the true Deity of Jesus Christ | Hosius (Bishop of Cordova) presided. Athanasius the chief defender of the faith. Homoousion. |
| II. 381 | Constantinople | Theodosius | Macedonius (Bp. of Constantinople) | Denial of the personality and Deity of the Holy Ghost | Meletius of Antioch, Gregory Nazianzen, and Timothy of Alexandria, successively presided. |
| III. 431 | Ephesus | Theodosius II. | Nestorius (Bp. of Constantinople) | That there are two persons in Christ | Cyril of Alexandria presided. Theotokos. |
| IV. 451 | Chalcedon (suburb of Constantinople) | Marcian | Eutyches Abbot in,, and Dioscorus Bp. of, Alexandria | That there is only one nature in Christ | Anatolius (Bishop of Constantinople) and the Envoys of Leo the Great, presided. Called the Monophysite heresy. |
| V. 553 | Constantinople | Justinian | Theodore of Mopsuestia | The "Three Chapters" | The vacillation of Pope Vigilius. |
| VI. 680—1 | Constantinople | Constantine Pogonatus | Sergius of Constantinople, Honorius of Rome | That in Christ there is only one will and one operation | Called the Monothelite heresy. |

## CHAPTER XXVIII.

#### THE EASTERN EMPIRE FROM THE DEATH OF JUSTINIAN TO THE EMPRESS IRENE.

THE great Justinian was succeeded (A.D. 565) by his nephew JUSTIN II. In his reign the Lombards and allied nations under Alboin overran the greater part of Italy, and for the next 200 years that country was unequally divided between the Eastern empire and the Lombard kingdom. The empire retained Ravenna, where the imperial power was represented by an exarch, who exercised a limited sovereignty over the dissevered provinces of Rome and Venice. The Lombard kingdom ruled the rest of Italy, with Pavia for its capital. In this reign also hostilities were recommenced with the Persian monarchy under the great Nushirvan. Justin, incapacitated by disease, resigned the purple, and, looking beyond the imperial house for the man most worthy, from his capacity and virtue, to sustain the state, appointed TIBERIUS (A.D. 574) as his successor. The choice was a happy one. Tiberius Constantine emulated the virtues of the Antonines, and, after an administration of eight years, followed the example which had placed him on the throne by choosing the worthiest for his successor. MAURICE (A.D. 582) justified the choice by a wise and vigorous reign of twenty years. During his reign Gregory the Great was Bishop of Rome. A revolution in Persia drove Chosroes, the grandson of the great Nushirvan, to seek refuge under the power of Rome. Maurice reseated the refugee on his paternal throne; but the diversion of his forces to the East left the West exposed to the Avars, and these ferocious Tartars ravaged Europe from the Danube to the walls of Constantinople, and from the Euxine to the walls of Rome. The cessation of the Persian wars left Maurice at liberty to turn his arms against this barbarian foe. Some considerable but transient successes were obtained, but the emperor's endeavour to revive the power of the empire, by restoring the discipline of the troops, roused a revolt, which replaced the virtuous Maurice by an ignorant and brutal centurion, PHOCAS, who massacred the family of his predecessor and their adherents, and imitated the vices and cruelties of the Caligulas and Domitians of the earlier empire.

HERACLIUS, the exarch of Africa, had refused to recognise the usurping tyrant, and was at length induced, by entreaties from the leading inhabitants of Constantinople, to attempt their deliverance. He committed the enterprise to his son, who sailed with the Egyptian fleet for the Hellespont; the tyrant was seized by his own guards and slain, and Heraclius was unanimously solicited to ascend the vacant throne. His reign was signalised by the conquest of Persia. Chosroes, on the murder of his benefactor Maurice, had declared war against his murderer, and, under this pretext, reopened the long contest between the two monarchies. The incapacity of Phocas and the disaffection of his subjects left the empire helpless before the great king. From the long-disputed boundary of the Euphrates and the Tigris, the Persians extended their conquests over Asia Minor, Syria, Palestine, up to the Thracian Bosphorus, where they established a camp over against Constantinople. Southward they penetrated into Africa, subdued Egypt and the province of Africa. The conqueror ruled his new subjects with an iron sceptre, drained their wealth by tributes, despoiled their temples of their treasures, and during a long reign was the most powerful and magnificent and absolute monarch of the world. In the midst of this power and magnificence he received an epistle from an obscure Arabian named Mohammed, inviting the great king to abandon the ancestral worship of the Persian monarchy, and to acknowledge him as the prophet of God. Chosroes rejected the invitation, and tore the letter with contempt. "It is thus," said Mohammed, when the reception of his message was related to him, "that God will tear the kingdom and reject the supplications of Chosroes."

The Avars, returned from the ravage of Italy, took advantage of the weakness of the empire, and pressed upon it from the north and west, while the Persian arms threatened it from the other side of the narrow strait. The empire was reduced to the walls of Constantinople with the remnant of Greece, Italy, and Africa, and some maritime cities from Tyre to Trebizond on the Asiatic coast. The capital was affected by famine and pestilence, and resistance appeared hopeless. Heraclius was about to abandon the city and transfer the seat of his government to Carthage, when the clergy and people entreated him to remain.

He now adopted a great resolution. Borrowing the accumulated treasures of the Church, he therewith hired the services of barbarians, mustered the native troops, and equipped a great army. Committing the powers of government to the patriarch and senate, and authorising them even to surrender the city if it should become necessary, he himself, putting off the purple, and clad as a warrior and penitent, embarked with his troops and sailed round to the Issic Gulf, in the north-east angle of the Mediterranean, and, having there organised and drilled his raw levies, he commenced a march which, in the course of three years, carried his victorious army through Cappadocia and the mountains of Armenia into the heart of Persia, up to the outskirts of the capital itself. Meantime the garrison of Constantinople had repulsed a siege of the Avars, and compelled them to retreat. A domestic conspiracy terminated the life of the Persian king. His son and successor gladly concluded a peace with the Romans, and Heraclius returned to his capital the deliverer of the empire. As Heraclius was returning from the Persian war he received at Emesa one of the ambassadors of Mohammed, who invited the princes and nations of the earth to the profession of Islam; and while the emperor was celebrating his triumph at Jerusalem, an obscure town on the confines of Syria was pillaged by the Saracens, who cut in pieces the troops sent to its relief. The robbers were the apostles of Mohammed, who had just emerged from the desert; and in the eight last years of his reign Heraclius lost to the Arabs the same provinces which he had rescued from the Persians.

From the conquests of the Arabs in the reign of Heraclius the limits of the Greek empire become permanently restricted to the city of Constantinople and the corner of Europe in which it is situated, but in those reduced dimensions it continued to exist for another 800 years, until the capture of the city by the Turks, A.D. 1453. The city, however, was the greatest, the most magnificent, the wealthiest, and the most civilised in the whole world; though its territory was small, it was the emporium of a considerable commerce; and the empire, though thus reduced, retained something of the dignity of its ancient greatness, and continued to be the great storehouse of the ancient learning and the ancient arts. The Crusades introduced some of this ancient civilisation of the East into mediæval Europe. The flight of the Greeks before the conquering Turk was the great means of the revival of this ancient learning in modern Europe.

The Heraclian dynasty lasted till A.D. 711, and then after a short interval of six years, in which three usurpers succeeded one another, it was followed by the Isaurian dynasty, whose founder, LEO THE ISAURIAN (A.D. 726), is known in ecclesiastical history as the Iconoclast. It is possible that the hatred of the Mohammedans for images, and their charge of idolatry against the veneration of images which had grown up in the Church, was one great cause of the rise of a party in the Church itself who were opposed to this veneration.

In the tenth year of Leo, the emperor, who had shared this dislike, felt himself strong enough to oppose the popular opinion, and issued a decree retaining the use of images, but removing them from the altar and sanctuary as objects of adoration; this was followed up by another edict proscribing the existence of religious pictures. Forthwith in all the churches of the East the statues of Christ and the saints were destroyed, and the pictures on the walls obliterated by a coat of plaster.

Under the next emperor, CONSTANTINE COPRONYMUS (A.D. 741), a council of the Eastern Church met, A.D. 754, in the suburbs of Constantinople; attended by 338 bishops, assembled from the emperor's dominions only, which unanimously decreed that all visible symbols of Christ, except the eucharist, were blasphemous or heretical, and ordered their destruction. The people resisted the execution of the decree, and insurrections ensued, which perilled the emperor's throne. The Eastern monks everywhere resisted the innovation, and suffered great indignities and cruelties in consequence. St. John Damascene, the last of the Greek fathers, wrote against it.

LEO IV. (A.D. 775) succeeded Copronymus; and his wife IRENE (A.D. 780), when the death of her husband left her empress-guardian of her infant son, A.D. 780, repealed the decree against images. Another council was convened at Nicæa (A.D. 787), at which the legates of Pope Hadrian and the Eastern patriarchs were present, which decreed that bowing, and an adoration of honour, should be paid to sacred images, but that this external and inferior worship should not be confounded with the true and supreme worship which belongs only to God. This council was recognised by the Latin as well as the Greek churches; but the Franco-German Church in synod at Frankfort, under Charlemagne (as we shall see), took a middle line between the opposing parties, allowing the use of statues and pictures as historical memorials and adornments, but forbidding to them any adoration of any kind. During the five succeeding reigns the strife continued, and at length the final victory was achieved by a second empress-guardian, THEODORA, the widow of THEOPHILUS, who had himself been the most cruel of the Iconoclasts.

Gregory II. was Pope when the decrees of Leo the Isaurian were issued; the emperor promised him the royal favour if he complied, and threatened him with degradation and exile as the penalty of disobedience. Gregory admonished the Italians of their danger, and urged them to resistance. Rome, Ravenna, Venice, and the cities of the exarchate, at once threw off their allegiance to the distant emperor, and prepared for their self-government and defence.

Rome consummated its final separation from the Eastern empire when Leo III. placed the imperial crown on the head of Charlemagne, and hailed him emperor of the West. Irene was then the empress of the East.

Amidst the dissensions caused by the controversy throughout the East, the Mohammedan power advanced almost unchecked.

## CHAPTER XXIX.

#### THE MOHAMMEDAN CONQUESTS.

MOHAMMED was born at Mecca, in Arabia, in the year A.D. 570. He was of the chief family of the tribe of Koreish, the most illustrious of the Arabian tribes, princes of Mecca, and hereditary guardians of the Caaba, the idol temple and place of pilgrimage of the Arabs. Left an orphan in his infancy, with a very small patrimony, at the age of twenty-five he entered the service of a rich widow, Khadijah, whose affairs he managed, and whom he shortly married, and lived the life of a well-to-do merchant till the age of forty. Then he entered upon his religious career, proclaiming the unity of God, and claiming to be the last and greatest of the prophets of God. First he converted his wife Khadijah, his faithful friend Abubeker, his cousin Ali, and his slave Seid. The circle of his believers very slowly increased; three years were occupied in making fourteen disciples. After seven years his followers were about 100. Warned of the resolve of the principal men of the city to kill him, he fled to Medina in the year A.D. 622. This flight (*Hejira*)\* is taken as the era from which the Mohammedan chronology dates. The people of Medina, among whom he had already some disciples, received him, embraced the faith he proposed, and accepted him as their chief. In 629 Mecca yielded to his arms; the Arabian tribes then flocked to his victorious standard, and by the year 632 all Arabia acknow-

\* It was the year in which Heraclius commenced his great war against the Persians.

ledged him as its king and prophet. On his death in A.D. 632, leaving no son, Omar and Ali, his cousins—the latter married to Fatima, the prophet's favourite daughter—seemed to have the strongest and equal claims to be the heirs of his greatness. Omar decided the contest by proclaiming Abubeker, the father of Ayesha, the prophet's favourite wife after Kadijah's death. After two years Abubeker died, naming Omar as his successor (A.D. 634). In the twelfth year of his reign Omar died by the hand of an assassin, and Othman, who had been Mohammed's secretary, was elected caliph (A.D. 644). After a feeble reign of eleven years, he too fell the victim of a conspiracy, and at length Ali succeeded to the throne (A.D. 660). Moawiyeh (of the house of Ommiyah, the rival branch of the family of the Koreish, and in his early days the fiercest opponent of Mohammed), who governed as the caliph's lieutenant in Damascus, set up a rival claim to the caliphate. A truce and compromise were arranged; the Syrian pretender gained the provinces of Persia, Yemen, and Egypt; Ali fell by the hand of an assassin; Moawiyeh induced the son of Ali to relinquish his pretensions; and finally secured the succession to his own descendants.

The religion of conquest began at a period favourable to its success, in the most degenerate and disorderly period of the Persians, the Romans, and the Barbarians of Europe. It boldly attacked at once the Persian monarchy and the Roman empire; and within a hundred years from the flight from Mecca, the power of the successors of Mohammed extended from India to the Atlantic Ocean, over Persia, Syria, Egypt, Africa, and Spain.

The conquest of Syria began in the year of the false prophet's death, and occupied two years. Damascus was the only city which detained the invaders long before its walls. The imperial troops were concentrated and marched to raise the siege, and were overthrown with great slaughter in the battle of Aiznadin, A.D. 633; and Damascus, after a brave resistance, capitulated. Its fate is an example of that of most of the cities which fell into the power of the Moslem. The majority of the inhabitants accepted the condition of tributary subjects of the caliph; seven of the churches were left to them, the rest were turned into mosques. A part of the people preferred exile, carrying with them their most precious possessions. In this case, after four days allowed for their departure, the fierce Kaled pursued them with a body of horse into the heart of the unconquered territory, massacred them, and returned with their spoils. Aleppo, Antioch, Cæsarea, city after city, submitted in despair.

The invaders marched next against Palestine. Jerusalem made a brave defence, and when it capitulated Sophronius, the patriarch, required that the caliph himself should come and ratify the treaty. Omar, who had succeeded Abubeker, consented, and rode from Medina on a camel which carried not only the sovereign of Arabia, Persia, and Syria, but all his baggage also, which consisted of a bag of corn, another of dates, a wooden dish, and a leathern bottle of water. He pitched his camel-hair tent in the Moslem camp, and received the envoys of Jerusalem seated on the ground. When the capitulation was completed he entered Jerusalem fearlessly, walked about with the patriarch, visiting the places of interest, knelt in worship on the steps of Constantine's Church of the Resurrection, and ordered a mosque (the mosque of Omar, still standing) to be built on the site of Solomon's Temple.

Persia was first attacked in the first year after Mohammed's death, and the Arabs marched victoriously to the Euphrates. Yezdegerd, the grandson of Chosroes, was raised to the throne, to unite the kingdom against its invaders. The royal forces were gathered together at Cadesia, and there in a four days' battle the strength of Persia was broken. A last stand was made among the hills south of Ecbatana, and the Arabs gained there the decisive victory of Navahend. Ctesiphon, the capital, was taken, sacked, and deserted, and a new capital, Cufa (Bagdad), rose upon the Tigris. Yezdegerd fled beyond the frontier, and died in A.D. 651, the last of the long line of the Persian kings.

After the conquest of Palestine, Amrou invaded Egypt; after a thirty days' siege he took Pelusium. This opened the road to Memphis. A seven months' siege and assault captured the fortifications of the bridge across the Nile, and the city surrendered. The native Christians were Monophysites, who, having been oppressed by the orthodox Greeks, were not much averse from a submission to new masters, by which they secured revenge for the past and toleration for the future. A wealthy Egyptian, who held the administration of the province, and who during Heraclius' Persian expedition had aspired to independence, made a treaty with the Arabs, on the condition of toleration, tribute, and submission.

Alexandria fell after a siege of fourteen months; it was twice rescued by the forces of the empire, which found easy access to it from the sea, and was as often retaken by the Arabs, and finally remained in their hands.

A successful campaign of fifteen months in North Africa, in A.D. 647-8, gave Tripoli and its spoils into the hands of the Arabs; but the conquest of North Africa was delayed for twenty years by the internal dissensions of the Saracens, and then its conquest proved more difficult than any which had preceded it. Akbar at length penetrated the length and breadth of the country from the coast to the desert, and from Egypt to the Atlantic Ocean, and conquered alike the Roman inhabitants of the cities and the savage heathen tribes of the interior. The emperor sent the forces of Constantinople to succour the fairest province of the empire, and engaged the assistance of a powerful body of Goths from the King of Spain, and the port and city of Carthage afforded a gate through which the reinforcements entered. The contest was protracted for twenty-four years (A.D. 665— 689), but the Arabs succeeded in establishing themselves permanently over the whole of this once flourishing province. The Church of Cyprian and Augustine maintained a feeble existence for a time, but at length utterly perished. North Africa is the only part of the world in which the Church, once planted and flourishing, has utterly ceased to exist.

Spain was the last of the great Mohammedan conquests. Ceuta, the single spot of Africa which had hitherto resisted the Saracen arms, was held by Count Julian on behalf of his sovereign, Roderick, king of the Goths. The licentious king had dishonoured Count Julian's daughter, and the injured father in revenge not only surrendered Ceuta, but joined the infidels with his forces, and acted as their guide in an invasion of Spain. The contending races met at Xeres; the Goths were defeated and dispersed (A.D. 711). Roderick fled, and was never more seen. The conquerors pressed forward to Toledo, the capital, which capitulated on the usual terms of toleration and tribute, and thence marched without serious opposition to the Pyrenees. Reinforcements crossed over from Africa and completed the subjugation of the country. The mountaineers of the north alone successfully resisted the invaders, and a Gothic and Christian kingdom maintained itself amidst the valleys of the Asturian mountains throughout the Moorish occupation of the Peninsula. The Jews, who were numerous in the Peninsula, aided the invaders, and were rewarded by the toleration of their religion, and the permanent favour of the conquerors, under whom they acquired wealth and dignities. The Moorish monarchy of Spain (the Spaniards called them Moors because they came to them from the opposite coast of

Mauritania) developed the resources of the country, cultivated learning and the arts during the period of their greatest depression in the rest of Europe, and flourished for 700 years.

In the year A.D. 750, the descendants of the house of Abbas, by a successful revolution, replaced the dynasty of the Ommyades upon the throne of Damascus. In the proscription of the Ommyades, a royal youth named Abdalrahman alone escaped destruction and fled from the banks of the Euphrates to the mountains of the Atlas; thence he was invited to Spain by the adherents of his family, who acknowledged him as their sovereign, and thus the dynasty of the Ommyades established a separate caliphate in Spain in opposition to the Abbasides reigning at Bagdad. The example of the Ommyades was imitated by the descendants of Ali, in Africa and Egypt, who established a separate caliphate, having Cairo for its capital, and the vast dominions of the followers of the prophet were thus permanently divided into three rival caliphates, which afterwards suffered further subdivisions.

In 721 the last wave of Mohammedan invasion at length dashed itself to pieces against the power of the Franks. Abdalrahman, Caliph of Cordova, conceived the idea of carrying the Mohammedan arms back in an eastward course, through France and Italy to Constantinople, and subduing all Europe to the faith of the false prophet. Their first attempt, upon that part of the south of France which had long been subject to the Gothic monarchy, was successful. A second effort carried them as far as the banks of the Loire. There at length they were met by Charles Martel and the Franks, routed, and driven back again behind the permanent barrier of the Pyrenees.

The religion of Mohammed was styled *Islam*, a word which implies submission to the will of God. In its first conception it regarded Judaism and Christianity as true but imperfect religions, and the Old and New Testaments as true but corrupted, and Mohammed as the last of the prophets, sent to complete the revelation of God's will. His revelations, collected and preserved in the Koran, were dictated by the prophet from time to time, as occasion required; they contain many striking coincidences with the Old and New Testaments, but many passages also which were derived from Talmudical legends and Apocryphal Gospels. In many respects Mohammedanism resembles the earlier forms of corrupt Christianity, and no doubt it was the large amount of truth which it contained, and the enthusiasm with which its converts embraced that truth, which gave the religion much of its early power. Its tenets were few and simple: the belief in the unity of God, and in the prophetic character of Mohammed; a belief in the providence of God and His predestination of all events which amounted to fatalism; and a belief in the resurrection of men and a future state of rewards and punishments. Its positive duties were also few—prayer, almsgiving, fasting, and the pilgrimage to Mecca once in the life-time. The moral duties and brotherly love were strongly insisted upon. Its principal doctrinal defect is the denial of the divinity and atonement of our Lord, and of the personality and eternity of the Holy Spirit. Its principal moral defect is the permission of polygamy and concubinage, and the facility of divorce. It retained the ancient Arabic rite of circumcision, administered at twelve years of age.

## CHAPTER XXX.

### THE GROWTH OF THE PAPACY.

WITHIN the time embraced in the Acts and the Epistles there was no Church—there were Christians, but no organised Church—in Rome. There is no positive evidence whatever of the time when, or the persons by whom, the Church was founded there. But the tradition that it was founded by the joint action, in some undefined way, of the two apostles St. Peter and St. Paul was so early and so widely current that the best historians accept it as a probable truth. The first names on the roll of Roman bishops—Linus, Anacletus, Clement— are not always given in the same-order; and they and the succeeding names down to the end of the second century are little more than names,[*] whose authentic history is a blank.

The Church, we have seen, adopted in its organisation the political divisions of the empire; this gave a certain pre-eminence to the churches of Rome, Alexandria, and Antioch, the capitals respectively of the European, the African, and the Asiatic divisions of the empire, and among these the primacy of honour was given to Rome, the Church of the imperial city. But this "primacy" of Rome was entirely titular and honorary. It did not entitle the Bishop of Rome to interfere in any other patriarchate than his own. It did not entitle him to exercise any other kind of authority within his own patriarchate than that which each of the other patriarchs might exercise in his. The metropolitan jurisdiction of Rome

---

[*] Linus, Anacletus, Clement, Evaristus, Alexander I., Sixtus I., Telesphorus, Hyginus, Pius I., Anicetus, Soter, Eleutherius, Victor I.

extended over the suburbicarian churches, *i.e.*, the churches in the civil diocese of Rome (viz., the seven provinces of middle and lower Italy, with the islands of Corsica, Sardinia, and Sicily), and was the same which every metropolitan exercised in his own province. Milan was another metropolitan see in Italy whose political prestige, while Gratian, Theodosius, and Valentinian held their court there, and Ambrose was archbishop, overshadowed that of Rome. Aquileia was another metropolitan see of Italy. Ravenna afterwards became a third centre of ecclesiastical government. In the early history of the Church we see each of these provincial churches entirely independent of Rome, and acknowledging nothing but a primacy of honour in the Roman see.

The idea of basing the primacy of Rome upon the alleged primacy of St. Peter among the apostles was an afterthought, and the claim of the Papacy to universal supremacy on this ground is of the weakest. It assumes—(1) That Christ gave to Peter the supremacy over the other apostles. (2) That Peter's see was at Rome. (3) That the supremacy which Christ gave Peter was to descend to his successors in that see.

We reply—(1) That there is no evidence in Holy Scripture or primitive antiquity that Peter possessed any such supremacy; on the contrary, at the Council of Jerusalem James presided, not Peter, and Paul claims to be not a whit behind the chiefest apostles. The three texts which Romanists adduce as Scripture evidence do not bear any such meaning. (*a*) In "Thou art Peter, and on this rock I will build My Church" (Matt. xvi. 18), the rock does not mean Peter, and if it did the text would not prove that Peter was to be universal bishop and supreme ruler of the Church. But the rock does not mean Peter. Of the fathers who have commented on this text, Origen, Chrysostom, Hilary, Augustine, Isidore of Pelusium, Cyril, St. Leo, Gregory the Great, Bede,

Gregory VII., interpret the rock to mean Peter's confession of Christ's deity, or the Person of Christ Himself. (β) "When thou art converted strengthen thy brethren" (John xxi. 17), does not indicate that Peter was the authoritative teacher of the whole Church. No single writer to the end of the seventh century dreamt of such an interpretation; all, without one exception—and there are eighteen of them—explain it simply as a prayer of Christ that Peter might not wholly succumb and lose his faith entirely in his approaching trial. (γ) Our Lord said to Peter, "I will give thee the keys of the kingdom of heaven" (Matt. xvi. 19), but so He said also to all the apostles; so whatever in that phrase Christ gave to St. Peter, He gave it not to him exclusively, but to him in common with the rest. The ancient fathers always speak of the keys of the Church, not the keys of St. Peter (Matt. xviii. 18; John xx. 21-23).

We reply to (2) That though there is so general and early a tradition that the Church of Rome was in some way founded by the joint action of St. Peter and St. Paul, there is no evidence that Peter ever acted as Bishop of Rome; on the contrary, Clement, the second on the list of Roman bishops, is said to have been appointed by St. Paul, and Linus and Anacletus, by St. Peter; but it does not appear that either St. Peter or St. Paul did more than thus exercise their apostolic authority in the appointment of others to the office of bishop there. If St. Peter did act as Bishop of Rome for a time, there is no evidence that he established his see there in any special sense. The other great patriarchates, Alexandria and Antioch, similarly claimed to be sees of St. Peter; and Gregory the Great, in replying to the complimentary letters of the patriarchs of these sees, sent him on his accession to the see of Rome, assumes that all three share the representation of the see of St. Peter. He writes to the Bishop of Alexandria: "Your Holiness has said much to me in your letters concerning the chair of St. Peter, chief of the apostles, declaring that he continues to sit in it himself in the person of his successors .... I have willingly received all that was said, because he who speaks to me concerning Peter's chair is the person who occupies it...." Then quoting the charge given to St. Peter, "Feed My sheep," he goes on: "And thus though the apostles may be many, yet the see of the chief of the apostles (which belongs to me, though it is in three places), prevailed in authority solely by virtue of his [Peter's] chiefship. For it is he which exalted the see on which he condescended to take his rest and finish the present life [*i.e.*, Rome]. It is he who adorned the see to which he sent the evangelist his disciple [*i.e.*, Alexandria]. It is he who established the see in which he sat for seven years, though he was to leave it [*i.e.*, Antioch]. Insomuch, then, as the see over which, by Divine authority three bishops now preside, is one man's [viz., Peter's] and one, whatever good I hear of you I lay to my own account, and if you hear any good of me lay this to the account of your own desert," &c. The compliment is rather an elaborate one, but the meaning is plain. Gregory assumed the truth of the theory, current before his time, that these three great sees attained their dignity not because they were the three great capitals of the empire, but because they were the three sees of St. Peter; and he assumes the other great patriarchs to be his equals in order and dignity; though no doubt he would have been ready to assert on proper occasion that the see of Rome was first in honour of the three.

(3) The third point, that a supremacy over the whole Church was to descend from Peter to his successors in the see of Rome, is a pure assumption, without a tittle of evidence in its favour from Scripture or primitive antiquity. In very early times the churches which had been founded by the apostles themselves were looked up to with considerable and natural respect, as a sort of models of apostolic faith and discipline.

It happened that Rome was the only apostolic see in the Western Church, and thus the reverence paid in the East to Alexandria and Antioch and Ephesus, and other churches, was in the West monopolised by Rome. Appeals on disputed points came naturally to be referred to these churches for solution; thus appeals from all the West were made to Rome. As Rome stretched her pretensions she asserted herself to be *the* apostolic see, and claimed to be a court of final appeal to the whole Church. Fathers had made reference to this respect for apostolic sees, and councils had recognised appeals to them. Rome, in later days, endeavoured to fortify her pretensions by the falsification of these evidences, making them speak of the apostolic see instead of the apostolic sees. Indeed it may as well be said here as elsewhere that the whole edifice of the Papal supremacy is, in the language of one of her own children [Père Gratry], "honeycombed and gangrened with falsehood." False documents are forged, genuine evidences falsified, so that in reading Roman books nothing can be accepted without previous verification.

That the great patriarchates were originally independent of one another we have the evidence of a canon of the Council of Nicæa. In reference to a question of ecclesiastical subordination which the Meletian controversy had raised in Egypt, it says: "Let the ancient custom, which has prevailed in Egypt, Libya, and Pentapolis—that the Bishop of Alexandria should have authority over all these places—be still maintained, since this is the custom also with the Roman bishop. In like manner at Antioch and in the other provinces the churches shall retain their ancient prerogatives"—*i.e.*, Rome, Alexandria, Antioch, and the other patriarchs had each the same autnority over their respective provinces. The origin of the precedence of Rome among the other patriarchates is distinctly stated on the highest possible authority, viz., that of two general councils, Constantinople and Chalcedon, to have been political and not religious; it was because Rome was the capital of the empire, not because Rome was the see of Peter. When the little town of Byzantium was made by Constantine the new capital of the empire, the Church of this "new Rome," which had been subordinate to Heraclia, the capital of Thrace, was raised by the second general council to the honorary dignity of the patriarchate, and precedence was assigned it above Alexandria and Antioch and next after Rome, "forasmuch as it is new Rome." The fourth General Council of Chalcedon, in adding to this honorary patriarchate jurisdiction over Thrace, Pontus, and Asia, said still more explicitly that "the fathers rightly conceded that rank to the episcopate of ancient Rome because Rome was the mistress city." Pope Leo the Great, indeed, was very angry with this assertion, and refused to recognise the canon; but the canon remained unaltered as one of the decrees of a general council universally received by the Church.

The primacy of Rome was based on the fact that Rome was the capital of the empire; to this fact we have the irrefragable testimony of two general councils. And not unnaturally, when the Western empire was destroyed, and Rome had been plundered and ruined by Alaric and Attila, and Constantinople had become the sole seat of the Roman empire, some of the patriarchs of Constantinople seem to have contemplated the assertion of the consequent transfer of the primacy to the see of new Rome. The assumption by the Patriarch John (585—595) of the title of Œcumenical bishop seems to have been suspected of being a step in this direction. And this supposition will explain the energy and temper with which Gregory the Great protested against it. His arguments against the ambitious designs which he attributed to John supply at least an insuperable argument against the usurpations of his successors in the see of Rome. He wrote to the patriarch himself against it, to the other Eastern patriarchs of Alexandria and Antioch, and to the Emperor Maurice. To the patriarchs he said that to allow the title to the Patriarch of Constantinople would be to derogate from their own rights, and would be an injury to the whole order. "Œcumenical bishop," he argued, must mean sole bishop; if, therefore, the Œcumenical bishop should err, the whole Church would fail; and for a patriarch of Constantinople to assume the proud and superstitious name, which was an invention of the first apostate, was alarming, since among the occupants of that see there had been not only heretics, but heresiarchs. The Bishop of Alexandria replied that he had ceased to use the title in addressing John, as Gregory had commanded (*sicut jussistis*), and in his reply addressed Gregory himself as "universal Pope"; whereupon Gregory wrote again, "I beg that you would not speak of 'commanding' since I know who I am and who you are. In dignity you are my brother, in character my father. . . . I pray your most sweet Holiness to address me no more with the proud appellation of 'universal Pope,' since that which is given to another beyond what reason requires is subtracted from yourself. If you style me universal Pope, you deny that you are at all that which you own me to be universally. Away with words which puff up vanity and wound charity." To John himself he writes : "What will you say to Christ (who is, you know, the Head of the universal Church) in the examination of the last judgment? You who endeavour to subject to yourself, under the name 'universal,' all its members? . . . Surely Peter, the first of the apostles, is a member of the holy universal Church. Paul, Andrew, John, what else are they but the heads of particular communities? And yet all are members under one Head; and to comprehend all in one brief expression, the saints before the law, the saints under the law, the saints under grace—all these, making up the body of the Lord, are dispersed among the members of the Church, and no one ever yet wished to be called 'universal.' Let then your Holiness acknowledge how great is your pride who seek to be called by that name by which no one has presumed to be called who was really holy."

The superior position of the Roman see grew out of natural causes. In the first two centuries we hear no claims to any superiority over other churches. The first evidence we have of any application from a foreign Church to Rome for the settlement of any question is in the synodical letter of Siricius in answer to Hunerius, Bishop of Tarragona, A.D. 385. The first attempts of the popes to exercise any authority over foreign churches are in the cases of the Easter controversy, the question of heretical baptism, and the question of the treatment of the lapsed. In the first case, Pope Victor's attempt, at the end of the second century, to enforce the Roman time of celebrating Easter in the churches of Asia Minor was an entire failure. He excommunicated those churches, but the other branches of the Church refused to concur with his sentence; the Asiatic churches disregarded it, Irenæus and other leading men of the time reproved Victor sharply, and, lastly, his excommunication was withdrawn, and the Asiatic churches retained their local custom till the Council of Nicæa decreed a uniformity of usage.

The question of heretical baptism arose in the middle of the third century in the African Church, which in a synod refused to recognise the validity of the baptism of heretics, on the ground that since they themselves were outside the pale of the Church their baptism could not admit any into it. This decision was adopted by an Asiatic synod. Stephen of Rome held the validity of baptism by men who, though heretical, were Christian, and pronounced excommunication against his opponents. He only drew down sharp censures on his unlawful arrogance. Both St. Cyprian, Bishop of Carthage, and St. Firmilian, Bishop of Cæsarea, denied that he had any right to dictate to other bishops and churches, declaring "that in respect of the internal government and particular custom of each diocese (= province) there was no one in the Church of God who could be bishop of bishops, or who could compel them by threats to forsake what they had found established by their predecessors." And again he says: "In which matter we do violence and give the law to no one, inasmuch as every bishop has the free choice of his own will in the administration of the Church, as he will give an account of his acts to the Lord."* The other Eastern churches, who were not directly mixed up in the dispute, quietly retained their own practice of rebaptizing, unmoved by the opinions or the fulminations of the Roman bishop.

In the Arian disputes which disturbed the whole Church for above half a century, and were discussed in more than fifty synods, the Roman see took no steps to settle the dispute by its own authority; and when at length Julius and Liberius (337—366) did take part in the controversy, they both fell into error. Julius declared, with his synod, the orthodoxy of Marcellus of Ancyra, who was an avowed Sabellian. Liberius purchased his return from exile by condemning Athanasius and signing an Arian creed. And this acknowledged apostacy of Liberius sufficed through all the Middle Ages for a proof that popes could fall into heresy like other people.

If we look at the history of the four general councils, which were the great events of the history of the Church

* St. Cyprian, Epp. lxxiii., iv., &c.

for 200 years, we do not see Rome playing any leading part. In the first and most venerable, of Nicæa, Rome was represented by two presbyters on account of the great age of the bishop, but they took no prominent part in the proceedings. In the second council, of Constantinople, the Roman see was not represented at all. The decrees of the council were communicated to Rome, in common with all other churches, and were received by her as by them. In the third council, of Ephesus, the council did not wait for the arrival of the Pope's representatives, who were behind their time, but deliberated and made their decree, and the papal envoys subscribed it at a subsequent sitting. In the fourth council the Pope's envoys took part in the previous " Council of Robbers," and the Pope had to disavow their assent to its proceedings. At the Council of Chalcedon Leo the Great was Pope ; he was one of the early assertors of the claims of the see; and for the first time the Pope took such steps unsuccessfully, as we should have expected him to have taken with success at the previous councils had the papal claims then been acknowledged. First he tried to get the council held in Italy, but the emperor declined; then he claimed that his envoys should preside in his name, and by way of compromise they were allowed to sit with Anatolius, the Bishop of Constantinople, as joint presidents, the emperor's commissioners being the real regulators of the proceedings.

The history of the fifth council is a less happy one for the see. Vigilius thrice contradicted himself on the subject under discussion ("The Three Chapters"), excommunicating first one side and then the other, and a long schism in the West was the consequence. The heresy of Honorius was one of the causes which necessitated the calling of the sixth general council (A.D. 649). He had pronounced in favour of the monothelite heresy and written two letters to the patriarchs of the Eastern Church in its defence, which for half a century were the strongest support of the erroneous opinions. The council, presided over by papal legates, pronounced the monothelite doctrines heretical, and solemnly anathematised Honorius by name as a heretic. In the acts of the council are the following passages: "We have caused to be read the letter of Honorius to Sergius, and have found it altogether alien from the apostolic teaching, the definitions of councils, the doctrine of the eminent holy fathers, and that contrariwise it follows the false teachings of the heretics. We altogether reject them, and abhor them as soul-destroying. . . . And those profane and soul-destroying writings we have caused to be burnt before us for their complete annihilation." The succeeding councils (the seventh and eighth), presided over by popes, and two Roman synods, repeated this condemnation and anathema of Honorius. And the Roman breviary down to its "reformation" in the sixteenth century, on the saint day of Leo II., recited in his honour that he had presided at the sixth council which had anathematised Honorius. And in the oath taken by the popes on their accession to the see, which may be seen in the old "Liber Diurnus," every pope declared Honorius a heretic and anathema.

A century later Pope Adrian approved the second Nicene Council in favour of the adoration of images, but the great council of Frankish and German bishops refused to receive it; and in 824 the bishops assembled in synod at Paris spoke without ceremony of the "absurdities" of Pope Adrian, who, they said, had commanded an heretical worship of images.

Political circumstances favoured the growth of the influence and then of the power of the bishops of Rome. The absence of the emperors and the court from Rome during the time that Christianity was becoming the religion of the mass of the people, and the adherence of the nobles of Rome to the ancient heathenism, left the bishop a conspicuous and influential person. He was the elect of the people; his wealth enabled him to maintain considerable state; his charities gave him extensive influence among the poor; his organisation of church officers gave him agents among all classes. The ruin of the great ancient families by Alaric and Attila left the bishop beyond question the greatest personage in Rome, and one of the greatest in Italy.

But moral circumstances still more efficiently commended the claims of Rome to general reverence and influence. While the other parts of the Church were distracted for centuries with successive heresies, the Western Church, saved by its unspeculative temper, had, on the whole, consistently held to the ancient faith, receiving the new definitions as they were definitively arrived at, without suffering from the contests by which the victories of the faith were won. This gave the Western Church, and the Roman bishop as its representative and mouthpiece to the rest of Christendom, a character for orthodoxy. Again, while the other parts of the Church were distracted by disputes for precedence—Constantinople seeking to establish a kind of primacy in the Eastern empire, and Alexandria opposing it—Rome had no rival in the Western Church, and grew continually more and more pre-eminent. These causes gave to Rome a very great prestige in the eyes of the whole Church; her advice was sought, her arbitration requested, her opinion on controverted questions solicited by both disputants. She welcomed all such references to her authority, and gave to her replies the tone of a judge giving sentence and a sovereign issuing decrees.

In the early part of the sixth century a Roman abbot, Dionysius Exiguus, published a work, in which he had collected the canons of the general and of the more important provincial councils, and to these he added a collection from the decisions (decretals) of the Roman bishops in reply to questions submitted to them, and this work soon obtained authority as a text-book of ecclesiastical law, and it had an important influence in shaping out the papal monarchy in the Western world that he had given so prominent a place to the papal decrees.

In the interval between the conquest of Italy by the Goths and the defeat of the Lombards by Pepin, the progress of the papal power was arrested and the bishops of Rome had a troublous time. Theodoric, while paying every respect to the Catholic clergy, exercised a control over the election and the administration of the bishops of Rome, to which under the later emperors they had not been accustomed. That king sent Pope John and five other bishops and four senators on an embassy to Constantinople (A.D. 525) to demand the same toleration for Arians which he allowed to Catholics. John was received with unbounded reverence at Constantinople, but on his return to Italy the king cast him into prison, where he soon after died. Again, in A.D. 536, King Theodahat obliged Pope Agapetus to go to the eastern capital to try to avert a threatened attack of Justinian. We have already related* how Agapetus died at Constantinople, and Justinian agreed with his archdeacon, Vigilius, who had accompanied him, to support his candidacy for the papacy on Vigilius undertaking, when Pope, to condemn the Council of Chalcedon.

After many variations of fortune, the Italian kingdom of the Goths was at length annihilated by the arms of Belisarius and Narses, and that nation disappears from the page of history.

In the following year, as we have already related,* Belisarius, who was then master of Rome, found Silverius

---
* Page 237.

guilty of correspondence with the enemy and banished him; and Vigilius at length was appointed, paying Belisarius 200 lbs. of gold for his interest. Vigilius hesitating to fulfil his secret engagements with the emperor, was ordered to repair to Constantinople. There he was detained upwards of seven years, trying in vain to steer a safe course through the religious dissensions which agitated the Eastern Church. He suffered from both sides—imprisonment from the emperor, and excommunication from the Catholics—came out of the matter with a ruined reputation, and died on his way back to Rome, having by his conduct greatly lowered the dignity and reputation of his see. These were further weakened by the subsequent schism of Aquileia and the other Italian provinces, which lasted nearly a century and a half. Justinian also established the right of the crown to a confirmation of the papal election, and greatly controlled the action of the popes. He even meditated the elevation of Constantinople to the primacy over the whole Church.

We have already related that in the reign of Justin II. the Lombards, having their seat in Pannonia, subdued the northern part of Italy, making Pavia their capital, and also established in the south the two powerful duchies of Spoleto and Benevento. The rest of Italy was governed by the exarch, deputed by the Greek emperor, and seated at Ravenna. Rome was nominally subject to the exarch of Ravenna, but his real authority in the city varied. There was always an imperial officer, under the title of prefect, to administer criminal justice; the people took an oath of allegiance to the emperor, and upon any irregular election of the bishop, a circumstance by no means unusual, the emperors held themselves entitled to interfere. The popes, as bishops, possessed some measure of temporal authority in the city. But the spirit and institutions of the Romans were republican, and the city appears to have possessed a municipal government by which its internal affairs were conducted.

On the issuing of the decrees of the Emperor Leo the Isaurian against images, the Italians refused to concur, and threw off their allegiance to the emperor. The Lombards took advantage of the opportunity and seized the exarchate of Ravenna. Rome was next assailed, and the Lombard kingdom might have been completed by its conquest, and permanently established in Italy, but that the Pope appealed to the Franks for aid.

The Pope had a weighty claim on the gratitude of the King of the Franks. The race of Clovis had gradually sunk into mere puppet kings, while the power of the state was wielded by an officer called the Mayor of the Palace. This office became elective, and at last hereditary. Pepin Heristal transmitted his authority to his son, Charles Martel, the hero who met the Saracens, flushed with their conquest of Spain and already advanced to the heart of France, and won the great victory (A.D. 732) which saved Europe from subjugation to the followers of Mohammed. Pepin succeeded to his father Charles Martel; and in A.D. 752, in the name and with the consent of the nation of the Franks, a solemn reference was made to the Pope, Zacharias, as to the state of the government. The question was proposed to him whether the royal name and dignity ought not to pass from the degenerate Merovingian race to that race which actually now for three generations had ruled the nation by its wisdom and defended it by its valour. Zacharias gave it as his decision that he who possessed the power should also bear the title of king. The unfortunate Merovingian prince was dismissed into a convent, and Pepin was raised to the throne, the founder of a new and more illustrious dynasty.

The Pope appealed to Pepin for aid against the Lombards.

Stephen II., who had succeeded Zachary, went himself beyond the Alps, and threw himself at the king's feet, humbly imploring his help. Pepin received him with extraordinary respect, prostrated himself in turn before the Pope, and walked by his side, holding his rein as he rode. The Pope returned to Italy, accompanied by Pepin at the head of an army of Franks, who drove the Lombards out of their recent acquisitions and bestowed them upon the Bishop of Rome. Some Byzantine envoys who were present at the conclusion of the treaty urged Pepin to restore the exarchate to the emperor, but Pepin replied that he had fought for St. Peter and not for the emperor, and that he could not take away from the apostle what he had given him. This donation was the beginning of the temporal power of the popes, though for many years to come this temporal dominion was held as a fief of the Frankish crown. The great reign of Charles, the son of Pepin, demands a separate chapter.

## CHAPTER XXXI.

#### THE EMPIRE OF CHARLEMAGNE.

THE genius of Charlemagne united under one head the various nations of central Europe which had risen out of the ruins of the Western empire; brought for the first time under the influence of civilisation and religion the barbarous tribes of Saxony, Bohemia, and Hungary; and during a vigorous and enlightened reign of nearly half a century fostered the growth of civilisation and religion over this vast extent of territory. His empire broke in pieces again after his great mind and strong hand had been withdrawn from it; but it left its impress in the political system of the European family of nations, and in their civil and social institutions, which has lasted to the present day.

Inheriting half the kingdom of Pepin, he seized the other half on the death of his brother Carloman (A.D. 772), and speedily subdued the kingdom of the Lombards. Next he conquered from the Saracens that part of Spain which lies between the Pyrenees and the Ebro. He prevented the danger of fresh irruptions of barbarous tribes upon the settled parts of Europe by his wars against the Saxons, which extended over thirty years before their sturdy independence finally succumbed. His successes against the Sclavonians of Bohemia and the Huns of Pannonia were equally important, and attained at far less cost. So that at length his conquests embraced the whole of Europe, from the Elbe to the Ebro, from the British Channel to the Mediterranean Sea. Two-thirds of the ancient Western Roman empire were subject to him, and his new conquests eastward made the new Western Empire territorially not less extensive than the old.

He had inherited from his father the title of Patrician of Rome, and exercised a real sovereignty over the papal states, and had visited Rome on several occasions. At length at the Christmas festival, in the first year of the ninth century, while Charlemagne was kneeling before the altar of St. Peter's Church, the Pope, Leo III., placed a crown upon his head in the presence of the assembled people, who saluted him with the grand old title of Augustus; and the Pope set the example of doing homage to him as the new Emperor of the West.

But the fame of Charlemagne does not rest merely on his conquests. His love of learning was, perhaps, the strongest trait of his character. He himself in mature age learned the arts of reading and writing, learnt to speak Latin with ease and accuracy, and to read Greek. He drew learned men to his court from Italy and from England, the only two countries of Europe which could then supply them. The greatest of these was our own countryman Alcuin, who had been educated in the cathedral school of York, under Archbishop Egbert, the brother of the Northumbrian king. Charlemagne established two great schools of learning—one at Metz; the other, called the Palatine school, of which Alcuin was the master, accompanied the movements of the court; in it were educated the members of the royal family, and the noble youths who formed part of the royal household; the emperor himself was one of its scholars. He urged his nobles to cultivate letters, required it of his clergy, and ordered that the clergy should open schools everywhere for all classes of the people. He took measures for the organisation of the Church throughout his dominions, gave liberal endowments to the clergy, and took a deep interest in religious questions. Among the conquered Saxons he founded eight bishoprics, whose sees were the first schools, and grew into the first cities of that savage land. Under his direction the ancient Roman law and the legal customs of the Franks were digested into a system of law, known as the Capitularies of Charlemagne. He gave liberal encouragement to commerce and agriculture, and to architecture and the arts.

Two brief sentences will enable us to synchronise the histories of the three great powers of the world at this period. The Emperor Charlemagne carried on a friendly correspondence with Irene, Empress of the East, and there seems to have been some idea of a re-construction of the ancient empire by a marriage between these two sovereigns. The emperor also exchanged compliments and presents with the famous Caliph Haroun al Raschid.

Three important ecclesiastical questions occurred in his reign. The second council of Nicæa established a reconciliation between Rome and Constantinople on the question of images, which had so long disturbed the peace of the Church. Pope Adrian sent a copy of the Acts of the council to Charlemagne, who forwarded them to Alcuin, then in England, and it is said the English bishops joined in requesting Alcuin to write against the council. He wrote a letter on the subject to Charlemagne, and out of this probably grew a treatise, in four books, put forth in the emperor's own name, and known by the title of the Caroline Books. In them the Frankish Church puts forth its objections to that reverence to images which the council had enjoined. It declares the only proper use of images to be for ornament or for historical memorial, and concludes by stating it to be the rule of the Catholic Church that images be allowed, but not worshipped.

A council of the Frank bishops held at Frankfort considered the question of "Adoptionism," which had been raised in Spain, and into which it is not necessary to enter here. It is enough to note it as an illustration of the fact, that the Church under the new Emperor of the West held councils important from the large area of the Church represented at them, and the learning of some of their members, and dealt with the doctrinal questions of the day.

A more important question, however, requires a fuller notice. We have seen (page 218) that at the Council of Toledo, at which King Reccared and the Arian party were reconciled to the Catholic Church, the Nicene Creed was put forth with the addition of the *filioque*. The Frankish Church also, we know not how, had taken up this form of the creed, and Charlemagne was very anxious to have it formally adopted. At a synod held at Aix in 809, complaints were made that Frankish pilgrims at Jerusalem had been accused of heresy for holding the creed with this addition, and had been forcibly ejected from some holy place. The synod approved of the addition, and Charlemagne sent a deputation to Rome to request the Pope to confirm its decision. The Pope (Leo III.), however, while admitting the correctness of the doctrine of the double procession, held it to be wrong to insert it in the Niceno-Constantinopolitan symbol; and as a precaution against its creeping into use in the Roman Church, had the creed in its proper form engraved on two shields of silver, and put up in St. Peter's as a lasting monument.

Charlemagne died in 814, and the European world relapsed into confusion and fell back towards barbarism for seventy years. His son, Louis the Pious, or the Debonair, subdivided the empire into four, intending to reproduce something like the constitution of Diocletian. But the divisions were taken as independent kingdoms; they soon became still further subdivided, and amidst the weakness and confusion of the government the empire was a prey to its foreign enemies. The Norman pirates ravaged the northern coasts of Europe throughout the ninth century, and their incursions only ceased when Charles the Simple (A.D. 918) ceded the province of Neustria to Rollo, the founder of the dukedom of Normandy. The Saracens made themselves masters of Sicily and Sardinia, and in the latter part of the ninth century, harassed the southern coasts of Europe; at the end of the ninth century the Hungarians, pouring in from the east upon Germany, Italy, and the south of France, recalled the memory of Attila by their devastations. These troubles replunged the western countries of Europe into confusion and barbarism.

At length, by the failure of collateral branches, the whole inheritance devolved under Charles the Fat; he was deposed by a diet (A.D. 888), and the governors, the bishops, and the nobles usurped as sovereigns the fragments of the empire which they held as fiefs. The term of seventy-four years from the abdication of Charles the Fat may be considered a vacancy of the empire till the establishment (A.D. 962) of Otho I. He recovered Germany, added to it part of France, conquered Italy, and extended civilisation and Christianity by his conquests among the Scandinavian tribes between the Elbe and the Oder, and in the peninsula of Sleswick and Denmark. On a second visit to Italy, in 961, he was solemnly crowned as emperor, after the title and its prerogatives had been suspended for nearly forty years. From that time the imperial dignity was fixed in the name and nation of Germany; the prince elected in the German Diet acquired also by that title the subject kingdoms of Italy and Rome; but he might not legally assume the titles of emperor and Augustus till he had received the crown from the hands of the Roman pontiff. He was assumed to succeed to all the rights of the Carolingian empire.

About the eleventh century the foreign invaders of Europe had been expelled, or incorporated and converted to Christianity, the nations had recovered peace and order, and the tide of civilisation so long checked began to flow again with a steady and accelerating course. During the whole period from the disruption of the Roman empire the Church in general was gaining in power. In the constitution of the Roman empire the clergy had never formed a part of the State; but the national councils of the new nations gave a constitutional position to the bishops as great landowners, while the superior civilisation of the bishops gave them a legitimate leading influence in those councils. The same facts gave the leading ecclesiastics of each nation a great influence in the private counsels of the king. The religious veneration entertained by these half-civilised men but faithful Christians for the hierarchy greatly increased the influence the clergy derived from their learning and their wealth. The result was that the power of the clergy in the nations of Europe during the ninth and tenth centuries was very great.

The power of the papacy also increased greatly. Rome had still to the rude nations of the north and west the prestige of a great name, and the Bishop of Rome was beyond question the head of the Western Church. The popes only followed the general example in asserting, as far as circumstances permitted, their sovereign independence in their own states. The disputes of other sovereigns, in which they were sometimes invited to arbitrate, and in which they sometimes interfered on the invitation of one side only, gradually gave the opportunity of putting forth the pretensions to crown and uncrown the kings of the earth, which afterwards found their greatest exponents in Gregory VII. and Innocent III.

The work of Dionysius had done a good deal through three centuries to favour the pretensions of the Roman see by publishing the doctrinal letters of the Roman bishops, together with the canons of councils, as authorities on ecclesiastical law. But about the middle of the ninth century a new collection of canons and decretals was issued (by an anonymous writer) under the venerated name of St. Isidore of Seville, which, besides the genuine canons of councils and letters of popes, contained new canons of hitherto unknown councils, above a hundred new letters of popes from the time of the apostles downwards, and a number of other documents. These documents greatly magnify the prerogatives of the bishops, but especially they exalt the authority of the Pope. They represent him as having from the earliest times acted as supreme head, lawgiver, and judge of the Church. Many of the forgeries are clumsy enough, but in an uncritical age they passed without detection, and were accepted as defining the principles of primitive ecclesiastical law and usage. At the time when the forged decretals came to general knowledge, Nicholas I. was pope (858—867)—a pope who exceeded all his predecessors in the audacity of his designs, in which he was favoured by the confusion which ensued on the break-up of the empire of Charlemagne. Nicholas grasped at the new weapon, silenced the doubts expressed by the Frankish bishops with the assurance that all these documents had long been preserved in the Roman archives, and proceeded to act upon the principles thus laid down.

For above two hundred years the Roman see was not in a condition to enforce new and extended claims, and, as we shall see in subsequent chapters, nearly three centuries passed before the seeds thus sown produced their full harvest.

## CHAPTER XXXII.

#### THE DARK AGES OF THE WESTERN CHURCH.

DURING the ninth and tenth centuries the Church was undisturbed by theological controversy; its history is chiefly filled with the tale of simony in the appointments to its benefices, and scandals in the lives of its prelates, and the general decay of religion.

With the growth of population, reduction of wild land under cultivation, and progress of wealth, the revenues of the great European sees had become very great, and, combined with their feudal rights over their own domains, had raised their occupants to the dignity of more or less independent princes. These great positions were often conferred by sovereigns as appanages upon their own relations, or bestowed as rewards of service or gifts of favour, or obtained by intrigues and gifts. The lesser benefices were bestowed on similar principles, and simony was rife throughout the Church. Again, the tendency of the feudal system was to make all offices and tenures hereditary, and this tendency showed itself in the dealings with the temporalities of ecclesiastical benefices. A few actual examples will illustrate these general remarks. In 990 a count of Toulouse sold the see of Cahors. About the same time a viscount of Beziers bequeathed the bishopric of that city and the bishopric of Agde as portions to his daughters. In 925 Herbert, Count of Vermandois, on the death of the archbishop of the great see of Rheims, not without suspicion of poison, compelled the clergy and people to elect his own son

Hugh, a child not yet five years old, and seized upon the temporalities. The election was confirmed by King Rodolph and Pope John X., and the boy prelate was committed to Guy, Bishop of Auxerre, for education, while a coadjutor-bishop administered the see. Seven years after (A.D. 932) Rheims fell into the power of another political party, by whom the claims of Hugh were disregarded, a monk named Artald was nominated archbishop, and invested with the pall by Pope John XI. Both claimants were backed by wealth and power, and the contest for the see continued with various fortunes for thirty years. It was the subject of discussions at provincial councils; and it will illustrate the confusion of the period to mention that, whereas Hugh had been acknowledged by one pope, and Artald by his successor, the rescript of a third pope, Agapetus II., was exhibited at one of these councils, peremptorily ordering the restoration of Hugh, while Artald exhibited to the assembly a letter of the same pope of exactly opposite tenor. The corrupt disposal of ecclesiastical benefices, the consequent intrusion of unfit men into the higher offices of the Church, and the scandal of their worldly lives, are the salient features in the history of the Church of continental Europe throughout this period.

These features are exhibited in the history of the papacy during this period, and unpleasant as are the revelations to be made and hinted at, it is necessary to an appreciation of the argument on the pretensions of the papacy that an outline of the facts should be here stated.

The see of Rome was the greatest ecclesiastical prize open to cupidity and ambition, and throughout the whole period it was contested by rival factions of the Italian nobles.

Formosus was raised to the papacy in 891, and held it for five years, and was a man of learning and probity. His successor was Boniface VI., a man who in youth had been of so scandalous life that he had been degraded from the priesthood. He attained the papal dignity by violence, and held it fifteen days, when he was in turn driven out by Stephen VI., a man of equally worthless character. Stephen having suffered some offence from Formosus in his early youth, now avenged himself by having the dead pope taken out of his tomb, arrayed in his pontifical robes, and formally tried for the offence of having been uncanonically translated from the see of Pontus to that of Rome. He was, of course, found guilty and degraded; then his body was stripped of its robes, the three fingers of the right hand, which had been used in giving benediction, were cut off, and the body was cast into the Tiber. On the death of Stephen (A.D. 897) the next pope, John IX., reversed the sentence, and restored Formosus to his papal dignity. A rapid succession of popes then took place. The marquises of Tuscany and the counts of Tusculum were the most powerful of the senators, and heads of rival factions, and their creatures were promoted to the see as one or other gained the upper hand. Elections, followed within a few months, or weeks, or days, by deaths, excited suspicion as to their cause; in some cases violence or poison appeared without disguise. At length Adalbert, Marquis of Tuscany, in league with a noble and wealthy Roman widow named Theodora, obtained a preponderance of power. Theodora had two daughters—Theodora and Marozia—both, like herself, beautiful, and all three seem to have assumed the licence of the noble men of their time in the unrestrained indulgence of their vices. For upwards of half a century these three women disposed of the Roman see, which they filled with their lovers, their illegitimate children and grandchildren. Sergius III., who was pope from 904 to 911, is described as a monster of rapacity, cruelty, and lust. He lived in open concubinage with Marozia. The next pope, Anastasius III., died in A.D. 913, and was succeeded by John X. Luitprand, the contemporary historian, gives the following account of the cause of his elevation: "In those days Peter, Archbishop of Ravenna, used frequently to send to Rome a deacon of his church named John, to pay his obeisance to his Holiness. As the deacon was a very comely and personable man, Theodora, falling passionately in love with him, engaged him in a criminal intrigue. While they lived thus together the Bishop of Bologna died, and John had interest enough to get himself elected in his room; but the Archbishop of Ravenna dying before he was consecrated, Theodora persuaded him to exchange the see of Bologna for that of Ravenna, and he was accordingly, at her request, ordained archbishop by Pope Lando. Lando himself died soon after, and Theodora exerted all her interest, as she could not live at a distance of 200 miles from her lover, and got him preferred to the pontifical chair. John proved himself a vigorous pope, and probably not subservient to the party which had elevated him. Accordingly some adherents of Guy, Duke of Tuscany, the second husband of Marozia, surprised the pope in the castle of St. Angelo, murdered his brother before his eyes, and put himself to death either by starving or by suffocation."

The illegitimate son of Pope Sergius and Marozia was then elevated to the papal seat under the title of John XI., but he was restricted to the performance of his ecclesiastical functions, while the government was administered by Marozia and Hugh the Great, King of Arles, Marozia's third husband, and afterwards by her son Alberic, who roused the Romans to revolt, expelled his stepfather, and kept his mother and his half-brother, the pope, prisoners in his palace. He seems to have sought to soothe a rising desire of the Romans for their old republican freedom by the creation of consuls and tribunes, but retaining to himself substantial power under the title of "Prince and Senator of all the Romans." He ruled tyrannically in Rome for two-and-twenty years, while the papal chair was filled with a succession of his creatures, whom he held in entire subjection. On the death of Agapetus II., in 956, Octavian, the son of Alberic, a youth of eighteen, who two years before had succeeded to his father's secular power, was advised to strengthen his position by assuming the papacy also. The young prince, however, regarded his episcopal functions as a mere adjunct to his character of prince and soldier, and continued to wear his former dress and live his former life; and no young prince of the time can have led a more dissolute life than Pope John XII. The Emperor Otho, a religious man, scandalised, with all Europe, at the life of the pope, came to Rome; but the pope withdrew from the city. The emperor wrote a letter, stating the charges—sacrilege, perjury, incest, murder—which were brought against him, and calling upon him to answer them. The young prince thereupon assumed the character of pope in the following reply: "John, servant of the servants of God to all bishops. We hear that you want to make another pope. If that is your design, I excommunicate you all in the name of the Almighty, that you may not have it in your power to ordain any other, or even to celebrate mass." A council decreed his deposition, and Leo, chief secretary of the see, a man of good character, was elected in his room by the clergy and people, and the Romans bound themselves by an oath never to choose a pope without the emperor's consent. After the emperor's departure, however, John regained possession of the city, another council deposed Leo, and the Tuscan party revenged themselves by the mutilation of their enemies. Shortly after John was killed in the act of adultery. The people, notwithstanding their oath, and notwithstanding the previous consecration of Leo VIII., proceeded to the election of a new pope in Benedict. But the emperor reappeared before the city and starved it into surrender. At a council Benedict formally surrendered his dignity to Leo and went into exile.

On Leo's death John XIII. was elected, with the emperor's approval (A.D. 965), but within three months was driven from Rome and imprisoned in a fortress in the Campagna by a party which had become very powerful, and which sought to establish a republican form of government in Rome. The emperor again interfered, restored the pope, and punished the heads of the revolt with death, banishment, and mutilation.

We need not enter into the subsequent struggle between the Romans and the emperors, nor follow the history of the succeeding popes, most of whom were respectable, and some of them men of learning and ability, till we come to the year 1033. In that year the Tusculan party, on the death of Pope John XIX., appointed to the popedom a boy of ten or twelve years of age, cousin of the preceding pope, under the title of Benedict IX. This youth soon appeared resolved to emulate the worst of his predecessors. In 1044 the Romans (for the second time) drove the debauched and tyrannical pope out of Rome, and elected John, Bishop of Sabina, in his place, under the name of Sylvester III. Within three months, however, John succeeded in regaining his position in Rome, and then, resolving to rid himself of the restraints and troubles of the papacy, he sold his interest to a priest called John Gratian, who had a great and deserved reputation for austerity of life. But after a short time Benedict grew tired of privacy, and resumed his claim to the see; so that there were three popes at once, each holding possession of one of the three principal churches of Rome

Benedict, supported by the Tusculan party, Sylvester by a rival faction of nobles, while Gratian, who had taken the name of Gregory VI., was supported by the people. Peter, the Archdeacon of Rome, went into Germany to request the interposition of the emperor, Henry III. At Piacenza Gregory met the emperor, and presided at a council. Benedict, having retired to a monastery, was not mentioned in the proceedings of the council; Sylvester was declared to be an intruder, and was deposed and condemned to be shut up in a monastery. Then Gregory was invited to state the circumstances of his own elevation. He explained that he had expended funds entrusted to him for pious purposes in what he considered the pious purpose of rescuing the Roman see from its calamities and disgrace. He was made to see that in the eyes of the council the transaction was simoniacal, and he resigned the papacy on the spot, or, according to other accounts, was deposed by the council. The papacy being thus made vacant, the emperor proceeded to fill it with a pope of his own selection in Clement II. (A.D. 1046).

The papacy of Clement introduces us to a new period of the history of the Church, and a very important one, which will be best commenced in a new chapter.

# CHAPTER XXXIII.

### THE CONVERSION OF THE NORTHERN NATIONS.

WE have seen how in the early times of Christianity the Gospel spread from country to country, and from city to city of the empire. In the third century we saw how the Church was planted in Armenia, Persia, Abyssinia, Britain. Again, in the fifth and sixth centuries, how the Goths, converted to the Arian form of Christianity, became the converters of the kindred nations which partitioned among themselves the fragments of the Western empire, and how the orthodox Franks succeeded the Arian Goths in Gaul and Italy, and Reccared healed the division in the Spanish Church, and Belisarius terminated the long persecution of the African Catholics, together with the sovereignty of the Vandals.

We have now to relate the history of the conversion, in the sixth and following centuries, of those nations which lay outside the area of the empire.

When Honorius withdrew the Roman legions and the imperial administration from the province of Britain, and left it disorganised and defenceless, the barbarous tribes from the opposite coasts of the North Sea—Jutes, Angles, Saxons, tribes addicted to piratical adventure—fell upon the land like wolves on a sick deer. The first adventurers having successfully established themselves, fresh swarms followed. The conquest extended over 100 years. By the end of that time the whole of England, except its western corners, Cornwall and Wales, had been conquered by the heathen barbarians. The civilisation and the Church of the

Roman province had been extinguished except in those last strongholds; and Saxon England was added to that vast extent of Northern Europe—the forests of Germany, the Scandinavian peninsula, and the plains of Russia—in which the Gospel was unknown.

To our own islands our attention is first to be directed. In A.D. 431 the attention of Pope Ce'estine was directed to Ireland, and he dispatched thither Palladius, whom he had previously consecrated as a bishop; but the object of his mission is not quite certain—whether to found a church or to preside over churches already existing. He landed with twelve companions, baptized a few converts, and erected three wooden churches; but his work did not prosper, and he retired to Scotland, intending to return to Rome, but was arrested by the hand of death.

Within a year he was followed by the missionary whose successful labours have given him the title of the Apostle of Ireland. The original name of St. Patrick was Succath. He was born of Christian parents, his father, Calphurnius, being a deacon, and his grandfather, Potitus, a priest. The place of his birth is disputed. He himself calls it *Bonaven Taberniæ;* Lanigan, Döllinger, and others, identify this with Boulogne, while others of our own antiquaries identify it with the present Kirkpatrick, between Dumbarton Castle and Glasgow. The date of his birth was, probably, A.D. 387. He was trained for his future labours in the monasteries of Southern Gaul. Amidst the conflicting legends it seems certain that he spent some time in the monastery of St. Martin at Tours, and submitted to the strict discipline of that famous seminary; afterwards studied with St. Germanus at Auxerre, and thence visited "one of the islands of the Tuscan Sea," probably Lerins, then a famous school of learning, in which St. Hilary of Arles and St. Lupus of Troyes had been educated. It had long been his desire to preach in Ireland, whither in youth he had been carried off in a piratical incursion, and had spent some years as a slave. On the abandonment of his mission by Palladius, Patrick was consecrated—there is reason to believe in Gaul —and sailed from Gaul with some fellow-labourers, A.D. 432.

We need not enter into the details of his successful work. After seven years his converts had so largely increased that he sent two of his original companions either to Gaul or Britain to receive consecration. One special feature in his work was the founding of monasteries, to which the native youth flocked for education; from which the clergy went forth preaching; which grew into great religious colonies and centres of civilisation and learning, as well as of evangelisation, to the surrounding districts. Most of the ancient sees of Ireland appear to have sprung out of these monasteries, each of which was presided over by a bishop— a fashion different from the custom of the Church in the civilised countries of the ancient empire, where the bishops were usually seated in the chief cities—a fashion which St. Patrick had probably learned in Gaul from the institutions of St. Martin, the Abbot-Bishop of Tours.

The fame of the Irish Church attracted, and was increased by, an influx of foreign Christians. The invasion of the empire by the barbarians drove thousands of its citizens from their homes to seek refuge anywhere out of reach of the fierce hordes who were filling the ancient world with ruin and blood, and crowds of these foreigners flocked to Ireland as a secure Christian, if uncivilised, place of refuge. But it soon ceased to be uncivilised. Learning and religion were so diligently cultivated that Ireland became one of the most famous schools of learning and the arts in Europe; and from this "Island of the Saints" went forth a host of missionaries whose labours in England, Gaul, and Germany we have briefly to record.

In the year 563, ninety-eight years after the death of St. Patrick, Columba, a native Celt, trained in one of the great Irish monasteries, left Ireland with twelve companions and founded a religious house on the little island of Iona, on the west coast of Scotland, near the Mull of Ross. Thence in frequent missionary journeys he converted the neighbouring Picts, and even extended his labours to the distant islands of Orkney and the Hebrides. The house of Iona is specially interesting to us as one of the chief centres from which our Saxon forefathers received their Christianity.

The native British Church had done nothing for the conversion of its heathen conquerors. So long as the war between the two races was still in progress—and it lasted for a century—the conquered race was organising armed resistance to the fierce heathen rather than missions for their conversion, and long before the strife of the races was over in the west and north, the settled tribes of the south-east had already received the Gospel at other hands.

What English youth does not know the charming story of the incident which first interested Pope Gregory the Great in this distant land? Long before he was bishop, while abbot of the monastery which he had founded on the Cœlian Hill, he was one day crossing the Forum when his attention was attracted to a group of youths of both sexes who were standing there exposed, like other wares, for sale. They had fair complexions, light hair, and blue eyes, and formed a striking contrast with the dark Italians about them. The abbot paused to ask who these children were, and was told that they were *Angles*, and came from the kingdom of *Deira*, and that their king was named *Ælla*; and, in fanciful play upon the words, he declared that they looked like *angels*, and ought to be saved *de ira* (from the wrath of God), and taught to sing *Alleluias*. The incident produced a deep impression on Gregory's mind; he resolved to undertake a mission to England, and had actually set out with the Pope's sanction, and gone three days' journey, when the people of Rome, who were warmly attached to him, refused to let him leave them, and he abandoned his journey. But long years of high employments, as ambassador to Constantinople and as Archdeacon of Rome, did not banish from his mind the recollection of the fair English slaves, and when at length he had succeeded to the papal chair, he carried out his intention of sending a mission for their conversion. For this enterprise he selected forty monks from his own monastery on the Cœlian Hill, with Augustine, the prior, at their head. He furnished them with books and everything necessary for their work, and gave them letters of commendation to the Frankish kings and to the Gallican bishops, and sent them forth to cross the Alps, and the breadth of Gaul, and the stormy channel, to their distant mission field.

A door of entrance into the land had been opened for them. Ethelbert, King of Kent, the earliest settled and the most civilised of the Saxon kingdoms, had married a Christian princess, Bertha, daughter of Charibert, King of Paris, who had been given to him on condition that she should retain the free exercise of her religion; and to this end a bishop and clergymen had accompanied her as her chaplains, and the king had fitted up one of the ancient British churches at Canterbury for their worship. No doubt the influence of his wife, and the conversation of her learned chaplains, had already prepared the mind of the Kentish king to give a favourable reception to this religious embassy which the great Bishop of Rome had sent him. After some cautious delay the king laid the subject before an assembly of the people, and with their concurrence it was agreed to abandon the faith of their barbarous ancestors, and embrace the religion which now for 200 years had been that of the civilised world; and the history assures us the Italian missionaries baptized the king and his notables, and 10,000 Kentish men, in the neighbouring river, in one day. The influence of Ethelbert obtained leave for the missionaries to preach in the neighbouring kingdom of the East Saxons, where they obtained some temporary success. In the kingdom of East Anglia they were tolerated, but made few converts. Edwin, the king of the leading kingdom of the northern part of England, sought the hand of a daughter of Ethelbert and Bertha, who was given to him on the same conditions on which her mother had been married, viz., that she should retain her religion, and have the ministrations of a staff of chaplains. Paulinus was entrusted with this new charge. The history repeats itself. After long delay and hesitation Edwin was persuaded in his own mind, and submitted the question of a change of religion to the assembly of the people. Bede, the historian of the Saxon Church, relates the way in which the proposal was received by the thoughtful old thane, glad to hear a religious teacher who offered a solution of the great problems of life—whence do we come, whither do we go? and by the worldly high priest, dissatisfied with the gods, who had insufficiently rewarded their chief votary with riches and royal favour, and who was willing to transfer his self-interested allegiance—specially, perhaps, since he saw that the new religion had already the king's support. The result again was, that the king, the thanes, and the people accepted the new religion, and Paulinus is said also to have baptized his 10,000 Northumbrians in a day. These wholesale conversions could hardly have been very safe ones, and we are not surprised to find that they were sometimes followed by wholesale apostasies.

Cœdwalla, a British prince, made an alliance with Penda, the King of Mercia, and defeated and slew the Northumbrian king, and regained the sovereignty over Bernicia and Deira, which he ruled cruelly for two years. Paulinus fled with the widowed queen and her child to the kingdom of Kent, leaving Jacob, a deacon, behind, to keep together the handful of Christians who still clung to their faith. Oswald, a prince of the family which had been dethroned by Edwin, set up the standard of revolt against Cœdwalla, and in the great battle of Hefenfeld the power of the British prince was entirely broken, and made head no more in the north, while Oswald established his family upon the Northumbrian throne. During his years of exile he had resided among the fathers of Iona, and had become an earnest Christian under their teaching. Instead, therefore, of recalling Paulinus, the partisan of the rival house and the teacher of the rival Church, he sent to Iona, and begged the monks to undertake the evangelisation of the north. Aidan was sent; he built a monastery, a second Iona, on the little island of Lindisfarne, off the coast of Northumbria, which became a missionary centre, from which the greater part of England was evangelised. The work accomplished by the two missions may be thus briefly described. The Italian missionaries Christianised Kent and Wessex; the Celtic missionaries Christianised Mercia; and a Northumbrian, with a Roman education (Wilfrid of York), introduced Christianity into Sussex. The work was begun by the Italians, and, after having lapsed, taken up and finished by the Celts, in Northumbria and Essex. The East Anglian Church was founded by Felix, a Burgundian, who was assisted in his work by Fursey, an Irish-Scot. And the part of the Gallican Church in sending Bishop Liudhard with Queen Bertha must not be overlooked. The two schools held the same doctrine, but some different customs. They had a different succession of bishops, kept Easter at different times, had a different liturgy, different customs in the consecration of the clergy, and other differences of lesser consequence. These differences served to divide the converts of the two sets of missionaries into two religious parties, and it seemed desirable to unite them by a general agreement on these minor points. Accordingly on the death of the Kentish Archbishop, Deusdedit, in A.D. 664, the two kings who were the special protectors of the two missions—Egbert king of Kent, and Oswy king of Northumbria—with the consent of the churches, agreed to select a man who should be acceptable to both parties, and to send him to Rome to receive consecration from the chief bishop of the Christian Church, that he might then return and regulate the English churches. Wighard, the man selected, died at Rome, and the pope, Vitalian, selected in his place Theodore, a Greek monk, and consecrated him Archbishop of Canterbury. Theodore, on his return, held a general council of the English churches at Hertford, A.D. 673, and there all the churches agreed in common customs, and were organised into a united Church of England, 150 years before the separate kingdoms of the heptarchy were united into one kingdom of England under the sceptre of Egbert.

Theodore, and Hadrian who had accompanied him to his English work, were both eminent scholars, and gave a great impulse to the cultivation of learning in England, so that the monasteries of Deira became famous throughout Europe for their learning. Bede, a monk of Yarrow, is reckoned among the great writers of the Church; his ecclesiastical history is an inestimable monument of the early Saxon history of our own country. In the next generation Archbishop Egbert, a man of princely birth, founded a noble library at York, and taught in the schools there, to which students flocked from all Europe. These schools produced Alcuin, one of the greatest scholars of the age of Charlemagne, who, as was stated above, was invited by that emperor to his court, and was one among the great men who were the counsellors and ministers of that able monarch. It happened that this brightest period of Saxon learning coincided with the darkest period of literature among the Franks.

Let us turn our eyes to the opposite continent of Europe. The Franks had been zealous converts, but the Frankish Church seems by this time to have lost much of its early zeal and energy, and many of the people were still in heathenism. Beyond the Rhine, their eastern frontier, stretched the vast forests in which the German tribes still maintained the freedom, the barbarism, and the paganism of their ancestors.

A great love of an ascetic life, combined with a great desire for missionary labours, possessed the religious mind of Ireland and England at that time; large numbers of monks and priests went out from both countries, like so many spiritual knights-errant, with a general intention of warring against ignorance, idolatry, and sin, and not insensible to the charm of the adventurous life into which their warfare led them.

Throughout the Continent, almost, the traces of these Irish missionaries are to be met with, in the names of saints to whom churches are dedicated and special local honour is paid. These foreign hermits and monks were very unpleasant visitors to the local clergy, not only because their life of poverty and self-mortification contrasted so strongly with the wealth and luxury and worldly habits of the local clergy, but also because of the different customs of their Celtic Church, to which they rigorously adhered, and because they acted very independently of the regular ecclesiastical authorities. Some of these British missionaries were men of superior powers, or had better opportunities, and accomplished results of great and permanent importance.

In 559 Columbanus, trained at the Irish Bangor, with twelve companions, journeyed to the south-east of France, refused the invitation of Guntram, the grandson of Clovis, to settle in his kingdom of Burgundy, and crossed into the wild district of the Vosges. This hilly country, once colonised and cultivated by Roman legionaries, was now overgrown again with forest and abandoned to the bear and wolf and to the tribes of pagan Suevi, who roamed through its defiles under the shade of its pine woods. Here Columbanus founded three monasteries, at Anegray, Luxeuil, and Fontaines. On their first settlement the monks had to endure great hardships, and were sometimes reduced to live on herbs and bark of trees. They cleared the forest and cultivated the land; people began to settle round them, to whom they taught the arts of life as well as the Christian faith. The Celtic monks maintained the customs of their own Church as to the time of the Easter festival and other peculiarities. This brought Columbanus remonstrances from the popes and from a synod of the local clergy; but the abbot begged the synod to leave him in peace, and suggested to the pope to reconsider the question of the paschal cycle, since it was his own calculation which was wrong; and he and his monks persisted in their own ways. The king, Thierry, held him in honour and used to visit him; but he rebuked his vices, and Brunehaut, the queen-mother, set herself against him; and at last Columbanus and his monks were marched by force down to the coast and bidden to leave the kingdom. He then made his way by the Rhine into Switzerland, and laboured first near Lake Zurich and afterwards at Brienz, on Lake Constance, and at length crossed the Alps into Lombardy, where he was received by Agilulf and Theodelinda, the sovereigns of Lombardy, and founded a monastery at Bobbio, where he died, A.D. 615. This monastery afterwards became famous throughout Europe. It existed till 1803, and its library possesed an Irish antiphonarium and missal, MSS. of the date of its foundation, and a very extensive and valuable collection of ancient books.

Gall, one of the companions of Columbanus, was prevented by sickness from accompanying his superior into Italy. He gathered together twelve companions and founded a monastery in the depths of the forest, and presided over it for twelve years. During that time he revived the faith in the ancient see of Constance and reclaimed from barbarism the district bordering on the Black Forest. After his death his humble cell became a great place of pilgrimage. His monastery was replaced by a more sumptuous edifice, under the auspices of the mayor of the palace, Philip l'Heristal; during the ninth and tenth centuries it was the asylum of learning and one of the most famous schools of Europe. Its library is still a storehouse of valuable ancient MSS.

Fridolin founded a monastery at Leckingen; Magnoald another at Füssen, in Swabia; Kilian, a monk of Iona, laboured successfully at Würzburg; Emmeran, a native of Poictiers and Bishop of Aquitania, resigned his see and preached in Bavaria; Rupert, Bishop of Worms, followed him in the same field and founded Saltzburg.

The monastic establishments of those ages were outposts of civilisation; the industrious monks taught the people by their own example the methods of agriculture and the arts of life, induced the roaming hunters to settle down around them to agricultural pursuits, and gradually Christianised and educated them into orderly, industrious communities. The kings and nobles gladly gave to any little company of monks a wide tract of the unreclaimed land on their estates, or a still wider district of a newly conquered territory, just as a colonial government now will give large grants of land to any industrious emigrants who will settle on it and reclaim it, or plant a military colony with great privileges on a disturbed frontier. This was the origin of the ecclesiastical greatness of the Middle Ages. The towns which sprang up about the monasteries became the great mediæval cities; the little oratory grew into the cathedral; the district of forest land, when cultivated and inhabited, became a principality; and the privileges of local government, originally given to the abbot to enable him to rule his rude dependants, made the mediæval bishop a sovereign prince.

The Franks maintained a border war for many years with their neighbours, the barbarous and fierce Friezlanders, who occupied not only the strip of country which still retains their name, but a considerable portion also of the Netherlands and adjacent districts. It was the policy of the kings of the Franks to encourage the introduction of Christianity among all these fierce barbarians on their borders as one means of civilising them, and even in many cases to force Christianity on a conquered people as one of the conditions of peace.

Hazardous as the adventure was, and fatal as it often proved to the adventurers, the zeal and courage of the missionaries led them to risk their lives in the foundation of these religious settlements among the hostile heathen. Thus when the conquests of King Dagobert had opened the way, Amandus of Aquitaine settled as a temporary bishop among the Frisians about the Scheldt, and ultimately succeeded to the see of Maestricht.

Eligius of Limoges, the goldsmith at the court of Clothaire II. and Dagobert, lived a holy life in the midst of a dissolute society, erected churches and monasteries, redeemed slaves, gave large alms to the poor, and at length, in 641, was elected Bishop of Noyon. His diocese was inhabited in great part by barbarous heathen tribes, among whom he laboured diligently and successfully, building churches and planting monasteries among them. Fragments of his sermons have been preserved by his biographer, St. Ouen,

Bishop of Rouen, and are interesting as examples of these missionary teachings. In one sermon, after protesting against the idea that men can win the favour of the Almighty by the mere performance of external ceremonies, he proceeds: "It sufficeth not, my brethren, that ye be called Christians if ye do not the works of a Christian. That man alone is benefited by the name of a Christian who with his whole heart keeps the precepts and laws of Christ, who abstains from theft, from bearing false witness, from lying, from perjury, from adultery, from hatred of his fellow-man, from strife and discord. For these commands Christ Himself vouchsafed to give us in His Gospel, saying, Thou shalt do no murder, thou shalt not commit adultery, thou shalt not steal, thou shalt not bear false witness, honour thy father and thy mother, and love thy neighbour as thyself; whatsoever ye would that men should do unto you, even so do ye unto them; for this is the law and the prophets. Nay, He adds stronger commands than these, for He says, 'Love your enemies, bless them that curse you, do good to them that hate you, pray for them that despitefully use you and persecute you.' Behold, this is a hard and difficult command, and seems impossible to men, but it has a great reward; for hear what He declares it is, 'That ye may be the children of your Father which is in heaven.' Oh, what grace is here! Of ourselves we are not worthy to be His servants, and yet by loving our enemies we become the sons of God. He, then, who wishes to be a Christian indeed must keep these commandments. He who keepeth them not deceiveth himself. He is a good Christian who putteth his trust not in amulets or devices of dæmons, but in Christ alone. . . . Neither heaven nor earth, nor stars, nor any other creature is deserving of worship. God alone is to be adored, for He created and ordained all things. Heaven, indeed, is high, and the earth wide, and the stars passing fair; but grander and fairer must He be who made all these things. For if the things that we see are so incomprehensible and past understanding, even the various fruits of the earth and the beauty of the flowers, and the diverse kinds of animals in earth, air, and water, the instinct of the provident bee, the wind blowing where it listeth, the crash of the thunder, the changes of the seasons, the alternations of day and night; if these things that we see with our eyes cannot be comprehended by the mind of man, how shall we comprehend the things we do not see? or what kind of Being must He be by whom all these things are created and sustained? Fear Him, my brethren, before all things, adore and love Him, cleave fast to His long-suffering, and never despair of His tender mercy."

In another sermon he gives a picture of the day of judgment: "Let us reflect what terror ours will be when from heaven the Lord shall come to judge the world, before whom the elements shall melt in a fervent heat, and heaven and earth shall tremble, and the powers of the heavens shall be shaken. Then, while the trumpets of the angels sound, all men, good and evil, shall in a moment of time rise with the bodies they wore on earth, and be led before the tribunal of Christ. Then shall all the tribes of the earth mourn while He points out to them the marks of the nails wherewith He was pierced for our iniquities, and shall speak unto them and say, 'I found thee, O man, of the dust of the earth; with My own hands I fashioned thee, and placed thee, all undeserving, in the delights of Paradise; but thou didst despise Me and My words, and didst prefer to follow the deceiver, for which thou wast justly condemned. But yet I did pity thee. I took upon Me thy flesh; I lived on earth among sinners; I endured reproach and stripes for thy sake; that I might rescue thee from judgment, I endured blows and to be spitted on; that I might restore to thee the bliss of

Paradise, I drank vinegar mingled with gall. For thy sake was I crowned with thorns, and crucified, and pierced with the spear. For thy sake did I die, and was laid in the grave, and descended into Hades, that I might bring thee back to Paradise. Behold, and see what I endured for thy sake! Behold the mark of the nails wherewith I was fixed to the cross! I took upon Me thy sorrows that I might heal thee; I took upon Me thy punishment that I might crown thee with glory; I endured to die that thou mightest live for ever. Though I was invisible, yet for thy sake I became incarnate. Though I knew no suffering, yet for thy sake I deigned to suffer. Though I was rich, yet for thy sake I became poor. But thou didst despise my lowliness and my precepts; thou didst obey a deceiver rather than Me. My justice, therefore, cannot pronounce any other sentence than such as thine own works deserve. Thou didst choose thine own ways; receive, then, thine own wages. Thou didst despise light; let darkness, then, be thy reward. Thou didst love death; depart, then, to perdition. Thou didst obey the evil one; go, then, with him into eternal punishment.'" We will only quote further the last words of this saintly seventh-century bishop: "Now lettest Thou Thy servant depart according to Thy word. Remember, O Lord, I am but dust, and enter not into judgment with Thy servant. Remember me, Thou that alone art free from sin—Christ, the Saviour of the world. Lead me forth from the body of this death, and give me an entrance into Thy heavenly kingdom. Thou who hast ever been my protector, into Thy hands I commit my spirit. I know that I do not deserve to behold Thy face; but Thou knowest how my hope was always in Thy mercy and my trust in Thy faithfulness. Receive me, then, according to Thy loving-kindness, and let me not be disappointed of my hope."

Our able, zealous, turbulent Wilfrid of York was among the

missionaries to Frisia. While on his journey to Rome to appeal against Archbishop Theodore, his ship was cast by a storm on the coast of Friezland in the year 678. He was hospitably received by the king, Aldgis, and the natives; and finding them still unbelievers, he stayed some time among them, and converted the king and several chiefs and some thousands of the people. But Wilfrid soon left them. Aldgis died, and Radbod, his successor, was a heathen, and the pagan customs were restored. In 690, Wigbert, a Northumbrian monk, spent two years in a vain endeavour to influence Radbod and his people. At this time Pepin l'Heristal gained some successes in Frisia, which appeared to afford a new opening to missionary enterprise, and Willebrord, a Northumbrian, who was educated in Wilfrid's monastery of Ripon, took eleven Irish companions, sailed to France, and offered his services to Pepin. Willebrord and his monks established themselves at Wilteburg, and succeeded in evangelising a considerable portion of Frankish Frisia, and was consecrated, by Pope Sergius, Archbishop of the Frisians. Many Anglo-Saxons came across the sea and worked under him, or attempted independent enterprises in the neighbouring countries. King Radbod fills a large share in the missionary annals of the time. Willebrord made a voyage into Denmark in a fruitless endeavour to find an opening for the Gospel there. On his return a storm drove him to take refuge in Heligoland, an island sacred to one of the Frisian deities. It was forbidden to kill any animal on the island, or to drink of the holy well except in solemn silence. The archbishop, being detained some time by the weather, killed some of the cattle for food for his crew and for thirty Danish boys whom he had bought and brought back to educate; and he baptized three of his company in the sacred well. King Radbod sent for Willebrord, and decreed that one of the three proselytes must die to atone for the desecration of the island. Some years afterwards, Wulfram, Bishop of Lens, with a company of monks also came on a missionary campaign into Frisia and baptized a son of Radbod, and preached with considerable success. Wulfram on one occasion found himself present at a great pagan festival at which human sacrifices were offered. A boy was about to be put to death by hanging on a gallows. Wulfram expostulated with Radbod on the cruelty of such practices, and prayed him to spare the boy's life. The chiefs standing round tauntingly said, "If your Christ can save the boy from death he shall be His servant and yours for ever." Wulfram fell on his knees as the boy was thrown off from the beam; the cord broke, and Wulfram, finding him still alive, claimed him for his own. The incident was accepted as a miracle, and the fame of Wulfram increased. Another time he was present when two boys were to be sacrificed by drowning. A stake was erected on the shore, the boys were fastened to it, and left to be overwhelmed by the rising tide. As the tide crept nearer, the elder tried to prolong the life of his brother a little while by taking him upon his own shoulders. The bishop begged Radbod to spare them, but was met with the old taunt, "If your God Christ will deliver them, you may have them." Wulfram prayed, and the story says the waves suddenly receded from the victims, and the bishop rushed forward and released the children, and brought them back by the hand. The Gospel gradually made its way among the people. Radbod's son, we have seen, was baptized, and the fierce old warrior himself at length listened to the bishop's teaching, and consented to be baptized. But at the last moment it occurred to him to ask whether, if he were baptized, he should meet the kings his ancestors in heaven; and on being told that they, being unbaptized, would not enter there, he drew back, declaring that he would rather share the company of kings and warriors than sit down in heaven with a handful of beggars. The king was half persuaded again to be baptized on his death-bed, but some vision was made the pretext of another delay, and ultimately the old pagan died as he had lived. On his death Charles Martel reduced the part of Frisia hitherto independent; and Willebrord was soon joined in his labours to extend the Gospel over the whole country by the fellow-labourer whose success soon eclipsed his own, and won for him the title of "the Apostle of Germany."

Winfrid (afterwards named Boniface), a noble Saxon, of Devonshire, of considerable reputation, had before him the prospect of a useful and honourable career in his own country, but his heart was set on missionary work among the heathen of the German forests. He first made a pilgrimage to Rome, and Pope Gregory II. gave him letters authorising him to preach the Gospel in Germany wherever he should find opportunity. At first he preached in Thuringia; but, hearing of Radbod's death and the new opening in Frisia, he repaired thither and offered his services to Willebrord, and laboured with him for three years. Willebrord, feeling the advance of age, desired that the able and energetic Winfrid should be his successor in the see of Utrecht. But Winfrid declined, and set out on an independent mission in Hessia. He met with great and speedy success among the Hessians; and Gregory, hearing of his labours, and foreseeing their probable extension and importance, sent for him to Rome, and consecrated him missionary bishop, taking from him an oath of obedience to the Roman see—a step which seems without precedent, except in the case of the bishops of the proper patriarchate of Rome. We have not space to detail his long, successful labours. He consolidated the work of the earlier Irish and Anglo-Saxon missionaries; he undertook, with the consent of Charles Martel, the reformation of the disorders of the Frankish Church, revived its councils, and gave new energy to its life. He covered Central and Western Germany with the first elements of civilisation and Christianity. Monastic seminaries—Amonëburg, Ohrdruf, Fritzlar, and Fulda—were founded amid the Teutonic forests. The sees of Salzburg, Freisingen, Regensburg, and Passau testified his care of the Church of Bavaria; the see of Erfurt told of his labours in Thuringia; that of Buraburg in Hesse; that of Wurzburg in Franconia; while his metropolitan see at Mentz, having jurisdiction over Worms, Spires, Tongres, Cologne, and Utrecht, was an evidence that, even before his death, the German Church had already passed beyond its first missionary stage. As age approached, instead of retiring, as he had once contemplated, to end his days among the brethren of Fulda, he set out on a last missionary journey into one of the earliest scenes of his labours, into Frisia. He appointed a great number of converts to meet him on the eve of Whitsunday, 755, to receive the rite of confirmation on the morrow; but, instead of the white-robed neophytes whom he expected, he found himself surrounded by a band of armed pagans. He forbad those with him to make any resistance, and they were massacred on the spot. The blood-stained copy of St. Ambrose on "The Advantage of Death," which the archbishop had brought, together with his shroud, to the shore of the Zuyder Zee, was long shown at Fulda as a precious relic of the great archbishop, than whom perhaps no one has added regions greater or more valuable to the dominion of Christ, and few exerted greater influence on the progress of the human race.

For thirty years, we have seen in a previous chapter, Charlemagne was engaged in war against the Saxons. Their savage country offered no temptations to a conqueror to be compared with those which might have induced him to extend his sway to the ancient boundaries of the Western empire in Italy and Spain; but it would seem that the sagacious monarch feared such an irruption of the barbarians who touched the eastern borders of his dominions as had proved fatal to the older empire, and spent his life in combating the danger. Part of his policy was to win the Saxons from their ancestral barbarism and ferocity by means of Christianity; and in spite of the remonstrances of men like Alcuin, who protested against the propagation of the Gospel, as Mohammed spread his false religion, at the point of the sword, Charlemagne persisted in his policy.

We need only give the most general sketch of the history. Whenever the emperor reduced the Saxons to sue for peace, he required the conquered to submit to baptism, and left monks and priests behind to carry on the work of their conversion. Sturmi, abbot of Fulda, Willehad, a Northumbrian, Liudger, a Frisian educated partly in the school of Alcuin at York, are among the most prominent agents of the Saxon conversion. As soon as the emperor was engaged in some distant part of his wide dominions the Saxons would break out into revolt, burn the churches and monasteries, and resume their ancient customs. Then the emperor would hasten back, and gather together his forces for another Saxon campaign. In the end the emperor gained his object. Slowly but steadily the wave of conquest passed on to the Weser, the Elbe, the sea. He established bishoprics richly endowed, and founded great monasteries as spiritual fortresses in the newly-annexed heathen country. His eight bishoprics of Osnaburg, Bremen, Münster, Minden, Halberstadt, Paderborn, Verden, and Hildesheim, grew into the great cities of mediæval Saxony.

Charlemagne's conquest of the Saxons brought him face to face with the Northern nations inhabiting the borders of the Baltic Sea, whose piratical expeditions made them then, and for two centuries later, the dread and scourge of Europe. The great emperor had contemplated the foundation of an archiepiscopal see on the Elbe at Hamburg, which should form a centre for the evangelisation of the North, but his death interrupted his plans.

Our limits do not admit of our relating the details of the conversion of Denmark and Sweden. Their evangelisation is to be attributed in great measure to the labours of Anskar, a monk of Corbie, who won the title of the Apostle of the North. Hamburg was made the centre of his work; there he built a church, monastery, and school. After many vicissitudes, after seeing Hamburg plundered and burnt by an incursion of the Northmen, he succeeded at length in obtaining the permission of King Eric of Denmark for his missionaries to preach throughout the land, and many of the people embraced the faith. Thence Anskar proceeded to the court of Sweden, and obtained leave to preach there from King Biorn and the popular assemblies; and there also, with some temporary checks, the Gospel slowly but surely made way.

The story of the evangelisation of Norway is one of the most striking passages in this part of our history. Until the ninth century Norway was still governed by numerous petty independent chiefs. The people were rough and fierce, with a spirit of sturdy independence. The younger sons of the chiefs mustered crews of hardy adventurers like themselves, sailed out of their fiords, and devastated the sea and river coasts of Europe. Those who stayed at home cultivated their bleak mountain farms, and lived in patriarchal simplicity, and waged frequent petty wars among themselves. About 860 arose the king who united all these principalities into one kingdom of Norway. He had already conquered several districts when he sought the hand of Gyda, but the ambitious damsel declared that she would only marry him who was king of the whole land; and

Harold made a vow never to comb his long beautiful hair—from which he took his name of Harold Haarfager (Harold the Fairhaired)—till he had become absolute king of Norway, like Eric of Sweden, or Gorm of Denmark. It was a long struggle, but he succeeded at last in reducing all the independent principalities to the position of tributary fiefs holding direct from himself. Then he cut and combed his beautiful hair, sent for and married Gyda, by whom he had one daughter and four sons. But the chiefs and bonders (*i.e.*, peasants), indignant at the new yoke, emigrated in great numbers, colonised the Orkneys and Hebrides, the Faroes and Iceland, invaded Russia and Normandy, and harried the coasts of England, Ireland, and Spain.

In 933 Harold Haarfager resigned the crown to his son, Eric "of the Bloody Axe." But the new king became involved in perpetual wars, and the people, groaning under his rule, sighed for a deliverer. The deliverer came in the person of Haco, his youngest brother. Haco had been living at the court of our Anglo-Saxon king, Athelstan, where he had been baptized, and educated in the faith and in manly exercises. Athelstan encouraged his design to offer himself to his countrymen as their king, and furnished him with men and ships, in which they sailed to Drontheim. The people welcomed him who promised to secure to the bonders their rights, and to restore the old customs. Eric found himself deserted by the people, and Haco was accepted by the whole country as king.

King Haco sent to England for bishops and priests, and their labours were not without success in the district about the capital, where several churches were built; and the king proceeded, at the great assembly of the people at the Froste-Thing,* to propose that the whole people should transfer their faith from Odin to Christ. The proposal, however, encoun-

* Winter assembly of the people.

tered opposition. "We bonders," said one of them, speaking for the rest, "do not know whether we have got back our freedom, or whether thou wishest to make vassals of us again by this proposal to abandon the ancient faith of our fathers. If thou wilt take this matter with a high hand, and try thy power and strength against us, we bonders have resolved to part with thee, and to take to ourselves some other chief, under whom we can freely and safely enjoy the faith which suits our inclinations." And Earl Sigurd was fain to quiet them by telling them that the king acquiesced in their wishes. But at the next Harvest-Thing the bonders demanded in turn that Haco should join in their sacrifices. When they gave him the mead cup to drink to the gods, he made the sign of the cross over it, and when the people asked what he meant by it, Sigurd told them it was the sign of Thor's hammer. Then they pressed him to eat of the horse-flesh of the sacrifice, and Sigurd persuaded him to make-believe to taste it. But in the following winter some of the chiefs bound themselves to root Christianity out of Norway, and they compelled the king to join in the sacrifices, and burnt some of the churches and killed their priests, and Haco was obliged to desist. His nephews, the heirs of King Eric, invaded the country, and Haco was mortally wounded in battle against them and died, expressing his remorse for his concessions to the heathens at the Drontheim feast.

Harold Ericson, who succeeded to the throne, had also, with his brothers, been baptized during their exile in England; and they proceeded to pull down the heathen temples, and forbid the sacrifices. The King of Denmark took advantage of the commotions which ensued, and conquered Norway, placing Yarl* Hacon over it as his viceroy. The King of Denmark was a Christian, and had given priests

* Earl.

and learned men to the Yarl, bidding him make all the people in Norway be baptized. But Yarl Hacon allied himself with the heathen party, and made himself independent of Denmark; before the great battle with the Jomsburg pirates, he offered one of his own sons to Thor for victory. But in spite of his compliances, his rule was unpopular, and the people welcomed Olaf, the son of Tryggve, as a deliverer.

Olaf's reign was the turning-point in the conversion of the country. In his youth he had been a viking,* and had travelled in England, Germany, Russia, Greece, as far as Constantinople. In Germany he had made the acquaintance of a priest of Bremen named Thangbrand, a typical specimen of the rude Teutonic priest—a man of noble birth, being a son of Willebald, Count of Saxony, "a tall man and strong, skilful of speech, a good clerk," but, withal, a good man-at-arms, hot-tempered, and dangerous when provoked. During one of his piratical voyages Olaf had touched at the Scilly Islands, and had there been converted and baptized with all his crew. Thence he sailed to England, and was confirmed by Elphege, Bishop of Winchester, in the presence of King Ethelred; thence he went to Ireland, where he married the sister of one of the Irish kings, and lived at the court of his royal brother-in-law. Here one of the northern vikings told him how all Norway was groaning under the cruelty of Hacon the Bad, and how they would welcome a grandson of Harold Haarfager. Olaf listened to the suggestion, sailed for Drontheim, and there was chosen by the Thing as king, and drove Yarl Hacon out of the land.

But as soon as Olaf was seated on the throne he proceeded to introduce Christianity. He destroyed the temples and idols wherever he could, and won over his relations and intimate associates, and then proclaimed his resolve that

* Sea-rover.

Christianity should be adopted as the national faith. All the inhabitants of the district more immediately subject to him were baptized. He went from place to place, holding assemblies of the people, and proposing to them to accept baptism or to fight, and in many places the people unwillingly submitted.

In the North he assembled the people of eight districts, and bade them accept baptism; but the people had come armed, and outnumbered Olaf's men, and they demanded of him to join in the customary sacrifices to the gods. The king temporised, and agreed to meet them at the midsummer festival at Mære. Meantime he assembled some of the chiefs, and told them if he was to sacrifice at Mære it should be a sacrifice of the most solemn kind—a sacrifice of men, and that not of criminals and slaves, but of the greatest men, and he commanded fifteen of the principal chiefs present to be seized and kept for the sacrifice. They rescued themselves from their danger by submitting to baptism. When the people assembled at Mære, Olaf and his men entered the temple, and while the sacrifice proceeded he suddenly struck the image of Thor from its place with his battle-axe; his men overthrew the other idols; and the king and his men going out to the people, he proposed his usual conditions, that they should be baptized or fight. They, disheartened by the powerlessness of their deities, surrendered to his will, gave hostages that they would be true to Christianity, and "took baptism." At one place he found eighty men who professed to be wizards. He made one attempt to convert them sober, and another over their horns of ale, and failing to convert them either drunk or sober, set fire to the place and burnt them. A young pagan hero named Endred agreed to decide the question of his faith by wager of battle, himself against a champion named by the king. Olaf himself appeared as the champion of

Christ. The contest lasted three days. Olaf beat him in swimming, in diving, in archery, and in sword play, and having conquered him, instructed him in the faith, and had him baptized. Olaf's zeal for Christianity at length cost him kingdom and life. Sigrid, the beautiful widow of a Swedish king, after refusing the hands of several princes, and burning one of them in his castle to cure the rest, she said, of their passion for her, visited the court of Norway in the hope of marrying Olaf—"the strongest, bravest, most beautiful of men." Olaf was inclined to the match; but on her refusing to embrace Christianity he treated her with contemptuous indignity. She soon after married Sweyn of Denmark, and stirred him up, in combination with the son of her first marriage and some disaffected Norwegians, to invade Norway. In the engagement which ensued Olaf was beaten, and with the last survivors of his crew he leaped overboard that he might not fall into the hands of his enemies. After his death the country was governed by the conquerors for fifteen years, when Olaf Haraldson, a descendant of Harold Haarfager, won the throne. He sent to England for a bishop and priests. Bishop Grimkil, "the horned man," as the people called him from the shape of his mitre, compiled a system of ecclesiastical law for the Norsemen. Olaf found that many of the people had relapsed into their old heathen customs, and went about the country reclaiming them to the Gospel by high-handed proceedings similar to those of his namesake. After his death he was canonised. When Canute had united the three crowns of Denmark, Norway, and England, he promoted the civilisation and evangelisation of his Scandinavian dominions; schools and monasteries were founded, bishoprics established, churches built; the old faith in Thor and Odin gradually disappeared, and the Northmen became the children of "the White Christ."

The evangelisation of the Sclavonic races was the work of

a later period and of the Greek Church, and will find a place hereafter.

The conversion of the races of Northern Europe has a special interest for us, because we were among the first converted, and then took a large part in the evangelisation of the rest. But independent of this the subject is one of great interest. The general features of the conversion of these barbarous nations differ from those of the Christianising of the civilised world of Greece and Rome. In the beginning of Christianity the Gospel was first preached among the humbler classes, and it spread imperceptibly from soul to soul. It was nearly three centuries before it became a subject of great political importance, and the conversion of the emperor was the culminating point of the conversion of the empire. In the conversion of the northern races the missionaries addressed themselves to the kings and chiefs in the very first place, and the question became at once one of first-rate political importance; the kings consulted the sages and warriors of their rude court, and then laid the matter before the free assemblies of the people. In some cases all agreed to receive the new religion, and were baptized by thousands in a day; in other cases the question divided the people into two factions—one in favour of Christianity and civilisation, the other resolved to maintain the religion and laws and customs of their ancestors against what they considered an enervating revolution. The dispute often led to bloodshed. In Norway especially, as we have seen, at one time the kings tried to force Christianity on the people at the point of the sword; and at another the sturdy bonders compelled the king to join in the heathen sacrifices; and the result was the wildest, wierdest chapter in the history of the spread of Christianity.

Two other features are conspicuous in the history. The first is the part which royal marriages played in the story. A pagan king seeks an alliance with the royal house of a Christian country, and receives the hand of the princess on condition that she be allowed to retain the free use of her religion, and to that end be allowed to have a chapel and a staff of clerics. The influence of the wife and the teachings of her chaplains naturally prepare the king's mind to receive the religion which he sees more and more is bound up with civilisation and good government, which he and his people must embrace if they desire to be included in the family of civilised nations. Thus Clovis was influenced by Clotilda, and Ethelbert by Bertha, and Edwin by Ethelberga.

The other feature is the machinery by which the conversion was effected—not by the teachings of individual missionaries going through the land and influencing one here and one there, so much as by the establishment of Christian colonies, in which civilisation and learning and religion were taught simultaneously, in whose schools the sons of chiefs were taught, and on whose lands the roaming hunters were induced to settle. In reading of these early monasteries the reader must not class them in his mind with the stately homes of learned leisure, whose very ruins are still among the architectural glories of our land, and whose reputation for inactivity and corruption have survived by three centuries their destruction. The first generation of these monks went through all the hardships of poor emigrants in an unreclaimed country. They with their own hands built their rude timber church and house, felled the trees and ploughed the ground, erected the watermill and ground the corn, sheared the sheep and made their coarse frocks and sandals. A monastery did not consist then of a dozen or two of studious recluses. It often numbered its inmates by hundreds and thousands; the Irish Bangor numbered 4,000; and the German Fulda, at the death of its founder, numbered 4,000. They were Christian colonies planted in the midst of heathen barbarism, from which civilisation as well as religion spread over the lands. One other feature of these northern missions which it is right to mention is their relations with the see of Rome. Rome in these seventh and eighth and ninth centuries was no longer the seat of empire, but in the eyes of these northern barbarians it still retained much of its old prestige. Its bishop was the Patriarch of the West; his primacy was universally admitted; he was the centre of the ecclesiastical organisation of the churches of Europe; he had taken the initiative in the organisation of missions to the barbarians; and he came to be looked upon as having a kind of right to regulate the labours of missionaries outside the territorial boundaries of the Church, to give them authority to preach, and to give them consecration as bishops in the new districts which they won, and to sanction the permanent organisations which grew out of their labours. Thus Celestine sent Palladius to Ireland, and probably sanctioned Patrick's subsequent mission; Gregory sent Augustine and his monks, and requested the Gallican bishops to consecrate him, and sketched out the ecclesiastical organisation of England, though it was not carried out. Thus Willebrord sought the pope's blessing on his mission in Frisia; Boniface received from Gregory II. an authorisation to preach in Germany, and subsequently, on receiving consecration from the same pope, he took an oath of obedience to the see of Rome; Ebbo received the authorisation of Pope Paschal I. to undertake his mission to Denmark; and Anskar, the Apostle of the North, on being consecrated Archbishop of Hamburg, was summoned to Rome, where he received the pall and a formal authority to preach to the nations of the North. Still, many of the missionaries settled among the heathen without seeking anybody's authorisation. The majority taught the neighbouring heathen by voice and the example of a holy and self-denying life, and passed away to their reward, leaving their rude cell and oratory to fall into decay, and their name to be forgotten; in other cases the oratory grew into a church, and the cell into a religious house, and the foundation found a place in the permanent ecclesiastical organisation of the country.

In all these transactions all parties were acting honestly for the best interests of the cause of Christ. It was clearly desirable that some order and method should be introduced into the labours of these volunteers from all quarters, and the primacy of the pope was supposed to carry with it the authority of general direction and supervision. There are many who think that in these days it might be well if our missionary embassies were accredited by some great recognised authority, such as the Primate of the English Church, to heathen kings and princes; if missionary work were done by the machinery of Christian colonies, something resembling, *mutatis mutandis*, the early monasteries; and if the volunteer missionaries recognised some authority which would wisely direct their efforts to the likeliest fields, and prevent rival missions from hindering one another's work.

## CHAPTER XXXIV.

#### CONVERSION OF THE SLAVONIC NATIONS.

The Teutonic nations had during three centuries been gradually yielding to the influences of Christianity, but scarcely any impression had been made upon the vast Slavonic population of rude, warlike, pastoral tribes which inhabited the rebarbarised provinces on each side of the Danube—Bulgarians, Moravians, Bohemians, Poles—and extended onwards into the heart of the modern Russian empire. In the early part of the ninth century, when Theodora was Empress of Constantinople, in the border wars the sister of the BULGARIAN Prince Bogoris fell into the hands of the Greeks, and while in captivity embraced the religion of the empire. Awhile after a Greek monk was taken by Bogoris, and an exchange made between the two captives. Bogoris, like Clovis, long listened unmoved to his sister's endeavours to convert him; but on the occurrence of a famine, prayers to his own deities having produced no effect, while prayers to the God of the Christians were followed by speedy relief, he received baptism at the hands of the patriarch, the emperor himself standing sponsor by proxy.

The divisions among Christians had the same evil results on the missionary work of the Church then as now. Missionaries from the Roman and Armenian churches visited the new convert, and sought to win his adherence to their communities. Political reasons made him for a time connect himself with the Western empire, and the interference of the Pope led to warm remonstrances from the Greek patriarch. Pope Nicholas claimed the Bulgarian Church, because it was within the limits of the ancient Western empire, the Patriarch Photius because the Eastern Church was the actual introducer of Christianity into the country. The controversy called forth works on the theological questions in dispute between the two churches from some of the greatest of the Western theologians, such as Hincmar of Rheims, Odo of Beauvais, Æneas of Paris, and Ratramn of Corbie. In the end the Bulgarians chose the Byzantine connection, and received a Greek archbishop and bishops.

The conversion of the Bulgarians led to the introduction of Christianity into neighbouring kindred tribes among the Chazars of the Crimea, the Slavic tribes in the interior of Hellas, and the Servians, who extended from the Danube to the Adriatic, and others. The kingdom of MORAVIA had acknowledged the supremacy of Charlemagne and his son Louis, and had received a regionary* bishop and some priests, who had not been very successful. When the empire of Charlemagne was breaking to pieces, Ratislav, the King of Moravia, sought to recover his independence, and in pursuance of the policy of withdrawing his people from Western influence, he wrote to the Greek Emperor Michael for religious teachers : " Our land is baptized," he wrote, " but we have no teachers to instruct us and translate for us the sacred books. . . . Send us teachers who may explain to us the Scriptures and their meaning." The emperor sent them Methodius and Cyril, who gave them an alphabet, and translated into their tongue the Gospels and Acts, the Psalter and others of the sacred books, and the Liturgy. The pope, Adrian, summoned the Greek missionaries to Rome, who obeyed the summons. The pope, after some hesitation, approved of their use of the Liturgy in the vernacular, appointed Methodius metropolitan of Moravia and

* A missionary bishop without a definite see.

Pannonia, and on their return, though the Greek clergy were hindered by the jealousy of the German clergy, they were very successful among the people. Before long Moravia was invaded by the pagan Magyars, and after the restoration of order was united to the kingdom of Bohemia and ceased to be an independent kingdom.

BOHEMIA received its Christianity through Moravia. Its heathen duke, Borziwoi, about 801, visited the court of the Moravian prince, and with his attendants received Christianity at the hands of Methodius, and on his return to his own country took with him a Moravian priest, who baptized the prince's wife and sons; and after various fluctuations, Boleslav the Pious, the great-grandson of Borziwoi, assisted by the influence of the Emperor Otho, established a Saxon bishop, Dietmar, at Prague, and the Church slowly won the people from their heathen customs.

The seeds of Christianity are said to have been wafted into POLAND from Moravia as early as the ninth century, and Christian refugees from the invasions of the Hungarians appear to have still further extended its progress during the tenth. In 965 the Polish Duke Mieceslav I. married the daughter of the Christian King of Bohemia, and embraced the faith, and a bishopric was erected at Posen. A fourth wife, Oda, the daughter of a German count, erected numerous monasteries and churches, and introduced French, German, and Italian ecclesiastics. Otho III. bestowed the title of king on Mieceslav II., and made Gnesen a metropolitan see, with authority over the sees of Breslau, Cracow, and Colberg. On the death of this king the affairs of Poland fell into confusion, and the heathen party regaining a temporary ascendancy, burnt the churches, and killed or drove away the clergy. At last the Poles agreed to restore the line of their ancient princes. Casimir, the son of the late king, was found in a Benedictine monastery, where he had taken the vows and received ordination. Pope Benedict IX. released him from his vows, and the new king abolished the remains of the Sclavonic Liturgy, and brought his Church into closer union with the Roman see.

The conversion of RUSSIA was the greatest missionary achievement of the Byzantine Church. Ruric, the leader of a band of Scandinavians, had founded a kingdom on the Baltic, of which Novgorod was the capital. As early as 867 Russian armies had appeared before Constantinople, but it was not till the close of the tenth century that Constantinople became fully aware of the importance of the great Sclavonic empire which had arisen round Novgorod and Kieff, and already extended from the Baltic to the Euxine. In 955 the Russian Princess Olga, the widow of the son of Ruric, with a numerous retinue, visited Constantinople, and there embraced Christianity, having the Emperor Constantine Porphyrogenitus for her sponsor. On her return she endeavoured to convert her son Swiatoslav and her grandson Vladimir. Some ambassadors whom Vladimir sent to Constantinople returned with their minds deeply impressed by what they had seen. The grandeur of the Divine service in the Church of Sta. Sophia; the impressiveness of the building—then, perhaps, the noblest in the world—the splendour of the service, the clergy, the processions, the music, the prostrate people overpowered their imaginations. "When we stood in the temple," said the ambassadors, "we did not know where we were, for there is nothing else like it on earth; there in truth God has His dwelling with men, and we can never forget the beauty we saw there. No one who has once tasted sweets will afterwards taste that which is bitter. We can no longer abide in heathenism." Thereupon the Boyars said to Vladimir, "If the religion of the Greeks had not been good, your grandmother Olga, the wisest of women, would not have embraced it." Soon after the prince besieged Cherson, the frontier city of the Greek empire, and when it fell into his hands he sent another embassy to Constantinople, demanding the hand of Anne, the sister of the Emperor Basil. His request was granted on condition of his embracing Christianity. As soon as the prince had become Christian he gave orders for the immediate baptism of his people. "Whoever on the morrow," ran the proclamation, "shall not repair to the river, whether rich or poor, I shall hold him for my enemy." Accordingly on the morrow the people of Kieff flocked in crowds to the river and were there baptized. The national idol was dragged to the river and thrown in; where the temple had stood, there the prince erected the Church of St. Basil. Michael, the first metropolitan, with his bishops and priests, travelled from place to place, baptizing and instructing the people. Churches were built and schools founded; the Sclavonic Scriptures and Liturgy, made ready to their hands by Cyril and Methodius, were introduced; sees were erected at Novgorod, Rostoff, Chernigoff, Vladimir, and Belgorod. Where trade and commerce had opened up the country to external influences and ideas their work was easy; but in the remoter parts of the country long labour and much persecution had to be endured before the Cross had triumphed over the ancient superstitions.

The ancient Sclavonic religion still maintained a firm ascendancy over a large tract of country; its hierarchy was powerful, and it was many years yet before Christianity obtained a complete conquest over it. It was not till the end of the first quarter of the twelfth century that the chief towns of POMERANIA received the Gospel, through the influence of the Suzerain Boteslav, Duke of Poland, and chiefly by the apostolic labours of Otho, Bishop of Bamberg

At the close of the twelfth century a new agency was employed in the conversion of these Sclavonic races. The mind of Western Christendom was full of the crusading spirit. At first its idea was to win back by the sword the lands which the Mohammedans had wrested out of Christian hands. Imbibing the spirit of Mohammedan proselytism, it proceeded to undertake the propagation of the faith in heathen lands at the sword's point. It was Innocent III. who directed the crusading spirit against the heretics of the south of France,* and the heathen of the north-east of Europe.

LIVONIA, on the east coast of the Baltic, was the first scene of these northern crusades. Meinhard and Berthold in the end of the twelfth century had successively for a dozen years (1186—1198) laboured in vain for the conversion of the stubborn heathen people, when in 1198 Berthold re-entered the country at the head of an army of crusaders. The people submitted to force, but, on the removal of the force, rose against the clergy and their converts. Berthold's successor, Albert of Bremen, came at the head of another crusading army and laid the foundations of the town of Riga; and when the crusading army broke up, he, with the pope's sanction, established a new military order, the Brethren of the Sword, as a permanent military force for the propagation of the Gospel. The new order, as the reward of its services, was to possess the lands they won, receiving the baptized natives as subjects, and those who refused baptism as slaves. From Riga, as a centre, the military evangelists spread out into the neighbouring country, erecting castles for the defence of their conquests, under the protection of whose walls German colonists settled, and gradually introduced civilising and Christianising influences into the land. The Bishoprics of Revel, Dorpat, and

* See page 361.

Pernau were at first so many ecclesiastical fortresses, founded by the Brethren of the Sword for the consolidation of their conquests, as well as centres for the propagation of Christianity.

The opening of the thirteenth century saw the PRUSSIANS still strongly adhering to their ancient heathenism, the missionaries who had from time to time penetrated into their country having paid for their rashness with their lives. In 1210, Christian, a Pomeranian monk, with several brethren, accredited by Pope Innocent III., laboured for four years and met with some success; but then the heathen party rose against them, destroyed their churches, and put many of their converts to the sword. A military order, after the model of the Order of the Sword, was then founded for the conquest and conversion of Prussia, but did not prove successful. Then the Order of Teutonic Knights, quitting the Holy Land, were incorporated, with the papal sanction, with the Order of the Sword, and undertook to expel the last remains of heathenism from the face of Europe. For fifty years the knights waged war against the Prussians, slowly making their way into the heart of the country, and securing their conquests by castles, around which arose the towns of Culm, Thorn, Marienwerder, and Eburg, which they peopled with German colonists. In 1260 the knights suffered a defeat at the hands of the neighbouring tribe of Lithuanians; the Prussians rose in revolt, burnt churches and monasteries, slew the clergy, and wasted the country far and wide. Twenty-two years of sanguinary war ensued, in which successive armies of crusaders came to the help of the knights, before the struggle between the rival faiths was ended.

The neighbouring province of LITHUANIA did not abandon its heathenism and embrace Christianity till the year 1386. And it was not till well into the fifteenth century that the

SAMAITES (of whom the Samoeids, now living within the polar circle, are probably the surviving representatives) received Christianity from a Lithuanian priest called Withold, who fixed his see at the town of Wornie or Miedniki. Among the LAPS Christianity did not become the popular religion till the sixteenth and seventeenth centuries.

## CHAPTER XXXV.

### THE HILDEBRANDINE PERIOD.

The religious abuses which we have narrated in chapter XXXII. had at length by a natural reaction given rise to a strong and widespread desire for a reformation of the Church. Among the clergy themselves there was a rising party intent on applying a remedy to the prevalent evils, and Gregory VI. had been the representative of their hopes. The emperor also, although he had procured the removal of Gregory, together with the other two rival popes, was himself resolved to fulfil the duty, which his office was understood to impose upon him, of reforming abuses. Among the people generally the state of the Church excited great discontent, and not a little disaffection, and any measures of reform were sure of their sympathy.

The emperor had selected one of his own ecclesiastics, Suidger, a Saxon by birth, and Bishop of Bamberg, as a man fit to be made, with the papal authority, the instrument of a reformation. On Christmas Eve (A.D. 1046) Henry desired the Roman clergy and people assembled in St. Peter's to proceed to the election of a pope. They replied that they were bound by oath not to elect another during Gregory's life, but begged the king to nominate one. Henry was then invested with the ensigns of the patriciate, and in the character of chief magistrate he presented Suidger to the people, and seated him in the papal chair, where he was hailed by the acclamations of the assembly as Pope Clement II.

Clement without delay summoned a council for the correction of abuses; but his plans of reform, whatever they may have been, were arrested a few months after by his death. The emperor then chose another German pope—Poppo, Bishop of Bixen—who was consecrated and installed in July, 1048, under the name of Damasus II., but survived his elevation less than a month. The emperor again named a German, his own cousin Bruno, Bishop of the humble see of Toul, a man of great reputation for piety, learning, and eloquence, and not without experience in public affairs. At a great assembly at Worms he was invested with the symbols of the papacy, and set out for Italy in all the state and splendour of pontiff-elect. At one of the halting-places of his cavalcade he was met by Hugh, the famous Abbot of Cluny, accompanied by one of his monks, an Italian named Hildebrand, a meeting which produced memorable results.

This Hildebrand was born of humble parents, but his uncle was Abbot of St. Mary's on the Aventine, and under him the youth was trained for the ecclesiastical profession. Embracing the severe ascetic notions which were spreading in the Church, and being discontented with the laxity of his monastery, he crossed the Alps and entered the society of Cluny, which had lately become famous for its revival of primitive monastic discipline. From Cluny he visited the court of Henry, and on his return to Rome he became chaplain to Gregory VI., whose pupil he had formerly been. On Gregory's deposition he accompanied him to Germany, and on his death returned again to Cluny.

In the interview between the pope-elect and the Abbot of Cluny and his monk, Hildebrand put forth the views of the reforming school among the clergy, which was adverse to the agreement which had been made between the Romans and the emperor as to the imperial nomination of popes.

The genius of Hildebrand at once obtained an ascendancy over the mind of Bruno. He adopted his views, he took him into his suite, and, pope-elect and cousin of the emperor though he was, he at once laid aside the pontifical symbols, adopted the dress of a pilgrim, entered into Rome barefooted and in a coarse frock, and addressing the people assembled in St. Peter's told them that he had been chosen by the emperor as pope, but had come to submit himself to their decision. He was rewarded by loud and universal acclamations, which hailed him pope under the name of Leo IX.

Leo ordained Hildebrand sub-deacon, and conferred on him the treasurership of the Church and other preferments, and Hildebrand became the soul of the reforming party among the Roman clergy, and the trusted adviser of the pope.

Leo undertook in earnest the work of reformation; and in imitation of the way in which the emperor moved from place to place, and personally superintended the affairs of every portion of his empire, the pope set out on a circuit of visitation. He crossed the Alps and passed through Germany, reforming abuses, redressing wrongs, reconciling foes, consecrating churches, conferring privileges on monasteries. Next he journeyed to Rheims, where he had promised, before his elevation, to consecrate the new church of the Abbey of St. Remigius, and announced his intention to hold there a council for the reformation of disorders in the Church and the general correction of morals, to which he invited the King of France, and summoned the French bishops. This was a novel assumption on the part of the pope, and an invasion of the rights of the French king and Church. The king tried to get the pope's visit deferred, and absented himself on the plea of a military expedition; but no one ventured to oppose the pope, and the synod was held. The bishops and abbots were required to swear that they had not been guilty of simony either in obtaining or administering their offices. The Bishop of Nantes, who confessed that he had purchased the succession to his father in the bishopric, was degraded to the order of presbyter; the bishops of Nevers and Coutances confessed that their preferment had been bought for them by their relations but without their own knowledge, and on making their submission they were allowed to retain their sees. The Bishop of Langres, accused of many vices, absconded in the night, and was deposed. Twelve canons were passed: one enacted that no one should be appointed to a bishopric without the choice of his clergy and people; another excommunicated the Bishop of Compostella, who had taken the title of "apostolic," and claimed an independent primacy over the Spanish Church; another summoned to Rome the Breton bishops, who had long been separated from Rome, and had not obeyed the summons to the present council.

From Rheims the pope proceeded to Mentz, and held another council there. He returned to Italy in triumph, having given a great impulse to the work of reform, and having greatly increased the prestige of the papal see. The system of visitation thus commenced was continued throughout his pontificate, and established the character and authority of the papacy as the acknowledged chief ruler of the Western branch of the Church, the powerful corrector of abuses in the hierarchy, and censor of the morals of the whole body of the faithful. During this pontificate, and in the year A.D. 1054, occurred the formal breach between the Eastern and Western branches of the Church, which will be related in a subsequent chapter.

Leo IX. died 1054, solemnly committing the Church to the care of Hildebrand; and the clergy and people were desirous of electing him as his successor. Hildebrand, however, induced the people to entrust him with a commission to the emperor, requesting him to nominate a pope who would be acceptable to the Romans, and he suggested Gebhard, Bishop of Eichstadt, one of the emperor's most trusted counsellors. On his arrival at Rome, he, like his predecessor, was formally elected by the clergy and people, and assumed the name of Victor II. In principle his papacy was a continuation of the last. The system of reforming synods was kept up, but instead of being held by the pope in person, they were presided over by his legates. In A.D. 1056 the pope was invited by the emperor to Germany, and was received by his old master with great honour. While he was still there the emperor died, receiving the last consolations of religion at the hand of the pope, and bequeathing to him the guardianship of his only son, Henry IV., a child of six years of age. The virtual government of the empire was thus vested in the same hands with the papacy, and great results might have followed, but the pope also died in the following year (A.D. 1057).

The Romans took advange of the minority of the young emperor to choose a pope for themselves. They chose Frederick, the brother of Duke Godfrey of Lorraine, who had married Beatrice, the widowed Marquess of Tuscany, and mother of the Countess Matilda, so famous in the subsequent history of Hildebrand. During his short reign, under the name of Stephen IX., synods were held which passed fresh canons against the marriage of the clergy. Hildebrand's influence continued unabated. It is probably at this time that he was ordained deacon and appointed Archdeacon of Rome; and when the pope's death drew near, Hildebrand being absent on a mission to Germany, he exacted an oath that his successor should not be appointed without Hildebrand's advice.

On Stephen's death, in Hildebrand's absence, the nobles of the Campagna took advantage of the opportunity; entered Rome, gained access to St. Peter's by night, and set up as pope a member of their faction under the name of Benedict X. Another party at Rome sent envoys to the empress-mother, requesting her to nominate a pope. Hildebrand, as he returned to Rome, met these envoys, and suggested the name of Gerard, Bishop of Florence, who accordingly was nominated by the empress, while Hildebrand secured a simultaneous election of the same man by the cardinals, who had fled to Sienna. Gerard took the name of Nicholas II., and was escorted to Rome by Godfrey of Tuscany, of whose capital of Florence he had been bishop, and who, it will be remembered, was the brother of the late pope. The anti-pope submitted to him, and passed the rest of his life in a monastery. In his papacy occurred a revolution in the religious affairs of Milan. The Church of St. Ambrose had long held a lofty position. Its archbishop was a great secular prince, and, in the absence of the emperor, the most important personage in the north of Italy; its clergy bore a high character for learning and morality, for the discharge of their pastoral duties and the education of the young. The church had a liturgy of its own, which it venerated as that of St. Ambrose, and its clergy was a married clergy—a privilege which they enjoyed under the sanction of that great father. The same custom was generally observed throughout the churches of Lombardy; and Peter Damiani, one of the most zealous advocates of celibacy, acknowledged that he had never seen a body of clergy equal to the Milanese; he bestows a very high commendation also on those of Turin, who were also a married clergy, having the sanction of their bishop, Cunibert, for the practice. An agitation was got up against the marriage of the clergy by some fanatical persons who inflamed the passions of the mob against them. A council was held at Rome (A.D. 1059) on the subject, and it was there enacted that no married priest should celebrate mass, and that the laity should not attend the mass celebrated by a married priest. The same council passed other important canons. One, that no clerk should take preferment from a layman, either for money or gratuitously, was aimed at the whole system of lay patronage ; another, that no layman should judge a clerk, claimed exemption for all the clergy from all civil courts; another established a new procedure for papal elections; it deprived the emperor of his recently acquired right of nomination, and the clergy and people of their primitive right of election, and vested the appointment substantially in the cardinals.

On the death of Nicholas II., in 1061, a contest ensued. One party of Romans sent envoys to the young emperor, who treated the recent canon as a nullity, and nominated Cadolaus, Bishop of Parma, as pope, under the name of Honorius II. The Hildebrandine party chose Anselm of Lucca, and after a bloody conflict enthroned him by night in St. Peter's as Pope Alexander II. A political revolution decided the question between the rival popes. The young emperor had hitherto been under the guardianship of the empress-mother, who ruled uprightly and firmly in his name. Hanno, Archbishop of Cologne, and Adalbert, Archbishop of Bremen, seized the emperor's person and the administration of government, and found it politic to enlist the Hildebrandine party on their side by the recognition of Alexander II. The empress-mother soon after acknowledged Alexander, and became a nun in the Roman convent of St. Petronilla. Honorius in 1063 gained possession of the Leonine* city, and was enthroned in St. Peter's, but after

* The new suburb of Rome beyond the Tiber, containing St. Peter's and the Vatican palace, walled in by St. Leo, and called after him the Leonine city.

much fighting was compelled to shut himself up in the Castle of St. Angelo, where he held out for two years, and then retired to his see of Parma, which he retained till his death, not formally resigning his pretentions to the papacy, but not making any active attempt to enforce them. [The Norman conquest of England occurred during this pontificate, in A.D. 1066.]

Alexander died in 1073, and while his funeral was being celebrated a loud outcry arose from the clergy and people demanding Hildebrand as his successor. The cardinals retired for a short time to make their election, and on their return presented Hildebrand as pope. He took the name of Gregory VII., thus at once testifying his gratitude to his first patron, Gregory VI., and proclaiming his acknowledgment of him as a legitimate pope. But Hildebrand, with a caution we should hardly have expected, declined consecration until the consent of the emperor had been first obtained; and his caution was justified by the event, for his appointment was dreaded by the emperor and the German bishops; and the envoys of the emperor were bidden, if they could find any irregularity in the election, to oppose the consecration.

Gregory soon began to develop the dazzling idea of a spiritual universal monarchy which his great genius had conceived. His theory was that the pope is chief governor of the Church; that bishops can only be appointed with his consent, and may be deprived at his will, and that his authority supersedes their diocesan authority; that he alone is entitled to make new laws for the Church; and that no council may be accepted as a general council without his decision to that effect. From this he deduced a control over sovereigns. Christ is the King of Christendom, and the pope is Christ's vicegerent, and has a right to watch over the conduct of kings as of other men, to correct their morals, to depose them if their government is unrighteous, and to absolve their subjects from their vows of allegiance. He claimed certain kingdoms as direct fiefs of the holy see—Spain, Saxony, Bohemia, Hungary, Denmark, Poland, Provence, Corsica, Sardinia, England, and Ireland. In cases of conquest and disputed or doubtful successions he assumed to confer a legitimate title on sovereigns, requiring them to accept their kingdoms as fiefs of St. Peter.

These monstrous claims were made possible by the state of the Church and the world. The general dissatisfaction of men with the tyranny and oppressions of kings and nobles, and with the abuses and corruptions of the Church, induced them to hail as a Heaven-sent deliverer this representative of Christ, who promised to cleanse the Church and to control the princes.

The question of Church patronage was the key of the position. The kings and nobles and lay patrons generally had abused their trust; Gregory sought to deprive them of it, and to vest it in the hands of the prelates, with a supreme control in the pope over all the ecclesiastical benefices of the whole Church. A canon against lay investitures had been made in the last pontificate; Gregory now renewed it with the resolve to enforce it.

But the quarrel of the investitures was postponed to other questions more pressing. Germany was in a miserable state of misrule and confusion. Henry IV., through the fault of his education, was dissolute and tyrannical. Saxony was in rebellion, many of the nobles were disaffected. The pope, after several remonstrances, at length summoned the emperor to appear at Rome and vindicate himself from the charges brought against him by his subjects. This assumption of authority over him naturally enraged the emperor, who replied by an exercise of the ancient imperial authority over the bishops of Rome; he summoned a council at

Worms (A.D. 1076), at which he entertained accusations against Gregory, and the council decreed his deposition. The pope replied by excommunicating the king, declaring his subjects released from their allegiance, and depriving him of his dominions. He also excommunicated those who had taken part in the proceedings at Worms. Germany was rent into two hostile parties. But the partisans of the emperor fell away from him, some influenced by private wrongs, some by political intrigues, some by superstitious fears, and the emperor found himself almost alone. The princes and prelates of Germany at length met at Tribur (A.D. 1076), and came to a resolution that if Henry could obtain the papal absolution within a year from the time of his excommunication they would accompany him to Rome, where he should be crowned as emperor, and they would aid him in driving out the Normans, who had seized part of his Italian dominions; but if unabsolved by the end of the year he should forfeit his kingdom. Meantime he was to lay aside the symbols of royalty, dismiss his excommunicated advisers, and live as a private man.

The year of grace was drawing towards its close when Henry left Germany, accompanied by his wife Bertha and their infant child, crossed the Alps in a winter of extraordinary severity, with great hardship and some danger, and found himself honourably received by his Lombard subjects, who were opposed to the Hildebrandine party, and hoped that the emperor would overcome and depose the pope. The pope was advancing northward, escorted by Matilda the Countess of Tuscany, to attend the council to which he had summoned Henry at Augsburg. On hearing of the approach of the emperor with a large train, he turned aside to Canossa, a strong Alpine fortress of the countess, and here he was joined by several persons of dignity.

At Canossa occurred that dramatic scene which the world

has regarded ever since with such strong and opposite feelings—one side with proud exultation at the display of the power of the Church, the other with indignation at the exhibition of priestly arrogance.

The emperor followed the pope to Canossa and sought his absolution in order to avert the forfeiture of his kingdom, offering to submit to any terms. At length the pope proposed that Henry should give proof of his penitence by surrendering to him the ensigns of royalty and acknowledging that he had rendered himself unworthy of the kingdom. Henry, driven to extremities, consented to these conditions. He was admitted, alone and unattended, clad in the coarse robe of a penitent and barefooted, within the second of the three walls which surrounded the castle, and there in the courtyard he remained the whole winter day fasting and neglected. A second day and a third day he spent in the same manner. On the fourth day he sought an interview with the Countess Matilda and Hugh Abbot of Clugny, who were present in the castle, and induced them to become sureties for his fulfilment of the conditions which should be imposed on him, and then he was admitted to the presence of the pope. The king, a man of tall and remarkably noble person, in his coarse robe and with bare feet, prostrated himself before the pope, whose small and slight person was now withered with austerities and bent with age. The pope was moved, and received him with tears; and on his promising to submit his conduct to an inquiry at a diet of German princes, at which the pope should preside, and to abide by its sentence, he received absolution. The pope celebrated mass, at which the emperor was present, and then the pope received him at his table and conversed with him in friendly fashion.

The German princes, however, set up a rival emperor—Rudolph, Duke of Swabia—and three years of war ensued, while Gregory kept himself neutral. At length the victory declared for Rudolph, and the pope declared for the victor. Henry again replied by summoning a council at Mentz and appointing a rival pope, Guibert of Ravenna, as Clement III. The loyalty of the Germans was rekindled by Henry's misfortunes; in another battle Rudolph was slain; Henry marched into Italy and besieged the pope in Rome. The siege lasted three years, when Henry took the city; Gregory took refuge in the Castle of St. Angelo; the antipope was enthroned in St. Peter's, and Henry and Bertha received their imperial coronation at his hand on Easter-day, 1084. In May the pope's Norman allies returned from an expedition in the East, and appearing unexpectedly before Rome took the city, and for three days plundered and ravaged its inhabitants. The people in despair rose in resistance, and Guiscard, the Norman leader, to quell their resistance, set fire to the city; and to this conflagration is to be attributed much of the desolation which still reigns over a large portion of ancient Rome.

Gregory left the capital in disgust and retired to Salerno, and in the following year (May 25, 1085) ended his eventful and memorable life.

Gregory VII. left behind him a powerful party resolved on carrying out his policy. The very men who were to lead the party for two succeeding popedoms were of his nomination; for on his death-bed he nominated Desiderius, Abbot of the great monastery of Monte Cassino, as his successor, or if he should refuse, then either Otho of Ostia, Hugh of Lyons, or Anselm of Lucca. Desiderius (after long reluctant delay) was the next pope, as Victor III., and Otho succeeded him as Urban II.

The quarrel between the emperor and the holy see continued, but with different fortune. Henry, taught by his misfortunes, exhibited vigour and firmness, recovered the allegiance of his nobles and the affections of his people. The popes did not withdraw their excommunication, but the German Church disregarded it, and its bishops received investiture from the emperor, in spite of the canons to the contrary. His life was troubled, however, by the rebellion of his sons. Conrad fled to his enemies, who used him as the tool of their opposition; and on Conrad's death Henry also rebelled, seized his father's person, and compelled his abdication.

Henry V., however, who had been lavish in professions of obedience to the Roman see, as soon as by its help he had secured the throne (A.D. 1106) proved a more determined and more successful opponent of the papal pretensions than his father. In 1110, having pacified Germany, he crossed the Alps, and occupied Rome with a great army, and demanded of the pope his coronation as emperor, and the recognition of his right of investiture. The pope hesitating, Henry carried him off with the cardinals, and for sixty days kept them prisoners in the castles of the neighbourhood, while his troops ravaged the country. The pope at length yielded, acknowledged the right of investiture, crowned Henry as emperor, and withdrew the excommunication on Henry IV., and the emperor returned in triumph to Germany. But the pope withdrew his concessions as soon as the emperor was gone, and the quarrel of investitures continued through the pontificates of Urban, Paschal, and Callixtus II. At length both parties were wearied out by the long contest of half a century, and a compromise was agreed upon at the Diet of Worms (A.D. 1123). On one side the right of free election and consecration to bishoprics and abbacies was secured to the clergy and monks; on the other hand it was yielded that the election should take place in the presence of the emperor or his deputy, and that the new prelate should receive investiture of the temporalities by the sceptre, without any payment, and should perform the feudal duties of his estates. The substantial victory remained with the papal see. It obtained that no bishop should be consecrated without its approval, and it used its right of approval to coerce the elections.

During the ensuing period of eighty years, down to the election of Innocent III., the pretensions of the papacy were maintained, and acted on from time to time according to the more or less vigorous character of the pope, and according to the opportunities which occurred. Innocent III. (A.D. 1178) carried the papal authority, during a reign of eighteen years, to a still greater height than Gregory VII. He assumed to himself a supreme authority over the kings of Christendom. His interference in their mutual quarrels, and in their several administrations, was often effectual, and his interposition was often sought by them. Philip of France appealed to him against Richard I. When Richard was imprisoned by the emperor, his mother, Queen Eleanor, appealed to the pope to procure his release. "Has not God," she asks, "given you the power to rule nations and kings?" He bade the kings of Castile and Portugal keep peace with one another, threatening them with excommunication and interdict; he enjoined the King of Aragon to restore his coin which he had lately debased; he excommunicated Sweyn for usurping the crown of Norway; he compelled the King of Leon to repudiate his wife, as being within the forbidden degree of relationship; he compelled Philip of France to take back the lawful wife whom he had divorced. Peter II., King of Aragon, voluntarily surrendered his kingdom to the pope, and received it back as a fief of the holy see, thus securing the powerful protection of the papacy against ambitious neighbours. He compelled John of England to lay his crown at Pandulph's feet, and to receive back his kingdom as a fief of the holy see.

The papal prerogative continued at the height to which Innocent had raised it throughout the thirteenth century. In the latter part of that period Boniface VIII. put forth still more extravagant pretensions. On the appeal of Scotland he claimed that country as a fief of the see, and forbade Edward I. to pursue his hostilities against it; but Edward summoned a parliament, which concurred with the king, in a firm repudiation of the papal claim. The pope forbade the clergy to pay taxes or to contribute, even voluntarily, to the revenue of their governments; but Edward retorted by withdrawing from his clergy the protection of the law, and Benedict explained that the clergy were at liberty to contribute to the expenses of the State with his permission, and gave them permission to pay what the king demanded. Germany made a similar stand against the papal encroachments, the Diet of Frankfort declaring (A.D. 1338) that the imperial dignity depended on God alone, and that he whom the electors chose was thereupon king and emperor without needing the approbation of the pope. The pope engaged in a still more serious quarrel with Philip the Fair of France, who also firmly withstood his pretensions. The pope had prepared, and was about to issue a bull deposing the king, when his minister, William of Nogaret, seized the pope's person, who was then staying at Anagni, a town in the Campagna; and although the pope was rescued, he died after a few days, of fever, brought on by the excitement through which he had passed.

Boniface had miscalculated the spirit of the time in trying to strain still higher the pretensions of the papacy. The great monarchies of Europe had all along maintained a steady protest against the papal invasion of the rights of the temporal sovereigns. They had been obliged to yield to the public opinion of Christendom. The authority of the popes had not depended on the number of their own subjects whom they could bring into the field against emperor or king, but upon the moral influence they exercised over the minds of the very subjects of king and emperor. It was the oppressions of kings and nobles, it was their abuses of their ecclesiastical patronage, which had made clergy and people welcome the interference of the popes of the eleventh and twelfth centuries as Heaven-sent deliverers. But as the popes of the twelfth and thirteenth centuries developed their extravagant pretensions to a universal temporal monarchy, their ambition shocked the common sense of the nations, their aggressions on the rights of national churches offended the clergy, the rapacity and venality of the Roman Curia alienated the whole Christian world, and from that time a steady reaction against the papal pretensions set in. This reaction was assisted by the revival of the study of the ancient Roman civil law, which dated from the latter part of the twelfth century. It was easy for the jurists, with the Pandects of Justinian in their hands, to show what in the ancient empire had been the relations of emperor and pope; and it was generally assumed that in Charlemagne the ancient empire of the West had been revived, and that the German emperors were the heirs of Charlemagne. The civil jurists were disposed to press the claims of the emperor to as great excesses as the canonists those of the popes; and the claims of the popes to universal temporal sovereignty were thus usefully balanced by similar pretensions on the part of the emperor. The empire at Canossa seemed to be under the feet of the papacy, but it was only a temporary triumph, and the recollection of Canossa only made the subsequent emperors the more stubbornly hold their own.

The other great European monarchies yielded nothing to the German emperor in their estimate of their own sovereign authority. A Peter of Aragon, or a John of England, might submit to the pope from interest or fear, but princes like Henry V., Edward I., and Philip the Fair, were bold enough to defy the superstitions which fenced the papacy; and when public opinion had once turned against the popes, the sovereigns were strong enough to gradually force back and limit the power which had once been so irresistible. The reaction, begun in the early part of the fourteenth century, steadily increased, till it produced the Reformation of the sixteenth century.

## CHAPTER XXXVI.

### THE CRUSADES.

AMONG the most remarkable religious movements of the Middle Ages were the expeditions for the recovery of the Holy Land from the power of the Mohammedans, which were called Crusades.

We have seen (p. 253) how Jerusalem capitulated to the Caliph Omar, and how the caliph peacefully visited the city, and the Patriarch Sophronius acted as his guide to the holy places, and how the caliph knelt on the external steps of the Church of the Resurrection at the hour of prayer. Jerusalem was a holy city to the members of all three of the great religions—to the Jew, the Christian, and the Mohammedan. Under the mild rule of the earlier caliphs the Jews retained their synagogues, the Christians some at least of their churches and their monasteries, while the Mohammedans appropriated some of the churches to their own worship, or built their mosques beside them. Pilgrims from all Christendom visited Palestine, and made the round of the sacred places without let or hindrance; and narratives* which returned pilgrims wrote for the edification of their home-staying fellows are still extant, and are full of curious interest.

In A.D. 969 the Fatimites severed Egypt and Syria from the caliphate of Bagdad, and set up an independent sovereignty,

---

\* Those of Eusebius, *circa* A.D. 360; Jerome, A.D. 380; Arculf, A D. 700; Willebald, A.D. 725; Bernard the Wise, A.D. 867; Sæwulf, A.D. 1103; Sigurd, A.D. 1111; Benjamin of Tudela, A.D. 1173, and others, down to the "Stacions of Rome" of the 14th and 15th centuries.

with Cairo for its capital. In course of time the Fatimite caliphs, like the late Merovingian kings, became mere puppets in the hands of their viziers. The Abbasside Caliph of Bagdad, to escape a like servitude, called in Togrul, son of Seljûk, chief of a Turkish tribe which had embraced Islam A.D. 1055, but found that he had only made an exchange of masters; for Togrul made himself temporal sovereign with the title of sultan, leaving to the caliph the dignity of representative of the prophet and religious head of his followers. This temporal power descended in the family of Seljûk to Alparslan, the nephew of Togrul, to Malek Shah, and to Tûtûsh. Under the last-named sultan the warlike and energetic Turks wrested Syria from the Fatimite sovereignty, and restored it to the caliphate of Bagdad. The government of Jerusalem was given to a fiery zealot called Orthok.

The Turks, with all the zeal of recent converts, were intolerant of Christianity. The Christian residents and the numerous pilgrims began to suffer indignities and injuries at their hands. Many of the holy places and things, the objects of enthusiastic reverence and devotion to the Christians, were wantonly defiled by the Turks. And the Western pilgrims on their return home filled Europe with their accounts of the profanation of the holy places, and the insults and dangers which the faithful had to endure in their visits to the birthplace and sepulchre of the Lord. The Byzantine emperors being unwilling or unable to afford help, Symeon, the Patriarch of Jerusalem, in A.D. 1093, commissioned Peter the Hermit, on his return home from his pilgrimage, to ask help from the Western Church.

The idea of a crusade was not altogether a new one. Nearly a hundred years before, Pope Sylvester had issued a letter in the name of Jerusalem to the universal Church, beseeching all Christians to sympathise with the afflictions of the Holy City, and to aid her by gifts if they could not do so by arms; and an expedition was fitted out which recovered Sardinia from the Saracen rule, but effected nothing further. Gregory VII., again, in 1074, in a letter to the emperor, Henry IV., stated that 50,000 men from both sides of the Alps were ready to march against the infidels of the East if the pope would be their leader, and said that he earnestly wished to undertake the expedition, especially as it held out a hope of reconciliation with the Greek Church.

Peter the Hermit, on his return to Europe, presented himself before the pope, Urban II., laid before him the request of the patriarch, and enforced it by a vision which he himself professed to have had in the Church of the Holy Sepulchre, in which our Lord bade him rouse the Western nations to the delivery of the Holy Land from the infidel. The pope authorised Peter to preach a crusade. Peter went through Italy and France, preaching in churches and highways, drawing an affecting picture of the desecration of the holy places by the infidels, and the indignities and injuries which they inflicted on Christian pilgrims, and so moving the masses of the people by his impassioned eloquence that a religious enthusiasm was kindled which spread like a contagion among all classes of people, gradually extended throughout Europe, and produced one of the most remarkable movements which Europe had witnessed. In the spring of 1095 the pope held a council at Piacenza, attended by 200 bishops, 4,000 clergy, and 30,000 laity. No building was capable of containing the multitude, and the sessions were held in the plain outside the city. The project of a holy war was proposed; ambassadors from the Greek emperor, Alexius Comnenus, stated the distress of the Christians and the danger of an invasion of Europe by the formidable and fanatical Turks. The people were moved to tears, and many on the spot bound themselves by oath to engage in the crusade. Another council was held at Clermont, in France, in the autumn of the same year, still more numerous and enthusiastic. Fourteen archbishops, 225 bishops, 100 abbots, and vast numbers of clergy and people filled the town and neighbouring villages, and encamped in the surrounding country. The pope addressed the people from a pulpit in the market-place; his exhortation to a crusade was interrupted by a cry from the whole assemblage: "God wills it!" and when he ceased thousands of the people took the vow and attached the cross upon their shoulders. The contagion seized all classes—knights and nobles, bishops and abbots, monks and clergy, artizans and peasants, old men and children, and women of all ranks. The order of society was profoundly disturbed. Landowners sold or pledged their lands and artizans their tools, and those who had nothing to sell begged, to raise funds for their equipment and expenses. Every one who assumed the cross was taken under the protection of the Church; the monk left his cloister, and the servant his master, and the debtor his creditors; women put on men's dress, and clerics appeared with armour and weapons. The impatience of the people could not be restrained. Before the nobles could complete their military arrangements, a vast crowd set out, with Peter the Hermit for their leader and a knight named Walter the Penniless for military commander; another followed under a priest named Gottschalk; a third under a priest named Folkmar. Each crowd was worse than that which preceded it. Without order or discipline, unprovided with arms or money, encumbered by numbers of infirm old people, women, and children, these companies of pilgrims straggled across Europe; no depôts of provisions or arrangements for their reception had been made; they were reduced to steal and plunder; their progress was consequently opposed by the inhabitants of the countries, and they perished in multitudes by the way. The strongest and best-provided found themselves at last at Constantinople. They were ferried across the Bosphorus, and marched on Nicæa, the capital of the newly-established Turkish sovereignty of Roum. A great battle was fought under its walls, and the Christians were defeated. A pitiless massacre ensued of the helpless multitude, and their bones were gathered into a great heap, which remained for many years a monument of the luckless enterprise.

Meantime the responsible chiefs of the crusade were maturing their preparations. Among them were Godfrey of Bouillon (son of that Count Eustace of Boulogne who was one of the chief followers of William the Conqueror in his invasion of England), with his brothers Eustace and Baldwin; Robert Duke of Normandy, the Conqueror's eldest son; Hugh of Vermandois, brother of the King of France; Count Raymond of Toulouse; Count Robert of Flanders; Stephen of Blois (whose son succeeded to the throne of England). They were subsequently joined by the Norman Bohemund of Tarentum, and his nephew Tancred the hero of the crusade. Each leader was in absolute and independent command of his own followers. They took different routes through Europe, some by land, some by sea, and rendezvoused at Constantinople. Nicæa fell before their arms, and a second victory at Dorylæum made them masters of the kingdom of Roum. Here Baldwin was induced to separate from the rest, and march with his followers upon Edessa, where he at once won himself a principality. The rest marched, with frequent skirmishes and much suffering from want of necessaries, as far as Antioch. For eight months they lay round Antioch, suffering the utmost extremity of famine, before the crafty Bohemund negotiated with a traitor an entrance for his troops into the town. They were in turn besieged by a Turkish army; but in an access of religious fanaticism they sallied out, defeated the Turks, and captured in their camp provisions and spoil.

While they lay before Antioch, they received news that the Fatimite caliph had taken the opportunity to attack the Turks, and had recovered Jerusalem out of their hands; and that he offered peace to the Christians and the old freedom of access to the sacred places. They, however, disdained to turn back without accomplishing the task for which Europe had already made such heavy sacrifices. After a siege of forty days, Jerusalem was taken and given up to slaughter and sack.

Godfrey was chosen king of the new kingdom. At its greatest extent, in the time of Baldwin II., the Latin kingdom of Jerusalem comprehended all the sea-coast from Tarsus, in Cilicia, to El Arish, with the exception of Ascalon and Gaza; in the north it extended inland to Edessa, beyond the Euphrates; and in the south the ranges of Lebanon and the Jordan formed its boundary. This territory was divided into four states, the county of Tripolis, the principality of Antioch, and the county of Edessa, which all owned fealty to the kingdom of Jerusalem. A code of law was drawn up called the Assizes of Jerusalem, which still remains, and is the completest monument we possess of the feudal constitution of the Middle Ages. The princes of these states subdivided the land among their followers and other adventurers who were willing to take service under them. Castles were built in commanding situations, and the fortunate European adventurers entered into the enjoyment of the Syrian fields and vineyards. The Latin conquest of this portion of the territory of the ancient Greek Church, instead of helping to heal the schism between the two communions, only served to widen and embitter it; for the crusaders got rid by one means or other of the Greek patriarchs of Antioch and Jerusalem, and everywhere substituted clergy of the Roman obedience.

The succession of Kings of Jerusalem was, Godfrey (A.D. 1099), Baldwin I. (A.D. 1101), Baldwin II. (A.D. 1118), Fulk (A.D. 1131), Baldwin III. (A.D. 1144), Amaury I. (A.D. 1162), Baldwin IV. (A.D. 1174), Baldwin V. (A.D. 1185), Guy of Lusignan (A.D. 1186), Conrad (A.D. 1192), Henry (A.D. 1192), Amaury II. (A.D. 1197—1205).

In 1118 was laid the foundation of an institution which supplied the kingdom with a standing army for its defence. In that year Hugh de Payens founded the order of the Knights of the Temple, and shortly afterwards the Hospitallers were reorganised on the same military basis. The two orders had their head-quarters in Jerusalem, and dependent houses, which were in fact castles, in various parts of the Holy Land. They were gradually endowed with estates in all the countries of Europe, and drew recruits from their noblest families. The two orders formed two divisions of a standing army, with whom war was not so much a profession as a religion.

The Latin dominions in the East owed their stability for so many years quite as much to the dissensions which occupied the Mohammedans as to the valour of their Frankish defenders. But in the time of Baldwin III. the cases became reversed; the Turkish power was reunited, and the Latins weakened by mutual jealousies and distrust, and the consequences were soon felt in the fall of Edessa (A.D. 1147), and the loss of all the territory which the Christians had held east of the Euphrates. This event, and the similar fate which menaced the whole of the Latin kingdom, again aroused the West. Pope Eugenius proclaimed a second crusade; at his request the illustrious St. Bernard preached it throughout Italy, France, and Germany, and it excited as wide and almost as wild an enthusiasm as the first holy war.

The second crusade consisted chiefly of French and Germans, who set out from their respective countries in the spring of A.D. 1147. The Germans were in number 71,000 knights and men-at-arms, with a great multitude of light horse and foot, commanded by the Emperor Conrad in person. The French army numbered about 60,000 harnessed knights and foot in proportion, and was led by its monarch, Lewis VII. Of these two armies a mere handful reached the Holy Land; the treachery of the Greeks left them without supplies, and the Turks harassed every foot of their march across Asia Minor. The great majority perished miserably by famine and the sword. The scanty remnant of crusaders assisted the Latins in a siege of Damascus, but when the attempt failed, through treachery as was believed, the Germans returned home in disgust. The French king wintered in Jerusalem, and returned home by sea at Easter without any further achievement. Europe had been drained of men and treasure with no results but defeat and disgrace.

The contest continued in the Holy Land in a series of battles and sieges, with occasional truces, between the Latins and their Turkish and Saracen neighbours. The kingdom was often indebted for timely assistance to the arrival of noble pilgrims who came with large armed trains, visited the holy places, fought a campaign against the infidel, and returned home again. But even these successes would hardly have sustained the kingdom, but for the contest carried on between the Turkish sultans of Bagdad and the Fatimite viziers of Cairo, which prevented both from giving their whole force to the prosecution of the Christian war. This old strife was now about to end. In A.D. 1173, Shawer was the Vizier of the Fatimite caliph, Noor-ed-deen was Sultan of Bagdad. The Arabs being hard pressed by the attempt of King Amaury, in conjunction with a Greek force, to seize Egypt, adopted the hazardous expedient of asking the Turks for help. Noor-ed-deen sent a large force into Egypt under Sheerkoo, his commander-in-chief, with whom was his nephew, the well-known Saladin. Meantime Shawer had got rid of the Christians by a treaty. But the Turks had not come to Egypt for nothing. They seized Shawer while on a visit to their camp. The Fatimite caliph in terror for himself sent to demand Shawer's execution, and named Sheerkoo vizier in his stead. Soon after Sheerkoo died, and Saladin succeeded him in both his offices—that of commander-in-chief of the Sultan of Bagdad and Vizier of the Caliph of Egypt. Shortly after the Fatimite caliph died and Saladin made himself undisputed master of Egypt. In the same year Noor-ed-deen died, and Saladin succeeded him as sultan, and thus united in his own person two of the long severed sections of the Mohammedan power—the Saracenic and the Turkish—a union which threatened speedy destruction to the kingdom of Jerusalem. The kingdom was ripe for destruction; the new king, Guy of Lusignan, had not the qualities needed at such a crisis, the princes were divided by rivalries, the nobles had fallen into the luxurious habits of the East, the two military orders were insubordinate, and the Templars suspected of treachery; the general state of morals was excessively depraved.

Saladin at first abstained from attacking the Christians, but at length, in A.D. 1187, provoked by their assaults upon his territory, and especially by their plunder of a caravan of travellers, of whom his mother was one, he invaded the country, defeated the Christian forces with terrible slaughter in the battle of Hittin, or Tiberias, marched to Jerusalem, which fell after a fortnight's siege, overran the country, admitting the Syrian Christians to submission and tribute, until the sea-port of Tyre alone remained in the hands of the Christians. Conrad, son of the Marquis of Montferrat, fortunately arrived in the port of Tyre with troops and money, after the city had been invested on the land side by the enemy, and enabled it to hold out.

Moved by this great misfortune the pope, Clement III., proclaimed a third crusade, and the great sovereigns of Europe responded to the call—Richard of England, Philip of France, Frederick of Germany, the Dukes of Austria and Burgundy, the Count of Flanders, and many lesser princes and nobles, and the great trading republics of Genoa and Pisa. But again these vast forces were wasted. The Germans marching by the old overland route were harassed by the old treachery of the Greeks, and by assaults of the Turks. The generalship of their great emperor however carried them successfully through both. They conquered the Turks with great slaughter in a battle before Iconium, took the city, and marched boldly through the rocky defiles of Cilicia. But in the passage of a river near Tarsus the emperor was drowned; the discipline of the army was no longer maintained after his death. On reaching Antioch many died of the heat and intemperance; many abandoned the enterprize and returned home. Out of all the German hosts the younger Frederick brought only 5,000 men to assist in the siege of Acre; and there he too fell a victim to the climate. Richard of England, who displayed a genius for military affairs, which has been eclipsed by the more popular fame of his personal achievements as a knight-errant, had built a great fleet, with which he sailed from Marseilles straight to Acre. Philip had been conveyed by the fleet of the Genoese. But when the various princes assembled at Acre, their operations were hindered by a thousand jealousies. For two years they were delayed before the town, between the garrison on one side and a great army under Saladin on the other. When Acre at length surrendered the French king returned home in disgust. Richard continued still another year and more, and recovered a large part of the coast from the enemy. But the Christian forces were thinned by war and disease; Richard's strength began to give way under the climate, and after having advanced within a day's march of Jerusalem, he was at last obliged to conclude a three years' truce with his great foe and leave his enterprise unachieved. Returning by land in disguise he was seized by the Duke of Austria and kept in prison for fourteen months until a large ransom had been paid, and, in the spring of 1194, returned to his distracted and impoverished kingdom.

Other crusades were from time to time undertaken.

On the death of the great Saladin (A.D. 1173), the inferior ability of his successor seemed to offer a prospect of success to a renewal of the crusade, and the new pope, Celestine III., urged it. Richard of England declined to take part in it; the King of France used it as a pretext for levying taxes from his people, which he diverted to other uses. The emperor, however, took up the project with some vigour, sent a considerable force to the Holy Land, which achieved some successes and recovered the sea coast; but there was no concerted action between them and the Latins of the East, and the conquests were ephemeral. On the death of Henry (A.D. 1197) the Germans concluded a six years' truce with the enemy and returned home.

Innocent III. on his accession to the papacy earnestly promoted the holy war. But Richard was now dead, Philip of France occupied with difficulties at home, and in Germany Otho and Henry were contending for the empire. A great excitement, however, was kindled in France by the preaching of a priest named Fulk, of Neuilly-on-the-Marne, and a number of the French princes took the cross, the chief among them being the young Count Theobald of

Champagne, brother of Henry, the late King of Jerusalem. They made an alliance with Venice—which at this period had surpassed her rivals, Genoa and Pisa, and was the greatest of the trading republics—for the transport and provisioning of their armies, on the condition that the conquests made should be equally divided between the allies. The great object of the crusade was an invasion of Egypt, which the statesmen of the West held to be the most vulnerable point of the Saracen monarchy. When the main body of the crusaders mustered in Venice, they were unable to raise the price agreed to be paid to the Venetians, and agreed, in lieu of the deficiency, to aid the Venetians in the recovery of Zara, in Dalmatia, which had lately been taken from the republic by the King of Hungary. Old Dandolo, the doge, a man of ninety-four years of age, thereupon took the cross and accompanied the expedition. At Zara they were invited by Alexius, the son of Isaac Angelus, the dethroned Emperor of Constantinople, to aid him in recovering his throne, who promised them in return the co-operation of the empire in the crusade, and the re-union of the churches. The crusaders accepted the offer, and sailed for Constantinople. The magnitude and strength and beauty and riches of the city astonished the Western visitors. After the first assault the usurper Alexius fled, the blinded Isaac was brought out of his prison, replaced upon the throne, and unwillingly ratified the terms which his son had made. Dissensions, however, soon arose between the Greeks and their foreign visitors. Another palace revolution placed Alexius Dinas on the throne. The terms on which the Latins had come to Constantinople were unfulfilled, and they resolved to take possession of Constantinople. They took the city in a second assault, and gave it up to slaughter and pillage. The plunder in gold and silver and objects of ancient art was immense, and Western Europe was enriched with the spoils. The Sainte Chapelle in Paris was built by St. Louis to enshrine the " crown of thorns," which was among the Constantinopolitan treasures, and the bronze horses which adorn the front of St. Mark's at Venice were part of the Venetians' share of the spoil. The conquerors elected Count Baldwin of Flanders to the vacant throne ; a Venetian, Morosini, was elected to be patriarch ; and the Greek empire and Church received a Latin sovereign and hierarchy.

The Latin empire, however, never established itself. Greek princes maintained themselves in Asia and Epirus ; Venetian and Frank nobles established little separate princedoms in the islands of the Levant. The anomalous power thus established endured, by help of the Venetians, through fifty-seven years, when the Greeks, in alliance with the Genoese, deposed Baldwin II., and restored the Greek sovereignty in the person of Michael Palæologus.

The celebrated Simon of Montfort, who was one of the princes of this crusade, refused to turn aside to the attack on Zara, and proceeded straight to the Holy Land, but with the scanty forces which he and others could collect nothing could be effected.

The successor of Innocent III. was equally bent on the prosecution of the holy war. Some reinforcements were sent to Acre. A larger body sailed for Egypt in November, A.D. 1219, and after a siege of sixteen months took Damietta ; but on their march thence to Cairo they found the way barred by the enemy, a pestilence broke out in their camp, the country round them was inundated by the opening of the sluices of the Nile, and the Christian army was compelled to make peace and return. In 1228 the Emperor Frederick sailed in person with a considerable force to Acre, and not by fighting, but by a treaty with the Sultan Kameel, he obtained possession of Jerusalem (with the exception of the Temple, which was to remain in the custody of the Saracens, but to be open to Christians), Nazareth, Bethlehem, Sidon, and other places, and entered Jerusalem in triumph.

Fifteen years afterwards, viz., in A.D. 1244, both Moslem and Christian succumbed before a new power. The Chorasinians, who had gained possession of Persia, were now pressed by the advance of the Tartars. The latter numerous race, inhabiting the plains of Asia, had been formed into a great empire by Genghis Khan in the early part of the thirteenth century; had appeared in a vast swarm and overwhelmed Russia in 1226; had been turned aside from Germany by a brave resistance; overran Poland, and poured down still towards the south. The Chorasinians, pressed on by this irresistible force, fell upon Syria and Palestine, captured Jerusalem, slaughtered the people, robbed the churches, and violated the tombs and sacred places. The pope vainly tried to rouse Europe to its rescue. At this time Lewis IX. of France (A.D. 1249) being hopelessly ill, desired to receive the cross, and from that time began to recover. In fulfilment of the engagement thus undertaken he displayed the Oriflamme, raised the forces of France, and sailed for Cyprus, and thence to Damietta. The history of the former Egyptian expedition was repeated. Damietta was taken with ease, but on the march to Cairo again famine, pestilence, and the cutting of the Nile, reduced the Christian army to the extremity of surrender to the enemy. St. Lewis undertook a second crusade in 1270, and landed in Tunis, but he died there, and the expedition came to nothing. Edward, the heir of England, who had taken the cross, did not arrive till after the death of the French king, and sailed to Acre, where he fulfilled his vow in the defence of the city. The Christians finally lost their last footing in the Holy Land A.D. 1291.

The two hundred years of the crusades dissipated the power and distributed the possessions of the great nobles, helped to build up a middle class with civil rights, to emancipate the peasants, and to establish the authority of the popes. It also introduced into the West something of the learning and arts of the East.

## CHAPTER XXXVII.

#### WALDENSES AND ALBIGENSES.

THEY err greatly who think that the mediæval Church was happily free from the erroneous doctrines and schismatical movements which have distracted us in these more recent ages. In the eleventh and twelfth centuries heresies sprang up sporadically in many parts of the Church, the natural growth of the times. There was a movement of religious earnestness among the people, but the abuses of the Church set earnest minds in antagonism to the established order, while their lack of sound religious knowledge left them a prey to error and fanaticism. The Paterines of the eleventh century were chiefly disaffected opponents of the clergy; the Cathari (or Puritans) of the twelfth century had derived from the East doctrines of a pronounced Manichæan complexion, such as that there are a good and evil principle; that matter is the source of evil; that the world was made by a secondary deity; that men's bodies are the production of the evil principle, and their souls imprisoned in them; that our Lord had not a real body, was not really born, or really died. Among the opponents of the existing order was Peter de Bruys, who during a twenty years' ministry in the early half of the twelfth century, in Languedoc and Provence, established a sect who were called Petro-Brussians. Some of his tenets were those of modern sectarianism. He preached against infant baptism and the grace of the Eucharist; and, since God will accept sincere worship wherever offered, advocated the pulling down of churches. He was at last seized and burnt by the populace. Henry, a monk and hermit, a little later held clandestine assemblies in Poitiers, Bordeaux, and Toulouse, in which he preached somewhat similar doctrines. He was at last brought before Eugenius III., at the Council of Rheims (A.D. 1148), and committed to prison. At the same period a sect of violent fanatics sprang up in Antwerp, who rejected all external ordinances of religion, and the ordinary ties of morality. They were suppressed by St. Norbert, the founder of the Premonstratensians. Arnold of Brescia was rather a seditious disturber of the public order in Church and State, and a man of free opinions, than a heretic, and it was for repeated endeavours to revolutionise Rome that he was at last seized by the prefect of the city and crucified.

The most remarkable of the sects of this century, for its doctrines and its popularity, was that of the Waldenses. These sectaries have excited much interest at various times among ourselves, from the fact that in the thirteenth century they claimed to have existed continuously as a distinct body, in the valleys of Piedmont, from the pure early ages of the Church, and to have maintained unbroken the primitive doctrine and discipline; and some of the continental reformers, who held the whole mediæval Church to have apostatised, regarded these Waldenses and their successors, the Wyclifites and Hussites, as a continuous chain of witnesses for Christ and the Gospel. The question has been very fully and carefully examined, and it seems certain that the sect of the Waldenses was founded about A.D. 1170, by Peter Waldo, a rich merchant of Lyons, who, having been deeply impressed by the sudden death of one of his fellow-townsmen, which took place at a meeting of the chief inhabitants of the place, turned his mind to the consideration of religious questions. He employed two ecclesiastics to translate for him the Gospels used in Divine service, and other portions of Scriptures, and passages of the Fathers. Captivated, as so many before and since have been, with the desire to live more closely after the example of our Lord and His apostles, he gave all his wealth to the poor, associated some others with him, and began to preach in the streets of the city and in the neighbouring villages. The Archbishop of Lyons forbad this unauthorised teaching, and, when Peter declined to desist, excommunicated and expelled him from his diocese. Peter sent two of his party to Rome to request the pope, Innocent III., to sanction their labours. Had he done so, the foundation of an order of preaching friars would have been anticipated by half a century. The pope refused, and they became a sect, under the name of the Poor Men of Lyons, and gradually developed doctrines in opposition to those of the Church. They spread into the south of France, Lombardy, Aragon, and Germany. The earliest real evidence which shows that they had spread also into Piedmont, is in the year 1198, when the Bishop of Turin obtained from the Emperor Otho authority to use forcible measures against them. Their adherents became very numerous; they taught publicly, established schools, proselytised energetically. Their first claim for laymen to preach rapidly developed, as in similar cases, into a claim for their preachers to administer all Christian rites. They went on in opposition to the Church and clergy, and finally limited salvation to their own sect, as being the only one which was like Christ and His apostles. It is admitted that they were sound in faith as to the doctrines which relate to God, and received all the articles of the creed; so that in many respects they bore a very striking resemblance to Protestant sects of modern times, who look back to them with natural interest.

In the latter part of the twelfth and beginning of the

thirteenth centuries various heretical sects multiplied to such an extent as to call for the serious notice of the authorities. In the south of France especially the doctrines of the Cathari had spread even among the princes and higher classes; the gentry ceased to put their sons into holy orders, the clergy were held in general contempt. The bishops issued sentences of excommunication and banishment, but the heretics were protected by the princes; the pope sent special legates, but their mission was not very successful.

It was in the midst of the age of crusades, and the precedent had already been set of applying the name of crusade to any expedition the pope might direct to be undertaken, and of giving the privileges of crusaders to those who joined it. The pope proclaimed a crusade against the heretics of the south of France, who were commonly known by the name of Albigeois, or Albigenses.

A large army was assembled of Frenchmen, Normans, and Flemings. Simon de Montfort, Earl of Leicester, was appointed chief in this holy war. The spirit in which it was carried on is sufficiently illustrated by a brief account of the fate of Beziers, the first town which they attacked. The townsmen, relying on the strength of their fortifications, refused to surrender, Catholics joining with Catharists in patriotic resistance to the invaders. The besiegers repulsed a sally, and pressing close on the retreating townsmen, entered the place with them, and a general massacre ensued. Arnold, Abbot of Citeaux, who was the pope's legate with the crusading army, when asked how the Catholics were to be distinguished from the heretics, answered, "Kill them all; the Lord knoweth them that are His." After the massacre the city was plundered, and then set on fire. At Carcassonne, which made a prolonged resistance, its viscount was decoyed into a conference by an assurance of safe conduct, and then treacherously seized, Abbot Arnold declaring that no faith was to be kept with one who was faithless to his God. He was cast into prison, where he shortly afterwards died. Raymond, Count of Toulouse, who had at first given a forced adherence to the crusade, was at length provoked into taking up arms in defence of his territory. He was aided by the King of Aragon, and the war continued for six years, with alternating fortunes, and with great cruelties on both sides. Raymond submitted in 1214. Simon de Montfort was confirmed by the Council of the Lateran in the possession of the greater part of his conquests, a small part being reserved for Raymond's son. The council also enacted (for the first time) that heretics of all sorts should be made over to the secular arm, which should assist in the extermination of heresy under pain of ecclesiastical censures.

## CHAPTER XXXVIII.

#### THE POPES AT AVIGNON AND THE GREAT SCHISM.

THE death of Boniface VIII., the result of the bold violence of William of Nogaret, the minister of Philip the Fair, closed the great period of the papacy which began with the rise of the Hildebrandine influence in the pontificate of Leo IX.

His successor, Benedict XI., hastened to recede from the domineering attitude and exaggerated pretensions of Boniface. He rescinded many of his predecessor's obnoxious acts, and conciliated the French king. His pontificate lasted only a few months, and Philip, after long intrigue, secured the election of a Frenchman, who was entirely in his interests. The new pope, Clement V., summoned the cardinals to attend his consecration, not at Rome, but at Lyons. He lived in various parts of France for five years, and at length fixed his permanent residence at Avignon; and here, nominally beyond the French territory, but entirely under the influence of the kings of France, the papal see continued for the next seventy years, the pope always a Frenchman, and the majority of the cardinals also of the same race. A papal delegate, usually the Bishop of Orvieto, represented the pope in Rome. A new race of noble families—the Colonnas and Orsini, Gaetani and Savelli, who had their domains and fortified castles near Rome, and their palace fortresses within the city—tyrannised over the imperial city. Dreams of an independent Italy occupied the minds of men; the short-lived tribunate of Rienzi was an attempt to realise these dreams by the revival of the ancient republic, an attempt which had the enthusiastic adhesion of Petrarch; Dante's mind turned rather to a restoration of an universal empire, with Rome for its capital; while both plans contemplated the reformation and maintenance of the spiritual authority of the pope. Rome was still the religious capital of Christendom, pilgrims still flocked from all countries to its shrines; but the court of Rome was at Avignon. The pope built a vast palace-fortress there, which still remains; the cardinals built noble houses around the residence of their sovereign. The papal officials had to find accommodation for themselves and their clerks. Ecclesiastical causes from all countries were brought there for decision; canonists attended upon the courts; crowds of suitors filled its streets, and the city grew to accommodate them; streams of gold flowed to this centre. Clerks seeking ordination, and clergy and prelates of all ranks seeking promotion, usurers and merchants, scholars and artists, swelled the crowd. The luxury of the papal court was great, and the license of the papal city shameless.

The popes,* in abandoning the grand pretensions of the previous period, consoled themselves with increased rapacity. John XXII., the most insatiate of pontiffs, reserved to himself all the bishoprics in Christendom. Benedict XII. assumed the privilege for his own life of nomination to all benefices vacant by cession, deprivation, or translation. Clement VI. continued the right for his time; and it soon became a permanent rule of the Roman chancery. And these benefices were sold without disguise, and were so managed as to bring in the greatest revenue possible. The vacancy of a rich benefice was

* The succession is: (1305) Clement V.; (1316) John XXII.; [Nicholas V., anti-pope, 1328-9;] (1334) Benedict XII.; (1342) Clement VI.; (1352) Innocent VI.; (1362) Urban V.; (1370) Gregory XI

only the first link in a chain of translations, each of which brought its own profit. John XXII. also first imposed upon all benefices the tax called annates, or first-fruits, being the first year's income, which was paid into the coffers of the pope.

The countries of Europe were by these and many other means drained of vast sums, which enriched the pope, the cardinals, and the court of Avignon. These extortions provoked remonstrance and opposition; and at length England, the last to submit to the papal pretensions and the first to oppose them, set the example of refusal to submit any longer to this rapacity. The Parliament of Carlisle, in the time of Edward I., addressed a strong remonstrance to the pope. A Parliament of Edward III. passed the Statute of Provisors, refusing to allow the pope to usurp the patronage of English benefices.

The absence of the popes from Rome had produced great dissatisfaction everywhere except in France. To the rest of Europe it seemed a monstrous anomaly that the popes, whose authority was professedly based on their occupancy of the Apostolic see of Rome, should leave Rome vacant and transfer their chair to Avignon. The higher class of Italians were discontented, for their families had been accustomed for centuries to derive wealth and honours from the possession of the great offices of the Church, which were now monopolised by Frenchmen; and the populace of Rome was dissatisfied with the loss of the wealth of which the absence of the court deprived them. Urban V. took up his residence in Rome, but after three years returned to Avignon. His successor, Gregory XI., also established himself in Rome, but it is said that he also had resolved to remove to Avignon, when death overtook him.

The death of Gregory XI. was the commencement of the Great Schism between two lines of popes, who for above forty years divided Western Christendom into two almost equal camps, and between whose rival claims it is to this day difficult, or impossible, to arrive at a satisfactory decision.

The origin of the schism was as follows. Gregory XI. dying in Rome, the cardinals proceeded to the election of his successor. The Roman populace surrounded the place of meeting with clamours for a Roman, or at least an Italian, pope. The cardinals elected a Neapolitan archbishop, under the name of Urban VI. (A.D. 1378). This satisfied the people. The cardinals announced the election to their absent colleagues and to the world, and treated Urban as pope for several weeks. But the pope began his reign by a sentence of excommunication against the cardinals who had been guilty of simony. The cardinals, in return, withdrew to a neighbouring town, declared the previous election null, because made under compulsion, and chose one of their own number, a Frenchman, under the name of Clement VII., who took up his residence at Avignon with the cardinals of his party, Urban remaining at Rome. In similar cases of rival popes in former times there had been little doubt who was the legitimate pope; the anti-pope was usually the creature of some prince or faction, and had only a scanty local recognition. But in the present case the question of right was really very doubtful, and each rival received a wide and conscientious support. To Urban adhered Italy, the German Empire, England, and the nations of the north. Clement received the recognition of France, Spain, Scotland, and Sicily. The general wish of Europe was that the difficulty might be solved by the abdication of both, and a fresh undisputed election. But personal ambitions and interests prevented the popes and cardinals of both lines from performing this act of self-denial. The Roman succession was continued by the successive elections of Urban VI. (1378),

Boniface IX. (1389), Innocent VII. (1404), and Gregory XII. (1406). The Avignon line was continued in Clement VII. (1378) and Benedict XIII. (Peter di Luna) (1394). One effect of the schism was that Christendom had to support two papal courts instead of one, both unwilling to submit to any diminution of the customary wealth and splendour. The exactions and venality of the earlier Avignon popes appeared light in comparison with the practices of both rivals during the continuance of the schism. The popes of both lines were continually pressed to abdicate; some of them solemnly swore to do so, and evaded their oaths. It was even said that there was a tacit collusion between them. The spectacle of two papacies, each anathematising the other as antichrist, and both behaving like antichrists, shook the authority of the papacy; there was universal uncertainty and distress of conscience throughout the Western Church. It was the opinion of the time that schismatical ordinations and sacraments were invalid, and who could feel sure that it was not his own party which was in the schism? Persons since accounted as saints by the whole Church were then arrayed against one another, and anathematised one another, while the whole Church cried aloud for a settlement and for a general reformation "in its head and in its members." At length the cardinals of both parties deserted their popes, and summoned a general council at Pisa for the solution of the difficulty.

The Council of Pisa (1409) began by deposing both popes, and then proceeded to elect a new pope in Alexander V. But the deposed popes continued their pretensions; both continued to find supporters, and the action of the council had only created a third line of rival popes. From 1378 to 1409 the Western Church was divided into two, and from 1409 to 1415 into three, obediences. Alexander V. was succeeded by John XXIII. (1410), who very reluctantly summoned another council to meet at Constance, in

A.D. 1414. This council at once deposed John himself, and then proceeded to consider fully the state of the Church. The proceedings of the council at Constance, and of the subsequent councils at Basle and Florence, are so important that they may be more conveniently considered in a separate chapter.

## CHAPTER XXXIX.

THE REFORMING COUNCILS OF THE FIFTEENTH CENTURY.

THE question of the schism had occupied men's minds for a whole generation, and its consideration had forced thoughtful men to adopt and insist upon principles of Church government opposed to those Hildebrandine principles which had obtained so universally for three previous centuries. As all the eminent saints of the period were outspoken and loud in their denunciation of the abuses of the papacy, so all the eminent theologians of the end of the fourteenth and beginning of the fifteenth centuries were substantially agreed on the principles on which a reformation of them must proceed. There was no question of Christian doctrine involved; it was entirely a question of Church constitution and of legislative and administrative authority. All were agreed that the Church must assert herself as against the Roman Curia; must maintain the superiority of a general council to that of the pope, and must undertake for herself, and not wait for the Curia to concede, a general reform of the Church " in her head and her members"; this was the watchword throughout Europe, and was understood to mean that the necessary reform must begin with the papal see. As Nicholas I. had enunciated the principle of the supreme sovereignty of the pope over the whole Church, and it had been left to the Hildebrandine popes to apply the principle and force it upon the Church, so the Council of Pisa had enunciated the theory that the Church represented in a general council was superior to the pope, and might depose him; and the Council of Constance forced the acceptance of this principle upon the popes.

The Council of Pisa had been a failure, and it was evident that it had failed, because as soon as it had elected a new pope, he, with the support of the cardinals, assumed the old attitude of supremacy, and at once arrested any further attempt at reformation. The Council of Constance was undertaken with a more developed idea of the ends to be attained and a more careful consideration of the steps necessary for their attainment.

The first step of importance was a return to primitive precedent by the appointment of the Emperor Sigismund to protect and preside over the council. The next important step was the holding of the council out of Italy, where the whole Church and people were pledged to the maintenance of the ancient abuses. A third was the admitting to the council, besides prelates and bishops, of whom the majority owed their positions to the abuses which it was desired to reform, representatives of universities, canonists, and theologians. There were actually assembled 300 bishops, deputies of fourteen universities, and 300 doctors. A fourth step was the method of voting by nations. The Italian bishops were then (as ever since) so much more numerous, in proportion to those of other churches, that their individual votes would have given them a very unfair advantage over the other branches of the Church. It was therefore resolved that the council should divide itself into four nations—the Italian, German, French, and English—each with equal rights, and that every proposition having been separately discussed the majority of the four should prevail. The first act of the council was to depose not only the rival pope, Gregory, but also the Pope John (XXIII.) who had summoned it. He had deserved deposition by his misconduct, and it seemed politic to do it, both to re-assert the principle of the power of a general council to depose a pope, and to leave a clear course for the contemplated reforms.

The famous decrees of the fourth and fifth sessions of this council declared that " every lawfully convoked œcumenical council representing the Church derives its authority immediately from Christ; and every one, the pope included, is subject to it in matters of faith, in the healing of schism, and the reformation of the Church." The decree was passed without a dissentient voice. That the council was œcumenical cannot be disputed. The two small fractions of the Church which still obeyed Gregory XII. and Benedict XIII. ultimately gave in their adherence to the council, as is shown in the concordat of Narbonne; Gregory XIII. resigned, and John XXIII. was deposed with universal consent. A committee of reformation sat and examined carefully into the abuses of the Church, and made recommendations to the council, which, if accepted and carried into effect, would have destroyed the machinery by which Rome had absorbed so much of the revenues and patronage of the Church, and corrected many of the evils which had so long oppressed the Christian commonweal. But the papistic party were astute and active. After Gregory and John had been put out of the way the council disagreed on the next great step. The Germans and English desired to proceed to settle the reforms before electing a new pope; the cardinals and Italians wanted to proceed at once to elect the pope; and the French, out of national jealousy of the lofty position and the leading part which the Emperor Sigismund took in the council, joined the Italians. The Latin party gained over the English, and it was decided to proceed at once to the papal election. Next the Germans and English joined the Italians in favour of an Italian candidate, the Cardinal Colonna, and he was elected as Martin V. The new pope acted as had been anticipated;

used all his power and influence to evade any real reformation, continued the policy of playing off the nations one against another; concluded separate concordats with them; and terminated the council as soon as possible. In the end only a few reforming ordinances came into force; most of the articles of these few were so drawn as to leave open a door for the renewal of abuses, and in a short time things reverted to their former course.

One important feature in the history of the Council of Constance must not be omitted here, viz., its action against Wyclif and Huss and Jerome of Prague. The council was, perhaps, influenced by a desire to balance its revolutionary action against abuses of constitution and administration by a striking evidence of its orthodoxy in questions of faith. The council accordingly considered the doctrines of Wyclif, and extracted forty-five propositions from his writings, which it condemned as unsound, and decreed that since Wyclif had died an impenitent heretic his bones should be exhumed and cast out of ecclesiastical sepulture. The sentence was duly executed by the English ecclesiastical authorities.

The council next dealt with the religious controversy which was disturbing Bohemia. Huss was a man of learning and distinction, Rector of the University of Prague, confessor to the queen, preacher at a chapel in the capital founded for the purpose of encouraging preaching in the vernacular tongue; he had adopted and taught the doctrine of Wyclif,* and his teaching on one hand found many adherents in Bohemia, and on the other excited great opposition. Cited to appear before the pope, he had excused himself and expressed his desire to appeal to a general council. The Emperor Sigismund wished that the council

* Except on the subject of the Eucharist, on which he held the current Roman doctrine.

should settle these religious difficulties of Bohemia, and requested his brother Wenceslaus, the King of Bohemia, to send Huss to Constance, promising him a safe-conduct. Jerome of Prague, one of his chief followers, hearing of this, also voluntarily joined him at Constance. Here the council induced Sigismund to allow his safe-conduct to be set aside, on the plea that the council was greater than the emperor and could overrule his safe-conduct, and that no safe-conduct extended to the protection of a heretic from the punishment of his heresy. The two men were imprisoned and treated with rigour, and ultimately were condemned and burnt at the stake—Jerome on May 30th, Huss on July 6th, 1416.

This act of the council provoked an outbreak of resistance to Rome throughout Bohemia, which brought the most terrible misfortunes upon the kingdom. The opposing parties engaged in a ferocious civil war, extended their hostilities into the neighbouring countries, and thus brought upon themselves repeated invasions in return.

Huss and Jerome were regarded by their party as martyrs, their pictures were placed in the churches, and the leading Hussites bound themselves by mutual engagements to maintain their doctrines. Nicholas of Hussinecz and John Ziska came to the front—the one as the political, the other the military, chief of the movement. The right of the laity to the sacramental cup was their watchword. Ziska gathered a powerful force, displayed the chalice embroidered on his banners, and wherever he went enforced the administration of the Eucharist in both kinds. On the 22nd July, 1419, a great number of the Hussites met on a hill near Aust, and formed a camp, and inaugurated their enterprise by a general celebration of the Holy Communion in the open air. The previous confession was omitted, the clergy celebrated without any distinctive vestments, the altars, 300 in number, were uncovered tables, the chalices of wood. Forty-two thousand persons—men, women, and children—communicated, and the celebration was followed by a great love feast. This camp became permanent, and grew into a town called Tabor —tabor being the Bohemian for tent. From this camp Ziska and his armed followers marched upon Prague, where they killed some of the magistrates, and attacked and plundered the convents. The excitement threw King Wenceslaus into an apoplexy, of which he died. Bohemia fell to his brother, the Emperor Sigismund, against whom the Hussites entertained a special hatred, as a traitor who had lured Huss to Constance by his safe-conduct and then abandoned him to his fate. They broke out at once into open rebellion, and proceeded to acts of violence; they renewed their attack on the convents of Prague, and slaughtered the monks. The movement spread to other places. Churches and monasteries were plundered, their ornaments destroyed, and in many places the buildings themselves reduced to ruin. The Bohemians were divided among themselves. A small proportion, especially among the higher classes, adhered to the Roman Church; the University, the inhabitants of the capital, and many among the middle classes generally were in favour of a moderate reform; a numerous party, chiefly of the populations of the towns and the peasantry, went to fanatical lengths in their views, and with their religious extravagances were mixed up political opinions of a republican and socialistic complexion. The more moderate reformers were called Calixtines (from calix, chalice); the more extreme Taborites, either from their original camp, or from the camp meetings which formed an important feature of their system, where the people assembled in tens of thousands to receive the Eucharist in both kinds, and where their fanaticism was kept alive by the well-known means of fervid oratory addressed to a vast and sympathetic multitude. This latter party, with Ziska at its head, was the party of violence. Ziska possessed extraordinary military genius, and by adopting modes of warfare suited to the rude arms and enthusiastic character of his followers, he made them into a formidable army, which was everywhere victorious in its enterprises. The war was carried on with horrible ferocity. On the taking of a town all the inhabitants were slain, except, perhaps, a few women and children; churches were burnt, with those who had taken refuge in them. Ziska was in the habit of burning priests and monks in pitch. The Catholics made equally cruel reprisals. By this warfare not only churches and monasteries, but palaces, castles, and even whole towns, were destroyed; manufactures and foreign commerce were ruined, tillage was neglected, adventurers flocked to both sides for the sake of adventure and plunder. The emperor collected a great army to subdue the country, but then the Bohemians suspended their mutual hostilities, and under the command of Ziska defeated the invaders. A second and a third time Sigismund invaded the country, but each time recoiled with disgrace before the heroic defence.

We anticipate the future, in order here to complete the Bohemian story. When the Council of Basle met, the Bohemians were invited to send a deputation for the discussion of their differences, and four articles, known as the *Compactata*, were agreed upon as terms of peace. The only concession they made was that the clergy should administer the Eucharist in both kinds to such adults as should desire it; in all other points the Bohemians were to conform to the Church The more moderate were willing to accept these terms, the more violent refused, and the disagreement led to a battle at Lipau between the two parties, in which the moderates were victorious, and the power of the fanatics was effectually broken. In 1436, at a great assembly at Iglau, Sigismund was met by all estates of the kingdom, the Bishop of

Constance being present as legate of the council, the *Compactata* were received as a settlement of the religious state of Bohemia, and a few days later Sigismund was formally accepted as their king. The troubles of Bohemia were, however, not yet concluded.

The death of Sigismund in the following year was followed by a disputed succession and a long minority. The Taborites were not silenced, and it was not until after a diet held at Prague in 1444 that the doctrine of the Calixtines acquired a general acceptance, and the Taborite practices gradually died out, until they survived only in the town of Tabor itself. But next the pope repudiated the *Compactata*, as having been agreed upon by the Council of Basle after its rupture with the pope, and therefore of no validity; and on the refusal of George Podiebrad, the king, to abandon the Bohemian liberties and reduce the kingdom to entire conformity, he fomented opposition to him, declared him a heretic, pronounced sentence of deposition, and proclaimed a crusade against him. Matthias Corvinus, King of Hungary, responded to the invitation of the pope and the papal party in the kingdom, to wrest the sceptre out of the hands of George, but the invader was unsuccessful. On the death of George the pope continued his patronage of Matthias; but the Bohemians elected Ladislaus, a Polish prince, who made good his claims by force of arms, and eventually succeeded Matthias in his Hungarian kingdom. In this reign a fresh settlement of religion was concluded. Each of the great parties was to enjoy perfect religious freedom, and on a vacancy in any parish the new incumbent was to be chosen from the same party to which the old one had belonged.

By one of the decrees passed at Constance it was provided that another general council should be held in five years, a second at the end of another seven years, and that from that time a general council should be assembled every ten years. Accordingly at the end of five years Martin V. summoned a council at Pavia, which, on account of the plague, was removed to Siena, and then dismissed by the pope on account of the fewness of those present. Shortly before his death, however, he summoned a new council at Basle. Eugenius IV., the new pope, could not avoid the meeting of the council, but immediately after its opening proceedings he pronounced it dissolved, with a view to its reassembling a year and a half later at Bologna. The council, however, relying on the decrees of Constance, refused to suspend its session. It received the adhesion of the kings, princes, prelates, universities, and bishops; many even of the cardinals and papal officials, in spite of his sentences of excommunication against them, deserted the pope and went to Basle; the public opinion of Europe was against the pope, and there was talk of suspending him, when he prudently gave way, retracted his hostile bulls, admitted that the council had been fully justified in continuing in session and passing decrees notwithstanding his bull of dissolution, and professed his devotion to the Universal Church and the holy Œcumenical Council of Basle. He sent four cardinals to preside over the council as his legates, who were admitted to the presidency on swearing, in their own names, to the decree already passed in the second session, that a general council has its authority immediately from Christ, and that all men, including the pope, are bound to obey it in matters relating to faith, to the extinction of schism, and the reform of the Church in head and members.

The subjection of the papacy to the authority of a general council seemed irrefragably established. For three years and a half the council continued its sessions; decrees of reform were drawn up, and the pope signified his agreement with them; but at the end of that time the struggle between the pope and the council broke out afresh. If the pope could remove the place of assembly to Italy his ultimate victory was tolerably secure. His first attempt to remove it to Bologna had failed, but now a plausible pretext arose for its removal, of which he took advantage.

The Emperor John Palæologus, threatened by the power of Amurath II., sought aid from the West for the preservation of the Greek empire and Church. The pope invited him to a conference with a view to the reunion of the churches, holding out the prospect of effectual temporal aid as the sequel of the healing of the religious schism which had so long kept the two halves of Christendom apart. The pope desired that the meeting should take place in some Italian city. A majority of the council passed a decree that the meeting should be north of the Alps; but the minority of the council also passed an irregular decree in accordance with the pope's wishes, got it by a stratagem signed with the seal of the council, had it read in one corner of the cathedral, while the decree of the majority was read from the pulpit, and sent it to the pope. The pope accepted it as the legitimate act of the council, and issued a bull transferring the council to Ferrara.

The pope's council opened at Ferrara, January 8, 1438. Of the fathers assembled at Basle only two transferred themselves to the rival assembly. Of the great nations only England obeyed the summons of Eugenius. The Basle council proceeded to declare Eugenius deposed, and elected in his place Amadeus, ex-Duke of Savoy, under the title of Felix V. The feeling of the Church was, however, opposed to the creation of another schism; the sovereigns, many of the bishops, and other important members of the council, absented themselves; and though the council continued to sit, it grew continually feebler. Nicholas V., the successor of Martin, induced Felix to resign, and the schism soon came to an end. The rival council of Ferrara meanwhile was busy with its negotiation with the Greeks.

The differences between the Eastern and Western divisions of the Church had grown up gradually. The foundation of a rivalry of honour was laid when Constantine removed the seat of empire to the shore of the Bosphorus, and this rivalry lay at the bottom of all the subsequent dissensions, and was the real cause of the final schism. The question of the worship of images was the first doctrinal question on which the two churches took opposite sides; but the controversy was only a temporary one. The addition in the Western Church of the "filioque" to the creed without the authority of a general council was, and has continued to the present day to be, the chief doctrinal cause of the division. There were other minor questions, as the use of leavened or unleavened bread in the Eucharist, the marriage or celibacy of the clergy; but on all these questions mutual explanations and mutual concessions often smoothed the way for a reconciliation; the great insurmountable obstacle was the pretensions of the Roman see to supremacy over the whole Church, and the refusal of Constantinople to surrender the liberties of the independent patriarchates to the ambition of the patriarch of Rome, and sacrifice the ancient constitution of the Church to the papal system of a monarchy.

Since the final breach in 1054, when the two churches formally excommunicated one another, several attempts had been made on both sides to effect a reconciliation. The emperors, when from time to time pressed by the invaders of the empire, sought a reconciliation as the means of securing the sympathy and help of the West. The popes from time to time endeavoured to complete their spiritual empire by negotiating for the annexation of the Eastern branches of the Church.

The present crisis offered a hope that the reconciliation might at last be effected. The emperor earnestly desired it, and was resolved to put considerable pressure on his Church to bring them to an agreement. The pope earnestly desired it; it would add greatly to the prestige of the papacy, so much lowered during the previous century. All Europe desired it, on the broad general ground of the wickedness of the schism.

In the existing relative position of the pope and the Council of Basle, each professing to be the true representative of the Western Church, it was of great importance which would obtain the recognition in that character of the Eastern churches. Each sent a pressing invitation to the emperor and the patriarch, each sent a fleet to convey them, and the rival fleets were with difficulty prevented from engaging in a naval combat within sight of Constantinople. The emperor and the dignified ecclesiastics and their numerous suites accepted the pope's invitation, and in due course arrived at Ferrara. Difficult questions of etiquette were settled by the pope occupying the highest seat, the Eastern emperor a place on his left on a lower chair, corresponding with the vacant chair of the Western emperor on his right, the patriarch a seat on the same level as those of the cardinals. The discussion of the disputed points occupied fifteen months, in the course of which the plague broke out at Ferrara, and the council was removed to Florence. The Greek theologians showed skill and courage, but they were not fairly treated. The pope had engaged to defray their expenses, but what he did was to dole out rations to them, and withhold supplies in order to coerce the unwilling, while giving bribes liberally to those who were open to such inducements; while their own emperor also put pressure upon them. In the end they arrived at an agreement on the four principal points debated: (1) The question of the procession of the Holy Spirit was compromised. The Greeks explained that in limiting themselves to the ancient words of the Niceno-Constantinopolitan Creed, "proceeding from the Father," they did not intend to exclude procession from the Son, but only procession from the Father and the Son as from two principles, while the Latins declared that they did not hold the double procession in this latter sense. Each party was still to retain its own form of the creed. (2) As to the Eucharist, it was decided that either leavened or unleavened bread might be used, and that each church should retain its own custom. (3) It was agreed that souls are purified by suffering after death, and that they may be benefited by the prayers and alms of the living; but on the difference as to the nature of purgatory nothing was decided contrary to the opinion of either Church. (4) The Roman pontiff was declared to have the primacy of the whole world, as being the successor of St. Peter, who was chief of the apostles and vicar of Christ; and that to him, in St. Peter, was given by the Saviour full power of teaching, directing, and governing the Church, according as is contained both in the acts of the œcumenical councils and in the sacred canons. The other patriarchal sees — Constantinople, Alexandria, Antioch, and Jerusalem—were to hold the same order as of old, to wit, with all their privileges and rights preserved.

The fourth decision was the critical one, and was arrived at with great difficulty.

The pope claimed a recognition of his supremacy over the whole Church, "according to Scripture and the sayings of the saints." The emperor pointed out that the sayings of the saints—*i.e.*, the courtly rhetoric to be found in the letters of ancient bishops and emperors to the bishops of Rome—could not be accepted as definitions of the legal relations subsisting between the two parties, and that the canons of councils ought to be taken as the rule. When the papal theologians sought to overwhelm the Greeks with the mass of forged and corrupted passages in the pseudo-Isidore and Gratian, they answered shortly and drily, "All these canons are apocryphal." The compromise at length effected was ambiguous. It ran that the pope had authority from Christ to rule and feed the Church "in the manner contained in the acts of the œcumenical councils and in the canons." But, first, the text of this famous passage has been corrupted; and next, whatever text be taken, its meaning is disputed. The Greeks say that they intended to acknowledge the pope's authority only so far as it was in accordance with the ancient councils and canons. The Latins say that the reference to ancient councils and canons was not a limiting clause, but only a confirmatory reference, and was not only an acknowledgment of the plenary authority claimed, but also that this authority was according to ancient rule and precedent.

This last attempt at a reconciliation of the schism between East and West utterly failed. Everywhere on their return journey the Greeks were met with marks of disapprobation. At Constantinople a storm of execration awaited them, and the people deserted the churches; the patriarch had died a month before the conclusion of the treaty, and the leading ecclesiastics refused to accept the vacant dignity; and when one was found to accept it the people turned their backs upon his benediction. The patriarchs of Alexandria, Antioch, and Jerusalem held a council, at which they denounced the Council of Florence, and declared the new patriarch of Constantinople, and all bishops appointed by him, to be deposed, and threatened the emperor with the censures of the Church.  The Primate of Russia, who had also attended the council and accepted its decrees, on his return was upbraided by the Prince Basil, at the public service of the Church, as a traitor; the clergy deserted him, he was imprisoned in a monastery, and at length escaped to Rome.

On the failure of the attempts at reformation by means of councils the sovereigns took the question into their own hands. The King of France, on the occasion of the quarrel between the pope and the Council of Basle, summoned an assembly, which was attended by the dauphin and princes of the blood, many of the nobility, bishops, and other ecclesiastics and laymen, at Bourges. At this assembly it was resolved to continue to recognise the pope, but also to accept the reforming decrees of the council, with certain modifications required by the circumstances of France. Thus originated the "Pragmatic Sanction of Bourges," the first comprehensive codification of what have since been called the Gallican liberties. They recognised the supreme authority of general councils, secured the freedom of Church elections, and rejected the papal encroachments on rights of patronage and the revenues of benefices. Twenty years after Pius II. (Æneas Silvius Piccolomini, who, as secretary to the Council of Basle, had written in its defence), at a council held at the Lateran, condemned the Council of Basle, and declared the Pragmatic Sanction to be heresy. Nevertheless it continued to be the law of France till Pius II. induced Lewis XI. to abrogate it, bribing the king by conceding to the Crown the patronage of the Church. The Parliament of Paris behaved with great courage, remonstrated with the king, refused to register his edict, and continued to act on the Sanction as legal, and it continued to be law till the time of Francis I. Leo X. induced that king to agree to a Concordat, and he, with great difficulty, coerced the Parliament and Church into its acceptance.

The German electors in like manner, at the Imperial Diet of Mentz (1439), recognised Eugenius as pope, but accepted the reformation decrees of Basle. But the pope, by intrigues and bribes, and through the influence of Æneas Silvius, the emperor's adviser, who had been won over by the pope, and by giving the princes large rights over the German churches, triumphed over the opposition; and soon after, in 1448, by the Concordat of Vienna the pope regained many of the advantages he had surrendered. In these concordats the popes bribed the sovereigns to allow the old exactions and the old invasions of the rights of the national churches to continue, by transferring to the sovereigns a large share of the patronage and power thus accruing.

On the whole, the Church relapsed into its old state of corruption. The popes steadily resisted any attempt to summon a new council. They had secured the sovereigns, they proceeded by honours and preferments to win over the men of literary talent; a new race of writers set themselves to rehabilitate the old theories of papal power. The popes never, indeed, assumed anything like the Hildebrandine attitude towards the Christian sovereigns, and the sovereigns were careful to maintain their power over their national churches, and their rights as against the pope; but the abuses of the court of Rome even increased, and from Rome, as from a centre of infection, corruption and vice spread over Europe. From 1464 to 1503 the Christian world endured the rule of such popes as Paul II., Sixtus IV., Innocent VIII., and Alexander VI., each of whom seems as if he had striven to exceed the vices of his predecessors. The Church cried out against the universal wickedness and corruption, but no one could see from what source it was possible for a reformation to arise. A Dominican preacher, about

1484, said, " The world cries for a council, but how can one be obtained in the present state of the heads of the Church? No human power avails any longer to reform the Church through a council, and God Himself must come to our aid in some way unknown to us."

# CHAPTER XL.

### THE GREEK EMPIRE AND CHURCH FROM THE EMPRESS IRENE, 780, TO THE FALL OF THE EMPIRE, 1453.

WE arrested our sketch of the Eastern empire in chapter XXVIII. at the reign of the Empress Irene, the contemporary of Charlemagne, the restorer of the worship of images. Irene was dethroned by her treasurer Nicephorus (802), and in exile on the Isle of Lesbos earned a scanty subsistence by the labours of her distaff.

A series of usurpations followed: Stauracius; Michael I.; Leo (V.), the Armenian; Michael (II.), the Stammerer; Theophilus; Michael (III.), the Drunkard, the Elagabalus of the Eastern empire. In his reign (842) occurs one of the chief points of contact between the Eastern and Western Churches. The Patriarch of Constantinople was deposed by Michael (or rather by his uncle, the Cæsar Bardas, who administered state affairs while his nephew wallowed in vice), and the able and learned Photius was consecrated in his place. Ignatius appealed to his brother Patriarch of Rome, Nicholas I., not to recognise the intruder. Nicholas espoused his cause and excommunicated Photius, who retorted the excommunication. The quarrel between the churches was embittered by their rival claims to the ecclesiastical obedience of Bulgaria.* Next came Basil, the Macedonian (867), who founded a dynasty which lasted through

* See page 319.

the reigns of five emperors, for one hundred and sixty years. Basil was succeeded by his son Leo, the Philosopher; he by his son Constantine (VII.), Porphyrogenitus; he by his son Romanus, who had two sons, Basil and Constantine, and two daughters, Theophano and Anne; the elder daughter was given in marriage to Otho II., Emperor of the West, and the younger to Vladimir, Duke (and Apostle) of Russia. On the death of Romanus his youthful sons, Basil II. and Constantine IX., succeeded, but in aid of their inexperience, first Nicephorus, and on his death John Zimisces, was associated with them in the purple. Basil II was the conqueror of the Bulgarians, who, though converted to Christianity, and owning ecclesiastical dependence on the see of Constantinople, had for many years past kept up an aggressive warfare upon the empire.

On the death of Constantine IX., the last male heir of the Macedonian family, its blood still occupied the throne in the person of his daughter Zoe, who brought the imperial title and power to her successive husbands, Romanus III., Michael IV., and Constantine Monomachus; and next in the person of Theodora, married to Michael IV., Stratisticus. It was while Theodora, now a widow, was sole empress, that the final rupture of the Eastern and Western branches of the Church was consummated. The swords of the Normans had terminated the Greek power in Apulia, which had formed part of the Greek empire since Justinian's reign, and brought its churches under the Roman obedience. The patriarch, Michael Celularius, issued a pastoral to the flock thus torn from his care, warning them against the errors of the Latins. The pope, Leo IX., sent ambassadors to complain of this insult, and obtaining no redress, the papal envoys laid on the altar of Sta. Sophia a formal sentence of excommunication, which the patriarch retorted (1054). The pretensions of the popes to sovereignty over the whole Church had by this time been matured; all future attempts at a reconciliation between the two churches failed in that point, and the breach continues to the present hour.

By a bloodless revolution the noble family of the Comneni succeeded to the throne; first Isaac Comnenus (1057), then, after an interval Alexius (1081), the emperor in whose reign the first crusaders passed through Constantinople on their way to the Holy Land. He was succeeded by his son John, the Handsome, an able and warlike sovereign, who ruled well, and kept the Saracens in effectual check. Manuel, his son, was the greatest hero of the imperial line of the East; he extended his conquests and influence in the West, strengthened himself by marriages and alliances with the Western princes; made overtures to the pope, Alexander III., for a reconciliation of the churches, and aimed at the reconstitution of the ancient grandeur of the Roman empire by the recovery of the obedience of the West. Andronicus, the last of the Comneni, the hero of a most romantic career, usurped the imperial throne in 1183. A revolt of the people dethroned him and raised Isaac Angelus to the purple. He was dethroned and imprisoned by his brother Alexius Angelus; but his son escaping fled to the West, repaired to Venice, where the warriors of Europe were assembling for the second crusade, and induced them by great promises to undertake his father's cause. The crusaders accepted the enterprise and sailed for Constantinople. After a brief assault they took the city and restored it and the European provinces to the Emperor Isaac. But the people of Constantinople rose against the Angeli and their Latin allies. A second siege put the city into the hands of the crusaders with the rights of conquerors (1204). They plundered the city of its wealth and its art treasures, the accumulation of a thousand years, and divided the empire among themselves; the French took the city and title of emperor, and seven Latin emperors succeeded one another during a period of fifty-five years. A Latin patriarch was appointed, and the Latin Church established as that of the new empire. The Greek nobles fled to the other great cities of the empire, and set up independent sovereignties. "Whatever was learned or holy, whatever was noble or valiant, rolled away into the independent states of Trebizond, Epirus, and Nice."

Theodore Lascaris set up the Roman standard at Nice, and he and his son-in-law and successor, Ducas Vataces, whose reigns extended over fifty years, gradually won back the whole of the European provinces, hemmed in the imperial city on every side, and reduced its Latin emperors to seek, and seek in vain, for Western succours to avert their impending fate. In 1261, under Michael Paleologus, the city itself was surprised, and the Greek empire restored at Constantinople in the family of the Paleologi. Several of the islands (Lesbos, Chios, Rhodes) were soon after wrested out of the hands of the Franks; but the Asiatic side of the empire was left exposed to the Turks.

Michael sought to avert a Western assault upon the restored empire by seeking an ecclesiastical reconciliation with the pope. This was effected (for the time) at the Council of Lyons (1274). But the subject despots of Ætolia, Epirus, and Thessaly, refused to accede to the union; the immediate subjects of Michael resisted it, and endured severe persecution; on the emperor's death the whole Eastern Church and people abjured the enforced and unreal union.

In the reign of John Paleologus (1341—1391) the Ottoman Turks conquered nearly all the empire, excepting only the city. The emperor again sought in person the succour of the West, offering the price of a reconciliation with Rome.

The history of the Council of Ferrara, in which this was effected with imperfect and transitory success, has been told in a previous chapter.

The emperor paid the price of submission to the pope, but failed to obtain the advantage which he sought; and on his return with empty coffers his person was detained at Venice for the sums he had borrowed there, till his son Manuel raised what money he could in Constantinople, and sailing with it to Venice relieved his father, and pledged his own person as a security for the debt. Thirty years later, when the empire was on the verge of ruin, Manuel again visited the chief states of Europe to beg for aid. He was received everywhere with imperial honours and respectful pity; but the King of France was a lunatic (Charles X.); the King of England (Henry IV.), a usurper, whose throne was threatened by internal discord, and who could not spare forces for a distant expedition; while the power of the papacy was paralysed by the great schism.

But the impending fate of the empire was postponed for another fifty years. The invasion of Timour (or Tamerlane) called Bajazet away to the defence of his own dominions, and his defeat and capture in the battle of Angora (1402) shattered the Turkoman power.

The severed portions of the Turkoman dominions were reunited in Mahomet I., who was succeeded by two warlike sovereigns. But the armies of Amurath II. and Mahomet II. were employed by John Hunniades, who at Belgrade arrested the westward progress of the Ottoman arms, and by Scanderbeg, the Prince of Albania, who for twenty-three years kept up a war of independence among his mountains.

The end of this long history of the empire of Constantine was, however, approaching. On the death of the Emperor Manuel Paleologus, his son Constantine was chosen as his successor (1448). Three years afterwards the young and enterprising Mahomet II. succeeded Amurath, and at once resolved on the conquest of the imperial city. The fall of the city is, perhaps, the noblest chapter of its history, and the last of the emperors died the death of a hero after a protracted and desperate defence in the breach, resisting the last overwhelming assault, and his body was found buried under a heap of slain, May 29, 1453.

The Turks tolerated the Church in their dominions, the sultans retaining the power which the emperors exercised of instituting and deposing the Patriarch of Constantinople. The organisation of the ancient churches has been maintained. There are still the four Patriarchs of Constantinople, Alexandria, Antioch, and Jerusalem, but they rule over a scanty, scattered, and oppressed people.

## CHAPTER XLI.

### MEDIÆVAL DEVELOPMENTS.

IF we try to bring together into one view some of the most striking features in which the general aspect of the Church and the popular religion of the Middle Ages differed from those of the present day, we shall perhaps find them in the following particulars.

In the general external aspect of the Church: (1) the papal supremacy, and all which flowed from it; (2) the disciplinary organisation of the Church; (3) the constitution of the various bodies of the clergy.

In the popular doctrinal system: (4) the popular idea of the Eucharist; (5) the cultus of the Blessed Virgin Mary; (6) the cultus of local saints, with the pilgrimages and indulgences which sprang out of it; (7) the belief in purgatory and masses for the dead.

A few words on each of these topics may help the reader to realise the religious condition of Christendom during these ages.

1. The papal supremacy. We must not suppose that people generally had any great personal veneration for the pope, or that they submitted willingly to the papal rule. On the contrary, we know that princes questioned and resisted his authority, that the national churches complained bitterly of the infringement of their rights, that the people generally complained of the venality and rapacity of the papal officials, and that some theologians questioned the Divine right of their rule. But the fact remains that the papacy had gra-

dually grown up to a spiritual empire over the whole West, which was practically recognised by all men, and made itself everywhere felt. People might murmur against papal tyranny and misgovernment, but they submitted to it as to a power they could not resist; they might complain of venality and rapacity, but they went on bribing the officials of the Curia when they had any business at Rome, and paying Peter's pence, all the same.

2. The disciplinary action of the Church then presents a striking contrast to the utter and lamentable absence of discipline among ourselves. Our fathers used to tell us about people being condemned to open penance for notorious sins, but for two generations perhaps the hand of discipline has not been stretched out against one single lay offender, and most Churchmen are unconscious that the Church even claims to exercise any control over their conduct. In those days the Church took cognisance of every man's life. The canonical obligation of confession at least once a year was the most wide-reaching practical part of this discipline, since it subjected every man to paternal rebuke for sin and private penance. This most disagreeable feature of the discipline was very frequently evaded, and the supposed salutary effect of it neutralised, by confession to a wandering friar. But besides this private exercise of discipline, open vice subjected the offender to open rebuke and Church censures as certainly as crime exposed him to the action and penalties of the civil law; in short, the Church had laws, which were adapted to the times, and those laws were regularly enforced. The archdeacon's apparitor, bearing a summons to some neighbour to appear before the ecclesiastical court for the scandal with which the neighbourhood was ringing, or for the Easter dues which he was backward to pay, was a familiar personage in town and village.

3. The outward status of the clergy more than anything else, perhaps, made the Church of those times differ in external aspect from the Church of this day. For, two whole organisations of clergy, three, if we include the military orders, have almost or entirely disappeared from several of the countries of Europe, and the status of the remaining order has been much modified in all. The great and wealthy monasteries, the palaces of the aristocratic order of the clergy, which were scattered over the face of Europe, are for the most part in ruins, and the learned and dignified members of the orders of Benedict and Cluny and Citeaux have disappeared from the face of modern Christendom. The friars, whose houses existed in the suburbs of every town, and whose frocks, black, brown, or grey, were familiar objects in town street, and on village green, in the castles of the nobles and the cottages of the poor, are no longer seen. The hermits and recluses have entirely vanished from their cells by roadside and churchyard. The prince bishops have all been reduced to the status of modestly-portioned officials of a struggling Church. The number of the secular clergy (except perhaps in Italy) is greatly reduced. The whole status and prestige of the Church is altered, not merely by the actual changes in the constitution of the clerical body, but also by the growth of other constituents of our modern society.

In the popular religion one great difference between those days and these is in public worship.

4. Then, the Church had put the Holy Communion in its right place, as the chief act of Divine worship, and all the people attended it. But the Church had allowed the sacrificial aspect of the Eucharist to attain exaggerated proportions, and the sacramental aspect of it to fall into neglect. The consequence was, that, though the great body of the people attended the eucharistic service every Sunday and holy day, they only communicated once a year. In these

days Morning Prayer and the sermon have come to be popularly regarded as the chief service, and Holy Communion as a supplementary and entirely voluntary act of special devotion; so that the vast majority of our church-going people have never once attended a celebration of the Holy Communion; but those who do attend it usually communicate.

5. The worship of the Blessed Virgin Mary entered very largely into the popular religion. Elevated in the popular theology into some such mid-way place between God and the mass of mankind as that into which Socinianism would depress our Lord, she was accepted as the favourite mediatrix between God and man. Her maternal relation and authority were supposed to give her special power with her Divine Son, while her sex and character were supposed to make her specially accessible to feelings of compassion. There may have been, there probably was, a distinction in the worshipper's mind between the worship which he offered to God and that which he paid to Mary, but it is not too much to say that the Virgin shared with God the worship of the people. The devout went to mass in the morning, and paid their homage to the Virgin in the evening. Sunday was the Lord's day, and Saturdays and all eves were devoted to the Virgin. The Psalter and the Book of Hours were adapted to the worship of the Virgin, and the Athanasian Creed parodied into an assertion of all the mediæval inventions about her, ending with the clause, "This is the faith concerning the Virgin Mary, which except every one believe faithfully he cannot be saved." The rosary consisted of ten aves* to every paternoster. There is one marked exception to this system—the liturgy† was not tampered with; the great act of Divine worship still showed forth Christ's sacrifice as the only

---

* The "ave" is an address to the Blessed Virgin Mary, the Paternoster is our Lord's Prayer.   † That is, the Communion Service.

atonement for the sins of the world, and Christ as the Great High Priest.

6. The special devotion to local saints was also a very prominent feature in the mediæval religion. Special saints were adopted by nations, families, individuals, as their special guardians—St. George of England, St. Denis of France, St. James of Spain, St. Bride of Douglas. The holy places of Palestine were, as early as the fourth century, objects of pilgrimage from all parts of the world; the shrines of the apostles and the other numerous holy places of Rome were next, in the popular estimation of Western Christendom, to the holy places of Palestine. Each country had its great shrines or relics which were famous throughout the West. Pilgrims came from all countries to visit St. James of Compostella, and the three kings of Cologne, and the crown of thorns at Paris, and the Holy house of Loretto, and the holy coat of Trèves, and the shrine of St. Thomas of Canterbury. Every country had, besides, a number of saints of merely national repute; every diocese, every neighbourhood, its tomb, or relic, or holy well. The pilgrimages to these places formed a considerable feature in the religious and social habits of the people, and connected with them were a multitude of superstitions.

7. Lastly, the notions about purgatory and the efficacy of masses for the dead exercised a considerable influence on the popular mind. No doubt these notions influenced, though not nearly so largely as is commonly supposed, the number of the donations which were given to the Church. Whenever a new monastery or a new church was built, the donor added the condition that prayers should be said there for himself and his relations, but it was not by any means the case that the sole object of his donation was to obtain those prayers. He would in many cases have founded the monastery or built the church independently of any such

consideration, but it was almost a matter of course that any one who was a considerable benefactor to the Church should ask its prayers in return. Still a considerable number of chantries were specially built and priests endowed for perpetual mortuary masses, and nearly everybody bequeathed some small sum to those who should attend and pray for him at his funeral. The whole subject of purgatory loomed large in the popular imagination. It probably did both good and harm. Some it would deter from sin by the belief that they would certainly have to pay for every sin by terrible suffering. It would undermine in others the resistance to a pressing temptation by the thought that they could pay for the indulgences of this life by posthumous penalties, and so win heaven at last.

There was much which was false and corrupt in the Church of the Middle Ages; but we must not fall into the notion that everybody held all these erroneous opinions just as they are laid down in the latest definitions, or that they believed all these superstitions, and carried them all to their logical conclusions. We see now people who are much better than their system. Their common sense escapes from the logical consequences of a bad system, their Christian instincts keep them right in spite of false theories. It is God's mercy which knows their honest intentions, and gives them grace and guidance, enabling them to use all that is right and true in their religious system and profit by it, and to pass through what is false and hurtful without taking much harm. And thus in this mediæval Church there was a widespread tone of earnest religious feeling, and it perhaps cultivated a high degree of saintliness of character more successfully than modern times have done; it especially kept alive two great ideas which in modern times have fallen into neglect—the idea of worship and the idea of self-sacrifice

This brief sketch may suffice for the general aspect of the

mediæval Church, but some of its developments are so important in their relation to our present religious controversies that even this little work would be incomplete if it did not give some adequate notion of the historical argument upon them. Such are the doctrine of Transubstantiation, of the Immaculate Conception of the Blessed Virgin Mary, of the Papal Infallibility.

*The Holy Communion.*—The Acts of the Apostles* has already showed us that our Lord's institution of the memorial of His sacrifice at once took its place as the great act of the worship of Christ's Church. St. Paul has briefly enunciated the doctrine: "The cup of blessing which we bless, is it not the communion (the partaking) of the blood of Christ? The bread which we break, is it not the communion of the body of Christ?" (1 Cor. x. 16). And in another place he has shown us the high estimation in which this sacrament, together with the other, was held by the primitive Church, when he thinks it needful to exhort them not to trust in them for salvation unless they live according to the privileges and grace given in them. Our fathers were baptized to Moses in the cloud and in the sea. They ate of that heavenly bread and drank of that spiritual rock, which was Christ. But when they sinned against God they were overthrown in the wilderness. Take heed—this is the meaning of the whole passage—lest ye likewise fall away and perish, notwithstanding that you have been baptized into Christ with water and the Holy Ghost, and have eaten and drunk of the bread and wine, and so have been partakers of Christ (1 Cor. x.).

The apostolic fathers speak of this sacrament in language which is vague as to doctrine, but shows that they held it in high estimation. Thus Ignatius says: "I desire the bread of God, which is the flesh of Christ; and His blood I desire

* Acts ii. See Chap. III.

to drink, which is love incorruptible." And again: "Breaking one and the same bread, which is the medium of immortality, our antidote that we die not, but live for ever in Christ Jesus."

Justin Martyr describes the Eucharist in his Apology to Antoninus. He speaks first of the bread and wine as blessed by the presiding presbyter, and then says: "This food is called by us Eucharist, which no one is allowed to take but he who believes our doctrines to be true, and has been baptized in the laver of regeneration for the remission of sins, and lives as Christ enjoined. For we take not these as common bread and common drink; for like as our Saviour Jesus Christ, having been made flesh by the Word of God, had flesh and blood for our salvation, so we are taught that the food which is blessed by the prayer of the Word that cometh from them, by conversion of which our flesh and blood are nourished, is the flesh and blood of Him, the Incarnate Jesus." We have not space to quote the long catena of passages from Irenæus, Tertullian, Origen, Cyprian, Athanasius, Cyril of Jerusalem, Jerome, Augustine, Theodoret, and later writers. They all speak in high terms of the sacredness and mystery and grace of the Sacrament. In their high conception of the sacredness of the Sacrament they speak in warm rhetorical language. They clearly believed in a real spiritual presence of Christ in the Sacrament; they believed that the faithful communicant did receive the body and blood of Christ in the Sacrament; and they sometimes use language of startling strength, and which at first looks like a plain assertion of modern Roman doctrine. But the truth is, this doctrine had not arisen in their days; they did not therefore speak with the caution which afterwards became necessary. Side by side with the most startling of these passages are others which serve to limit and define the meaning of the writer.

The modern Roman doctrine was not put forward till towards the middle of the ninth century. Paschasius Radbert, a monk of the Abbey of Corbie, was master of the monastic school, and a commentator on the Scriptures, and had attained some celebrity among the theological scholars of the age. He afterwards became abbot of his monastery. At the request of the abbot of the daughter house of New Corbie, Paschasius drew up a treatise on the Eucharist for the instruction of the younger monks of that house. The treatise obtained a reputation, and the Emperor, Charles the Bald, requested a copy of it. In this treatise the rhetorical phrases of the Fathers were turned into hard material definitions, and the doctrine of transubstantiation broadly expressed. Paschasius professed to lay this down as the received doctrine of the Church, but this assumption was immediately contested. Rabanus Maurus, Archbishop of Mentz, Walafrid Strabo, Florus, and Christian Druthmar, all of them among the most learned men of the age, declared that there was no other than a spiritual change in the Eucharist, and that Paschasius' teaching was a novelty. On the other hand, Hincmar, the great Archbishop of Rheims, uses language which seems to show more or less sympathy with Paschasius' view, and Haymo, Bishop of Halberstadt, a commentator of great reputation, strongly supports the novel doctrine. At the request of the emperor the book was answered by Ratramnus, another monk of Corbie, in a work which still remains, and which had a great influence on the minds of the English reformers. He holds that "the change in the elements is not wrought corporally, but spiritually and figuratively; under the veil of the material bread and wine, the spiritual Body and Blood of Christ exist. . . . Both (the bread and wine), as they are corporally handled, are in their nature corporal creatures, but according to their virtue and what they become spiritually, they are the mysteries of Christ's Body and Blood." "By all that hath been hitherto said, it appears that the Body and Blood of Christ, which are received by the mouths of the faithful in the Church, are figures in respect of their visible nature; but in respect of the invisible substance, that is, the power of the Word of God, they are truly Christ's Body and Blood. Wherefore, as they are visible creatures, they feed the body; but as they have the virtue of a more powerful substance, they do both feed and sanctify the souls of the faithful."

The tendency of the age was towards superstition, and the doctrine of Paschasius rapidly gained ground; less rapidly in the Gallican Church; and in the Saxon Church, which had little intercourse with the rest of the world, the primitive doctrine still held its ground down to the time of the Norman Conquest.

A new controversy on the subject broke out a hundred years later. Berengarius had been the master of the cathedral school of Tours, and was now Archdeacon of Angers. He had a clearness and vivacity of method in his teaching, an originality and independence of mind, and had a high reputation throughout France for learning and piety. Berengarius was an opponent of the doctrine which Paschasius had introduced, and which had now become generally accepted. Some of his friends used to remonstrate with him. In 1049 Berengarius wrote a letter on the subject to Lanfranc, who was then Abbot of Bec, in Normandy, expressing his surprise that he should maintain the doctrine of Paschasius. Lanfranc was absent, and the letter fell into other hands, and its contents became known at Rome. At a council held at Rome by Leo IX., in 1050, the subject was brought before the council, and Berengarius was condemned unheard as a heretic. From this time to the end of his life in 1088, Berengarius lived a life of controversy and persecution. Twice he made his submission to a council of the Church, overborne, not by arguments, but by clamour and threats, but did not cease to retain and to teach his own opinions. He entered into a controversy with Lanfranc on the subject. Lanfranc's book has been always preserved, and that of Berengarius has recently been recovered. Lanfranc supports the doctrine of Paschasius. Berengarius's doctrine is not that mere figurativism which is sometimes attributed to him. "He distinguishes between the visible sacrament and the inward part or thing signified; it is to the outward part only that he would apply the terms for which he had been so much censured—sign, figure, pledge, or likeness. He repeatedly declares that the elements are 'converted' by consecration into the very body and blood of our Saviour; that the bread, from having been something common, becomes the beatific body of Christ, not, however, by the corruption of the bread, or as if the body, which has so long existed in a blessed immortality, could now again begin to be; that consecration operates not by destroying the previous substance, but by exalting it. It is not a portion of Christ's body which is present in each fragment, but He is fully present throughout." *

Successive councils condemned the views of Berengarius, and the doctrine of transubstantiation became the accepted doctrine of the Western Church. When the Norman Conquest threw England more open to continental influences, and Lanfranc, one of the foremost champions of the new doctrine, became Archbishop of Canterbury, the doctrine spread into England also.

It was not, however, until the early part of the thirteenth century that the full doctrine was formally defined and put forth as part of the authoritative teaching of the Roman Church. This was done under Pope Innocent III., by the

* Robertson, iv. 363.

famous Lateran Council, A.D. 1216. Its first chapter declares that in the sacrifice of the mass " Christ's body and blood are really contained under the species of bread and wine, the bread being transubstantiated into His body and the wine into His blood." Lastly, the Council of Trent, A.D. 1551, decreed that by consecration "there is a conversion of the whole substance of the bread and wine into the substance of Christ's body and blood;" and the creed of Pope Pius IV. (A.D. 1563) declares that "the body and blood of Christ, together with His soul and divinity, are truly and really and substantially in the Eucharist, and that there is a conversion of the whole substance of the bread into His body, and of the whole substance of the wine into His blood, which conversion the Catholic Church calls transubstantiation."

Still, as Bishop Harold Browne remarks, under all these definitions there is room for different phases of belief. In scholastic language the substance of a thing is that by which it is that which it is; the accidents comprise its form, texture, colour, taste, &c., all by which it is cognisable by the senses. Now the definition of transubstantiation is, that it is only the substance of the elements which is changed, the accidents remaining. But it is questionable whether the accidents do not comprise all the properties of matter. If so, the change may still be spiritual rather than material. And as a matter of fact, while the unlearned multitude of the Middle Ages, and of modern times, have held the doctrine in the grosser form, the more learned and liberal-minded have from time to time put forth statements which indicate that there have always been those who interpreted the definition of transubstantiation in a sense which differed little if at all from that of the primitive Church. St. Bernard of Clairvaux (A.D. 1115) acknowledged no feeding but a spiritual feeding. Peter Lombard, the famous master of the Sentences (A.D. 1141), though speaking of the conversion of the bread and wine, declines to define whether that conversion be formal or substantial, or of some other kind. Thomas Aquinas (A.D. 1255) spoke of Christ's body as present, not bodily, but substantially—a distinction not easy to explain. Durandus (A.D. 1320) said that though we believe the presence, we know not the manner of the presence. Cuthbert Tonstal, Bishop of Durham, said that "before the Lateran Council it was free to every one to hold as they would concerning the manner, and that it would have been better to leave curious persons to their own conjectures." Cardinal Cajetan, "the classical theologian of the Roman court," writes that "the real body of Christ is eaten in the Sacrament, yet not corporally but spiritually. Spiritual manducation, which is made by the soul, reaches to the flesh of Christ, which is in the Sacrament." And Gardiner, in his controversy with Cranmer, says: "The Catholic teaching is, that the manner of Christ's presence in the Sacrament is spiritual and supernatural, not corporal nor carnal, not natural, not sensible, not perceptible, but only spiritual, the how and manner whereof God knoweth." \*

The dogma of transubstantiation has never been adopted by the Greek Church.

*The Temporal Power.*—"The ecclesiastical hierarchy never received any territorial endowment by law, either under the Roman empire or the kingdoms erected upon its ruins."†
"The early endowments of the Roman see consisted of estates, not only in Italy and the adjacent isles, but also in distant countries, as Gaul, Africa, Asia, the gifts no doubt of many different benefactors. The letters of Pope Gregory I., who was a careful steward of this patrimony of St. Peter, as it had come to be called, give much curious information as to its management." ‡

\* Bishop Harold Browne's "Exposition of the Thirty-nine Articles," ii. 468.
† Hallam, "Europe during the Middle Ages." ‡ Robertson, ii. 376.

The first accession to the Roman see of temporal authority over cities and provinces came through the connection of the popes with the Carolingian family. Pope Zachary's solution of the case of conscience proposed to him had sanctioned Pepin's assumption of the dignity of King of the Franks. When the pope asked Pepin's protection against the aggression of the Lombards, Pepin not only freed Rome from its immediate danger, but he wrested the exarchate of Ravenna out of the hands of the Lombard invader. The keys and the hostages of the principal cities were surrendered to the Frank ambassador, and he in his master's name presented them before the tomb of St. Peter.

If it was the intention of Pepin to give this territory in supreme and absolute dominion, the subsequent history shows us that his son, at least, exercised sovereign rights over it, and treated the popes as feudatories. And the popes accepted the position, conferring on Charlemagne first the title of patrician and subsequently that of emperor, and acknowledging themselves his subjects.

In the dissolution of the Lombard kingdom the inhabitants of the duchy of Spoleto sought a refuge from the storm by declaring themselves the subjects and servants of St. Peter, and completed by this voluntary surrender the circle of the ecclesiastical state.

At the same time that the forged Isidorean decretals were issued there appeared also another remarkable literary forgery, perhaps by the same hand, of a document which is known as the "Donation of Constantine." This document was introduced to general notice in an Epistle of Pope Hadrian the First, in which he exhorts Charlemagne to imitate the liberality and revive the name of the great Constantine. According to the legend, the first of the Christian emperors was healed of leprosy, and baptized by Pope Sylvester, and in gratitude Constantine withdrew from the seat and patrimony of St. Peter, declared his resolution to found a new capital in the East, and resigned to the popes the free and perpetual sovereignty of Rome, Italy, and the provinces of the West. This gross fiction was in those uncritical days generally accepted without opposition; and it enabled the popes to represent all their future claims to territory and sovereignty in the West as being only a resumption of the rights which the first Christian emperor had conferred, and which had been lost by the invasion of the barbarians. It is not improbable that this claim had some influence in the history of the next great acquisition which we have to record.

The Countess Matilda, daughter and heiress of Boniface, Duke of Tuscany, the powerful supporter of Gregory VII. against the Emperor Henry IV., settled all her vast estates upon the see of Rome. The possession of this splendid inheritance was disputed by the Emperor Henry V., and by several other princes, and some portions of it were lost; but the Roman see remained in possession of a considerable part of it, which it continued to hold down to the present century. It is in our own day, and within the recollection of most of us, that this temporal sovereignty of the popes has been reduced to the dimensions of a palace, a church, and a garden.

*The Papal Infallibility.*—There is no trace of the doctrine in the early centuries. The early Church believed that the promise of Christ that the indwelling Spirit should guide His disciples into all truth, and that Christ would be with them always to the end of the world, involved the belief that the Church would be supernaturally preserved from error and kept in the truth. In primitive times it was held that this authoritative and infallible voice of the Church was to be looked for in a general council, and this opinion derived support from the words of the decree of the Council of Jerusalem: "It seemed good to the Holy Ghost and to us" to make this decree. Accordingly, when questions of doctrine arose which troubled the Church, councils were summoned to determine them. The history of the general councils is an evidence of this belief that a general council was the Church of Christ by representation, and that it possessed these promises of Christ.

The opposite theory that this infallibility of the Church resided in the pope could not originate till the pope had begun to be regarded as in some sense the organic head of the Church, accordingly we hear nothing of it for the first eight centuries of the Church's history. It was not till the forged Isidorean decretals had laid a foundation for the papal assumptions that Nicholas I. ventured to claim that the decrees of a pope were a rule for the whole Church, and to pronounce an anathema on all who should refuse to receive them. The circumstances of the papacy for the next 200 years prevented any further growth of the seed thus planted. It burst into leaf in the Hildebrandine period. Gregory VII. assumed that the pope in uttering his decrees had the Divine guidance, and that his utterances were therefore infallible. The writers of the period, Anselm of Lucca, Cardinal Damiani, Cardinal Gregory of Pavia, writers of the Hildebrandine party, supported the papal pretensions, began to claim a sort of vague infallibility for the popes, and sought authorities and arguments in support of this position. Pope Agatho had said at a Roman synod in 680 that all the English bishops were to observe the ordinances made in former Roman synods for the Anglo-Saxon Church. Cardinal Damiani represented this as a decree issued by Agatho to all bishops in the world, saying they must receive all papal orders as though attested by the very voice of Peter, and therefore of course infallible. A passage of St. Augustine said that all those canonical writings (of the Bible) were preeminently attested which apostolical churches had first received and possessed. He meant the Churches of Corinth, Ephesus, &c., which had received St. Paul's Epistles. Anselm of Lucca took the passage and corrupted it into "the epistles issued by the apostolical see are part of the canonical Scriptures." This corruption was adopted by subsequent writers, by Gratian and Peter Lombard, whose works were the text-books of the mediæval Church; and so the Church was taught that St. Augustine had declared every papal decree to stand on a level of inerrancy side by side with the apostolical epistles. One of their favourite arguments in its support was the text, "I have prayed for thee that thy faith fail not; and when thou art converted, strengthen thy brethren," which, they argued, involved a promise to Peter and to his successors the popes that they should be sound in the faith, and should be the authoritative teachers of the faith to the whole Church. It is enough to repeat that no single writer to the end of the seventh century dreamt of such an interpretation; they all without exception—and there are eighteen of them, including all the Fathers of the Church—explain it simply as a prayer of Christ that the apostle might not wholly fail in his approaching trial. The first to quote it as a promise of inerrancy to the see of Rome was Pope Agatho in 680.

The two great authors of the infallibility are, however, Gratian and Aquinas—the one the great authority for the mediæval canon law, the other for mediæval scholastic theology. Gratian in his "Decretum" adopted in good faith all the forgeries and falsifications of the previous ages. His work became the great repertory and manual from which the succeeding canonists and theologians derived all their knowledge of fathers and councils. Gratian plainly lays down that the pope is the source of all law, and himself above all law, and compares him in this respect with Christ. As Christ submitted to the law on earth, though in truth he was its Lord, so the pope is high above all laws of the Church, and can dispose of them as he will, since they derive all their force through him.

When Aquinas wrote his "Summa Theologiæ" (about 1250), which became the theological text-book of the succeeding ages of the Church, he assumed the truth of all that Gratian had written, and adopted all the mass of matter which had accrued or been invented in the intervening period in support of the papal pretensions. Especially he adopted the forgeries which were published in his own time of a collection of passages from Greek councils and fathers, which were calculated to establish that the Roman Bishop was from primitive times recognised as the sole authority on doctrinal questions. Aquinas probably believed these extracts to be genuine; and influenced by them, he, for the first time, lays down that the pope is not only the absolute ruler but also the infallible teacher of the Church. "Christ," he says, "is fully and completely with every pope in sacrament and authority. The apostolic see rules, ever remaining unshaken in the faith of Peter, while other churches are deformed by error; and thus the Roman Church is the sun from which they all receive their light. A council derives its whole authority from the pope; he has the right of establishing a new confession of faith, and whoever rejects his authority is a heretic, for it belongs to him alone to decide on every doctrinal question."* The popes were delighted. John XXII. declared that Thomas (Aquinas) had worked as many miracles as he had written articles, and could be canonised without any other miracles, and in his bull affirmed that Thomas had not written without a special inspiration of the Holy Ghost. Innocent IV. said that

* Summa, ii. 2, Q. I., Art. 10; Q. XI., Art. 2, 3.

whoever assailed his teaching incurred suspicion of heresy.

Still the doctrine met with much opposition. The Dominican order were the special champions of all that Aquinas (one of their order) had taught, and among these of the papal infallibility. But the great theologians, notably those of the University of Paris, the great theological university of the Middle Ages, opposed the doctrine. Besides, it was a received maxim of the Church that popes could err, and the error of Liberius was constantly quoted as an illustration of it. Only the papal champions invented a theory that as soon as a pope erred he, *ipso facto*, ceased to be pope.

The great schism, however, brought the doctrine of the Pope's infallibility into disrepute, and the councils of Constance and Basle formally enunciated the doctrine that a general council is superior to a pope, and obtained the assent and submission of the contemporary popes. For 130 years (1320—1450) not a single book was written in support of the papal claims until Cardinal Torquemada resumed the defence of the ultramontane theory. Cardinal Cajetan and others followed, and the infallibility was rehabilitated. The new Order of Jesus became its influential champions. The two theories continued to be held by two parties within the Roman Church down to the present day, when the pope's infallibilty was proclaimed as a dogma of the Christian faith in the Vatican Council of 1870.

*The Cultus of the Blessed Virgin Mary.*—After the history of the Nativity the Gospel histories contain very few notices of the Virgin Mother, and several of these seem to be introduced for the express purpose of showing that her maternal relation to Jesus did not give her any relation to His redeeming work. "Thy Mother and Thy brethren stand without, desiring to speak with Thee. . . . And He stretched forth His hand to His disciples, and said, Behold My mother and My brethren; for whosoever shall do the will of My Father which is in heaven, the same is My brother and sister and mother."* And still more clear, both as the first expression of the feeling which afterwards ran into such excesses of veneration, and in the warning response to it, "Blessed is the womb that bare Thee, and the paps which thou hast sucked. . . . Yea, rather, blessed are they that hear the Word of God and keep it."†

The book of the Acts of the Apostles only mentions her once, as being present with the other disciples on the day of Pentecost.‡ The Church writers of the first four centuries say nothing more of her than the Gospels say, and speak of her in the same tone. In the fourth century we find it was the received tradition that the Virgin had accompanied St. John to Ephesus, and died there. And the Council of Ephesus, which assembled to determine the controversy which Nestorius had raised about the title Theotokos commonly attributed to her, held its sittings in the church dedicated to her memory, and in which she was supposed to have been buried.

The prominence given to the subject by this council called the attention of all Christians to it, and from this time we find titles of reverence and affection, gradually growing in extravagance, attributed to her, and a legend growing up about her.

Sophronius (Bishop of Jerusalem when it fell into the hands of the Mohammedan conquerors) in the fifth century mentions that the notion of her Assumption had already been suggested: "Many of our people doubt whether Mary was taken up with her body, or went away leaving the body. But how, or at what time, or by what persons her body was taken hence, or whether removed, or whether it rose again, is not known, although some will maintain that she is already revived, and is clothed with a blessed immortality with

* Matt. xii. 47.   † Luke xi. 27.   ‡ Acts i. 14.

Christ in heavenly places, which very many affirm also of blessed John the Evangelist." The belief in the Assumption gradually became popular. In Italy a festival in honour of it was introduced as early as the seventh century. It was adopted in France and Germany in the ninth. The reverence for the Virgin continued to increase. In the time of Gregory VII. offices in her honour were said in some of the monasteries. It became a pious custom to repeat frequently the angelical salutation, " Hail, Mary, full of grace! blessed art thou among women." The title " Queen of Heaven " was attributed to her. St. Bernard encourages the idea of her being invoked as a mediatrix by those who feared to approach the Saviour directly.

The first idea of any mystery in the birth of the Virgin occurs in the twelfth century; and St. Bernard, highly as he was accustomed to exalt the Virgin, vigorously opposed this new step. Some monks of Lyons were desirous of establishing a festival in honour of the immaculate conception of the blessed Virgin. Bernard wrote to them a letter, which is still extant, and furnishes us with sound and sufficient arguments against the doctrine. He is willing to grant that the Virgin, like John Baptist and Jeremiah, may have been sanctified from the womb, but he denies that she was conceived without sin. He shows that if freedom from sin in conception were required for the Virgin, it must equally be required for the parents of the Virgin; and so it must be carried back to all her ancestors, which would be absurd. He calls the doctrine a " novelty," an " error," and a " superstition." He sums up thus : "Wherefore, though to some few of the sons of men it has been given to be born in sanctity, it has not been given them to be conceived in sanctity, that the prerogative of a holy conception should be reserved for One who Himself should sanctify all, and bring remission of sins. It is only the Lord Jesus Christ who was conceived of the Holy Ghost, who alone was holy in conception. With that exception God looks upon all as born from Adam; as one truly and humbly says of himself, 'I was born in iniquity, and in sin hath my mother conceived me.'"

For a long time the doctrine did not make way in the Church. Peter Lombard, Hugo de St. Victor, St. Thomas Aquinas, even Buonaventura, the author of the "Psalter of the Virgin" and of the "Creed of the Virgin," are all opposed to it. We may include three popes—Innocent II., III., and V.—among its opponents. Innocent II. says in a sermon on the Assumption, "The glorious Virgin was conceived in original sin." Innocent III., comparing Eve and Mary, says, "Eve was formed without sin, but she conceived in sin; while, on the contrary, Mary was conceived in sin, but she conceived without sin." Innocent V. (towards the close of the thirteenth century), attempting to explain the mystery, says she was sanctified before her birth, but not in her conception, for "if that had been so, she would have been exempt from original sin." Aquinas enters at great length into the argument, and concludes that ".Christ in no way contracted original sin, but His very conception was holy, according to St. Luke i., 'That which is born of thee shall be called the Son of God'; but the blessed Virgin did contract original sin, although she was cleansed from it before she was born from the womb." Buonaventura proves that St. Thomas (Aquinas') opinion was most agreeable to the faith, piety, and the authority of the Fathers, and that Mary was not sanctified until after she had contracted original sin.

In the fourteenth century the doctrine began to spread. Duns Scotus took up the question as the subject of a scholastic thesis; admitted that it was not an accepted doctrine of the Church, but argued that God might have done it, and that it may possibly be true. Duns was a Franciscan, and his order, devoted to the honour of Mary, took up the doctrine as a new jewel in her crown. The two great orders of friars were thereupon divided upon the question, the Dominicans maintaining the conclusions of their champion Aquinas. The contest rose into a flame. Sixtus IV. issued a bull in 1476, censuring the disputants on both sides for their violence against each other, and condemning them equally for charging each other with heresy, since the point was not yet decided by the Roman Church and the apostolic see. Pius V., in 1570, issued another bull, in which he allows both sides to discuss the question freely, but forbids either side to condemn the other. Still later Paul V. (1617) and Gregory XV. issued bulls forbidding any to assert in private conversation or in sermons that the blessed Virgin was conceived in sin; but at the same time forbidding the use of the word "immaculate" as applied to her conception in any public office of the Church. In the Council of Trent it was attempted to get the dogma defined, but the opposition to it was successful, and nothing was determined either way.*

So the two opinions existed side by side in the Church till the year 1854, when the present pope astonished the world by the issue of a bull, in which at length he decreed that the doctrine of the immaculate conception was an article of the faith, and that any one who from that time should deny it would be guilty of heresy, and imperil his salvation.

* This section is chiefly extracted from the Rev. J. E. Bennett's "Broken Unity of the Church."

## CHAPTER XLII.

#### THE REFORMATION.

IN the year 1517 Leo X., of the great Florentine family of the De Medici, was pope, a young prince of ability and education, with a taste, like all his family, for literature and the arts, and an equal taste for splendour and luxury; who might have passed as a very respectable sovereign prince of any other of the Italian cities, but was a very unsuitable person for head of the Church of Christ. The three chief sovereigns of Europe were, Maximilian I., Emperor of Germany; Francis, King of France; and Henry VIII. of England, powerful and gallant princes, rivals in European politics, in the splendour of their courts, and in personal fame.

The state of the Church was peaceful. Francis had successfully imposed the concordat in France; the English King maintained the laws which his predecessors had enacted, restraining all encroachments of the pope on the rights of the crown. Germany had its concordat, but allowed greater privileges to the pope than any other country. In Spain the king had from an early date possessed the rights which other sovereigns had only recently and hardly won. The pope and the Curia, on the other hand, derived a very large revenue from all the countries of Europe, through bulls of confirmation to bishoprics, annates, appeals, &c.; and a jubilee every twenty-five years brought in a vast sum in the shape of offerings at the shrines of Rome; and if between times a Julius wanted money to maintain his wars, or a Leo to support his magnificence, he issued an indulgence, and farmed it out to the different countries, and so replenished his exchequer.

The Church was at peace indeed, but it resounded with complaints. The venality and exactions of Rome, the wealth and uselessness of the monasteries, the non-residence of the secular clergy, the rapacity of the friars and their defence of superstitions and abuses, the general decay of discipline and corruption of morals, filled all lands with complaint. The revival of learning, and the study of antiquity and the Scriptures, had made the learned acquainted with the falseness of the foundation on which the system of the papacy was reared, and had led men to question some of the received religious doctrines; and the discovery of the art of printing was spreading this disquieting knowledge among the people. The Church was at peace; so much so that the popes could afford to disregard the murmurs of the people, and any attempts at opposition to the prevalent system were easily suppressed. Every now and then a man of note, condemned by the papal court, would enter a vain protest, and appeal to a general council, which the popes were resolved should never be held so long as they could prevent it. The Church was at peace, and seemed likely to continue so; but it was on the eve of the greatest convulsion which had happened to it for a thousand years. And what princes and councils, universities and doctors, prelates and saints had attempted in vain during two hundred years was effected at last through an obscure German friar.

The magnificent young pope wanted money, and issued an indulgence, nominally for the rebuilding of St. Peter's. The indulgence was farmed as usual. A Dominican friar called Tetzel was engaged to conduct the sale in Germany. The indulgences were at best a strain on the good sense of Christian people, for in them the pope professed out of the plenitude of his power to give pardons for all the sins which a man had committed, and even for sins which a man might hereafter commit. But Tetzel made them still more offensive as he travelled from town to town, attracting the attention of the people by the grossness and profanity of his addresses, outraging common sense and Christian feeling by his assertions of the efficacy of the papal pardons, and deluding the ignorant and superstitious people into the purchase of his dangerous wares.

Wittemberg, the chief town of Saxony, was the seat of a university, in which Doctor Martin Luther, an Augustine friar, was Professor of Philosophy. Doctor Martin, familarly so called, was a man who had drunk of that stream of spiritual religion which flowed deep and clear through all the corruptions of the mediæval Church. He had read the great work of the mystic Tauler, and knew his Thomas à Kempis, and was already engaged in translating some of St. Paul's Epistles into German. He was one of very many holy souls who were grieved and shocked at the corruptions of religion and the wickedness of the people; and this sale of indulgences was one of the most shameful of the corruptions, and one calculated to encourage men in their wickedness. But Doctor Martin was a man who acted boldly on what he felt strongly. On the eve of All Saints, the day on which Tetzel was to begin his exhibition of relics and sale of pardons in the Church of Wittemberg, in the presence of the pilgrims who had come from the neighbouring villages, and of the townspeople and the students of the university, he posted upon the door of the church a paper containing ninety-five theses against indulgences, which he undertook to defend in disputation.

This was the commencement of that movement for the Reformation of the Church which shook all Europe, which produced immediate consequences of the greatest magnitude and importance, and which has not yet completed its work or expended its force.

The challenge of the Wittemberg Doctor was taken up by several papal champions, and a sharp controversy followed; it attracted wide attention and keen interest. Leo summoned Luther to appear before him at Rome. Frederick (surnamed the Wise), Elector of Saxony, who sympathised with the Reformer and steadily protected him, interfered in defence of his subject, and represented that the cause was one which ought to be decided by the ecclesiastical laws of the empire. Luther was accordingly ordered to appear before the Diet of the Empire at Augsburg, where Cardinal Cajetan appeared as Papal Legate. The Cardinal Legate made the mistake of trying to overbear the Wittemberg friar by mere authority, insisting upon his immediate and humble submission to the holy see. Luther refused, and appealed to the pope "when better informed." The pope in turn made the same mistake, thinking to settle the controversy by the issue of a bull, in which he commanded all men to acknowledge his power to deliver from all the punishments (eternal as well as temporal) due to sin and transgression (not against ecclesiastical ordinances only, but) of every kind. On hearing of the bull, Luther appealed to a general council. The pope next tried conciliation, and Luther was induced to write a submissive letter to the pope, and to promise silence on the controversy, provided the other side were also silenced. But Eckius, one of the papal champions, challenged Luther to a disputation at Leipsic on the authority and supremacy of the Roman pontiff. Luther accepted the challenge, and no doubt, opposing such a thesis, would say many things which would be heretical to the ears of the papal partisans. Moreover he published a vast number of popular tracts, preached constantly, and renewed the old demand for a Reformation of the Church in its head and members, in a book entitled the *Reformation of Christendom*.

The reply came from Rome in the shape of a bull of excommunication, unless he retracted within sixty days. Luther having drawn the sword, now threw away the scabbard. On the 10th of December, 1520, outside the city of Wittemberg, in the presence of a great concourse of people, he formally committed to the flames, not only the bull of excommunication, but also the Book of Decretals and Canons, the basis of the whole papal system.

We have seen how, with the spread of learning, men had broken the bonds of mere precedent, and ceased to limit their studies to the mediæval text-books, and had begun to study for themselves the Scriptures, ancient history, and the Fathers. The bold act of Luther fanned into flame the doubts which were smouldering in men's minds. Wittemberg became famous; students from all parts flocked to its university to read Greek with Melancthon and theology with Luther; and their principles passed with great rapidity throughout Europe, and excited a great and general ferment.

Not long after the commencement of these divisions Maximilian died, and Charles V. of Spain, his grandson, was elected to the imperial title and authority. Leo demanded of the new emperor the punishment of the audacious friar, who had set all ecclesiastical authority at defiance, and was disturbing the whole Church. Luther was accordingly summoned to appear before the Diet assembled at Worms (A.D. 1521). Here he was condemned and declared an enemy of the empire, and it was forbidden to all men to give him aid or shelter. But the Elector Frederick had provided for his safety. As he returned homeward he was seized by agents of the Elector in disguise, who carried him to the Castle of Wartzburg, where he lay concealed for ten months, occupying himself in study and writing, especially his German translation of the Scriptures.

Luther, however, tired of his absence from the active conduct of the movement, which was rapidly spreading, left his retreat, and returned to Wittemberg. In 1522 he left Wittemberg, and in 1524 abandoned his monastic vows and costume, dressed like a secular priest, and married an ex-nun. The progress of the reform was disturbed and imperilled at this time by the excesses of the Anabaptists and the revolt of the peasants. The peasantry, oppressed by the feudal system of Germany, broke out into open war, and Munzer, a leader of the new sect of Anabaptists, threw himself into the revolt and gave it the air of part of the general movement for reformation, and frightened men as to the possible consequences of Luther's movement. The revolt, however, was suppressed, and the Reformation went on.

In 1525 the Elector Frederick died. He had protected and encouraged the Reformers, but maintained the existing ecclesiastical order, aiming at a gradual and peaceful reformation of the Church without any violent disruption. He was succeeded by his brother John, who adopted a bolder policy. He at once assumed the supremacy over the ecclesiastical affairs of his own dominions; engaged Luther and Melancthon to draw up a body of laws relating to the form of ecclesiastical government, the method of public worship, the rank, offices, and revenues of the clergy, and other matters of that kind; established it as law, and proclaimed it by heralds throughout his dominions (1527). Other princes and states of Germany followed his example; renounced the papal supremacy, and established a like form of worship, discipline, and government. Some of the princes who had joined in the cry for a reformation drew back from this avowed abrogation of the papal supremacy, and an open rupture ensued among them—one party embracing the Reformation, the other adhering to the old order. The papal party soon gave indications of an intention to proceed to hostilities against the Reformed states. The Reformed princes in turn began to consider measures of mutual defence. In the midst of these preparations the Imperial Diet met at Spires (A.D. 1526), presided over by Ferdinand, the brother of the emperor, who was himself fully occupied in regulating the troubled state of his dominions in France, Spain, and Italy. These political troubles favoured the cause of the Reformers. The imperial ambassadors had orders to keep the affairs of Germany quiet, only requiring the execution of the decree of the Diet of Worms against Luther and his adherents. But the majority of the princes declined to assent to the execution of the decree, until the whole question had been determined by a general council; the diet unanimously requested the emperor to summon such a council; and in the meantime it was agreed that the princes and states of Germany should be at liberty to manage the ecclesiastical affairs of their several dominions as they should think expedient.

Political events still further aided the Reformation, for the pope, after the defeat of Francis I. at Pavia, apprehensive of the growing power of the emperor in Italy, entered into a treaty with the French and Venetians against him; and the emperor in return repudiated the papal authority in his Spanish dominions, made war upon the pope, laid siege to Rome, and blockaded the pope in the Castle of St. Angelo. These events encouraged others of the German princes to join the reforming party.

This promising aspect of affairs was only of short duration. The emperor came to an agreement with the pope. Another Diet was held at Spires (A.D. 1529). The liberty of the princes to manage ecclesiastical matters as they thought proper was revoked by a majority of votes; and it was declared unlawful to introduce any changes in doctrine, discipline, or worship, until a general council had been held. The Elector of Saxony, the Landgrave of Hesse, and others, entered a solemn protest against this decree, appealing to the emperor and a future council. Those who adhered to this protest were first called by the name of Protestants, which since that time has received a wider popular application to all who protest against the supremacy of Rome.

The next important step in the history was the holding of the Diet of Augsburg, at which the emperor was present in person. The question of religion took precedence of all other matters. The Protestants, at the emperor's desire, had had prepared for submission to the diet a formal statement of their case, in twenty-eight chapters, of which twenty-one consisted of a clear enunciation of the chief doctrines of their belief, and seven pointed out the errors and abuses which had occasioned their separation from Rome. This important document, known as the Confession of Augsburg, was signed by John, the Elector of Saxony, and four other princes of the empire, and by the imperial cities of Nuremberg and Reutlingen. It was afterwards adopted by other bodies of seceders from Rome as the expression of their faith, and was largely used in the articles of religion drawn up by the English Reformers under the guidance of Cranmer and Ridley.

A series of conferences followed in the endeavour to reconcile the differences of the two parties. Luther was debarred from being present, but the case of the Reformers was argued by Melancthon and others, while Luther, in safe keeping in the Castle of Coburg, kept up a constant communication with his friends and influenced their proceedings. This method failing, the diet made a decree, in the absence of some of the chief Protestant princes, censuring the changes which had been made in religion; ordering all the princes, states, and cities of the empire to return to their allegiance to Rome; ordering that no judge refusing to accept this decree should sit in the imperial chamber of Spires, the supreme court of the empire; finally, the emperor and the popish princes engaged themselves to enforce the observance of the decree (Nov. 19, 1531).

The Protestant princes entered into a defensive league, and sought to engage in their confederacy the aid of other sovereigns and states, especially the King of England, then engaged in that controversy with the pope on the question of his marriage, which tended towards, and shortly ended in his rejection of the papal supremacy; the King of Denmark, who had already broken with the pope; and the King of France, who sometimes favoured and sometimes burnt the Reformers, but whose political antagonism to the emperor might lead him to join any confederation against him. The emperor, threatened on one side by this confederacy, and on the other by the advancing power of the Turks, arranged a peace, in which, in return for the help of the princes in his Turkish war, he conceded freedom of religion till a rule of faith should be fixed either at a general council or, failing that, in a diet of the empire.

Clement VII. died in 1534, having to the last evaded the emperor's pressing demands for a general council. Paul III., his successor, convoked one at Mantua, but the Protestants solemnly protested against an Italian council, claiming that a controversy which had its rise in the heart of Germany should be decided within the limits of the empire. The pope subsequently proposed Trent as the place for the council, and the emperor assented; but the Protestants still refused to attend it. The emperor and the pope thereupon resolved to reduce the recusants by force of arms. The Elector of Saxony and the Landgrave of Hesse raised their forces in self-defence:

but at the battle of Muhlberg, on the Elbe (April 24, 1547), the Protestant armies were defeated, and the elector and landgrave fell into the emperor's hands. At the diet held soon after, the emperor required the Protestants to leave the decision of these religious matters to the council then sitting at Trent. But the council was soon after adjourned from Trent to Bologna, and thereby in effect dissolved, and the pope could not be induced to reassemble it.

The emperor then fell upon another device. He engaged a number of divines to draw up a formulary, which might serve as a rule of faith and worship for both parties within the empire till the decision of a council could be obtained; and this *formula ad interim*, which satisfied neither party, and was not very strictly observed by either, yet served to tide over the difficulty for a few years.

The emperor was believed to be playing an ambitious game. It was the policy of the emperors to endeavour to weld the hundreds of independent sovereignties held by electors, bishops, princes, barons, knights, and free cities, over which they exercised an indefinite elective suzerainty, into a united hereditary monarchy, and it was believed that Charles was making use of the religious divisions among the princes and states to strengthen himself at their expense; while, on the other hand, he was using the religious dissensions to coerce the pope into a general council, by which also his imperial authority would be aggrandised. His plans, if he entertained such, were frustrated by a bold move on the part of Maurice Duke of Saxony. He suddenly marched a powerful army, and surprised the emperor at Innsbruck, and obtained from him, under this disadvantage, terms which were ever after considered by German Protestants as the basis of their religious liberty. It was agreed that the rule of faith called the *Interim* should be void; that all should enjoy the free exercise of their religion till a diet should determine amicably the present disputes; and that if it should be found impossible to arrive at an uniformity in doctrine and worship, then this religious liberty should continue always. The diet alluded to met at Augsburg in 1555, when it was finally decreed that the Protestants who followed the Confession of Augsburg should be for the future considered as entirely exempt from the jurisdiction of the Roman pontiff, and from the authority and jurisdiction of the bishops; that they should be at liberty to enact laws for themselves relative to their religious sentiments, discipline, and worship; that all the inhabitants of the empire should be at liberty to join themselves to that Church which they preferred; and that any one injuring another on account of his religious opinions should be proceeded against as an enemy of the empire, an invader of its liberties, and disturber of its peace.

The Lutheran body thus by the force of circumstances became a rival community, existing side by side with the unreformed ancient German Church. But Luther always regretted this, acknowledged the authority of the episcopacy, and would gladly have restored his followers to their obedience to a reformed national Church.

*The Reformation in Switzerland.*—The followers of Zuingle, a canon of Zurich, claim for him that he anticipated Luther, and had already begun to preach a reformation before the great German reformer posted his famous theses on the doors of the Church of Wittemberg. He opposed the sale of indulgences in Switzerland, after the example of Luther in Germany, and thus began the movement for reform in the Helvetic cantons. His revolt from the ancient system of doctrine and discipline was more violent than that of Luther. In doctrine he denied the grace of sacraments; in discipline he attributed to the civil magistrate such authority in ecclesiastical affairs as is inconsistent with the Divine constitution of the Church. The disputes which took place between the followers of Luther and Zuingle, chiefly on the doctrine of the Eucharist, weakened the reform movement. A conference was arranged at Marburg (1527) between the chief reformers—Luther, Melancthon, and Justus Jonas on one side, Zuingle, Œcolampadius, and Bucer on the other—but it failed to produce an agreement. Many of the German cities embraced the Zuinglian system, and it was not until the year 1577 that a *Form of Concord* between the two parties was arrived at which allowed both to hold and preach their own views within the same Church.

What Zuingle effected at Zurich, Œcolampadius carried through at Basle, the system of the latter being, however, in doctrine more nearly in agreement with Luther than with Zuingle.*

The reputation of the school of Zurich was, however, soon eclipsed by that of Geneva, organised by the genius of Calvin.

John Calvin, the son of a notary of Picardy, was educated with the sons of the neighbouring noble family of De Montmor, and went with them to the University of Paris. His father destined him for the priesthood, and had procured a benefice for him, when the talent which he developed led his father to think that such extraordinary abilities might find a more profitable career in the law. Calvin, who had already come under the influence of Olivetan, the first translator of the Scriptures into French, willingly abandoned the ecclesiastical career, and continued his law studies in Orleans and Bourges, where he became still more decidedly attached to the reformed doctrines then widely spreading in France.

It was now twelve years since Luther had published his thesis—years of great excitement, not only in Germany,

* The mass was abolished in Zurich in 1525. By 1529 the reformed doctrines were established in Berne and other of the Swiss cantons.

but in nearly all the adjacent countries. In France there had been no open revolt against Rome, but multitudes of people of all ranks had lent a favourable ear to the reforming teachings, and some had secretly embraced them, and held private meetings. With these Calvin had associated at Orleans, and at Bourges his abilities had made him noted as a leading spirit among them. When he returned to Paris he abandoned the study of law, gave himself once more to theology, became a teacher of the reformed doctrine, and was soon regarded as the head of that party in France. In 1532 his friend Nicholas Cop was elected rector of the Sorbonne, and engaged Calvin to write for him the customary oration, in which he gave an exposition of the new doctrines. Both were summoned before Parliament, but fled and took refuge at the court of the Queen of Navarre, the sister of Francis I., who had embraced the Reformation, and gave shelter to the Reformers.

In 1536, being then only twenty-five years of age, he published his "Institutes of the Christian Religion," which contains a full development of the theological system known by his name. Returning from a visit to the court of the Duchess of Ferrara, another favourer of the Reformation, he was stayed at Geneva, which had thrown off the yoke of Rome, by a request that he would devote himself there to the organisation of religion. Here he spent the remainder of his life, establishing and administering the system of doctrine and Church government which he had already laid down in his Institutes.

In doctrine Calvin adopted, on the whole, the platform laid down by Luther. He believed in the grace of sacraments, though he is not always consistent in his utterances on the subject, and many of his followers adopted the Zuinglian theory upon it. The great feature of his system is his teaching on election. This was founded on the teaching of St. Augustine on this obscure and dfficult subject, which had been generally received, though not authoritatively sanctioned, in the Western Church. It will be enough here to state as briefly as possible Calvin's theory, and to point out where it is an advance upon St. Augustine's doctrine. Calvin's teaching on predestination may be summed up in what are called the Five Points—viz., (1) election (and non-election or reprobation); (2) redemption; (3) the bondage of the will; (4) grace; (5) final perseverance. "He maintained that God not only foresaw, but from all eternity decreed the fall of Adam and the total corruption of his posterity by sin; all from birth inherit his fallen nature, with its hereditary bond of sin and guilt, and are in a state of utter alienation from God; free-will can do nothing but sin, and that continually. God is pleased, for reasons known to Himself and independently of the foreseen merits of the objects of His mercy, to elect some from the fallen race to salvation. They are made willing by His grace, which is irresistible, or necessarily effectual, to obey the Gospel call; are regenerated by His Spirit, and live in holiness and obedience to His will, and cannot finally fall from a state of grace. The rest of mankind God predestines to eternal destruction, not on account of foreseen sin, though it may aggravate their doom, but in fulfilment of His sovereign purpose or decree." Augustine did not teach that God had predestined the fall of Adam and the ruin of his race. He did hold that the guilt of Adam, as well as his sinful nature, was inherited by his posterity. But, unlike Calvin, he believed that Christ died for all men, and he believed that all who are baptized are regenerated and receive grace. But there is another grace—the grace of perseverance—which he believed that only the elect receive. The great difference between the two systems is, that Calvin makes God chargeable with the fall of man, Augustine does not. Augustine believes in the universal bestowal of baptismal grace, and that a man may fall away from it and be lost; Calvin believes that it was only bestowed on the elect, and that they would necessarily be saved.*

Calvin also introduced a novel system of Church government, which, as developed under his own superintendence, became a stern spiritual tyranny. The government was vested in a Consistory, composed of six clerical and twelve lay elders, of whom Calvin retained the presidency to the end of his life. This body met weekly and took cognisance of doctrine and morals. It only professed to enforce its discipline by spiritual censures; but when these were insufficient it handed over the offenders to the secular arm, to be dealt with in no gentle way; and it was a principle of the system that the State was bound to give its support to the Church, and to enforce her censures by temporal penalties. The model which Calvin followed was the Jewish theocracy. A gloomy asceticism was the prevalent tone. Not only crimes but sins were severely punished; not only libertinism but innocent merriment were sternly checked. Some young persons were punished for playing a Twelfth Night game. Men were imprisoned for reading the old romances. Unchastity was sternly punished. One case is recorded of a person who had been sentenced to a whipping for adultery, and appealed to a higher court; the court, in revising the process, found that he had before been guilty of the same thing, and at once sentenced him to death. One child was beheaded for striking his parents, and another condemned to death for an attempt only to strike its mother, and with difficulty escaped the sentence. All kinds of blasphemy were visited with heavy

* The English Reformers put predestination and election into an important place in their theological system, but their theory was that of Augustine, or nearly so, not that of Calvin.

penalties, and it was held to be blasphemy to speak against the Reformers. Witchcraft was severely dealt with. Watchmen—*i.e.*, spies—were established, whose duty it was to report all breaches of discipline. There was an annual visitation of every house in the city; not a quiet, pastoral call, but a formal inquisition by a minister and a lay elder into the habits of the household. To this in 1550 was added a system of catechising from house to house, and attendance on sermons was insisted upon. The idea of religious toleration had no more entered the mind of Calvin than of any of his contemporaries, and the burning of Servetus for Socinianism is the historical illustration of this truth. Calvin's system had a great attraction for the sterner minds among the Reformers, and Geneva for many years was the centre to which from all quarters they sought refuge from persecution in their own countries, and from which emissaries went forth propagating this system throughout Europe. In the end the Palatinate, several German cities, the Seven United Provinces, seven of the Swiss Cantons, Scotland, and the large and powerful body of Huguenots in France adopted the Calvinistic doctrine and discipline.

In France the doctrines of the Swiss Reformers were secretly disseminated, and gained a ready hearing; but at first no distinguished leader of a reform movement arose, no very notable outward demonstrations occurred, and consequently the matter did not excite the fears or call forth the opposition of the authorities. Francis, like all the sovereigns of Europe, was not averse to some reform of Church abuses, and he encouraged or frowned upon the Reformers according to the political exigencies of the moment. Two or three solitary executions, indeed, acted as a warning of the danger of preaching new opinions, and at length the massacres of Vaudois at Calvrières and Merindol stained France deeply

with "the blood of the saints." Henry II. ascended the
throne with the determination to prevent the Reformation
from spreading in France, and among the festivities on the
coronation of the queen were horribly interposed four burn-
ings, at which the king and court attended; and shortly after,
in 1552, he issued the edict of Chateaubriand, which dis-
qualified all persons holding reformed opinions from holding
any civil office, and established a censorship of books. All
this time the doctrines were spread secretly, and those who
held them were ministered to in secret meetings by Swiss
emissaries. It was not till 1555 that a reformed church
with a settled pastor was opened in Paris. On one occasion
the worshippers were suprised, and five of them were condemned and burnt; nevertheless congregations were organised
in the provinces. In the next year the reformed made a
public demonstration by walking in procession through the
streets to the number of 4,000, singing psalms of the version
of Clement Marot, which did so much to popularise the
cause. Two of the Bourbon princes, who had been summoned to the marriage of the Dauphin with Mary Queen
of Scots, joined openly in this demonstration. The Reformers held a synod in 1559, and issued a Confession of
Faith. After the accidental death of Henry II. by the
splinter of Montgomery's spear, the antagonism of the two
parties became still more embittered. The reformed, under
the Prince of Condé, tried to possess themselves of the
person of the young king at Blois. The king, on the other
hand, issued the Edict of Romorantin, which declared all
who attended the reformed worship traitors, and transferred
the jurisdiction in their causes from the civil to the ecclesiastical courts. At the assembly of notables which met at
Fontainbleau soon after, the Admiral Coligny, with a retinue
of 800 horsemen, presented a petition from Normandy,
demanding freedom of religious opinions. On the death of

Francis II., at the meeting of the States General, under the regency of the queen-mother Catherine of Medicis, a theological discussion on the reformed doctrine took place, in which Beza was the champion of the reform, and a more tolerant edict was issued.

An accidental collision between the two parties at Vassy, in which sixty of the reformed were killed and two hundred wounded, was the prelude to the civil wars of religion, which, with occasional truces and treaties, lasted for nearly 40 years. The first war ended with the Peace of Amboise, which gave the reformed party several towns in which they might freely exercise their religion, of which Rochelle was the most important, and gave to the nobles a right to have reformed worship in their own houses for their families and tenants. Our space does not permit us even to sketch the subsequent wars. We must briefly mention the famous Massacre of St. Bartholomew, A.D. 1572, in which, with the king's assent, the troops were let loose on the Huguenots in Paris, and they were hunted out and killed on the spot. Similar massacres occurred in other towns, and the number of the killed is variously estimated at from 30,000 to 100,000. When news of the massacre reached Rome, by the pope's order it was received with a salute of artillery, a general illumination, a thanksgiving service, and a medal struck to commemorate the event. Attempts have been made in later times to palliate and explain away this barbarous rejoicing over a treacherous and cold-blooded massacre, but the contemporary evidence leaves no doubt of the facts or of their meaning.

The murder of Henry III. by Jacques Clement placed Henry IV. of Navarre upon the throne. Jeanne d'Albret, the sister of Francis I., the widowed Queen of Navarre, had established the reformed religion in her little independent sovereignty of Bearn about 1570, which became a refuge for the persecuted Reformers, and had brought up her son Henry in the reformed religion. The Roman party opposed his accession to the throne; but, supported by his own gallantry and warlike skill, and the wisdom of his counsellors, and the forces of the Huguenot party, he made good his claims, and though he was induced for the peace of France to conform to the established religion, yet by the Edict of Nantes (May, 1598) he gave large freedom of opinion and worship to the reformed, and removed all disqualification for civil office.

Richelieu, by the capture of Rochelle, the chief stronghold of the Huguenots, broke their strength as a political party, but left them toleration of religion and worship.

Louis XIV., in the later part of his reign, under the influence of Madame de Maintenon, resolved to reduce them to conformity. He began to oppress them in various ways, forbad their ministers to preach, and destroyed their places of worship; and when they began to emigrate, in order to escape these persecutions and enjoy religious freedom in other countries, he forbad them to quit the kingdom on pain of the galleys. In 1684 and 1685 Roman ecclesiastics were sent among the reformed to convert them, attended by troops of dragoons. The soldiers were quartered in the houses of those who refused to conform, and were allowed to insult and plunder and harass them, in the hope of compelling them to yield. At length, in 1648, the Edict of Nantes was revoked; all the privileges of the reformed were withdrawn, their preachers were banished, and the exercise of their religion entirely forbidden. The consequence of these persecutions was that many were driven to conform; many still in secret maintained the religion made still dearer to them by persecution, and some half million or more emigrated from France within three years, and enriched England, Holland, and North Germany, with that number of intelligent, industrious citizens, who brought some wealth, and still more valuable trades with them.

Louis XIV., however, strenuously upheld against the pope his own royal authority and the rights of the Gallican Church. In 1681—82 he summoned an assembly of the French clergy, which was attended by thirty-five bishops and as many representatives of the other orders, at which the following propositions were laid down and accepted by the whole assembly: 1. That the pope's power only extends to spiritual things; that kings are not subordinate to popes; and that the doctrine that kings may be deposed by them is contrary to God's Word. 2. That the pope's authority in spiritual things is subject to the limitations defined by the Council of Constance. 3. That the authority of the holy see can only be exercised in France according to the laws and usages and ordinances of the Gallican Church. 4. That the pope's decisions on matters of faith are only valid when received by the Church.

In Sweden the doctrines of the Lutheran Reformation were early introduced, and the reorganisation of its Church was effected by the king, Gustavus Vasa. The Church had been very wealthy; the king deprived it of two-thirds of its revenues, which he divided between the crown and the landowners. The legal succession of its bishops is disputed, the first bishop of reformed opinions, Archbishop Lawrence Pearson, received his consecration in 1531 from Peter Manson, the Bishop of Westerus (the actual record of Manson's consecration is not found in the episcopal registers, but there is no ground to doubt the fact). A second Lawrence Pearson bore the title of bishop; no record of his consecration is forthcoming; but it seems highly probable that he was consecrated by the first Lawrence Pearson. From this time the stream flows clear to the nineteenth century. The one peculiarity about these Scandinavian consecrations is that there is usually only one consecrating bishop, with two assistant canons, who may be presbyters; but the validity of consecration by one bishop is universally allowed. King Sigismund, favouring the party of reaction towards Rome, was dethroned; a council was held at Upsal in 1593, whose acts, establishing the Lutheran doctrine as the religion of Sweden, are regarded as the Magna Charta of the Swedish Church. The Church is now governed by the Archbishop of Upsal, eleven bishops, and one superintendent—a kind of chaplain-general of the navy. To fill a vacant see the clergy of the see present three candidates, out of whom the king selects one. The bishop has a consistory of clergy and laity, who assist him in the discipline of the diocese. The king is the head of all the Church courts, assisted by an ecclesiastical council of laymen.

In Denmark the doctrines of the Lutheran Reformation, introduced about 1526, spread from the lower to the upper classes of society till, at the Assembly of the Estates, held at Odensee, 1527, a legal sanction was given to them. The Reformation was not, however, established till 1544, and the constitution of the Church as it at present exists is the work of King Christian V. in the year 1683. Only Lutheranism is tolerated; no man can fill any office, civil or military, unless of the national religion. The government of the Church (including Iceland) is by nine bishops, of whom the Bishop of Zealand is metropolitan, and one superintendent-general—all appointed by the king. Each diocese has a consistory, in which the lord-lieutenant presides, the bishop being answerable to the Assembly for the ecclesiastical discipline of the diocese. The Danes retain many of the customs of the ancient Church. Confession before Communion; at the celebration a cross and lighted candles on the altar; the clergy wear surplice and chasuble of red velvet, with a cross embroidered in gold on the back; wafer bread is used; the sentences of administration are the ancient ones: "*Hoc est verum Jesu corpus; Hic est verus Jesu sanguis.*"

The Church of Norway was anciently part of the Church of Denmark. At the cession of Norway to Sweden in the early part of the present century the Danish Church became independent.

By the cession of Finland to Russia in 1809 another independent Lutheran Church was created, and an Archbishop of Abo created as its ecclesiastical head.

The so-called Jansenist Church of Holland presents an interesting and important episode in modern Church history. When in 1665 A.D. the pope required all bishops to subscribe the condemnation of Jansenius, the Archbishop of Utrecht and his suffragans demurred. They were willing to condemn the incriminated propositions, but not to aver that those propositions were held by Jansenius. The result was that the popes endeavoured to prevent the continuance of the line of bishops thus refusing submission to the demand of Rome. The bishops, however, took care to continue their succession; each successive bishop dutifully reports his election and consecration to Rome, and Rome returns an excommunication as its reply. Still the ancient Church of Holland maintains itself, and presents the spectacle of a Church Catholic but not Roman. It has become of additional importance in our own day when the Old Catholics of Germany have obtained episcopal consecration from the Archbishop of Utrecht.

In all the provinces of Italy the reformed doctrines found many adherents, especially in Venice, Tuscany, and Naples, Ochino and Peter Martyr being the most conspicuous of the preachers of the reform. But the popes put in motion the machinery of the Inquisition in all the provinces over which they had control with such searching rigour that many sought safety in exile, and the rest dissembled their opinions and conformed to the established order. In Naples the viceroy was ordered by the emperor to introduce the Inquisition; but the people, who had on several previous occasions resisted the introduction of that horrible tribunal, again took up arms against it with such success that the emperor was glad to accommodate matters and issue a general pardon.

In Spain the new doctrines were introduced by stealth; but the Inquisition, already long established here, acted with such promptitude and vigour that the movement made less way than in any of the other countries of Europe.

In England the reformation of the Church took a more regular course than in other countries, and came to a happier conclusion. England was the last country in the West which fell under the Roman supremacy in the eleventh century; it was the first country which in the fourteenth protested against the papal abuses, and restrained them by legislative enactments. Its insular position and strong nationality helped its independent action. The reforming doctrines spread at once from Germany into England, and, falling on favourable soil, became popular with all classes. Wolsey, the great minister of Henry VIII., was in favour of a general reformation, and had taken steps in that direction in the visitation of the monasteries, the encouragement of the new learning at the universities, and his lenient treatment of those who were charged with heretical opinions. Warham, the Archbishop of Canterbury, and a great number of the prelates and clergy inclined in the same direction. The king at first took up the defence of the ancient order, and, proud of his ecclesiastical knowledge, wrote an answer to one of Luther's early books; but the affair of the divorce enlisted his passions against the papal supremacy and engaged him in the Reformation. The special feature of the English Reformation was that it was not, as in Germany, the setting up of a rival system in opposition to the ancient ecclesiastical organisation, or, as in Geneva or the United Provinces, the total subversion of the old organisation and the planting of a new one in its place, but it was a real reformation of the Church undertaken by those to whom the work properly belonged—the sovereign and the clergy; and the result was that in England alone the historical organisation and status of the Church were preserved, while its doctrine and discipline were reformed.

We must refer to other works for a fuller account of the English Reformation; we can only here point out its salient features. In 1534 Cranmer, the new archbishop, declared the king's first marriage null and void, and thus virtually set aside the pope's supremacy by deciding a cause which had long been before the papal court. Already, in 1531, the Convocation, with Archbishop Warham at its head, had petitioned the king to relieve the clergy of the payment of annates, and of the fees for bulls for consecrations of bishops, and requested that, if the pope refused, the obedience of England might be withdrawn from the see of Rome. An Act of Parliament was accordingly passed which abolished annates, offered five per cent. on the value of the see as fees for bulls of consecration, and enacted that if the pope should in consequence refuse the bulls, bishops should be consecrated by the archbishop of the province and other bishops; and that if the pope should proceed to excommunication and interdict, his sentence should be disregarded. Two years afterwards, by Acts of Parliament, all reference to the pope, and all interference on his part, in the appointment of bishops was done away, all appeals to the papal courts and all applications to Rome of any kind were forbidden. And in the same year (1534) the two Convocations endorsed what the Parliament had done, declaring that the Bishop of Rome has no greater jurisdiction conferred on him by God in this kingdom of England than any other foreign bishop. There seeems to have been no difficulty in obtaining the assent of the clergy generally, even in the monasteries, to this final repudiation of the papal supremacy, and the bishops were zealous in preaching it to the people. Thus the English Church and nation declared that it would pay no taxes to the see of Rome; that the pope should have no judicial authority in England; that his assumed rights of patronage to bishoprics and other benefices should be abolished; that his licence and authorisation should not be required for any ecclesiastical appointments; and, finally, that he should have no spiritual authority in England.

Having thus effectually thrown off the papal supremacy and asserted its independent position, the Church proceeded to regulate its own affairs. First the mendicant orders were suppressed in 1535, and five years later the monastic institution altogether was abolished, and the king seized the bulk of their possessions for his own use, and distributed them in grants to his nobles and courtiers. The chantries were suppressed and their property confiscated in 1547. The Convocation drew up ten articles of religion in 1536, in which the doctrines of the English Reformation were briefly set forth. Several translations of the Bible were published—Coverdale's Bible in 1535 and the Great Bible in 1539, besides others—and the Service Book was slightly altered. On the accession of the young King Edward VI. a new Book of Common Prayer, prepared during the last reign, was published, thus completing the first stage of the English Reformation. The young king fell, however, into the hands of the Duke of Somerset, the Lord Protector, who was influenced by the Calvinistic Reformers Calvin himself entered into correspondence with the king and

Cranmer; Bucer and Peter Martyr were invited to England, and made divinity professors at Cambridge and Oxford; John a Lasco, a Zuinglian, was allowed to establish a congregation in London, and Calvinistic views of doctrine and discipline were encouraged. The doctrines and liturgy of the Church of England were then revised. A new Prayer-book was drawn up, with alterations in the Genevan direction, abolishing the ancient vestments of the clergy, and making many alterations in the Holy Communion service in the direction of Zuinglian doctrine. The second Prayer-book, however, did not get into general use, for before the day fixed for it to come into use an order in council suspended its further issue, and before anything further was done the young king died.

Mary on her accession obtained from Parliament the repeal of all the Reformation laws, and things reverted to the state in which they stood before the Reformation began, and steps were taken to root out the Reformation by the fires of persecution. Many of the most conspicuous or the most earnest fled abroad—some to Frankfort, some to Geneva. During the three years that the persecution continued it is computed that 277 persons were brought to the stake, besides those who were punished by imprisonment, fine, and confiscation. The majority of the people, terrified by the persecution, conformed; but the fires of Smithfield burnt into the heart of the nation an undying hatred of Romanism. Mary died November 17th, 1558, and Cardinal Pole died on the following day.

Elizabeth and her advisers desired to go back, not only over the reign of Mary, but over that of Edward VI. also, and to take up the Reformation as it stood at the end of its first and English stage, accepting the first Prayer-book of Edward as the standard of doctrine and ritual. But it was desirable to conciliate the Puritan party, which, encouraged in the reign of Edward VI., had become much more influential through the return of the Marian exiles, who had brought Genevan ideas and fashions back with them. Accordingly, the second book was taken as the standard, and some few alterations made as to vestments and eucharistic observances, which raised the tone of its orthodoxy. A large proportion of the dignified clergy declined to accede to the changes; the great bulk of the parochial clergy (one hundred only excepted) accepted them; and the mass of the people received them with joy. The Thirty-nine Articles of Religion received the assent of Convocation in June, 1563. Pope Pius V. it is said, made overtures for a reconciliation, offering to accept the English Reformation and approve of the Prayer-book on condition of the recognition of his supremacy, acknowledging that the book contained nothing contrary to the truth, while it comprehended all that is necessary to salvation. Finding that a return of England to the obedience of the Roman see was hopeless, Pius V. (1570) published a bull of excommunication and deposition against the queen, fomented conspiracies against her, and called upon Spain to execute the pope's sentence. The queen was strong in the affections of her subjects, the conspiracies proved abortive, and God delivered us from the Spaniard by the wreck of the Armada.

The antagonism between England and Scotland prevented the English Reformation from spreading into the northern country. John Knox, a disciple of Calvin, is the hero of the Scottish Reformation, and it was chiefly by his influence that the Genevan system was established there. The first overt act of the Scottish Reformation was taken in 1559 by the presentation of a petition to the queen-mother, Mary of Guise, regent on behalf of her daughter, Mary Queen of Scots, praying for prayer, sacraments, and preaching in the vulgar tongue, and for reformation of the lives of the clergy. The petition not meeting with a favourable answer, some noblemen and gentlemen formed an association, and entered into a covenant to stand by one another with life and fortune in the attempt to obtain a reform. The clergy held a provincial council at Edinburgh, and passed some constitutions for the improvement of discipline; the synod also condemned several persons of heresy, and required them to make recantation at the market-cross; but the mob riotously broke up the procession and rescued their friends.

The reforming party, who styled themselves "the Congregation," in allusion to the Old Testament name for the ancient Church of God, made Perth their head-quarters, and there introduced on their own authority the novelties in religion which they had in vain asked of the authorities. Then, after a sermon by Knox, the mob rose and defaced the images of the Church, and attacked and plundered the monasteries, an example which was followed at Coupar, in Fife. The regent ordered troops to move upon Perth, whereupon the Lords of the Congregation summoned their friends there to the number of 7,000, besides the burgesses of Perth. An accommodation, however, was arrived at, and the forces on both sides disbanded. But the regent violating the conditions of the agreement, the Congregation met again a few months after at Crail, when, after one of Knox's inflammatory addresses, they proceeded to destroy the altars and images, and proceeding to St. Andrews committed the same violence. The regent hereupon ordered troops to march towards St. Andrews; the Congregation mustered their forces to oppose them, and open war began. The insurgents marched upon Perth, and obliged the garrison to surrender; thence they marched upon Edinburgh, defacing the churches and destroying the monasteries on their route. The mob of Edinburgh, encouraged by their approach rose against the magistrates, despoiled the churches, and plundered and destroyed the religious houses of the capital. The regent not being strong enough to put down the outbreak by force concluded a truce with the Congregation, on the conditions that Edinburgh should be restored into the hands of the government, that no further violence should be done, that the preachers and the reformed should not be disturbed, pending a meeting of Parliament. The regent, however, fortified Leith, the port of Edinburgh, and garrisoned it with French soldiers; and the Congregation on their part concluded a treaty with Queen Elizabeth, and with the help of English troops laid siege to Leith. The queen regent died during the siege, whereupon a peace was concluded, on the ground of an act of oblivion for the past, and a promise of a settlement of religion to be made at the next Parliament. The King of the French and the Queen of Scots refused to ratify the treaty, but the Parliament was held without their authority, and proceeded to a settlement of religion. In brief, it abrogated the ancient ecclesiastical order and doctrine, and established a system of doctrine and government framed after the model of that of Geneva, but adopting the second Book of Common Prayer of Edward VI. for general use. An order for destroying the monastic churches and houses having been issued, the mob took up the work and included in it many of the churches also, on the ground that the places where idols had been worshipped ought to be destroyed. " Thus every building with a steeple was a mark of the beast, a seat of idolatry, and a house of devotion of the Amorites. By the help of this divinity the churches were all rased or battered, the beauty of the great towns scandalously blemished, and the public ornaments of the kingdom laid in rubbish. The communion plate was made prize, and the bells, timber, and lead sent to sale in the market. Registers and libraries were destroyed, and the remains of learning and antiquity thrown into the fire." (Collier, Book vi.) Mary Queen of Scots, her husband having died, returned to her own dominions, 1561, and was received with every mark of loyalty and regard. But in the following year she was petitioned to refuse toleration to the adherents of the old religion, and two years after (1564) the General Assembly of the Church again petitioned her " that the mass, with all the appurtenances of popish idolatry, should be suppressed through the whole kingdom; that the Queen's person and family should be included in this reformation, and that offenders upon conviction should be punished according to law." The queen, in reply, claimed for herself the same liberty of conscience which she allowed to others. The queen's marriage with Darnley, her having her son baptized with the ancient ceremonial, the death of Darnley, and her marriage with Bothwell, brought the queen into such ill odour that the Lords of the Congregation were encouraged to seize her person, and confine her in the Castle of Lochleven; and, lastly, to cause her to resign the crown, and appoint the Earl of Morton regent during her son's minority (1567). In the following year she effected her escape from Lochleven, and took refuge in England, where she was kept in confinement by Elizabeth until her execution in 1587.

In 1581 James and his nobles and all ranks of people subscribed the Covenant. In 1610 James, having meantime succeeded to the throne of England and adopted its religion, endeavoured to restore the apostolical form of government in his native country. Three bishops were consecrated in London to three of the ancient sees; they consecrated an archbishop of St. Andrews, and he proceeded to fill the other sees. The step was unpopular and occasioned riots, but it was maintained by the civil authority. Charles I. on his accession to the throne endeavoured to complete the rehabilitation of the Scottish Church by the introduction of a Book of Common Prayer, taken, with some modifications, from the English Book. When the Dean of Edinburgh (1633), in obedience to the new order, appeared in the cathedral church in a surplice and began to read prayers from the book a riot broke out*; the resistance thus initiated spread throughout the country. The Covenant was again brought forward and signed by the Assembly of the Kirk, and the Scots Parliament (1640) ratified the act of the Assembly; Charles was now embroiled with his English subjects, and was obliged to connive. The Covenant slightly altered was adopted by the Westminster Assembly of Divines and the Parliamentary party. When Charles II. was restored, the Scots Parliament (1661) rescinded the Covenant, and left the settlement of religion in the king's hands. It was resolved to re-establish the Church of Scotland, and Sharp was consecrated Archbishop. A resolute resistance was maintained by a section of the people, who under the name of Covenanters refused to conform, and continued to meet for public worship. They were persecuted with great cruelty—fine, torture, and death being freely applied against them, with the result of keeping up their own enthusiasm, and prejudicing mankind in favour of a cause which produced so many "martyrs." It was not until the Revolution that the persecutions ceased, and William III. established in Scotland the Presbyterian form of Church government and doctrine, of which he was himself an adherent.

* Jenny Geddes has become an historical character as the leader in this outbreak; when the dean began to read, Jenny threw her three-legged stool at his head, exclaiming, "Thou false loon, wilt thou read the mass at my lug?"

## CHAPTER XLIII.

#### THE PRESENT STATE OF THE CATHOLIC CHURCH.

WE conclude our task with a brief comprehensive glance at the present state of the Church of Christ.

The gradual decline of the Eastern Churches under the unfriendly rule of Mohammedan powers, while the nations of Europe have gradually grown to be the great and influential nations of the world, has given to the Western Church a vast predominance over the other branches of the ancient Catholic Church. The Greek Church is only saved by its Russian branch from comparative insignificance. The great Patriarchate of Antioch is represented by a chief pastor, who still bears that grand historic title, ruling over a handful of Jacobite Christians scattered about Syria and Mesopotamia. The Eastern Church, which once ruled in Persia without a rival, and spread its branches over the whole northeast of Asia up to the wall of China, is represented by a Catholicos, who rules a few tribes of mountaineers in Kurdistan, and a group of villages in Persia. The great Church of Egypt survives in a few Coptic Christians, whose head still bears the great name of Patriarch of Alexandria. The ancient Church of Abyssinia survives—now, as in the first day of its existence, receiving its head from the Alexandrian Patriarch—but in a state of ignorance and superstition. Still, these feeble remnants of the great ancient churches survive, their roots still occupy the ground, they still bear a few leaves and a little fruit; it is within the possibilities of God's providence that they might yet take new root downward and bear fruit upward, if the people, who still cling passionately to their ancient faith, were once delivered from the domination of a foreign religion and power, under which they have so long and so cruelly been oppressed. As it is, in all their present feebleness, they are the representatives of the ancient churches which once flourished in these eastern and southern lands, and the irresistible witnesses of the fact that Rome never was the mistress of the whole Church of Christ, or of anything more than her own Patriarchate of the West. Rome has made great endeavours to win these ancient churches to submit to her supremacy. We have seen in the preceding history how she has steadily aimed at this ever since the time of the Hildebrandine popes, and used intrigue and bribe and violence, and always failed. And in these modern days she is still as anxious as ever, and as persistent in her endeavours to obliterate these evidences against her claim to the universal monarchy of the Church. We in our little island, moored off the north-western side of the European continent, seem to have been hidden by its bulk from sight of, and interest in, these ancient churches. From time to time, once in a couple of centuries or so, some slight communication has passed between the English and the Greek Church. Surely it is our interest to open cordial relations with these our allies against the revived pretentions and augmented errors of Rome; surely it is our duty as a great, learned, wealthy branch of the Church—our duty to Christ and to mankind—to do our best to help these ancient churches to recover purity, unity, and prosperity.

But if the great ancient churches have withered away and left the Roman Church predominant, these modern times have seen the growth of the great Anglican communion, which promises to be an efficient counterpoise to the power of Rome, and so to save the Christendom of the future from the utmost evils of her ambition. The offshoot of the English Church planted in the United States of America has grown into fifty-two dioceses. Her four dioceses in India have planted the standard of our Church in that vast empire; the fifty-five colonial bishoprics created within our own generation have planted the Anglican Church in those countries probably destined in a very few generations to be among the great nations of the world. As we now look back to the conversion of the empire in the first three centuries, and to the conversion of the nations of Europe in the fifth and sixth, and of the northern nations in the ninth and tenth, so our posterity will look back to the founding of new nations and churches in the waste places of the world by the Anglican race in this nineteenth century as to one of the great periods of ecclesiastical history. It is a great period of the world's history we live in; it is a great part we are called upon to play in it; may God give us faith to grasp the grandeur of the situation, and love and self-denial to fulfil our duty.

Our great weakness arises from a cause which the course of the history has not called upon us to notice hitherto, the division of the force of English Christianity by Dissent. It came into being at the time of the Reformation; it was insignificant in its power and influence until the present century. The great increase of population in the early part of the century was the cause of the growth of Dissent. The establishment was not prepared to adapt its religious machinery to the religious needs of the increasing population. The Church failing to build places of worship and provide pastors, and to gather the new generation into her fold, the people built places of worship for themselves, accepted the services of those who offered themselves as religious teachers, and organised themselves under various forms of Dissent. The Wesleyans are the most numerous, and in doctrine and discipline least removed from the Church; if they adhered to the principles or retained the spirit of their founder they would reunite themselves with the Church, which earnestly invites their return. The bulk of the remainder of the Dissenters are included within the organisations of the Independents and the Baptists, who are sufficiently alike in doctrine and discipline to be classed together in our present view. Their principles of organisation are fundamentally opposed to those of the Church of all ages; they reject the belief which the Church of all ages has held on the fundamental questions of the ministry and the sacraments. The Wesleyans may be regarded as estranged friends, of whose reconciliation there is good hope; but the Independents and Baptists are necessarily, by force of their principles, the irreconcilable opponents of the Church. There remain the Romanists in England, who have made the most strenuous efforts during the last generation to win adherents here. They are not very numerous; their efforts have seduced a few clergymen from the Church, and a few lay people of high social position, and have attracted great notice throughout the kingdom; but their success has not been commensurate with their efforts. The mind and heart of England are as averse from the papal supremacy and the Roman corruptions of doctrine as ever; not so blindly and passionately averse, perhaps, but more intelligently, resolutely, and therefore more irrevocably, opposed to a system antagonistic to human freedom, to the primitive constitution of the Church of Christ, and to the faith of Christ.

This division in our Christianity has unhappily been propagated everywhere, together with our Christianity, to the United States and the Colonies, and to every heathen country to which our missionary labours have extended. Nothing, probably, would so tend to further the cause of

Christ and His Gospel, to re-unite His divided and distracted Church, as a re-union of English Christianity, and that re-union can only take place, so far as human wit can foresee, by a re-absorption of the Dissenters into the body of the English Church.

The ancient historic Church of England stands in the midst of 198 sects. Should she give up all which divides her from the Wesleyans in order to unite herself with them, she would cease to be the Church of England, and become Wesleyan, and still the Independents and Baptists and the rest of the 197 sects would be as irreconcilable as ever; the ancient historic Church of England, the link which unites the present generation with the Apostolic Church, the stronghold of English Christianity against Rome, the centre round which it is possible for the great ancient churches one day to rally, would cease to be; and English Christianity would be almost as far from the desired unity as ever. But the Wesleyans could unite themselves to the Church; not perhaps without some sacrifice of feeling and predilections, but without any sacrifice of their fundamental principles.

Among the dissenting communities, even among those whose principles are most opposed to those of the Church, there are thousands of individuals who are what they are from early training or accidental preferences, not from any conscientious objection to anything in the Church; they might—they would, if they saw all the evils created by division—re-unite themselves to the Church, without any sacrifice at all. In short, this re-union of English Christianity by the re-absorption of the English people into the body of the English Church is the key of the ecclesiastical position. The example of England would be followed in the countries and colonies which are influenced by England. This course would give such strength and prestige to the Anglican communion as would affect the whole

Church of Christ. It is the divisions and ecclesiastical disorders of English Christianity which make the ancient churches afraid to follow the example of our self-reformation. It is these divisions which weaken the cause of Christ in all those English-speaking countries in which the various denominations are rivals for the adhesion of the people. These divisions, more than anything else, paralyse the preaching of the Gospel to the heathen:—Our blessed Lord prayed for those who should believe through the preaching of the Word "that they all may be one . . . . . that the world may believe that thou hast sent Me" (John xvii. 21).

LONDON:
PRINTED BY JAS. TRUSCOTT AND SON,
Suffolk Lane, City.

# PUBLICATIONS

OF THE

Society for Promoting Christian Knowledge.

---

### THE FATHERS FOR ENGLISH READERS.
Fcap. 8vo., cloth boards, 2s. each.

**LEO THE GREAT.** By the Rev. CHARLES GORE, M.A.

**GREGORY THE GREAT.** By the Rev. J. BARMBY, B.D.

**SAINT AMBROSE:** his Life, Times, and Teaching. By the Rev. ROBINSON THORNTON, D.D.

**SAINT AUGUSTINE.** By the Rev. E. L. CUTTS, B.A.

**SAINT BASIL THE GREAT.** By the Rev. R. T. SMITH, B.D.

**SAINT HILARY OF POITIERS AND SAINT MARTIN OF TOURS.** By the Rev. J. GIBSON CAZENOVE, D.D.

**SAINT JEROME.** By the Rev. EDWARD L. CUTTS, B.A.

**SAINT JOHN OF DAMASCUS.** By the Rev. J. H. LUPTON, M.A.

**THE APOSTOLIC FATHERS.** By the Rev. Canon HOLLAND.

**THE DEFENDERS OF THE FAITH;** or, The Christian Apologists of the Second and Third Centuries. By the Rev. F. WATSON, M.A.

**THE VENERABLE BEDE.** By the Rev. G. F. BROWNE.

## THE HOME LIBRARY.

Crown 8vo., cloth boards, 3s. 6d. each.

**BLACK AND WHITE.** Mission Stories. By H. FORDE.

**CHARLEMAGNE.** By the Rev. E. L. CUTTS, B.A. With Map.

**CHURCH IN ROMAN GAUL, THE.** By the Rev. R. TRAVERS SMITH, B.D. With Map.

**CONSTANTINE THE GREAT:** The Union of Church and State. By the Rev. E. L. CUTTS, B.A.

**GREAT ENGLISH CHURCHMEN;** or, Famous Names in English Church History and Literature. By W. H. DAVENPORT ADAMS.

**JOHN HUS.** The commencement of Resistance to Papal Authority on the part of the Inferior Clergy. By the Rev. A. H. WRATISLAW, M.A.

**JUDÆA AND HER RULERS,** from Nebuchadnezzar to Vespasian. By M. BRAMSTON. With Map.

**MILITARY RELIGIOUS ORDERS OF THE MIDDLE AGES;** the Hospitallers, the Templars, the Teutonic Knights, and others. By the Rev. F. C. WOODHOUSE, M.A.

**MITSLAV;** or, The Conversion of Pomerania. By the late Right Rev. R. MILMAN, D.D. With Map.

**NARCISSUS:** A Tale of Early Christian Times. By the Rev. Canon BOYD CARPENTER, M.A.

**SKETCHES OF THE WOMEN OF CHRISTENDOM.** Dedicated to the Women of India. By the Author of "The Chronicles of the Schönberg-Cotta Family."

**THE CHURCHMAN'S LIFE OF WESLEY.** By R. DENNY URLIN, Esq.

**THE HOUSE OF GOD THE HOME OF MAN.** By the Rev. Canon JELF.

**THE INNER LIFE,** as Revealed in the Correspondence of Celebrated Christians. Edited by the late Rev. T. ERSKINE.

**THE LIFE OF THE SOUL IN THE WORLD;** Its Nature, Needs, Dangers, Sorrows, Aids, and Joys. By the Rev. F. C. WOODHOUSE, M.A.

**THE NORTH AFRICAN CHURCH.** By the Rev. J. LLOYD, M.A. With Map.

**THOUGHTS AND CHARACTERS:** Being Selections from the Writings of the Author of the "Schönberg-Cotta Family."

## DIOCESAN HISTORIES.

**CANTERBURY.** By the Rev. R. C. JENKINS. With Map. Fcap. 8vo., cloth boards, 3s. 6d.

**CHICHESTER.** By the Rev. W. R. W. STEPHENS. With Map and Plan. Fcap. 8vo., cloth boards, 2s. 6d.

**DURHAM.** By the Rev. J. L. LOW. With Map and Plan. Fcap. 8vo., cloth boards, 2s. 6d.

**LICHFIELD.** By the Rev. W. BERESFORD. With Map. Fcap. 8vo., cloth boards, 2s. 6d.

**OXFORD.** By the Rev. E. MARSHALL, M.A. With Map. Fcap. 8vo., cloth boards, 2s. 6d.

**PETERBOROUGH.** By the Rev. G. A. POOLE, M.A. With Map. Fcap. 8vo., cloth boards, 2s. 6d.

**SALISBURY.** By the Rev. W. H. JONES. With Map and Plan. Fcap. 8vo., cloth boards, 2s. 6d.

**WORCESTER.** By the Rev. I. GREGORY SMITH, M.A., and the Rev. PHIPPS ONSLOW, M.A. With Map. Fcap. 8vo., cloth boards, 3s. 6d.

**YORK.** By the Rev. Canon ORNSBY, M.A. With Map. Fcap. 8vo., cloth boards, 3s. 6d.

## COMMENTARY ON THE BIBLE.

With Maps and Plans. Crown 8vo., cloth boards, red edges, 4s.; half calf, 10s.; whole calf, 12s. per vol.

### OLD TESTAMENT.

Vol. I., containing the Pentateuch.
Vol. II., containing the Historical Books
Vol. III., containing the Poetical Books.
Vol. IV., containing the Prophetical Books.
Vol. V., containing the Apocryphal Books.

### NEW TESTAMENT.

Vol. I., containing the Four Gospels.
Vol. II., containing the Acts, Epistles, and Revelation.

|  | s. | d. |
|---|---|---|
| **ALONE WITH GOD; or, Helps to Thought and Prayer.** For the Use of the Sick; based on short passages of Scripture. By the Rev. F. BOURDILLON, M.A., Author of "Lesser Lights." 12mo., cloth boards | 1 | 6 |
| **A MODE OF CATECHIZING.** By the Rev. TEMPLE HILLYARD, Rector of Oakford, Devon. 18mo., cloth boards | 1 | 0 |
| **BEING OF GOD, SIX ADDRESSES ON THE.** By C. J. ELLICOTT, D.D., Bishop of Gloucester and Bristol. Small post 8vo., cloth boards | 1 | 6 |
| **BIBLE PLACES; or, The Topography of the Holy Land.** By the Rev. Canon TRISTRAM. With Map and numerous Woodcuts. Crown 8vo., cloth boards | 4 | 0 |
| **CALLED TO BE SAINTS** · the Minor Festivals Devotionally Studied. By CHRISTINA G. ROSSETTI, Author of "Seek and Find." Post 8vo., cloth boards | 5 | 0 |
| **CHRISTIAN MISSIONS BEFORE THE REFORMATION.** By the Rev. F. F. WALROND, M.A. With Four full-page Illustrations on toned paper. Post 8vo., cloth boards | 2 | 6 |

|  | s. | d. |
|---|---|---|

**CHRISTIANS UNDER THE CRESCENT IN ASIA.** By the Rev. E. L. CUTTS, B.A., Author of "Turning Points of Church History," &c. With numerous Illustrations. Crown 8vo., cloth boards ............................................ 5 0

**CHURCH HISTORY IN ENGLAND,** from the Earliest Times to the Period of the Reformation. By the Rev. ARTHUR MARTINEAU, M.A. 12mo., cloth boards ............ 3 0

**CHURCH HISTORY, SKETCHES OF,** from the First Century to the Reformation. By the Rev. J. C. ROBERTSON, M.A. With Map. 12mo., cloth boards ........................ 2 0

**DAILY READINGS FOR A YEAR.** By ELIZABETH SPOONER. Crown 8vo., cloth boards............................... 3 6

**DEVOTIONAL (A) LIFE OF OUR LORD.** By the Rev. E. L. CUTTS, B.A. Post 8vo., cloth boards........................... 5 0

**ENGLISHMAN'S BRIEF, THE,** on behalf of his National Church. New Edition. Small post 8vo., paper boards ...... 0 6

**GOSPELS, THE FOUR,** arranged in the Form of an English Harmony, from the Text of the Authorized Version. By the Rev. J. M. FULLER, M.A. With Analytical Table of Contents and four Maps. Cloth boards ........................ 1 6

**HEARTS AND LIVES GIVEN TO CHRIST.** Twenty-four Bible Lessons for Young Women's Classes. By ELINOR LEWIS. Post 8vo., cloth boards ...................................... 1 6

**HISTORY OF THE ENGLISH CHURCH,** in Short Biographical Sketches. By the Rev. JULIUS LLOYD, M.A., Author of "Sketches of Church History in Scotland." Post 8vo., cloth boards ............................................ 2 0

**HISTORY OF THE JEWISH NATION, A,** from the Earliest Times to the Present Day. By the late E. H. PALMER, Esq., M.A. With Map of Palestine and numerous Illustrations. Crown 8vo., cloth boards .................................. 4 0

**JOHN WICLIF; his Life, Times, and Teaching.** By the Rev. A. R. PENNINGTON, M.A., Canon of Lincoln, &c. Post 8vo., cloth boards ............................................ 8 0

PUBLICATIONS OF THE SOCIETY

|  | s. | d. |
|---|---|---|
| **LAND OF ISRAEL, THE.** A Journal of Travel in Palestine, undertaken with special reference to its Physical Character. By the Rev. Canon TRISTRAM. Fourth Edition, revised. With two Maps and numerous Illustrations. Large post 8vo., cloth boards | 10 | 6 |
| **LECTURES ON THE HISTORICAL AND DOGMATICAL POSITION OF THE CHURCH OF ENGLAND.** By the Rev. W. BAKER, D.D. Post 8vo., cloth boards | 1 | 6 |
| **LESSER LIGHTS;** or, Some of the Minor Characters of Scripture traced, with a View to Instruction and Example in Daily Life. By the Rev. F. BOURDILLON, M.A. First and Second Series. Post 8vo., cloth boards, each | 2 | 6 |
| **LITANY, THE.** With an Introduction, Explanation of Words and Phrases, together with Illustrative and Devotional Paraphrase. By the Rev. E. J. BOYCE, M.A. Fcap. 8vo., cloth boards | 1 | 0 |
| **MODERN EGYPT;** Its Witness to Christ. Lectures after a visit to Egypt in 1883. By the Rev. HENRY B. OTTLEY. With Illustrations. Fcap. 8vo., cloth boards | 2 | 6 |
| **NARRATIVE OF A MODERN PILGRIMAGE THROUGH PALESTINE ON HORSEBACK, AND WITH TENTS.** By the Rev. ALFRED C. SMITH, M.A. Numerous Illustrations, and four Coloured Plates. Crown 8vo., cloth boards | 5 | 0 |
| **ON THE NATURE AND OFFICE OF GOD THE HOLY GHOST.** By the Rev. S. C. AUSTEN, Vicar of Stokenchurch, Oxon. Fcap. 8vo., cloth boards | 1 | 0 |
| **PALEY'S EVIDENCES.** A New Edition, with Notes, Appendix, and Preface. By the Rev. E. A. LITTON. Post 8vo., cloth boards | 4 | 0 |
| **PALEY'S HORÆ PAULINÆ.** A New Edition, with Notes, Appendix, and Preface. By the Rev. J. S. HOWSON, D.D., Dean of Chester. Post 8vo., cloth boards | 3 | 0 |
| **PEACE WITH GOD.** A Manual for the Sick. By the Rev. E. BURBIDGE, M.A. Post 8vo., cloth boards | 1 | 6 |
| **"PERFECTING HOLINESS."** By the Rev. E. L. CUTTS, Author of " Pastoral Counsels," &c. Post 8vo , cloth boards | 2 | 6 |

|  | s. | d. |
|---|---|---|

**PLAIN REASONS AGAINST JOINING THE CHURCH OF ROME.** By the Rev. R. F. LITTLEDALE, LL.D., &c. Revised and Enlarged Edition. Post 8vo., cloth boards ...... 1 0

**PLAIN WORDS FOR CHRIST.** Being a Series of Readings for Working Men. By the Rev. R. G. DUTTON. Post 8vo., cloth boards ...... 1 0

**PRAYER-BOOK, HISTORY OF THE.** By Miss PEARD, Author of "One Year." Cloth boards ...... 1 0

**PROMISED SEED, THE.** Being a Course of Lessons on the Old Testament for School and Families, arranged for every Sunday in the Year. By the Rev. C. R. BALL, M.A. Post 8vo., cloth boards ...... 2 6

**PROPHECIES AND TYPES OF MESSIAH.** Four Lectures to Pupil-Teachers. By the Rev. G. P. OTTEY, M.A. Post 8vo., cloth boards ...... 1 0

**READINGS ON THE FIRST LESSONS FOR SUNDAYS AND CHIEF HOLY DAYS, ACCORDING TO THE NEW TABLE.** By the Rev. PETER YOUNG. Crown 8vo. In two volumes ...... 6 0

**RELIGION FOR EVERY DAY.** Lectures for Men. By the Rev. A. BARRY, D.D., Bishop of Sydney. Fcap. 8vo., cloth boards ...... 1 0

**ST. CHRYSOSTOM'S PICTURE OF HIS AGE.** Post 8vo., cloth boards ...... 2 0

**ST. CHRYSOSTOM'S PICTURE OF THE RELIGION OF HIS AGE.** Post 8vo., cloth boards ...... 1 6

**SCENES IN THE EAST.** Consisting of Twelve Coloured Photographic Views of Places mentioned in the Bible, beautifully executed, with Descriptive Letterpress. By the Rev. Canon TRISTRAM. Cloth, bevelled boards, gilt edges... 7 6

**SEEK AND FIND.** A Double Series of Short Studies of the Benedicite. By CHRISTINA G. ROSSETTI. Post 8vo., cloth boards ...... 2 6

**SERVANTS OF SCRIPTURE, THE.** By the Rev. JOHN W. BURGON, B.D. Post 8vo., cloth boards ...... 1 6

PUBLICATIONS OF THE SOCIETY.

|  | s. | d. |
|---|---|---|
| **SINAI AND JERUSALEM; or, Scenes from Bible Lands.** Consisting of Coloured Photographic Views of Places mentioned in the Bible, including a Panoramic View of Jerusalem, with Descriptive Letterpress. By the Rev. F. W. HOLLAND, M.A. Demy 4to., cloth, bevelled boards, gilt edges ......... | 7 | 6 |
| **SOME CHIEF TRUTHS OF RELIGION.** By the Rev. E. L. CUTTS, B.A., Author of "St. Cedd's Cross," &c. Crown 8vo., cloth boards .................................................................. | 2 | 6 |
| **THOUGHTS FOR MEN AND WOMEN.** By EMILY C. ORR. Post 8vo., limp cloth ................................................ | 1 | 0 |
| **THOUGHTS FOR WORKING DAYS.** Original and Selected. By EMILY C. ORR. Post 8vo., limp cloth ...................... | 1 | 0 |
| **TURNING-POINTS OF ENGLISH CHURCH HISTORY.** By the Rev. E. L CUTTS, B.A., Vicar of Holy Trinity, Haverstock Hill. Crown 8vo., cloth boards .................... | 3 | 6 |
| **TURNING-POINTS OF GENERAL CHURCH HISTORY.** By the Rev. E. L. CUTTS, B.A., Author of "Pastoral Counsels," &c. Crown 8vo., cloth boards ...................... | 5 | 0 |
| **UNDER HIS BANNER.** Papers on Missionary Work of Modern Times. By the Rev. W. H. TUCKER. With Map. Crown 8vo. New Edition. Cloth boards ...................... | 5 | 0 |

---

**Depositories:**
LONDON : NORTHUMBERLAND AVENUE, CHARING CROSS, W.C.;
43, QUEEN VICTORIA STREET, E.C.; 26, ST. GEORGE'S PLACE, S.W.
BRIGHTON : 135, NORTH STREET.

www.ingramcontent.com/pod-product-compliance
Lightning Source LLC
Chambersburg PA
CBHW051851300426
44117CB00006B/350